# The European Union and Supranational Political Economy

The financial crisis – originated in 2008 in the United States – had a dramatic impact on the world economy. The European Union was immediately involved, but its reaction to the crisis was clearly inadequate. The misgovernment of the European economy not only put at risk the European Monetary Union (EMU), but it also caused further hindrances to the recovery of the global economy.

The global financial turmoil shook deep-rooted beliefs. The doctrine of international neo-liberalism is more and more criticized. Nevertheless, the critics of neo-liberalism focus their attention on the relationship between the state and the market, as if the nation states, with their international organizations, have enough power for an effective global governance of the world economy. The model of European supranational integration, though seriously imperfect, can suggest some new way out from the crisis – even at the world level – based on a new relationship between the supranational government of the Union and the market.

In this book, several academic disciplines are involved: international economics, international political economy, international law, international relations, political theory and democratic theory. Adopting such a multidisciplinary theoretical perspective, the volume tries to answer the following questions: Is a more supranational Europe able to provide a better government of the EMU? Does this reform involve more European democracy?

**Riccardo Fiorentini** is Associate Professor of International Economics at the University of Verona, Italy.

**Guido Montani** is Professor of International Political Economy at the University of Pavia, Italy.

# Routledge Frontiers of Political Economy

# The European Union and Supranational Political Economy

Edited by Riccardo Fiorentini and Guido Montani

Routledge
Taylor & Francis Group

LONDON AND NEW YORK

First published 2015
by Routledge
2 Park Square, Milton Park, Abingdon, Oxfordshire OX14 4RN

and by Routledge
711 Third Avenue, New York, NY 10017

First issued in paperback 2016

*Routledge is an imprint of the Taylor & Francis Group, an informa business*

*British Library Cataloguing in Publication Data*
A catalogue record for this book is available from the British Library

*Library of Congress Cataloguing in Publication data*
Fiorentini, Riccardo.
The European Union and supranational political economy / Riccardo Fiorentini, Guido Montani.
    pages   cm. – (Routledge frontiers of political economy)
1. European Union countries–Economic conditions–21st century.
2. European Union countries–Economic policy–21st century.   3. Europe–Economic integration.   4. Neoliberalism–European Union countries.
5. Global Financial Crisis, 2008–2009.   I. Montani, Guido.   II. Title.
HC240.F4567 2014
337.1'42–dc23
2014025243

ISBN 13: 978-1-138-22684-5 (pbk)
ISBN 13: 978-1-138-78664-6 (hbk)

Typeset in Times New Roman
by Out of House Publishing

# Contents

# Figures

# Tables

# Contributors

**Richard Connolly** is the Director of the Centre for Russian, Eurasian and European Studies at the University of Birmingham and Senior Lecturer in Political Economy. His research focuses on the political economy of Russia and its role in the global economy. He is author of several scientific articles published in leading academic journals and of the book *The Economic Sources of Social Order Development in Post-Socialist Eastern Europe*, London, Routledge.

**Riccardo Fiorentini** is Associate Professor of International Economics at the University of Verona. He is Director of the Master's in International Markets and Firms and a member of the Scientific Board of the Centre for International Studies at the University of Verona. His main research interests include international monetary institutions, international macroeconomics, European integration and monetary policy. He has published several scientific articles in Italian and international academic journals and is author (with G. Montani) of the book *The New Global Political Economy: From Crisis to Supranational Integration*.

**Ulrike Guérot** is Senior Associate for Germany, Berlin, Open Society Initiative for Europe (OSIFE). She has been directing the Berlin office of the European Council on Foreign Relations for seven years, and is a frequent commentator in German and European media on European affairs. She is also Founding Director of the European Democracy Lab, an experimental new think tank aimed at redesigning European democracy along the lines of division of power in the sense of Montesquieu. She has been awarded with the prestigious French *L'Ordre pour le Mérite* for her European engagement. Her special competences are Franco-German and euro-translatlantic relations, and her research interest are the future, the conditions and the strain on European democracy and the social and political implications of the euro-crisis.

**Fernando Iglesias** is Chairman of the World Federalist Movement Council, Director of Campaña por una Corte Penal Latinoamericana, founding member of Cultura Porteña and Director of Spinelli Chair at CUIA. He was a member of the Parliament of Mercosur. His main research interests include world federalism, European federalism and integration. He has published several books on the topic of globalization and democracy.

**Fabio Masini** is Professor of Theories and History of International Economic Relations at the University of Rome. He is Secretary General of the Italian Council of the European Movement, Managing Editor of the *History of Economic Thought and Policy* journal and Managing Director of the International Research Centre on European and Global Governance. His main fields of research are: economic and monetary integration; economic policy and public intervention in the economy; the history of economic thought; and the economics and policy of tourism and local resources. He has published many academic articles and papers and is the author of 'Luigi Einaudi and Italian Liberalism, 1940–1960', in Schulz-Forberg H. and Olsen N. (eds) *Reinventing Western Civilization: Transnational Reconstructions of Liberalism in Europe in the Twentieth Century*.

**John McCormick** is Jean Monnet Professor of European Union Politics at the Indianapolis campus of Indiana University in the United States, and a former Fulbright-Schuman Chair in US–EU Relations at the College of Europe in Bruges. He has a particular interest in the dynamics of transatlantic relations, in the dynamics of the debate over European integration (explored in his book *Why Europe Matters: The Case for the European Union*), and in the qualities that define the meaning of being European (explored in his book *Europeanism*). He has also written two textbooks on the politics and policies of the EU: *Understanding the European Union* and *European Union Politics*.

**Guido Montani** is Professor of International Political Economy at the University of Pavia. He has published many papers on the theory of value and distribution, especially on Ricardo, based on Piero Sraffa's reconstruction of the classical approach. A second field of study concerns the theory of political and economic integration in Europe and in the global economy. He is honorary member of the Union of European Federalists. His books (with R. Fiorentini) include: *The New Global Political Economy: From Crisis to Supranational Integration*.

**Tibor Palánkai** is Emeritus Professor of Economics, International Relations and European Studies at the Corvinus University of Budapest, where he was Rector in the period 1997–2000. He has been Jean Monnnet Professor since 1994 and Jean Monnet Professor ad Personam at CUB since 2004. In 2010, the EU Commission awarded him with the Jean Monnet Prize. His main research topics include: world economy, theory of international integration (measuring integration), and Global and European integration. He is the author of a large number of publications, including ten books, many of them published in foreign languages. Recently, in 2014, he published the book *Economics of Global and Regional Integration*.

**Heikki Patomäki** is Professor of World Politics at the University of Helsinki and member of the boards of seven academic journals in international relations, global political economy, globalization and other fields. His research interests include philosophy and methodology of social sciences, peace research, futures studies, economic theory, global political economy and global political theory. He has published a large number of papers in international journals and is the author of several books, including the recent *The Great Eurozone Disaster: From Crisis to Global New Deal (Economic Controversies)*.

**Zoltán Pogátsa** is Director of the Master's in International Economics and Business at the University of West Hungary. His research interests focus on development economics and the political economy of European integration, especially with regards to the Northern, Eastern and Southern Periphery. He is the author of many scientific articles and of *The Political Economy of the Greek Crisis* (2014).

**Daniela Preda** is Full Professor at the University of Genoa, Jean Monnet Chair ad personam in History and Politics of European Integration since 1995 and director of the degree course Diplomatic and International Studies at the University of Genoa. Former president of the Associazione Universitaria di Studi Europei (Italias section of ECSA), she is a member of the Board of the Centre for Studies on Federalism (Turin). Her main research interests concern the history of the European Community and the history of the federalist movements. She is the author of a large number of papers and books written in Italian and French. In English she recently published (with Daniele Pasquinucci) *Consensus and European Integration: An Historical Perspective*.

**Roland Sturm** has held the Chair of Political Science at the University of Erlangen-Nürnberg in Germany since 1996. From 1991 to 1996 he was Professor at the Institute of Political Science in Tübingen, Germany. He taught as Visiting Professor at the Universities of Washington, Seattle, and Peking, and at the Pompeu Fabra University, Barcelona. He has published widely on German politics; comparative politics and comparative public policies; political economy; and European integration.

**Vito Tanzi** is Honorary President of the International Institute of Public Finance. After an initial academic career he joined the IMF, where he was the Director of the Fiscal Affairs Department for almost 20 years. He has also been President of the International Institute of Public Finance (1990–94) and State secretary for Economy and Finance in the Italian Government. He is the author of some 20 books and of hundreds of articles in professional journals including the *American Economic Review* and the *Journal of Political Economy*. His major recent interest is the economic role of the state, on which he has published two books, with Cambridge University Press. An 'effect' in economies, the 'Tanzi effect', is named after him.

# Abbreviations

| | |
|---|---|
| AfD | Alternative für Deutschland |
| CAP | Common Agricultural Policy |
| CECE | Comité d'Etudes pour la Constitution Européenne |
| CFC | chlorofluorocarbon |
| CFSP | Common Foreign and Security Policy |
| CSDP | Common Security and Defence Policy |
| CUIS | Common Unemployment Insurance System |
| ECB | European Central Bank |
| ECJ | European Court of Justice |
| ECSC | European Coal and Steel Community |
| EDC | European Defence Community |
| EEAS | European External Action Service |
| EEC | European Economic Community |
| EESF | European Employment Stabilization Fund |
| EFTA | European Free Trade Area |
| EIA | Energy Information Administration |
| EMS | European Monetary System |
| EMU | European Monetary Union |
| EP | European Parliament |
| EPU | European Payment Union |
| ERP | European Recovery Program |
| ESM | European Stability Mechanism |
| EU | European Union |
| FN | Front National |
| GDP | gross domestic product |
| GIIPS | Greece, Ireland, Italy, Portugal, Spain |
| GVCs | global value chains |
| G7/8 | Group of Seven or Eight |
| G20 | Group of Twenty |
| ICC | International Criminal Court |
| IEA | International Energy Agency |
| IMF | International Monetary Fund |

| | |
|---|---|
| IPE | international political economy |
| LAO | limited access order |
| LNG | liquefied natural gas |
| LT | Treaty of Lisbon |
| MEPs | Members of European Parliament |
| MNCs | multinational corporations |
| NAFTA | North-American Free Trade Agreement |
| NATO | North Atlantic Treaty Organization |
| NGOs | non-governmental organizations |
| OCA | optimum currency areas |
| OECD | Organisation for Economic Co-operation and Development |
| OEEC | Organization for European Economic Cooperation |
| OMT | Outright Monetary Transaction programme |
| SEA | Single European Act |
| SGP | Stability and Growth Pact |
| SME | small- and medium-sized enterprises |
| SRM | Single Resolution Mechanism |
| TANAP | Trans-Anatolian natural gas pipeline |
| TAP | Trans-Adriatic pipeline |
| TFEU | Treaty on the Functioning of the European Union |
| TNCs | transnational corporations |
| UN | United Nations |
| VAT | value added tax |
| WTO | World Trade Organization |

# Introduction

*Riccardo Fiorentini and Guido Montani*

## The international and supranational political economy

A book called *The European Union and Supranational Political Economy* runs the risk of being considered a useless academic exercise at a time in which the European Union (EU) is undergoing a serious crisis and its survival is even in doubt. But, in our opinion, research on the supranational point of view is necessary not only to understand the innermost workings of EU institutions and its unique position in the history of international relations, but also to find the way out from the present deadlock. Effective reforms in the EU are crucial with the introduction of new rules for a more secure, just and sustainable global order.

A popular handbook defines international political economy (IPE) as 'the study of the interplay of economics and politics in the world arena' and specifies that 'political economy' has a variety of meanings:

> For some, it refers primarily to the study of the political basis of economic actions, the ways in which government policies affect market operations. For others, the principle preoccupation is the economic basis of political action, the ways in which economic forces mold government policies. The two focuses are, in a sense, complementary, for politics and markets are in a constant state of mutual interaction.
>
> (Frieden and Lake, 2000: 1)

This definition gives a fairly good description of the field of human activities studied by IPE; but in order to get a better understanding of the scope of a discipline which is neither politics nor economics, but an integration of the two, it is useful to remember that IPE emerged during the years after the collapse of the Bretton Woods system, when several scholars understood that in international affairs it was no longer possible to separate political and economic phenomena in watertight compartments. The study of the interplay between the two was needed in order to understand new problems such as economic integration, political interdependence, the birth of international civil society and the increasing importance of international institutions.

The historical circumstances prompting the birth of an academic discipline also determine its methods of inquiry and theoretical framework. IPE inevitably reflects the political ideologies of the time: we cannot do without them when we look for sense and meaning in the world we inhabit and wish to change (Freeden, 1996). And, in fact, the leading studies of IPE very soon came under one of three umbrellas: Liberalism, Marxism and Realism. In domestic politics, liberals generally believe that the market is the best mechanism to allocate resources and that the state should not interfere, or interfere only in order to guarantee the smooth functioning of the market. 'At the level of international economy, liberals assert that a fundamental harmony of interests exists between, as well as within, countries' (Frieden and Lake, 2000: 10). For liberals, cooperation among nations does not require intricate regulations and large institutions. Marxists possessed a sophisticated theory of history, capitalism, imperialism and the class struggle, but the breakdown of the Soviet Union prompted an in-depth theoretical review, which is still ongoing. Today Marxists are concerned with two main issues: 'The first is the fate of labour in a world of increasingly internationalized capital', the second is 'the poverty and continued underdevelopment of the Third World' (Frieden and Lake, 2000: 11). Realists, the third school of thought,

> believe that nation-states pursue power and shape the economy to this end. Moreover, they are the dominant actors within the international political economy. According to Realists, the international system is anarchical, a condition under which nation-states are sovereign, the sole judges of their own behaviours, and subject to no higher authority.
>
> (Frieden and Lake, 2000: 12)

These three ideologies, singled out by Frieden and Lake, should be joined by nationalism, the ideology of the nation state, since realism – according to scholars of IPE – without sovereign nation states, the true subjects of internationalism, is an empty box.

Recent IPE studies, especially after the financial crisis, abandon ideology in favour of an eclectic point of view. The aim of this book is to look for a more comprehensive approach: to sketch out a background in which a new historical phase for the implementation of the fundamental values of traditional ideologies becomes possible. According to Hannah Arendt, the history of civilization, from antiquity to the modern age, is characterized by a distinction between the public and private spheres of community life. 'The distinction between a private and a public sphere of life corresponds to the household and the political realms, which have existed as distinct, separate entities at least since the rise of the ancient city state', she says. This feature of the human condition becomes more complex in modern times, but persists: 'the emergence of the social realm, which is neither private nor public, strictly speaking, is a relatively new phenomenon whose origin coincided with the emergence of the modern age and which found its political form in the nation-state' (Arendt,

1958: 28). In a political essay, Norberto Bobbio (1985) considers the public/ private 'dichotomy' as crucial for all social sciences. Bobbio explains that the dichotomy – where what is public is not private and what is private is not public – is adopted by the main political ideologies, such as Liberalism and Marxism (and Socialism). Liberals advocate the supremacy of the private sphere of individual life, and hence human rights, including the economic freedom of the market, over and above the public power of the state. Socialist thinkers support the primacy of the public sphere, since the common good cannot be considered the simple summation of private goods. There should be a balance between the two. The absolute primacy of the public sphere leads a community toward totalitarianism, Stalinism or Nazi-fascism. Bobbio concludes by observing that the modern democratic state is based on the search for the peaceful and balanced coexistence of the two principles. It could be added that the public/private dichotomy is not a feature of only Western civilization. Francis Fukuyama, in his study on the origins of political order, considers China the first example of the state in history, because 'many of the elements of what we now understand to be a modern state were already in place in China in the third century BC, some eighteen hundred years before they emerged in Europe' (Fukuyama, 2011: 19). Analysing Zhou China, a kind of patrimonial society in the seventh century BC, he says that 'there is no distinction in this society between public and private; each ruling lineage raised armies, imposed taxes, and dispensed justice as it saw fit. All this, however, soon changed' (Fukuyama, 2011: 109).

The public/private dichotomy is a very useful tool to inquire into the most pressing problems of the present international order and to test the ability of international institutions to solve them. Some scholars of IPE have done so. John Ravenhill (2014: 18) says: 'Global political economy is a field of enquiry, a subject matter whose central focus is the interrelationship between public and private power in the allocation of scarce resources.' The debate on the need to provide global public goods is already under way. Establishing what new institutions could be endowed with the power to provide global public goods, should therefore be the goal of future research. However, a realist approach – adopted by many liberal and socialist scholars – falls short of this task because it is locked into the straitjacket of national sovereignty. For instance Robert Gilpin defines global political economy as the 'interaction of the market and such powerful actors as states, multinational firms and international organisations', in order to adapt the traditional definition to the new international context, in which new actors, and not only states, are prominent. But Gilpin adds that in the last resort, 'the state is the *only* important actor' not only in the global system, but also in the European Union because 'whatever the ultimate shape of the European Union, national governments will continue to be important actors within this regional arrangement' (Gilpin, 2001: 17–18, original emphasis). This statement, although not entirely inaccurate, confines important institutions in the European Union to the backstage. One of them is the Court of Justice, which has the power to apply European legislation over and above national legislation. Another is the European Parliament, which has the power to co-legislate with the European Council. Consider the European Central Bank, which determines monetary policy for the euro-area. Are these international or supranational institutions? In our opinion, they are supranational institutions – because their function is to provide supranational public goods, such as justice, democracy and monetary stability, to a community of national peoples – although – as many papers in this book demonstrate – the penumbra (Burgess, 2013) between international and supranational institutions is yet to be clarified.

A first step to shed light on this penumbra is to distinguish between realism, dating back to Thucydides and Machiavelli (unfamiliar with the international order that emerged in the modern age after the Westphalia Treaty), and the current theory of international relations based on the existence of sovereign nation states. In other words, is a realist political theory possible outside the ideological framework of nationalism? Is the supranational political economy a realistic way to understand the European Union and the world political and economic order? An initial answer is provided by Michael Zürn (2013: 416) who says:

> The shape of more recent inter-, trans-, and supranational institutions is hardly compatible with the traditional notion of state sovereignty in the national constellation. … the debate as a whole accepted the analytical shackles of 'methodological nationalism'. The study of global governance needs to go beyond methodological nationalism.

Let us now examine why, in modern international theory, national sovereignty is an unavoidable dogma and supranational institutions are considered a utopia. In his classic treatise, *Politics among Nations*, Hans Morgenthau asks this very question. In the chapter on the 'World State' he writes:

> No society exists coextensive with the presumed range of a world state. What exists is an international society of sovereign nations. There does not exist a supranational society … the people of the world are not willing to accept world government, and their overriding loyalty to the nation erects an insurmountable obstacle to its establishment.
>
> (Morgenthau, 1973: 501)

Moreover, he states that a citizen of the world willing to act in favour of a world state would inevitably be considered a traitor by his fellow citizens: 'a man who would want to act as a citizen of the world would by the conditions of the world be forced to act as a partisan of another nation and as traitor to his own' (Morgenthau, 1973: 502). The first edition of Morgenthau's book was published in 1948, before the creation of European institutions and, of course, a realist can be forgiven for ignoring what does not exist. But after the Second World War the 'loyalty' of European national peoples towards their nation states changed dramatically. The catastrophe of European civilization had been provoked by their own governments, which in many countries were fought as an enemy. After the war, European peoples yearned for 'peace among the nations' and no more wars. The new governments of Europe understood the popular feeling and set about building European supranational institutions to guarantee a peaceful future. These institutions were limited to some sectors of European society and were clearly defective compared to the federal model cited in the founding pact, the Schuman Declaration. But transferring some national power to European institutions was considered evidence of the will to press on to a more perfect union. In other words, scholars of the supranational political economy are not traitors to their countries but, in a world destined to become a community of faith, they are European (Latin-American, African, etc.) citizens convinced that fundamental values and rights can better be upheld by a supranational system of government, with limited but adequate power to provide supranational public goods.

## This book

The above remarks explain the content and structure of the book. Its authors share the feeling that supranational institutions deserve to be investigated, but have different points of view on the nature of the EU. Therefore the Editors set out in the following rections their own opinion on the present problems of European integration and its future.

The aim of Part I – Birth of the Supranational Project – is to show that the creation of European institutions was the outcome of the desire for peace in Europe: as Daniela Preda explains in her historical reconstruction of the birth of the first supranational polity, the European Coal and Steel Community (ECSC) was not a truce between France and Germany but the first step towards a lasting peace based on institutions whose aim was to make war impossible. It was not until the failure of the European Defence Community that the economic aspects of integration came to the forefront, allowing some scholars to adopt a neo-liberal interpretation of the European integration process. However, as functionalists, neo-liberals and federalists debated the foundation of the European institutions, Fabio Masini's inquiry into the history of economic thought on European integration casts doubts on the fact that neo-liberal thinking did prevail among the founding fathers, as some believe.

The chapters in Part II – Europe between Confederation and Federation – have the difficult task of clarifying the penumbra between confederation and federation, where the dividing line of responsibilities and powers between the differing levels of governments is difficult to find. John McCormick clarifies the main issues at stake for the future of the EU. There are three: the return to the era of the nation state, the creation of the United States of Europe, or the creation of a confederated union. The Author considers the last of these the most realistic and practical solution to the present crisis. Roland Sturm gives an in-depth examination of the difficulties the German political system faces in dealing with European integration. Germany has the dilemma of safeguarding national interests while furthering European integration. At the moment, Germany may be reluctant to take a lead, but it has the duty to act as a benevolent hegemon. Zoltán Pogátsa, a heterodox scholar of IPE, presents a critique of the neo-liberal EU, today one of the building blocks of the Washington Consensus. According to the Author, attempts to build a social or federal EU are doomed to fail, if the neo-liberal project is not defeated by renewed policies at both the national and supranational levels. In order to overcome these difficulties, a new relationship between national and European democracy is crucial. Here, the remarks of Morgenthau concerning the loyalty of the citizens to their national government are relevant: experience shows that the degree of solidarity among national peoples is usually lower than that existing among citizens of the same nation. The problem is vital for the future of the EU. Heikki Patomäki observes that a careful analysis in terms of political economy and power relations is necessary to move toward a democratic Union. The euro crisis and related economic problems of the Union can be explained by post-Keynesian economic theories, implying the need for common fiscal policy, drastically revised central bank mandate and redistributive mechanisms in the Union. These kinds of reforms could, however, aggravate the legitimation problems of the Union, unless they are accompanied by further democratization of the Union. According to Ulrike Guérot the present techno structure of the EU provides a breeding ground for Euro-populism, because citizens who are against EU policy stand against the EU polity. The Author recommends the creation of a European Republic, with a fully fledged Parliamentary system with two-chamber structure, in which the European Parliament has full rights of initiative and full budgetary sovereignty over tax revenues. There would be a clear division of power between the legislative and the executive. Members of the eurozone could then agree on further integration, creating a new fiscal capacity. Common unemployment insurance schemes should be created.

In Part III – Policy Issues – the chapter by Tibor Palánkai presents a general framework of macroeconomic parameters for the guidance of European policies. On the basis of detailed quantitative analysis, the Author finds that member states of the EU have reached a very high level of integration. The EU is the only organization which has created a single market and a single currency, has extended the principle of cohesion and solidarity to the Union level and, finally, is a model of regional supranational integration. In the following chapter, Riccardo Fiorentini underlines the latent deflationary bias of the EMU caused by the Stability and Growth Pact (SGP) and the Fiscal Compact. Fiscal austerity exaggerated the original deflationary bias during recession and has been one of the causes of the recent rise of Eurosceptical movements. The Author argues that a federal fiscal union is necessary to overcome the limits of the EMU and suggests the creation of a collective insurance fund as a vehicle for greater solidarity between EU countries combatting cyclical unemployment. Finally, Richard Connolly examines the world energy market, especially how the deep and rapid transformation of the global gas market is shaping European energy security. These changes are crucial for the understanding of the trade relationship between Europe and Russia. The Author remarks that the recent financial crisis caused an increase in the use of carbon-intensive coal in the EU and concludes that EU dependence on Russian gas looks likely to remain unchanged for years to come.

Finally, in Part IV – Political Economy: from Internationalism to Supranationalism – the proposal of a new scientific paradigm – Supranational Political Economy – is expressly analysed by Guido Montani. While the debate about the confederal/federal nature of the European Union is open and unlikely to reach consensus in the near future, less disagreement exists among scholars of European integration on its supranational features. Sometimes, the term 'supranational' is also utilized for international institutions such as the UN or the WTO. Therefore the distinction between the two terms needs to be defined. Moreover, a good exercise consists in examining the major international problems of the global age from a supranational perspective, extending the crucial paradigm of political economy – the state/market relationship – to the international and supranational level. Of course, this is a sensible procedure only if the experiment of the European Union is taken as the starting point and the EU proves able to recover from the present crisis. Vito Tanzi takes on the difficult task of comparing the relative abilities of the USA and the EU to fight the negative impact of the financial crisis on their economies. He observes that while at first sight the USA appears to have better institutional arrangements and rules, the value of the euro has risen against the dollar; the euro is also increasingly used as a reserve currency; and public debt for general government expenditure has increased more in the USA than in the EMU area. According to the Author, in spite of recent difficulties, the EMU will survive. Finally, Fernando Iglesias provides an assessment of European integration from a Latin-American point of view. He recognizes that, whatever the road the EU will take, post-war European experience remains the turning point in the dialectic between socio-economic processes, political institutions and territory. The EU is the missing link between the order of nation states and the post-national world order of the future. In his conclusions, the Author says that, in order to face the challenges of the twenty-first century, humanity needs to build the institutions of a global democracy, which does not mean a concentration of power, but democratic decision-making at every level.

## The crisis of the European Union and Euroscepticism

European institutions were conceived by the founding fathers as a mixture of federalism and confederalism. So, from the very outset, the quarrel was left open between advocates of greater political integration – whose final goal was the federal system – and advocates of intergovernmentalism – whose aim was to keep sovereign powers in the hands of national governments. The controversy can be seen in the opening speech of Jean Monnet, the first President of the High Authority, at the Parliamentary Assembly of the ECSC in August 1952. Monnet said that all European institutions could be reformed in the future, but

> what is beyond dispute is the fact that they are supranational institutions and, let's say the word, federal. They are institutions that within the limits of their competences are sovereign, that is endowed with the right to decide and execute.
>
> (Monnet, 1955: 56–8)

The fundamental ambiguity of the founding act has caused several crises and provoked some successes in the process of European integration. Sometimes intergovernmental forces have prevailed, such as in the times of de Gaulle, sometimes the federalist project had the upper hand, such as during the Delors presidency of the European Commission. Today, after the EMU crisis, European citizens and political parties are divided into Eurosceptics and pro-Europeans. Roughly, all political parties with candidates for President of the European Commission in the European elections of 2014 were pro-Europeans, even if critical of the present EU and its governance, which they believe can be reformed. Eurosceptical parties want to dismantle the EU, especially the EMU, which is considered the primary cause of unemployment and poverty. The clearest example of a Eurosceptical party is the *Front National* (FN) headed by Marine Le Pen in France. The FN wants France to leave the EU, prevent any further steps towards a federal Union, and restore the *franc* and protectionism at the national border. The political aim of the FN is to destroy the EU and to recover full national sovereignty.

Those who wish to save the European Union need to understand the causes behind the rise in Euroscepticism, which are recent but come from afar. Recent causes are clearly related to the poor governance of EU institutions during the financial and sovereign debt crises. The Maastricht Treaty established a monetary union without a fiscal union and a European government, a patchy compromise with France happy to divest Germany of the Deutsche Mark and Germany anxious to unite West and East Germany. 'A united Germany in a united Europe' was considered to be a reassuring prospect. However, European governments, the Commission and the European Parliament were all well aware of the incomplete nature of the EMU. They were confident that, in an emergency, a step towards more powerful Union could be achieved. But when the difficulties arose – the first serious sign was the Greek threat to default – instead of entrusting to the Commission all the powers (mainly financial resources) needed to deal with the emergency, national governments, and the Council, decided to manage the crisis situation directly. Council meetings, normally three a year, became more and more frequent, but the decisions coming out of them were often partial, confused and even inappropriate. 'Too little too late' was the most common comment on this new policy-making mechanism. A survey sponsored by the European Parliament on the effect of Troika policies noted that the macroeconomic impact of fiscal measures 'was underestimated in some programmes' and that 'the depressed situation in partner EU countries was not anticipated and weighed heavily on programme countries'. The survey concludes by observing that

> the current mood, which tends to focus on exit as measure of success, is understandable, but should be partly resisted … because many problems remain, even if countries succeed in exiting their programmes. In particular, unemployment rates and (private and public) debt levels are still very high.
>
> (Sapir *et al.*, 2014: 58–9)

After five years of poor European governance, the outcome has been that the German government has taken over government of the Union. Instead of a united Germany in a united Europe, today we have a strong Germany in a divided Europe. However, Europe's reluctant hegemon, as some call it (The Economist, 2013), provides only a temporary balance.

A turning point is necessary and will be possible only if the remote causes of the derailment of Europe are identified and removed. There are two main causes: one is the asymmetric relationship of European institutions; the second is a more general political change in world politics after the fall of the Berlin Wall. The first is related to the role of the European Parliament in the process of European integration. During the severe Community crisis of the 1970s, European governments favoured the direct election of the Parliamentary Assembly, as established in the Treaty of Rome, since they understood that European institutions required democratic legitimacy. On the eve of the first direct European elections (1979), Willy Brandt said that the European Parliament needed to become a permanent constituent assembly. During the first Parliamentary term, a group of Members of the European Parliament (MEPs), led by Altiero Spinelli, was able to work out and gather a wide majority for a Treaty of European Union, a project for the transformation of the European Commission into a European democratic government responsible before Parliament and the Council, where unanimity was required only in foreign and security policy. In 1984, the European Parliament presented a draft of a Treaty of European Union to the Council. France, Germany and Italy supported the project, but Mrs Thatcher opposed it. The outcome was the humiliation and abasement of the European Parliament, the only institution that actually represents European citizens. After this defeat European political parties no longer had the courage to propose a comprehensive reform of the Union and in the following years, the Council alone decided the schedule and contents of reforms. And as the European Parliament increased its power, citizens nonetheless lost hope in their representatives. Turnout decreased with each election.

The second factor to consider is the change of international politics after the collapse of the Soviet Union. During the Cold War, international politics was dominated by the ideological and military confrontation of the two superpowers.

Within the Western and Eastern hemispheres satellite countries accepted the doctrine – whether explicit or tacit – of 'limited sovereignty'. The end of the Soviet Empire opened the way for the revival of nationalism in Eastern countries, where a peaceful settlement of their differences had not been agreed since the First World War. The Soviet Empire split into numerous nation states, of which the largest was Russia, and old national rivalries resumed, such as in Yugoslavia and Chechnya. The tragedy of ethnic cleansing returned to bloody Europe.

The revival of nationalism is linked with two other phenomena: the relentless increase in globalization and the appearance on the international scene of emerging giants, China, India and Brazil. Slowly the traditional landscape of international politics changed: immediately following the collapse of the Soviet Union many scholars proposed the new scenario of a world led by the USA as the one indispensable superpower. Some years later, at the dawn of the twenty-first century, most observers thought the USA was in decline: its failure to export democracy to Iraq and Afghanistan, its inability to end the Israeli-Palestinian conflict and the eruption of the financial crisis of 2008 persuaded many in Europe and elsewhere that security and economic stability had to be guaranteed nationally. This new mood – the outcome of the end of the doctrine of limited sovereignty in the West – had a crucial impact on relations between the member states of the EU, especially on the Franco-German relationship. The process of European integration started because France offered Germany – the defeated power – a shared destiny of peace. The partnership was founded on the tacitly accepted leading role of France, as de Gaulle made clear. France was a member of the Security Council, an atomic power, was able to propose a 'tout azimuth' military strategy and Community foreign policy was conceived as a kind of intergovernmental cooperation led by France. The strategic military role of France in Europe persists, as on the occasion of the Iraq war in 2003, the war in Libya in 2011 after the Arab Spring, the intervention in Mali in 2013 and in the Central African Republic in 2014. But the de Gaulle era is over and forever. The effect of the intergovernmental approach for European foreign policy was to make each member state think of itself as an imaginary great power. Inside the EU, the poison of national revival and the illusion of a national foreign policy divided and weakened the EU in a world when only continental power had a voice. At a certain point, France – which (with the UK), fostered intergovernmentalism to the detriment of the federal method of government – had to face facts: during the financial crisis, when monetary and financial problems were uppermost, reunified Germany, not France, was clearly the leading country of the EU. This change of leadership is no longer in doubt: for European citizens and many politicians Berlin is the real political capital of the European Union.

This came as a surprise to those who cultivated the illusion of national sovereignty. European peoples will be able to recover the power to decide their future only if united in a federal Union. In a global market and a multipolar political world, the EU needs a government. All the main political issues – security, welfare, growth, defence of the environment, inequalities within and among countries – are supranational and can be tackled only through cooperation. A divided EU is weak and unable to react to global challenges. When the financial crisis began, the European Commission had no powers to control it or assist troubled countries. Owing to the primacy of intergovernmentalism over the communitarian method, the Council took the lead because of Germany's financial ability to aid countries in distress. The Council imposed strict austerity rules for countries not in compliance with the SGP and the European commission acted as the agent of the Council. Usually a power that imposes sacrifices on citizens is unpopular and this was no exception: Euroscepticism is not a movement of the left or right. In 2005, the French referendum against the European Constitution was led by a coalition of the far left with Front National. First and foremost, Euroscepticism is a protest against obscure, non-democratic European governance; nationalist and populist political parties seek to dismantle the EU by exploiting the protest. The EU is at a crossroads. German Europe is rejected, because it is thought of as a return to dangerous German domination. The EU, as it is managed today, is rejected, because it is deemed a bureaucratic body at the service of the German government. Therefore, political parties and citizens who want to recover the power to decide their future look to a democratic European government.

### Is a democratic European government possible?

The fact that Berlin, and not Brussels, is today considered the true capital of the European Union shows that the European Union needs political leadership to face the challenges of globalization and preserve unity and cohesion for its member states. However, a German-led Europe can only be accepted as a transitory solution. In the long run it will spur anti-German reaction. Here, our task is to detect the main political obstacles to a genuine democratic European government and to point to some issues.

As we already said, the problem of a democratic European government is complicated by the fact that the European Union is not a federal state yet. A debate on European democracy must take into account not only the reforms required for creating a more direct link between the citizens and the executive or the government, but also the power that this body must have in order to provide the public goods required by the citizens. Therefore, our first step is to clarify the main institutional gaps that the European Union must fill: fiscal Union and a European Defence Community.

A 'fiscal capacity for the EMU' was the main issue of the so-called Report of the four Presidents (Van Rompuy, 2012), in order to complete the construction initiated at Maastricht. However, after this declaration, nothing happened. Indeed, the European Council should have tackled the problem at the onset of the 2008 financial crisis. The silence of the Council and European leaders reveals how sensitive the issue is: fiscal policy is considered a crucial national power, which national governments do not want to share with a supranational government. But the budget of the EU, at present 1 per cent of EU GNP, is clearly insufficient for an appropriate European economic policy, especially for investments in R&D, in transnational energy networks and for counter-cyclical growth policies. Expressed with the jargon of fiscal federalism, in the EU there is vertical and horizontal imbalance. The vertical imbalance comes from the fact that only 2 per cent of the fiscal resources of the EU go to Europe and this very modest amount is paid by national contributions, not from Europe's own resources. The horizontal imbalance consists in the inability of the EU budget to guarantee a process of convergence of poor and disadvantaged regions and states toward the EU average. This problem was hotly debated during the financial crisis because austerity policies were imposed on all troubled states under the assumption that 'the German model' was a suitable target for everyone. The EU budget should be increased in order to provide a European policy for sustainable growth, full employment and more solidarity for disadvantaged regions and states.

The Common Foreign and Security Policy (CFSP) and the Common Security and Defence Policy (CSDP) are the best examples of the conservative role of the intergovernmental system. The assumption that these policies can emerge from intergovernmental cooperation is a pure illusion: like assuming that a common European monetary policy can be achieved without a European Central Bank. The CFSP and CSDP are wishful thinking without a common European military capability. A Report of the European Parliament clearly says that 'no single member state can achieve the level of security required for its citizens by acting alone' and that the lack of Europe's defence capacity 'might be tolerated so long as the US supply what the EU lacks' but that 'these factors are less certain than in the past'. The cost of non-Europe caused by the lack of integration of the military structure of the member states and a truly integrated market ranges from €26 billion to €130 billion. But of course, this economic cost does not take into account the significant political cost, the lack of a common strategic and European vision on the world stage (Ballester, 2013: 7–9). After the Ukraine crisis, the time has come to seriously reconsider the old proposal of a European Defence Community, rejected by France in 1954.

Let us now consider the most important political imbalance of the EU, the supremacy of the confederal system over the federal system. One of the constitutional pillars of the EU is the principle of dual democratic legitimacy: citizens are represented in the European Parliament and member states in the European Council and Council of Ministers (Article 10 of the Lisbon Treaty). Indeed, in every federation an intergovernmental (or horizontal) system exists side by side with a vertical democratic system. In the USA a so-called 'federalism without Washington' and in Switzerland a 'federalism without Bern' decides some cross-border issues. But in the USA and Switzerland the horizontal dimension of the decision-making system is balanced by a vertical dimension, i.e. a federal government democratically accountable to a two-chamber Parliament. In Europe, as we saw in the previous section, internal and external causes produced the present almost hegemonic German governance, with the transformation of the European Commission into the bureaucratic executive of the policies decided by a body outside the control of the citizens. The supporters of the intergovernmental method hold that the European Council is composed of representatives of their citizens and therefore may legitimately decide the most important policies of the Union. However they forget to add that the European Council comprises only members who draw their legitimacy nationally; nobody in Europe (not even the European Parliament) can vote against or dismiss this body of so-called European governance.

This anomaly has been pointed out by scholars of federalist systems. For instance, Ronald Watts observes:

> In a federation the executive and first legislature chamber in the common institutions are composed of representatives directly elected by and accountable to the *citizens*, and in exercising its legislative and taxing powers the federal government normally acts directly on the citizens, paralleling the direct relationship of the regional governments to their electorates. In this way they minimize the apparent 'democratic deficits' and technocracy that have characterized contemporary confederal political systems. In the latter, major central institutions are not directly elected but are composed of officials and ministers who serve as delegates of the constituent governments. This 'indirect' relationship with the electorate of the central confederal institutions has tended in practice to create difficulties for generating public support and loyalty for confederal institutions, a problem that has become apparent, for instance, in the European Union.
>
> (Watts, 2008: 135–6, original emphasis)

This statement shows how to overcome the democratic deficit of the European Union: strengthen the vertical decision-making system of the European Union in order to create a federal government which 'normally acts directly on behalf of European citizens'. The task is not impossible: the European Commission already exists and is accountable to the European Parliament, directly elected by the citizens. If this federal core is strengthened a more balanced union, between the federal and the confederal system, can emerge.

The 2014 European elections were a first step in the right direction. European parties finally found the courage to present to the electorate their candidate for President of the European Commission. Despite the confused post-electoral debate, due to the ambiguity of the Treaty, a tug-of-war between the European Council and Parliament became visible to public opinion and was hotly debated in the media: the issue was 'who represents the European citizens?'. People's sovereignty was at stake. For the first time, the Council needed to heed the European Parliament and its choice of President. Citizens were asked to choose the man or woman for the top job, not merely rubber-stamp a candidate chosen by diplomatic bargaining behind closed doors. Consequently, the President of the European Commission can no longer be considered a bureaucrat. Moreover, during the present Parliamentary term a double majority exists: the Commission will be supported by a coalition of right and left parties, and this majority, the so-called pro-European parties, will face so-called anti-European parties or Eurosceptics. The double majority will be a challenge but also an incentive for democratic reform in the European Union.

A step toward the Parliamentary government of the EU is also a good starting point for constitutional reform of the EU. The new European Parliament could give birth to a new democratic Union if the Council understands that, failing reform, the future of Europe is at stake. It is not necessary to start from scratch. The outgoing Parliament has already drafted two important documents, which can be very useful as a starting point for the new legislative term. The first is 'A Fundamental Law of the European Union', drafted by the Spinelli Group, comprising more than 200 MEPs from across the board of pro-European political parties in the last Parliament. The *Introduction* says that after the inadequate response of the Council to the financial crisis

> it is hardly a surprise that 'Europe' is getting blamed, although the precise target of the blame remains unclear because the governance of the Union is diffuse and opaque. [Therefore,] in response to the crisis, the federalists argue that the European Union must deepen its integration or risk falling apart. 'More of the same' is not an option. The historic mission to unite Europe's states and peoples needs to be refurbished. Reform needs to be driven not by a retreat to old nationalisms but by a fresh assertion of the values and principles on which the Union is founded.
>
> (The Spinelli Group, 2013: 12)

The crucial reform proposed by the 'Fundamental Law' is the transformation of the European Commission into a truly democratic European government, accountable to a two-chambers Parliament. The second legacy of the outgoing Parliament is a collection of policies approved by the EP but not yet implemented, i.e. 'The Cost of Non-Europe'. This Report includes 24 policies, showing that 'the absence of common action at European level may mean that, in a specific sector, there is an efficiency loss to the overall economy and/or that a collective public good that might otherwise exist is not being realised'. The conclusion of the Report is that

> if the policies listed were to be pursued effectively, the economic benefit would build up annually to a point where, on this initial estimate, around

800 billion euro – or currently about six per cent of EU GDP – might be added to the European economy.

(EPRS, 2014: 3)

If these two proposals are taken seriously into account by the new European Parliament, the Commission and the Council – even if some national governments stand on the sidelines – a more balanced and democratic Union can be built.

## Europe and the world

The deplorable state of European foreign and security policy is evident in the fact that the only official statement of a European security strategy was written by Javier Solana (2003), the former High Representative for the EU Common Foreign and Security Policy, a decade ago. In this document Solana says: 'Large scale aggression against any member state is now improbable. Instead, Europe faces new threats which are more diverse, less visible and less predictable.' Among these threats, the document mentions regional conflicts, state failure, organised crime and, of course, international terrorism. With the new threats, says Solana, 'the first line of defence will often be abroad … moreover, none of the new threats is purely military; nor can any be tackled by purely military means'. Therefore, 'our task is to promote a ring of well governed countries to the East of the European Union and on the borders of the Mediterranean with whom we can enjoy close and cooperative relations'. More generally, in international politics 'the best protection for our security is a world of well-governed democratic states. … the EU should support the United nations as it responds to threats to international peace and security'.

The Solana proposal for a European foreign and security policy has no teeth as long as national governments are left the freedom to pursue national strategies with national means. In the face of a severe international crisis, Europe generally falls into disarray. The survival of the myth of a EU policy based on the coordination of national policies is the main cause of the failure of the CFSP. Despite numerous declarations, neither the European Rapid Reaction Force nor the European Defence Agency for armament standardisation and procurement became operative; nor has a common immigration policy been agreed. The only hard power of the EU is its economic position in the world economy. Via its aid policy, economic sanctions and its commercial and financial policy, the EU is sometimes able to reach satisfactory results in foreign affairs.

In the present international order hard powers are necessary, but soft powers are no less significant. The international political system is based on the ideology of the sovereign nation state, whereas the European Union is based on the principle of the gradual overcoming of national sovereignty through the transfer of some national powers to supranational institutions. The supranational goal of the EU negates nationalism and affirms positive values such as peace, respect of the rule of law, human dignity, freedom, democracy and human rights, including the right to belong to minorities (Article 2 of the LT). It is on the basis of this set of fundamental values that the EU can contribute to changing international relations and building a new world order. At present, the active contribution of the EU in world politics is limited by its imperfection. Only two important supranational public goods are provided: the single European market and the Economic and Monetary Union. But if the EU is able to endow itself with a democratic European government a new model of international relations will become active and visible all over the world.

We would like to end this *Introduction* with an observation about IPE in Europe. In a comprehensive survey on IPE in the world, Benjamin Cohen says: 'European IPE still lacks visible cohesion ... the Continent still resembles an archipelago – a series of dots on a map. However, that does not mean that there are no commonalities at all among the islands' (Cohen, 2014: 92). In our belief, the Supranational Political Economy is a proposal that can contribute not only to joining the dots on the European map, but also to prompting some bold ideas for the reform of the world economic and political order. For example, the Economic and Monetary Union could be taken as a model for the reform of the present international monetary system, based on the dollar, which nobody would claim played no part in the recent world financial crisis. The transition from the old international order to a multipolar order, with several great powers and competing currencies would produce a precarious balance and potentially lead to further serious monetary and financial crises. Today, the proposal for a supranational world monetary union, with a world central bank, considered utopia at Bretton Woods, is being taken seriously not only by some European scholars (Fiorentini and Montani, 2012), but also by Chinese economists (Lin, 2013). If similar proposals are debated in other continents, especially the USA, the Supranational Political Economy could fulfil a fundamental role on the European Continent and bring together IPE scholars the world over.

## References

Arendt, H. (1958). *The Human Condition*. Chicago: Chicago University Press.

Ballester, B. (2013). *European Common Security and Defence Policy. Cost of Non-Europe Report*. Brussels: European Parliament.

Bobbio, N. (1985). *Stato, Governo e Società. Per una Teoria Generale della Politica*. Turin: Einaudi.

Burgess, M. (2013). 'The Penumbra of Federalism: a Conceptual Reappraisal of Federalism, Federation, Confederation and Federal Political Systems.' In Loughlin, J., Kincaid, J. and Swenden, W. (eds.). *Routledge Handbook of Regionalism and Federalism*. London: Routledge, pp. 45–60.

Cohen, B. J. (2014). *Advanced Introduction to International Political Economy*. Cheltenham: Edward Elgar.

The Economist (2013). *The Reluctant Hegemon. A Special Report on Germany*, 15 June.

EPRS (2014). *Mapping the Cost of Non-Europe 2014–19*. Brussels: European Parliament.

Fiorentini, R. and Montani, G. (2012). *The New Global Political Economy. From Crisis to Supranational Integration*. Cheltenham: Edward Elgar.

Freeden, M. (1996). *Ideology and Political Theory. A Conceptual Approach*. Oxford: Clarendon Press.

Frieden, J. A. and Lake, D. A. (eds.) (2000). *International Political Economy. Perspectives on Global Power and Wealth*. London: Routledge.

Fukuyama, F. (2011). *The Origins of Political Order*. New York: Farrar, Strauss and Giroux.

Gilpin, R. (2001). *Global Political Economy. Understanding the International Economic Order*. Princeton: Princeton University Press.

Lin, J. Y. (2013). *Against the Consensus. Reflections on the Great Recession*. Cambridge: Cambridge University Press.

Monnet, J. (1955). *Les Etats-Unis d'Europe ont commencé*. Paris: Laffont.

Morgenthau, H. (1973). *Politics among Nations. The Struggle for Power and Peace*. New York: Alfred A. Knopf.

Ravenhill, J. (2014). 'The Study of Global Political Economy.' In Ravenhill, J. (ed.). *Global Political Economy*. Oxford: Oxford University Press.

Sapir, A., Wolff, G., de Sousa, C. and Terzi, A. (2014). *The Troika and Financial Assistance in the Euro Area. Successes and Failures*. Economic and Monetary Affairs Committee, European Parliament.

Solana, J. (2003). *A Secure Europe in a Better World*. European Security Strategy, Brussels.

The Spinelli Group (2013). *A Fundamental Law of the European Union*. Gütersloh: Verlag Bartelsman Stiftung,

Van Rompuy, H. (2012). *Towards a Genuine Economic and Monetary Union*. Report by the President of the European Council. Brussels, 5 December.

Watts, R. L. (2008). *Comparing Federal Systems*. Montreal & Kingston: McGill-Queen's University Press.

Zürn, M. (2013). 'Globalization and Global Governance.' In Carlsnaes, W., Risse, T. and Simmons, B. A. (eds.). *Handbook of International Relations*. London: Sage.

# Part I

# Birth of the supranational project

# 1 The birth of the European Community

## Supranational ideals and national interests

*Daniela Preda*

### The historiography of European integration

In recent years there has been a considerable development in studies on the history of European integration.[1] The fall of the Berlin Wall is clearly to be considered as in some ways 'liberatory' for this area of research. With the end of bipolarism through the disappearance in the East of the endogenous glue that forcibly held together diversity, and in the West of the exogenous glue (the Soviet threat) which for a long time represented the background to the integration process and was the reason for the crystallization of the system, the studies on European integration were finally liberated from a superficial interpretation that equated Europeanism and Atlanticism and from their long subjection to the history of international relations.

The strengthening of the European Union and the prospects for its enlargement within the context of a system that is by now clearly multipolar brings into question not only Europe's place in the new global system but also the change in how Europeans live and feel about themselves. Still obscure in many regards, because interpreted for the most part – by a culture steadfast in its nationalistic point of view – as the continuation and development of the national phase of European history, the European Union can today become the focus of a broader reconstruction that takes into account Europe in all its complexity and, at the same time, as the offspring of national interest and ideals, in line with the conception of the state in the second half of the twentieth century.

If it is commonplace to state that the Second World War, with the collapse of the European system of states, the disappearance of European centrality in the world and the birth of bipolarism, created a true division in the history of Europe by decreeing the transition of 'European unification' from utopia to reality and marking the beginning of the process of European integration, the consequences of this interpretation are not always considered. Thus despite the broad consensus on this point, it is not uncommon that the recounting of historical events tends rather to emphasize those elements of continuity with the past.

The difficulty that historiography encounters in adopting a different point of view is analogous to a difficulty that involves culture as a whole, which is still in large part conditioned, in its way of analysing facts and its proposals for action, by the eighteenth-century idea that sees the national state as the natural outlet for the self-determination of peoples.[2] Accustomed to using the national state as the all-embracing canon of interpretation, immutable and absolute, history, economics, literature, art and, in a broad sense, culture have based their thought and development on this concept.

The meticulous construction of the national myth, which was superimposed on the spontaneous nationalities and supernationalities (Albertini, 1960, 1961a, 1961b, 1965) of the past, was developed during the nineteenth century through monumentalized works and theories. Historiography played a non-marginal role in this process. As Stuart J. Woolf emphasized, the obstacles historians have encountered, and will continue to encounter, in distancing themselves from the dogmas of nationalism are due to the fact that, on the one hand, 'it has always been the historians themselves who have selected and structured the events and memories of the past that constitute the fabric of the national narrative on which the plot of national and nationalistic myths is woven', and on the other the incontrovertible formulations of nationalism 'have entered so deeply into our *Weltanschauung* as to become a category by which we classify our observations' (Woolf, 1996: 7): a dogma, in fact.

Even historiography, which, with respect to other disciplines, clearly should have been more prepared, due to its own methodology, to renounce any presumption regarding the existence of permanent substantial entities proper to teleological determinism, has not been able to avoid the difficulties of dealing with the revolutionary process represented by European integration, by the creation of a new state, in an area, moreover, already organized into national states on the basis of an agreement among the latter. Instead historiography undertook the task with obsolete instruments. In dealing in-depth with these historical transformations it has encountered the same difficulties that political scientists and legal scholars are forced to face on the theoretical and legal-constitutional level. The obstacle is clear: that which is revolutionary under the existing order by definition lies outside that which is codified.

It is understandable how the differing perceptions of the modern, post-1945 era have caused some people – the majority – to base their research on the chameleon-like concept of the reconstruction of national states (Milward, 1992; Milward *et al.*, 1993) while others – few and for the most part heavily impeded by a strong nationalist orthodoxy closed to change – have operated inside the new context provided by the transition from the European system to the world system of states, striving to interpret the parable of the national states from this perspective.

What is missing, and there is still a need for today, is a unitary view of post-1945 Europe capable of interpreting the advancement of the new order (European integration) alongside the continuation of the old order (the neo-colonial uprisings, the grandeur); a view that is able to identify and motivate the coexistence in the political culture and in the action of states of ambivalent, ambiguous, at times contradictory and even incoherent attitudes that reflect the indecisive action of sovereign states, wavering between resignation over the de facto loss of their political independence and the foolish attempt to regain a bygone power.

After the Second World War there was a convergence between national interests and the process of European unification. If before the two World Wars national interests were pursued by means of a policy of national strength, starting from the Second World War only the policy of European integration can in some ways claim to be an authentic national policy. 'Europe must federate or perish', said Clem Attlee, leader of the Parliamentary Labour Party, in 1939.[3] In March 1954, on the eve of the rejection of the EDC by the French National Assembly, Luigi Einaudi wrote:

> The need to unify Europe is clear. The present states are dust without substance, none of which is capable of bearing the cost of its own defense. Only the union can allow them to continue on. The problem is not between independence and union, but between being united or disappearing.
>
> (Einaudi, 1966: 89)

The apparent strengthening of the national states from the European integration process in reality hides their effective decline. The process of European integration has allowed the national states to strengthen themselves, but at the cost of a progressive shift of power toward the 'community' level. The state that is reconstituted is no longer the old sovereign national state, whose main task was to guarantee the security and, beginning in the twentieth century, the welfare of its citizens. This task has now been transferred to the higher level of the supranational state.

Only when historiography has favoured its dynamic and pragmatic character it has succeeded in correctly analysing the process under way. Europe is an unresolved problem that emerges where, procedurally, unification advances. The European Union, though created through the classically international procedure that is the treaty among sovereign states, was conceived from the start according to a plan far different from the normal one used in diplomatic relations; that is, from one which, by means of treaties, gives rise to situations purely of international cooperation. In other words, the European integration process cannot be viewed as merely an intergovernmental process destined to create an increasingly closer alliance among states which, though cooperating in several political-economic sectors, intend to preserve intact their sovereignty. From the beginning the Monnet project was by nature a true constitutional project, even if limited to a single sector. In fact, the states did not limit themselves to drawing up a simple international treaty but yielded part of their power to a structure that, composed of the fundamental institutions of democracy – those which Jean Monnet indicated as 'les premières assises concrètes de la fédération européenne' ('the first concrete foundations of the European federation')[4] – possesses more than a few features of statehood.

The final result – the construction or breakup of the Union, the creation of a world political order as a corollary to the globalization process under way, or the perpetuation of anarchy – is unknown to us. What is important is that until now it is clear that, far from being dogma, the historiographical reconstruction of the modern era depends on elements of uncertainty: writing history – especially during periods of change such as the present one – means distancing oneself from explicative-predictive models and avoiding constructing 'laws' that govern and explain transformations.

We are asked to interpret a Europe in flux, considered in terms of the advancement of the unification process, thereby questioning the previous territorial arrangements; a nomadic, regionalist, pluralist, 'integrated' Europe that allows for flexible statehood models and variants in terms of membership, the Europe of unity in diversity. Knowledge of this Europe requires the adoption of a diachronic view of reality, of a methodology capable of adapting to change, one which broadens the horizons, leaving room for imagination and creativity. Such knowledge entails reference not only to institutions and diplomacy but to civil society and the complex phenomenology of its behaviour: economic, political, social, cultural and religious.

This approach obliges the historian to adopt appropriate conceptual tools – 'overturning the previous point of view' (Albertini, 1973), to use an effective image of Albertini's – and a methodology that allows him to shift from a synchronic interpretation of historical processes under way to a diachronic one. As a result there is the need to adopt a new historiographical point of view, one that is 'European' and no longer national, pluralist and no longer centralist, interdisciplinary and no longer monothematic, historicist and no longer static. A point of view that leaves room, on the one hand, for the new international context characterized by the death throes of the European system of states and the shift to the world system of states, and on the other for the emergence of a group of actors, reflecting the achievement of a mature conception of the democratic participation of the masses in political power.

The leap, in itself revolutionary, of the national states to a supranational state, which by its nature does not fall within the boundaries of the present order, is the result of converging actions aimed at clearly indicating the final objective and mobilizing the necessary political and social forces as well as at making the hypothetical aims politically viable and acting to achieve them. Mario Albertini theorizes in this regard about the existence of two factors: initiative (thinkers, theorists, movements, precursors of the times), which is able to perceive the new but does not possess the power to achieve it, and execution (governments, diplomacy, institutions, administrations, interests), which has the power but is constrained by its role to move daily along the existing ground. In this way, according to the situation factors of 'construction' or of 'integration', acts of 'initiative' or of 'execution' can be favoured in the historical reconstruction of European integration.

Moreover, as in any episode containing revolutionary elements, in the European unification process as well the actions of individuals within or on the margin of governments and movements are often decisive in influencing and at times provoking events. The movement, if it ever takes place, from sovereign states to the United States of Europe cannot but appear, even in its initial phases, as in large part the result of the action of men who, having identified in advance the crisis points, and for this reason feeling 'called on' to undertake an historical task, work from inside the crisis to alter the context, with more than one even dedicating his life to achieving the goal.

## The historical origins of European union process in the context of the new international order

The interwar period marked a change in international relations. The First World War represented the breakdown of the system of equilibrium among the states which for several centuries had dominated international relations, basing itself on the system of European public law; the Second World War sanctioned its end. The slow and gradual transformation of the historical setting generated over the centuries by powerful factors of integration such as growing economic interdependence and the lingering death throes of the European system of states had already been set in motion, both vertically (the removal of class barriers, the strengthening of the states) and horizontally (among the various economic-political areas). The decline of European national states began to concretely manifest itself during this period, when it became clear that the size of the states represented a decisive obstacle to the complete development of the productive forces. On the other hand, political unification progressed much more slowly than economic unification. The war had become increasingly larger in scope; the destructive potential of new arms made it practically impossible to distinguish belligerents from non-belligerents, military objectives from civil ones, thereby making the entire world a single community with a common destiny. In the new European and international context, political thought gradually broke away from doctrines that could not keep pace with history, abandoning false solutions, utopias and, from a new perspective, examining the paths to take to construct peace and the approach to adopt to deal with the question of the relations among states and the conception itself of state and nation.

The Second World War marks a watershed. By accentuating the weaknesses due to the division of the continent and amplifying the crisis of the nineteenth-century nation state, the Second World War appeared to make choosing valid and immediately applicable alternatives unavoidable. The unitary ideal, which had always been a counterpoint to the evolution of the modern state and the progressive division of Europe, ceased to belong to the ethereal realm of utopia and began to embody a precise political project able to act on reality and deeply modify the course of events. Starting in 1945, these projects took on a new concreteness, imperiously entering the political struggle, acting as strongly on government policy as on the hopes and expectations of the people. The Second World War spawned the minute diffusion of unitary ideals. Organizations and movements for union were formed in various European countries amongst several peoples, and resolutions in favour of European unity were presented in many parliaments and even adopted by some, the issue being discussed by politicians and public opinion alike. The changes it brought in the European context are of such importance as to make those projects of federal unification which between the two wars had appeared overly ambitious, immediately realizable.

In 1945 there were many who believed they had won the war. Over the following months, however, it soon became clear that the biggest loser of the Second World War was not Germany, but in reality the whole of Europe. Reconstruction was provoking apparently intractable economic problems everywhere, including those countries, like France and the United Kingdom, which boasted of a recent past as Great Powers. The 'Great Four' were still on the stage but in reality the destiny of the world had been taken over by the American and Soviet superpowers. Behind the scenes the last act of an evolution with distant roots was being played in the development of productive forces which demanded ever wider markets and the growth of weaponry whose costs were becoming ever harder to meet for traditional nation states.

Awareness of the new internal and international situation was not immediate, but it would become inevitable. Inherent contradictions and difficulties which arose when solving certain problems within the ambit of the single nation state began to push Europeans in the direction of unification.

On 5 June, 1947, the plan presented at Harvard University by the US Secretary of State, General George Marshall, hit hard the stagnant reality which was the Old Continent. If the original objective of the *European Recovery Program* (ERP), as the Marshall Plan was called, was to restore balance to and ensure the political stability of the European states, it was quickly transformed into the desire to adopt the US federal model, with its advantages, on the Old Continent (Hogan, 1987). In fact, the US did not limit itself to promising aid but subordinated this to the creation of a common European programme of reconstruction and development. The Marshall Plan even expressed, and was the first to apply, the political theories formulated in the context of Atlantic federalism, and promoted through the *Federal Union* movement and, in particular, through the activities of Clarence Streit (Stella, 2005). Despite the rejection of William Fullbright's proposal, which called for the inclusion of European political unification among the objectives of the Marshall Plan,[5] the latter contributed to setting under way the European integration process, thereby creating the conditions for a relatively autonomous European political action.[6] The United States interest in European unification gave new credibility to the arguments of the advocates of unity, inducing the European governments, the offspring of a common wartime experience and not deaf to the exalted claim for unity from the Resistance movement, to consider limits to national sovereignty in favour of gradual integration. On the one hand, this entailed the need for some type of unity of a concrete nature, as the governments necessarily favoured, and on the other it obliged them to consider the various consequences of the Cold War under way, thereby geographically limiting the 'Europe of the possible' to those states willing to accept this reality. Thus the first phase of the European unification process began, which has also been defined as the 'psychological' phase of the process.

The first attempts at collaboration certainly did not stand out in terms of clarity of intentions or boldness, but they nevertheless contributed to creating widespread sentiment for Europe. On 16 April, 1948 the Organization for European Economic Cooperation (OEEC) was created, whose main objectives were to manage the aid from the Marshall Plan and the liberalization of European trade. In 1950 the birth of the European Payments Union (EPU) would complete the OEEC from the monetary point of view.

On 17 March, 1948, the Brussels Pact was signed by France, the UK, Belgium, the Netherlands and Luxembourg, with the aim of providing mutual defence aid in cases of aggression in Europe. The pact also called for economic, social and cultural cooperation among the signatories. Born out of the traditional alliances such as the Treaty of Dunkerque – which Britain and France signed in 1947 as an anti-German measure – the Brussels Pact suffered more than marginally from the understandable slowness of France in adapting to the new bipolar context, within which the former enemy Germany became an ally, and from its obstinate, anachronistic clinging to the patterns of political behaviour of a European power, almost as if the Second World War had not changed anything with regard to international power relationships and Europe was still the arbiter of the world's destiny. The pact also suffered from a similar British predilection for bilateral agreements in which Europe ended up being considered the necessary basis, in the new international context, of a leadership that otherwise could have wavered.

The culmination of this initial phase of government integration, which, though lacking in concrete progress along the 'uphill road' toward unification, was rich in ideals (even though these were not yet well defined), is represented by the creation of the Council of Europe, a body composed of a Council of Ministers and a Consultative Assembly, which could be defined as Europe's first representative assembly. However, from the start compromises undermined the Council of Europe's potential. Devoid of effective powers due to British resistance and at the mercy of the Council of Ministers – that is, the intergovernmental institution which became overcautious from the participation of Britain and the Scandinavian countries, which shared a lukewarm attitude to the European issue – the Assembly soon was reduced to impotence. Nevertheless, the Council of Europe represented the maximum level possible of collaboration among that nucleus of nations that emerged with the creation of the OEEC, as well as the expression of a desire for union which, though in varying forms, involved all of Europe beyond the 'iron curtain', which Churchill identified in his famous 'Iron Curtain Speech' at Westminster College in Fulton, Missouri on 5 March, 1946 (Churchill, 1995: 298–302). Moreover, from its creation it clearly brought out the distinction between bold and cautious nations, between those asking for the immediate creation of a united Europe and those opting for a more gradual and less revolutionary process, which brought up the problem of the UK and its choice of battleground.

This initial phase of integration had thus laid the basis for and initiated the process, but it had reached a standstill. Though pro-European sentiment had unarguably taken root, many wondered what strategy should best be adopted; what model Europe should strive towards. Federation, along American or Swiss lines? Confederation? Perhaps a form of institutionalized cooperation between states, starting from a handful of sectoral competences? It was not just a matter of what to aim for, but also how to attain it. It goes without saying that the only recognized democratic way of creating a new state was by the constituent method. However, its implementation in a Europe of sovereign states was troublesome.

As the 1950s dawned, governments opted for a functionalist approach to creating Europe, based on a theory of slow, gradual steps. The progressive integration of industrial sectors would hardly hinder the eventual success of the constituent approach, starting from the more advanced purlieus of Europe. Indeed, a gradual process might foster even greater success, by highlighting the increasingly serious political and institutional deficiencies brought to light by broader integration and a more extensive transfer of power. Even for Jean Monnet, federation was in any case the final leg of European unification, consisting theoretically in a gradual expansion of functions to be handed over to supranational institutions. The question was: what would trigger such a process? Where and how should it be embarked upon?

## The 'Monnet Memorandum'

The opportunity to lead Europe towards overcoming its divisions was not late in coming. The crucial issue which persuaded Europeans to work towards unity in the post-war period was the problem represented by Germany. This country was the most forward and exposed outpost of the new rivalry created by the division of the world into two spheres of influence. The Soviet blockade of Berlin, starting in June 1948, had been the first disturbing signal, despite being effectively countered by the prompt American response. To contain Soviet encroachment in Europe, a 'normalization' of the area was needed, and the Americans were in favour of it.

Any decision to rebuild the pre-war German state apparatus, however, provoked controversy in France, where both fear of the past and a willingness for reconciliation led to the formulation of a hesitant foreign policy, sometimes following, but often also opposing that of the other Allies. But, how to oppose the rebuilding of the German state, then apparently called for by the looming 'Red peril', without creating the bases for the acquiescence of Central Europe to Soviet demands? Conversely, how then to agree to the rebuilding of the German state, its economy and its army, without fashioning the premises for a new *revanche*? Fear of Germany and the possibilities of aggression from that quarter was expressed in France as resistance to any agreement which would allow Germany to regain the two big foundations of its power: its economy – particularly coal and steel, the keys to economic power and weapons production – and the army. Thus it is not by chance that the first two supranational European Community projects – the European Coal and Steel Community (ECSC) and the European Defence Community (EDC) – were to involve precisely these two sectors.

These were the parameters of an objective difficulty: that of creating a bond between France and Germany capable of neutralizing the two greatest sources of the German power: heavy industry in the Rhine region and the army. The aim was to disarticulate the complex system of protected and autarchic economies of the European states which had just emerged from a war regime and its associated malaise of exasperated nationalism, starting from the coal and steel sector.

New ideas were needed to disentangle the complicated situation to finally overcome the obsolete schemes of the pre-war era. In the new geo-political context of the bipolar system, neighbouring states, natural enemies of the past, had to become natural partners in the future. Indeed, if the fear of the German industrial domination could be overcome in France, the greatest obstacle to the unification of Europe would have been removed. There was need for a solution which would place French industry on the same starting line as German industry, whilst freeing the latter from those encumbrances born of its military defeat. This would create the economic and political conditions for a understanding vital for the future of Europe.

It was Jean Monnet (Monnet, 1976; van Helmont, 1981; Duchêne, 1994; Roussel, 1996) who proposed what that we could define a Copernican revolution in European national relationships.

Facing the worsening Franco-German dispute, Monnet began to realize that the only way to prevent Germany from getting its hands back on the material bases for its military power was to place them under the control of an authority which France also had to recognize. This would have avoided exposing Germany to discriminatory unilateral controls in the future. But Monnet went even further, creating the foundation for a new era in European history: the unification process. While this plan succeeded in isolating the coal–steel problem and solving it through an intergovernmental agreement, for Monnet this first attempt at forging the European Community still appeared to be lacking in imagination. Therefore, he aimed at linking the solution of that crucial, but specific problem, to a greater historic plan: that of creating European unity. For Monnet the point of departure of the European federation was Franco-German union. To attain it, he believed that the first step had to be the creation of common bases for economic development, at first for coal and steel, then for other sectors. Later, in developing his ideas, he anticipated he could extend this Franco-German union to the other countries of Europe. Thus the creation of a European pool for coal and steel was transformed by Monnet into the first step towards the gradual building up of a European federation.

Jean Monnet knew that the Atlantic Council meeting fixed for 10 May, 1950 in London to resolve the German question, would give the French Foreign Minister, Robert Schuman, the chance to meet his British counterpart, Ernest Bevin, as well as the American Secretary of State, Dean Acheson. Hence, on 28 April he sent a memorandum to the French Prime Minister Georges Bidault and Schuman himself. In it, Monnet proposed the creation of a specialized Supranational Authority with powers limited to the sector of coal and steel production. He was not concealing his real objectives: 'cette proposition réalisera les premières assises concrètes d'une fédération européenne indispensable à the préservation de la paix' ('this proposal will be the occasion for the first Assembly of a European federation indispensable for the maintenance of peace') (Monnet, 1976: 353). The key word in his proposal was 'peace'. In a second memorandum, dated 3 May, he explained his theory for gradual but also radical development. Europe could not be created in one step, nor could it be a hotchpotch of states; it would have to be the result of concrete realizations capable first of all of creating solidarity in fact. He emphasized in particular that the problem of European organization could be faced and solved only by 'resolute action on a limited but decisive point, that will cause a fundamental change on this point and progressively modify the terms themselves of the whole set of problems'. 'Thus – continued Monnet – one will be able to give the peoples of the "free world" hope even for the most distant objectives which will be entrusted them and will create in them the active determination to pursue them.'[7]

Within a few days, the Monnet project earnt the support of Schuman, the French Cabinet and the German Chancellor, Konrad Adenauer. It was formally presented by Schuman in Paris, in the Hall of the Clock, on 9 May, causing acute irritation in Bevin but attracting the support of Acheson.

On 9 May, 1950, the French Minister of Foreign Affairs, Robert Schuman presented a memorandum to the French National Assembly, and indeed, to the whole world: it was to be the so-called Schuman Plan (Diebold, 1959; Gerbet, 1962; Schwabe, 1988; Gillingham, 1991; Spierenburg and Poidevin, 1993; Dell, 1995; Ranieri and Tosi, 2004; Wilkens, 2004). It anticipated the creation of the first European Community: the European Community of Coal and Steel.

It is not by chance that 9 May was chosen as the symbolic date for the inception of the unification process of the European Community, the 'European' day *par excellence*. 9 May takes on a meaning which goes beyond that of the ECSC: it identifies a project, it traces a path. It means: we can start with the ECSC to build something different and more substantial. The ECSC was the first stage in a journey that today Europeans are still travelling, a long and tortuous road, which is slowly leading towards overcoming the division between sovereign nation states and is unifying the continent. The Schuman Plan, as it was then presented on 9 May, 1950, began as follows:

World peace cannot be safeguarded without the making of efforts proportionate to the dangers which threaten it.

The contribution which an organized and living Europe can bring to civilization is indispensable to the maintenance of peaceful relations. ...

Europe will not be made all at once, or according to a single, general plan. It will be built through concrete achievements, which first create a *de facto* solidarity.

With this aim in view, the French Government proposes to take action immediately on one limited but decisive point.

The French Government proposes to place Franco-German production of coal and steel as a whole under a common higher authority, within the framework of an organization open to the participation of the other countries of Europe. The pooling of coal and steel production should immediately provide for the setting-up of common foundations for economic development as a first step in the federation of Europe.[8]

The time for the birth of the Community European had come.

In order to study and carry out the plan a diplomatic conference was convened in Paris on 20 June, 1950, in which France, the Federal Republic of Germany, Italy, Belgium, the Netherlands and Luxembourg took part. For its part Britain, where the government was committed to nationalizing the coal and steel industries and which was wary of free market concepts, had no intention of placing its resources in common with other European countries and of subordinating them to a High Authority with sovereign powers, as called for under Monnet's plan. It thus declined the invitation. The required commitment eliminated any doubt about the concept of European unity and clearly indicated which states intended to take concrete measures in favour of unification. A new barrier for the 'Europe of the possible' was thus determined through a division among those states willing to move forward up the hill of supranational unification and those not yet ready to give up their sovereignty.

As is well known, the Treaty project drafted by the conference was signed in Paris on 18 April, 1951, and the first supranational European organization came into effect on 25 July, 1952.

The event was epoch breaking, since it marked the beginning of the European integration process and introduced a new player to world politics: Europe, even if only partially integrated territorially and politically.

In the preamble the contracting parties affirmed their resolution to create 'the first assembly of a larger and deeper community among a people who for long have been opposed by bloody divisions' and 'to lay the basis for institutions capable of guiding what has already become a common destiny'.

## From the European Defence Community to the European Political Community

At the same time as the events concerning the ECSC were unfolding at the start of the 1950s, Europe had to deal with problems regarding its defence. The worsening of the Cold War made the situation dramatic. In August of 1949 the Soviets exploded their first atomic bomb, throwing into crisis the theory of nuclear deterrence and holding out to the West the frightening prospect of a European war that would be fought using only conventional arms. The start of the Korean War on 25 June, 1950, demonstrated in turn, and in a concrete way, that the Cold War could lead to a 'hot' war and appeared to represent a sort of test by which the Soviets gauged US reactions to communist expansion while waiting to strike against the crucial sector of Europe.

In everyone's eyes Germany became the new Korea, the weak link in the Western defence system. On 8 September, Harry Truman approved the so-called *one package*; that is, the formation of an integrated army in which Europe would participate with sixty divisions under US command, with an international general staff. This army would contain a number of German divisions, at the time undefined but which would turn out to be ten. The US president thus came out in favour of a US commitment in Europe but on the condition that the Europeans accepted collaborating on the basis of the American proposals.

On 12 September the French, British and American defence ministers met in New York to prepare the work for the Atlantic Council. Dean Acheson, along with Rear Admiral Thomas H. Robbins, proposed the one package to Bevin and Schuman. In the three-part conversations on 13–14 September no agreement was reached, however, as Schuman held his own against the US secretary of state, accepting the creation of a unified command and an increase in forces and in arms production in Europe, but not German rearmament. The same scenario occurred at the meeting of the Atlantic Council on 15 September, where Schuman, though isolated, held fast to his position. However, there was no time for delay: a way had to be found to proceed with German rearmament. It was Jean Monnet who suggested a way out of the impasse.

While the New York Conference was under way he reunited the group that had already developed the bases for the ECSC project: Hirsch, Uri, Clappier and Reuter, to which Hervé Alphand would be added. Regarding the political-institutional model for the ECSC, Monnet proposed linking German rearmament to the European integration process, including the German military forces within a European army which would be unified at the lowest possible level of military units with regard to command, organization, equipment, and the financing and managing of common supranational institutions, with an Atlantic Supreme Command. Monnet sent a memorandum in this sense to Premier Pleven on 14 October. On 24 October, Pleven announced to the French National Assembly the country's intention to work toward the creation of a European army, stating that it was necessary to overcome the national coalitions and to aim toward a common army, which would mean the complete merging of Western Europe's human and material elements and a linking up to the political institutions of a united Europe. The project presented indicated the institutions that were to be created: an assembly, a defence ministry appointed by the governments and accountable to both the assembly and ministry, and a Council of Ministers of the member states, which would serve as an intermediary between the Community and those states. There was also talk of a common budget to finance the army. The process to create a European Defence Community (Aron and Lerner, 1956; Fursdon, 1980; Clesse, 1989; Preda, 1990; Dumoulin, 2000) was thus already under way. The uniqueness of the French project, and the aspect that distinguished it from the *one package*, was its supranational character, which went far beyond traditional military alliances and brought into play the very same sovereignty of the states regarding a crucial sector of their existence, thereby providing a chance for Europe.

Hence on 26 February, the Paris Conference for a European Army was held, attended by France, the Federal Republic of Germany, Belgium, Luxembourg, Italy and later on the Netherlands. The Americans supported the parallel talks at Petersberg between themselves and the Germans that were being held to reach agreement over the inclusion of German contingents in NATO forces. In the Summer of 1951, however, the Americans changed their minds following the failure of the Petersberg talks and because of French (especially Monnet's) insistence[9] and so began to openly support EDC.

On 27 May, 1952, after difficult diplomatic negotiations the foreign ministers of the states that had participated in the Paris Conference signed the treaty creating the European Defence Community. The project then moved on to the ratification phase.

Between autumn 1951 and winter 1952, as the ECSC came into being and negotiations on the EDC wound down, there was a groundswell of support for the creation of a European political community (Preda, 1994). The newly hatched functionalist process, spreading from sector to sector, offered glimpses of deep contradictions, and supplied increasingly convincing arguments in support of a struggle for European unity. One prime issue was how to create an effective common army – not just a mere overlap of national armies – before creating the federal state it should serve. Another was how to appoint a specialized authority to create it, since a unified army had ramifications affecting other crucial public sectors such as foreign policy and the national budget. And again: could such specialized authorities remain divided from one another and totally separate without the risk of generating confusion, and worse still, getting bogged down in inefficiency? In other words, could the EDC precede the constitutional foundation of a European state? These are the issues that Altiero Spinelli quite rightly raised in a memorandum to the Italian premier Alcide De Gasperi in August 1951.[10]

Having entered into an area as sensitive as defence, functionalist integration needed to deal with the question of political unification, creating the conditions for a smooth transition towards a constitutional approach.

De Gasperi (Preda, 2004) took steps to have the draft treaty of the EDC include an article – number 38 – entrusting the provisional Assembly of the EDC with the task of drafting a project for the Statute of the European political community, at the same defining the principles which should inspire the Assembly in the course of its inquiry: 'l'organisation de caractère définitif qui prendra la place de la présente organisation provisoire – the article stated – devrait avoir une structure fédérale ou confédérale. Elle devra comprendre notamment une Assemblée bicamérale et un pouvoir exécutif'.[11] De Gasperi was able to provide a leap in quality to the unification process by moving beyond the functionalistic approach to adopt a federalist one.

In the spring of 1952, the forces in favour of a united Europe weighed up the possibility of bringing forward the calling of the Constituent Assembly. In May, the Belgian Paul-Henri Spaak, after having consulted with Monnet (who, in December 1951 had given up his post as president of the Consultative Assembly of the Council of Europe), proposed giving the task of drafting the project for a European Constitution, pursuant to art. 38, to the ECSC Assembly (suitably enlarged to include the members of the EDC), which was soon to meet as the ratifications of the Schuman Plan were about to be completed.

The proposal to bring forward the Assembly was immediately welcomed at the highest levels, leading to a Franco-Italian government initiative that was discussed and approved on 9 September by the six ECSC Foreign Ministers meeting in Luxembourg.

On 10 September, Adenauer formally requested that the ECSC Council – at its maiden meeting – draw up a Constitution of the European political community. Three days later, the Assembly agreed to the governments' request and went to work, naming itself the *ad hoc* Assembly.

With the convocation of the *ad hoc* Assembly the EDC had achieved its metamorphosis: an event that involved the sectoral integration of Europe, which was managed by the national diplomatic authorities, had acquired the features of an adventure that envisaged the potential existence of a European democratic and federal state. What before had only been illusion now became hope. In the space of only a few months, the European Constituent Assembly had become a reality and Europe found itself – albeit only fleetingly – on the brink of unification.

What just months earlier had seemed a pipe dream was now not only within reach, but could not materialize fast enough. There was a need to deal promptly with new challenges, the most demanding undoubtedly being the need to create a supranational political authority, uniting not thirteen former British colonies, or a handful of cantons, as in the case of the United States or Switzerland, but the great sovereign national states of the modern era. So as the project advanced at the government level, the Movements were taking action not just to ensure the successful fulfilment of the task at hand, but also to prepare to deal with the new challenges lying ahead, proposing themselves as a viable force driving government action.

In March 1952, Altiero Spinelli pushed for the creation of a *Comité d'Etudes pour la Constitution Européenne* (CECE) – Committee for the Study of a European Constitution, of which Paul-Henri Spaak became the Chairman and Fernand Dehousse the secretary. The aim of the group was to explore the problems raised by the political unification of Europe, and draw up plans for a European Constitution which – given the novelty of the subject and the little time available – would have provided valuable support to the 'official' constituent assembly. The results achieved by the CECE, also aided by a group of Harvard University experts led by Karl Friedrich and Robert R. Bowie, were published in the form of nine resolutions in November 1952.[12] That same month, the *Travaux préparatoires* were also published, which contained the minutes of the CECE proceedings.[13] There is evidence of close links between the CECE and the *ad hoc* Assembly: Paul-Henri Spaak chaired both bodies; Fernand Dehousse was secretary of the CECE and *rapporteur* for the Political Institutions subcommittee of the *ad hoc* Assembly (chaired by Paul-Henri Teitgen), and also a member of the latter's *Groupe de Travail*; Lodovico Benvenuti was a distinguished member of the CECE and a *rapporteur* for the Attributions subcommittee in the *ad hoc* Assembly chaired by the Dutchman Blaisse.

The *ad hoc* Assembly went straight to work under the guidance of Chairman Paul-Henri Spaak, and six months later, within the deadline that had been set for 10 March, 1953, the draft statute of the European Political Community had been unanimously approved, except for five abstentions.

Though the draft was not explicitly federalist, it nevertheless proposed very progressive solutions. The Community was supranational in nature and was declared to be indissoluble; it was a legal entity that incorporated the ECSC and the EDC, it exercised powers conferred to it in respect of the statute or additional acts, in close co-operation with national organizations – through the governments of the latter – and with international organizations that shared similar aims. The exercise of its duties was entrusted to five institutions: a Parliament, a European Executive Council, a Council of National Ministers, a Court of Justice, an Economic and Social Council.

The Community institutions were given over the competences of the ECSC and the EDC, in addition to several new ones. As regards international relations, the Community could sign international treaties and accords, or comply with them insofar as their responsibilities allowed, send or receive ambassadors, and ensure that the foreign policies of the member states were coordinated. As regards finance, the Assembly decided to empower the Community to impose taxes on citizens and member states, buy and sell property and assets, and borrow money (subject to the Parliament's approval). The contributions of the states were fixed by the Council of ministers, by unanimous vote, on the proposal of the Executive Council. The procedures for setting the basis, rates and conditions for direct tax liability were to be set out by the Executive Council and submitted to Parliament for its approval. The Community budget, proposed by the Executive Council, was voted annually by Parliament. The Community was also given the task of gradually forging a common market, i.e. the free movement of goods, services, people and capital. The Community also had other powers, such as the power to support member states, on their request, or on its own initiative, to ensure respect of the democratic liberties; to set up its own administrative system independent of that of the member states. The statute approved by the *ad hoc* Assembly then went to the attention of the national governments, but the fate of the political Community – necessarily influenced by the ups and downs of the EDC – was becoming more and more uncertain. The context that served as a background to these events had by now changed. Stalin's death, which opened up the prospects for détente, and France's growing difficulties in Indochina made ratification difficult. During the initial meeting of the six nations in Paris on 12 May, where once again De Gasperi showed he was the true propulsive force of the Community, the ministers unanimously recognized the need to create a political Community and to move toward this goal through the proceedings under way. However, on 21 May the Mayer government fell in France, with immediate repercussions, even for De Gasperi, who, after being defeated in the 7 June elections (which would shortly lead to his ouster from the government) was about to leave the scene.

After shuffling along for months, and staging countless Summit meetings (Strasburg, 9 March; Paris, 12 May; Paris again, 22 June; Baden Baden, 7 August), the ministers handed over the project to a Conference of experts (Rome, 22 September–9 October), who had neither the competence nor the power to draft a European Constitution. The Statute was drastically amended and gradually came to lose many of its federal characteristics. By the time the Hague Summit was held on 20 November, the ministers realized it would be impossible to achieve significant results in an historic context that was no longer pressing for unification, but they were reluctant to put a sudden end to the proceedings and did not wish to shoulder responsibility for failure, so they decided to entrust a Commission with the task of further exploring the issue. The Commission dragged on meeting after meeting until late June, when someone came up with the idea of adjourning the proceedings 'with the maximum caution and without noise', by simply neglecting to set a date for resuming discussions after the summer break. With the collapse of the EDC, even the plan of a Statute for the Political Community was abandoned indefinitely.

The destiny of the political Community was thus linked to that of the EDC, which was ratified in 1954 by four European countries: the Netherlands (the first signatory), Belgium, Luxembourg and Germany. Uncertainty came from Italy, where the ratification process was under way, and France. On 30 August, 1954, the French National Assembly, without engaging in a lengthy debate, rejected the project based on a *question préalable* (a preliminary question) presented by General Aumeran, with 319 votes in favour, 264 against and 12 abstentions. The Communists and Gaullists voted unanimously against the project, while the Socialists and Radicals were divided. In a historical period characterized by détente, these political forces formed an unlikely coalition and managed, through a newly discovered national pride and economic recovery, to block the first attempt at creating a European army. The project for a European political community followed the same destiny, though indirectly.

However, quite apart from the failure of the initiative, the constitutional experience of the European Political Community that stemmed from the functionalist project of the EDC, for the first time in the process of European unification, actually merged two parallel strategies for achieving European unity, functionalism and constitutionalism; on this basis the first attempt to create a federal European state took place.

Although this first attempt at constructing a European federation failed, it highlighted the possibility of involving a large range of political forces and broad social classes in the attempt to end, with the help of a European democracy, the nefarious Nazi era. To this end the vigorous activities of statesmen such as De Gasperi, Schuman and Adenauer were indispensable; men who rose above party and national interests to create new political structures to keep pace with the economic, civil and social progress. Equally indispensable was the thinking and actions of individuals such as Spinelli and Monnet, who made such goals their mission in life.

## The 'turning point'

After the failure of the EDC, Europeanists immediately 'relaunched' the idea of continental integration. The ministers of the original six nations met in Messina on 1–2 June, 1955, to begin the process which, on 27 March, 1957, would lead to the signing in Rome of the Treaties that created the EEC and Euratom.

The Treaties of Rome (Serra, 1989; Preda, 2013) represented an important turning point in the European integration process. The path toward the idealistic Europe turned toward a pragmatic Europe made up of markets as well as new common policies that would become the pillars of the future European Union. If, from 1952 to 1954, horizontal and vertical integration had progressed in parallel fashion, the start of the so-called 'European relaunching' definitely ended the moment of convergence: institutional strengthening was set aside and the tendency toward a broadening of competencies became predominant.[14]

This did not preclude the existence of strong elements of continuity that bound together the Europeanist elements of the second half of the 1940s: the beginning of Community construction and the Treaties of Rome. Rather, by means of a greater focus on the twofold nature of the approach, we can emphasize the existence of this continuity right from the start. In fact, we would not be able to explain the rapidity with which, on 25 March, 1957, the governments signed the Treaties of Rome and implemented them on 1 January, 1958, if we did not also refer to the experience of the European political Community, not so much as regards its constitutional aspect but its functionalist ones, which also were well present in that experience.

Nevertheless, the fact remains that, due to the failure to make the issues of peace and the overcoming of the Franco-German disagreements a central focus (issues which had inspired the initial projects for European integration), during the period of détente and decolonization a functional approach was favoured in the belief this could gradually lead, as a final stage, to political integration.

Therefore, the Treaties of Rome represented a hybrid. The two spirits already present in the OEEC, the federalist one and the functionalist one, the 'bold' and the 'cautious', were reflected in the two new Communities. The European Community proposal for atomic energy (Euratom) (Dumoulin *et al.*, 1994), presented by Monnet, responded to a sectoral vertical integration strategy characterized by the creation of supranational institutions with sweeping powers; a sort of constitutional gradualism that, as the final stage, called for a process to create a European federation. The European Economic Community responded instead to a different idea of integration: a horizontal, broader integration in which the supranational institutions existed only as a function of the organization and management of the market. The economic decision-making power was assigned to the Council of Ministers, the expression of the national governments, which concentrated in itself the legislative power and a good deal of the executive power. However, no resources were provided for the Community budget.

Of the two Treaties, the one that would have the most impact in subsequent decades would be the EEC; that is, the one that was horizontal in nature and which responded to the canons of the *functional approach*. The Euratom, on the other hand, would be left without its more advanced features.

Despite this, the Treaties were from the beginning viewed as a sort of *passe partout* to European political integration, an interpretation which would continue to exist up to the present day. In my opinion, this has occurred for two main reasons, one subjective and one objective. Interpreting the spirit and will that had led to 'Europe's relaunching', the president of the Commission Spaak, who was charged with studying and drawing up the Treaties of Rome, would state that the men entrusted with drafting the Treaties of Rome 'croyaient que l'intégration économique les conduirait immancablement à l'union politique', viewing economic integration as nothing other than 'l'accessoire, ou tout au moins la première étape d'une révolution politique plus importante encore' (Spaak, 1969: 100). Based on this conviction, Spaak could claim, in the same way as many other contemporary statesmen, that 'le Traité de Rome marquait le triomphe de l'esprit de coopération et la défaite du nationalisme égoïste' (Spaak, 1969: 99). For his part, Fernand Dehousse, during the debate in the Belgian senate on the ratification of the Treaties of Rome (session of 26 November, 1957), could underscore, in stating that the only solution to the problem could come from the political Community, that an effective merging of the markets and economies (positing the irreversibility of the process) was at risk due to the insufficient powers of the Community and the possible crisis being experienced by one of the signatory countries.

Le couronnement indispensable des Communautés européennes que nous construisons c'est, tôt ou tard, la Communauté politique ... C'est dans cet esprit-là – en vue de ménager les souverainetés qui commencent à se rapprocher et qui se fédéreront un jour – que j'accepte et que la grande majorité du groupe socialiste accepte les deux traités qui nous sont proposés.

(Dehousse, 1960)

Thus, political integration was part of the 'spirit' of the Treaty but not of its substance.

The objective reason can be found, I believe, in the international context in which the Treaties came about. In 1955 the member states had already been reconstructed (that period witnessed the Austrian state treaty, the creation of the UEO and Germany's inclusion in NATO), the war was far removed in time, and even the Cold War, markedly Stalinist in nature, had given way to détente and competitive coexistence. Decolonization was progressing inexorably while a world composed of non-aligned nations began to appear on the horizon. Within the bipolar world US leadership guaranteed Europe its essential instruments of sovereignty: security and a common defence through NATO and the nuclear umbrella; and monetary stability, at least since 1971, through the dollar and the gold exchange standard. Moreover, strong economic expansion favoured economic liberalization and the convergence of economic policies.

During the Cold War European integration was imperfectly achieved. The reasons for the union were constantly at odds with those upholding the preservation of national sovereignty, without a resolution of this contrast in favour of one or the other position. The existence of an objective momentum toward unification and a *de facto* statehood of reference – the US – permitted the European Community to set aside the institutional aspects of unification and not to untie the Gordian knot between federation and confederation, instead maintaining an ambiguity regarding the objectives, an ambiguity that still remains today.

## Notes

1 If the historiography regarding European topics became generalized only beginning at the end of the 1980s, it had already for some time become influenced by the studies of the German historian Walter Lipgens (1968–1991).
2 In this regard Stuart Woolf underscores that nationalism has succeeded, through a constant *nation-building* activity, in transmitting to all citizens an interpretation of the state – the identification between the individual nation and individual state within a single territory – contrary to both the course of European history and the increasing migrations of its peoples (Woolf, 1996).
3 Attlee's speech at the Caxton Hall on 8 November, 1939, was quickly printed as *Labour's Peace Aims*. See Corthorn and Davies (2008: 96).
4 This represents not only the hopes of Monnet, who saw in that limited Community the seeds of a future Europe without borders. In fact, it must be remembered that Robert Schuman as well, in presenting on 9 May, 1950, the project for the first specialized Authority, also held out the prospect of a federal evolution.

5  On the US attitude, see the excellent works by Mélandri (1980) and Bertella Farnetti (2004). The idea to promote the creation of a true European federation, starting with the Marshall Plan, appears officially in January of 1948, when Elbert Thomas, Fullbright and Boggs proposed an amendment in this direction to the congressional Foreign Affairs Committee. Fullbright would later withdraw the amendment, though after having succeeded in including in the final report of the committee that the plan should not be limited solely to economic cooperation, as the aid plan aimed also at producing progress in creating political and cultural ties. During a plenary session on 3 March it was once again proposed to include political unification among the objectives of the Marshall Plan. After further debate in Congress, in 1949 the preamble was modified by the addition of the following sentence: 'It is the policy of the American people to encourage the unification of Europe.' After a prolonged discussion in Congress, the proposal to substitute the term unification with federation was abandoned (Mélandri, 1980: 145 and *passim*).

6  Through his adjunct Joseph Jones, Marshall was probably inspired in this 'ideological' extension of the Plan by two convinced advocates of Europe's economic and political integration: Ben T. Moore and Harold van Buren Cleveland, who, while proposing in the immediate term what to them was an insufficient monetary and commercial unification, believed it possible to foster in Europe an opinion favourable to the supranational idea of European unity (van Buren Cleveland, 1988, Geiger and van Buren Cleveland, 1951). Cleveland, as well as Ayers Brinser, Robert G. McCloskey, Edward McWhinney, Louis B. Sohn and Arthur E. Sutherland, would be part of the team of Harvard University scholars, led by Robert R. Bowie and Carl J. Friedrich, who would collaborate with Spaak and Spinelli in the proceedings of the Study Committee for the European Constitution, publishing the results in Bowie and Friedrich (1954). In this regard see also Preda (1996).

7  The 'Monnet Memorandum' of 28 April, 1950. The quotation in the text was published by *Le Monde*, on 9 May, 1970, with a comment from which the quotation has been drawn.

8  The translation of these two paragraphs of the Schuman Plan of 9 May, 1950, was taken from Acheson (1969: 383–384).

9  During a dinner in Paris at the end of June, in the presence of the American Chief of Staff Gruenther, and the President Truman's adviser Harriman, Monnet managed to convince Gen. Eisenhower of the importance that the EDC would have in Europe. On 3 July, in London before Attlee and Churchill, Eisenhower made a speech where he committed himself without reservations to European unity considering it an essential basis for the security and prosperity of Europe. 'Europe' – declared Eisenhower – 'cannot attain the towering material stature possible to its peoples' skills and spirit so long as it is divided by patchwork territorial fences. They foster localized instead of common interest', and added: 'but with unity achieved, Europe could build adequate security and, at the same time, continue the march of human betterment that has characterized Western civilization' (Geiger and van Buren Cleveland, 1951: 83–85).

10  *Promemoria sul Rapporto provvisorio presentato nel luglio1951 dalla Conferenza per l'organizzazione di una Comunità europea della difesa*, an appendix to Albertini (1977).

11  *Projet de Traité de la CED*, 14 February, 1952, in Ivan Matteo Lombardo papers, filed with the Historical Archives of the European Union, Florence.

12  *Brochure No 1* of the Comité d'Etudes, Brussels, November 1952.

13  *Projet de Statut de la Communauté politique européenne. Travaux préparatoires*, Brussels, November, 1952.

14  It is significant that the term *intégration* contained in the Benelux Memorandum was replaced by the more neutral term *construction* (Gerbet, 2007: 86).

# References

Acheson, D. (1969). *Present at the Creation. My Years in the State Department.* New York: Norton & Company.

Albertini, M. (1960). *Lo Stato nazionale.* Milano: Giuffré.

Albertini, M. (1961a). 'Per un uso controllato della terminologia nazionale e supernazionale.' *Il Federalista*, III (1) and *Le Fédéraliste*, V (3), 1963.

Albertini, M. (1961b). 'Idea nazionale e ideali di unità supernazionali in Italia dal 1815 al 1918.' In *Nuove questioni di storia del Risorgimento e dell'unità d'Italia.* Milan: Marzorati. Republished in Mosconi, N. (ed.) (9 vols. 2006–2010). *Mario Albertini. Tutti gli scritti.* Bologna: Il Mulino, vol. III, *1958–1961*, pp. 775–851.

Albertini, M. (1965). 'L'idea di nazione.' *Giornale del Censimento*, I (4).

Albertini, M. (1973). 'L'integrazione europea, elementi per un inquadramento storico.' In Levi, L. and Pistone, S. (eds.). *Trent'anni di vita del Movimento federalista europeo.* Milan: Franco Angeli, pp. 13–34.

Albertini, M. (1977). 'La fondazione dello Stato europeo.' *Il Federalista*, XIX (1).

Aron, R. and Lerner, D. (eds.) (1956). *La querelle de la CED.* Paris: A. Colin.

Bertella Farnetti, P. (2004). *Gli Stati Uniti e l'unità europea 1940–1950. Percorsi di un'idea.* Milan: FancoAngeli.

Buren Cleveland, H. van (1988). 'Reflections on the Marshall Plan: Then and Now.' In Ellwood, D. W., *The Marshall Plan Forty Years After: Lessons for the International System Today.* Bologna: The Bologna Center of the John Hopkins University School of Advanced International Studies.

Bowie, R. R. and Friedrich, C. J. (1954). *Studies in Federalism.* Boston; Toronto: Little, Brown.

Churchill, W. (1995). 'The Sinews of Peace.' In Kishlansky, M. A. (ed.). *Sources of World History.* New York: Harper Collins.

Clesse, A. (1989). *Le projet de la CED du Plan Pleven au 'crime' du 30 août: histoire d'un malaintendu européen.* Baden Baden: Nomos Verlag.

Corthorn, P. and Davies, J. (2008). *The British Labour Party and the Wider World.* London: Tauris Academic Studies.

Dehousse, F. (1960). *L'Europe et le monde. Recueil d'études, de rapports et de discours 1945–1960*, vol. II. Paris: L.G.D.J.

Dell, E. (1995). *The Schuman Plan and the British Abdication of Leadership in Europe.* Oxford: Oxford University Press.

Diebold, W. (1959). *The Schuman Plan: A Study in Economic Cooperation 1950–1959.* New York: F. Praeger.

Duchêne, F. (1994). *Jean Monnet. The First Man of Interdependence.* New York: Norton & Company.

Dumoulin, M. (2000). *La Communauté européenne de défense, leçons pour demain?* Bruxelles: Peter Lang.

Dumoulin, M., Guillen, P. and Vaïsse, M. (1994). *L'énergie nucléaire en Europe. Des origines à l'Euratom.* Berne: P.I.E. Peter Lang.

Einaudi, L. (1966). *Lo scrittoio del Presidente.* Turin: Einaudi.

Fursdon, E. (1980). *The European Defense Community: a History.* New York: St. Martin's Press.

Geiger, T. and Buren Cleveland, H. van (1951). *Making Western Europe Defensible: An Appraisal of the Effectiveness of United States Policy in Western Europe.* Washington: National Planning Association.

Gerbet, P. (1962). *La genèse du Plan Schuman*. Lausanne: Fondation Jean Monnet pour l'Europe.

Gerbet, P. (2007). *1957. La naissance du Marché Commun*. Paris: Complexe.

Gillingham, J. (1991). *Coal, Steel and the Rebirth of Europe, 1945–1955. The Germans and French from Ruhr Conflict to Economic Community*. Cambridge: Cambridge University Press.

Helmont, J. van (1981). *Jean Monnet comme il était*. Lausanne: Fondation Jean Monnet pour l'Europe.

Hogan, M. (1987). *The Marshall Plan. America, Britain and the Reconstruction of Western Europe 1947–1952*. Cambridge: Cambridge University Press.

Lipgens, W. (1968). *Europa-Föderationspläne der Widerstandsbewegungen 1940–1945*. Munchen: R. Oldenbourg.

Lipgens, W. (1977). *Die Anfänge der europäischen Einigungspolitik 1945–1950*. Stuttgart: Klett.

Lipgens, W. (1982). *A History of European Integration*. Oxford: Oxford University Press.

Lipgens, W. (ed.) (1985–1991). *Documents on the History of European Integration*. Berlin; New York: De Gruyter (Vol. I, 1985. *Continental Plans for European Union 1939–1945*; Vol. II, 1986. *Plans for European Union in Great Britain and in Exile 1939–1945*; Vol. III, 1988. *The Struggle for European Union by Political Parties and Pressure Groups in Western European Countries 1945–1950*; Vol. IV, by Lipgens, W. and Loth, W., 1991. *Transnational Organizations of Political Parties and Pressure Groups in the Struggle for European Union, 1945–1950*.

Mélandri, P. (1980). *Les États-Unis face à l'unification de l'Europe*. Paris: A. Pedone.

Milward, A. S. (1992). *The European Rescue of the Nation State*. London; New York: Routledge.

Milward, A. S., Lynch, F. M. B., Romero, F., Ranieri, R. and Sorensen, V. (1993). *The Frontier of National Sovereignty. History and Theory 1945–1992*. London; New York: Routledge.

Monnet, J. (1976). *Mémoires*. Paris: Fayard (*Memoirs*, translated by Richard Mayne, foreword by the Rt. Hon. Roy Jenkins, London: Collins, 1978).

Preda, D. (1990). *Storia di una speranza. La battaglia per la CED e la Federazione europea*. Milan: Jaca Book.

Preda, D. (1994). *Sulla soglia dell'Unione. La vicenda della Comunità politica europea (1952–1954)*. Milano: Jaca Book.

Preda, D. (ed.) (1996). *Per una costituzione federale dell'Europa. Lavori preparatori del Comitato di Studi presieduto da P. H. Spaak*. Padova: Cedam.

Preda, D. (2004). *Alcide De Gasperi federalista europeo*. Bologna: Il Mulino.

Preda, D. (2013). *Avanti adagio. I Trattati di Roma e l'unità europea*. Padova: Cedam.

Ranieri, R. and Tosi, L. (eds.) (2004). *La Comunità europea del carbone e dell'acciaio (1952–2002). Gli esiti del Trattato in Europa e in Italia*. Padova: Cedam.

Roussel, E. (1996). *Jean Monnet*. Paris: Fayard.

Schwabe, K. (ed.) (1988). *The Beginnings of the Schuman-Plan*. Bruxelles: Bruyant.

Serra, E. (ed.) (1989). *The Relaunching of Europe and the Treaties of Rome*. Bruxelles: Bruyant, Baden Baden: Nomos Verlag, Paris: L.G.D.J., Milano: Giuffré.

Spaak, P. H. (1969). *Combats inachevés*, vol. II, *De l'espoir aux déceptions*. Paris: Fayard.

Spierenburg, D. and Poidevin, R. (1993). *Histoire de la Haute Autorité de la Communauté européenne du charbon et de l'acier. Une expérience supranationale*. Bruxelles: Bruyant.

Stella, T. (2005). 'Euro-atlantismo. L'eredità del federalismo americano del secondo conflitto mondiale.' In Preda, D. and Rognoni Vercelli, C. (eds.). *Storia e percorsi del federalismo. L'eredità di Carlo Cattaneo*. Bologna: Il Mulino, vol. II, pp. 1043–1090.

Wilkens, A. (ed.) (2004). *Le Plan Schuman dans l'histoire. Intérêts nationaux et projet européen*. Bruxelles: Bruyant,

Woolf, S. J. (1996). 'Vecchi dogmi e nuovi approcci: il nazionalismo in Europa.' *Passato e Presente*, XI (39), pp. 7–14.

# 2 European integration

## Contrasting models and perspectives

*Fabio Masini*

### Introduction

The European Union is a very peculiar institutional architecture. It is better labelled for *what it is not*, rather than for *what it is*. It is no longer a mere *confederation* of States, as many policy areas are tackled with a democratic decision-making process, involving both citizens and national governments, where a majority rule is adopted for some collective choices. It is not even a *federation*, as some crucial competences that are usually attributed to the central government in the existing federations are still retained by nation States either directly or indirectly through the use of a veto power over collective decisions.

Unlike traditional nation States, the European Union has no constitutional law, but is ruled according to a variable geometry of treaties, some of which are enforceable only for a limited number of member States. At the same time, it cannot be said to be a mere international agreement among sovereign states, for some European laws possess a higher degree of enforceability towards the European peoples than the national laws.

This ambiguous structure is also manifest in the diverse and contradictory critiques it receives, especially as concerns the euro-area. Some claim against its alleged federal structure, actually targeting European monetary govern- ance which is supposed to be part of a strategy to challenge the capability of each State to finance the welfare state at the national level (Gillingham, 2003; Harmes, 2012: 67): the transfer of monetary sovereignty from nation States to an independent supranational Central Bank with the limited scope of targeting price stability obliges national budgets to shrink in order to avoid speculation and rising costs for the service of the public debt, therefore press- ing governments to reduce the standards and costs of welfare. Others, on the contrary, claim against the lack of an effective and complete federal structure in the euro-area, underlining that the very absence of a federal budget and government hinders the reversal of the austerity stance in economic policy now prevailing in most nation States (e.g. De Grauwe, 2013).

Such radically opposite assessments can coexist because the European Union is an unfinished project, a precarious and unstable process, rather than a mere international agreement or a robust constitutional structure (Montani, 2008). This judgement of 'exceptionality' of the European Union is not unanimously shared. Some (Hermann, 2007; Harmes, 2012; Palley, 2013) believe it is a very common 'neo-liberal mainstream' structure. As Hermann (2007: 1) claims: 'the European integration process was used to adopt mainstream neo-liberal policies and thereby to circumvent and erode those state traditions and national compromises, which in the past gave Europe its distinctiveness compared to other countries'.

Although this claim received recently much attention and support, it is hardly attributable to the *founding fathers* of the European integration,[1] a very heterogeneous group, in which several intellectual sources converged on the need to start the integration process in Europe after the Second World War. They all shared a common goal: European integration was to serve the urge to stop forever any possibility to make wars among European people. The main goal of European integration was to provide a European-collective good such as perpetual peace in Kantian terms. Some thought this should be achieved through the foundation of a genuine political union based on the constitutional principles which rule the United States of America. Some others thought that a political integration process might be premature, and struggled to pave the way for an economic integration process in order to ease a further deepening of the political links among European peoples and States. The former shared the intellectual sources rooted in the proposals for a European federation that had flourished in the inter-wars years. The latter started a new strategy of supranational integration, which would be named *functionalism*, following David Mitrany's works (in particular 1933, 1943) of the same period, in which he suggested to integrate single functions *against* the utopian alternative of a struggle for a political union.

Before we discuss this in further detail, we would like to anticipate that the claim concerning the intellectual influence of the neo-liberal approach, in particular of the economists Mises and Hayek, to the alleged present federal structure of Europe and to European integration (Gillingham, 2003: 6–15) is substantially wrong. Not only because Europe is far from being a federation, even in economic matters, but also from the intellectual point of view: not only regarding the *founding fathers*, but also regarding the end of the 1980s, when the process towards the euro was launched, leading to the present architecture of monetary governance. At the same time, functionalism, in the making of the European project, was not necessarily intended as an anti-federalist solution, as Mitrany himself had suggested, but it was often meant as a tool aiming at setting the path towards a federation. In synthesis, our impression is that these explanations are simplistic and do not grasp the true nature of the question we are going to tackle: what are the intellectual models in the history of economic thought that shaped the EU?

A further point concerns the relevance of economic ideas in forging European integration. The interpretations above suggest that it was overwhelming. Nevertheless, although economic theories certainly exerted a major influence on the debates concerning European integration, their role should be better qualified. In order to enquire into all this, we shall first describe the nature and significance of the three most relevant approaches to supra-national integration (instrumental federalism, constitutional federalism, and functionalism), whose weight in the European integration process evolved in time. Each of them will be treated in the next three sections.

We have further identified three major phases in such process. The first is the period before the foundation of the European Common Market, between the end of the Second World War and 1957. The second is the 1970s, when the debates on monetary integration revitalized the more general debate on the aims and scope of European integration. The third phase is the one starting at the end of the 1980s, when the Delors' Report paved the way to the build-ing of the euro. Each of them will be illustrated in the third, fourth and fifth sections, before we provide some concluding remarks.

## Austrian libertarianism and instrumental federalism

The end of the First World War marks a dividing line within all major ideologies. Most intellectuals understood that their efforts should be directed to the understanding and changing of international relations, with the aim of designing a more stable international order. Economists were among the protagonists of this effort, in particular as concerns liberal thinkers.

Between the two world wars, liberalism tried to evolve quickly to face the new challenges posed by increasing demands for social protection and greater interdependence worldwide. A key contribution to such reflections was given by those who became later known as a 'neo-liberal thought collect-ive' (Mirowski and Plehwe, 2009). It is widely recognized that among its main protagonists were Ludwig von Mises and Friedrich August von Hayek. They shared important social, political and philosophical views, also as concerns the role of international institutions and the global public goods they are sup-posed to provide.

In *Liberalismus*, Mises (1927: 111) tackles the crucial question of 'how to create the social conditions that will eliminate the causes of war'. In *Nation, Staat, und Wirtshaft* he had already given an answer to that: 'The first require-ment in this regard is private property. When private property must be respected even in time of war ... an important motive for waging war has already been excluded'. According to him, 'liberalism ... is indifferent towards the State itself' (Mises, 1919: 66) unless it proves detrimental to the establishment of a free-market international framework. In that case, the problem becomes 'limiting State power to a minimum' (Mises, 1919: 126). In *Nation, Staat, und Wirtschaft*, Mises had indeed underlined the political aspect of economic freedom but also the economic goal behind political action: 'Liberalism, which assumes full economic freedom, tries to solve the difficulties which the different political institutions pose to the development of the market, detach-ing economics from the State' (Mises, 1919: 35). Liberalism implies, under this point of view, a political struggle designed to free economics from the influence of politics.

Peaceful international relations are, therefore, as in Bentham and Mill, the by-product of economic freedom: 'The starting-point of [the liberal] entire political philosophy is the conviction that the division of labor is international and not merely national' (Mises, 1927: 148). Indeed, when criticizing the Covenant of the League of Nations, Mises (1927: 149–150) argues against it because it does not adequately guarantee private property and economic freedom from the political power, not because it is ineffective to make, pass and enforce the international law. The solution lies in the general acceptance (to be pursued in each country) of the *liberal principles*:

> This frame of mind can be nothing less than the unqualified, unconditional acceptance of liberalism. Liberal thinking must permeate all nations, liberal principles must pervade all political institutions, if the prerequisites of peace are to be created and the causes of war eliminated. As long as nations cling to protective tariffs, immigration barriers, compulsory education, interventionism, and etatism new conflicts capable of breaking out at any time into open warfare will continually arise to plague mankind.
>
> (Mises, 1927: 150–151)

Mises' vision is what Sally (1998a, 1998b) defines as *liberalism from below*, according to which the goal of international peace can be served through a liberal agenda to be pursued at the level of single national countries, eventually supported by international economic institutions to guarantee the best operation of the market.

Building on these concepts of the nature and scope of international institutions, Hayek started to reflect in the early 1930s on these topics, later claiming in favour of federal supranational institutions. Although rooted in previous works (Hayek, 1931, 1933a, 1933b) his first book on these questions is *Monetary Nationalism and International Stability*, published in 1937. He would later return on these matters in 1939 with 'Economic Conditions of Inter-State Federalism' and in 1944 with the world-known *The Road to Serfdom*, where he deals extensively with federalism in Chapter XV on 'The Prospects of International Order'.

Hayek started to think about federalism because he was looking for institutional tools that could reduce the room for public intervention into the economy. The degeneration of the political debate in fascism, nazism, corporatism during the 1930s made it more and more urgent to raise obstacles to the arrogant distortions of politics in economic matters. The defence of the free interplay of the market was a way to defend individual freedom from the State. But in Hayek's view, even more detrimental was the alternative, within liberals themselves, defended by economists like Harrod and Keynes who argued in favour of monetary (and economic) nationalism. Not yet radically critical about rationalist constructivism, Hayek thought that advocating a European federation might be a good opportunity to limit the power of nation States over the economy.

The starting point of Hayek's argument is that international monetary cooperation was both responsible for the 1929 crisis and for the high price volatility with no reference to the underlying market conditions, which resulted in a dangerous and arbitrary redistribution of resources: 'the conscious cooperation between Central Banks certainly played a great role' (Hayek, 1932: 124) to create the conditions which degenerated in the 1929 collapse, a cooperation aimed to 'avoid the inevitable fall in the national level of prices' (Hayek, 1932: 123).

Hence an apparent contradiction between his strong claims: a) against any international monetary cooperation and; b) in favour of an international system of economic and political institutions designed along federal principles (Hayek, 1937, 1939). In fact, such contradiction disappears if we observe that Hayek's reference to the international institutional framework based on a federal political structure in his writings of 1937 and 1939 is clearly aimed at strongly reducing the intervention of (national) public authorities in the realm of economic relationships. In *Monetary Nationalism and International Stability*, when discussing the prospects for a new international monetary system, he writes:

> The rational choice would seem to lie between either a system of 'free banking', which not only gives all banks the right of note issue and at the same time makes it necessary for them to rely on their own reserves, but also leaves them free to choose their field of operation and their correspondents without regards to national boundaries, and on the other hand, an international central bank.
>
> (Hayek, 1937: 77)

The transfer of monetary sovereignty from nation States to a supranational authority is clearly and merely a means to minimize public interventions into the working of the global market, not a matter of conflicts resolution. Under the intellectual influence of Mises, international institutions are for Hayek the best substitute to avoid any public (national) intervention in the economy.

Along the same lines he publishes an article in *New Commonwealth Quarterly*, also in 1939, titled 'Economic Conditions of Inter-State Federalism', where he argues in favour of federal supranational institutions to support the principles of economic freedom (Hayek, 1939). But, again, it is clearly a negative-sum game as concerns public interventions into the economy:

> the conclusion that, in a federation, certain economic powers, which are now generally wielded by the national states, could be exercised neither by the federation nor by the individual states, implies, that there would have to be less government all around if federation is to be practicable.
>
> (Hayek, 1939: 266)

This approach would later evolve in a more radical concept of federalism where the federal authority is a sort of functional, technical organism constraining national policy-making into narrow paths of public spending, as would later be for Friedman (1962) and Buchanan.

In synthesis, apart from a very short period in his life, not only could Hayek's political liberalism be labelled as 'instrumental' (Kley, 1994), but also his claim for political federalism can be said to be *instrumental* to an economic and social *Weltanschauung* aimed at preserving the spontaneous social order expressed by the market from the interference of any collective political body. This is the attitude that would exert a major influence on the neo-liberal thought in the following decades and which, for reasons that we shall later explore, is sometimes said to have exerted some influence in the integration process of the European Union in the last thirty years.

## Sovereignty, liberal planning and constitutional federalism

The main feature of Mises' *liberalism from below* and Hayek's *instrumental federalism* is that any effort to design some international institution is devoted only to elicit national State sovereignties from interfering with the operation of the free market. This is a different question from the one addressed by two other major exponents of the early neo-liberal thought collective, Lionel Robbins and Luigi Einaudi, who both played an important intellectual role in the Founding Fathers of the EEC.

Their approach to the crisis of civilization after the First World War was quite different from those of Mises and Hayek. They both found the crisis to be attributable to the existence of absolute and exclusive national sovereignties, which make it intrinsically impossible to rely on diplomatic arrangements for international conflict resolution and therefore to solve the problems of collective action which are necessary to provide international public goods, first of all *peace*.

Einaudi had extensively dealt with this problem soon after the First World War, although his first contribution on this point dates back to 1897, when he writes an article in an Italian newspaper where he comments on the view expressed by Thomas Stead, a renowned British journalist who had considered the joint intervention of the six major European powers to defend peace in Crete (after the outbreak of a violent anti-Turkish revolt) as 'the birth of the United States of Europe' (quoted in Cressati, 1992: 35). The most interesting part of Einaudi's article is the reason why such an idea could be agreed upon: the fact that the six powers had agreed not to decide 'according to the rule of the *liberum veto*' (Einaudi, 1897: 37).

Anticipating Sen (1970) on the 'impossibility of a Paretian liberal', and building on his intellectual background deeply rooted in the British liberals (Cressati, 1992: 34; Giordano, 2006: 65), Einaudi claims that freedom, at the international level, does not depend on the possibility to act according only to national sovereign choices but on a set of rules where international decisions are taken by majority principle and where, therefore, 'State sovereignty has to be limited' (Morelli, 1990: 21). His crucial point is that the absolute and exclusive sovereignty of each national State, embodied in the veto rule at the international diplomatic level, makes it impossible to pursue any collective action and hence to provide a collective public good such as international peace, which is in turn fundamental in providing other liberal values such as the effective operation of the markets.

If this is the analysis, the way out is a system where supranational choices are the result of a democratic decision-making process:

> From this imperfect phase when even only one of the six powers, with its opposition, could make any plan accepted by all the others inapplicable, we will slowly come to a point when the majority will be able to impose decisions on the minority without making recourse to the *ultima ratio* of the war.
>
> (Einaudi, 1897: 37–38)

Such concepts would be further restated several times, especially soon after the First World War (Einaudi, 1918a, 1918b, 1919) and after the Second World War (Einaudi, 1943, 1944, 1947, 1948).

Between the wars, Einaudi is engaged in an intellectual struggle against the fascist regime and his priorities change. Nevertheless, in the second half of the 1930s, Einaudi returns to the questions concerning the institutional architecture for international liberalism. During these years, one of the most influential books to him is Robbins' (1937a) *Economic Planning and International Order*. After reading it, Einaudi immediately sends it to the friend and colleague Ernesto Rossi, imprisoned for anti-fascism on the Island of Ventotene, where the book becomes the reference volume for the elaboration of the federalist *Manifesto for a United Europe* – written with Altiero Spinelli – and for the foundation of the European Federalist Movement, in 1943, to which Einaudi immediately adheres.

It is exactly via Einaudi and Rossi that Altiero Spinelli comes in touch with Robbins' contributions to European federalism. Spinelli re-elaborated Robbins' federalist ideas for his political project about the reconstruction of post-war Europe and in his *Manifesto* he implicitly (and in many other political documents explicitly) referred to Robbins' works as a crucial source for his intellectual building-up.

Robbins' key point is that peace is not a mere and temporary absence of conflicts but a permanent condition that requires a specific economic, political and institutional structure. The causes of war are therefore to be found both in inefficient institutions and in market failures depending on a perverse concept of *sovereignty*, which is exclusively attributed to nation States: 'The ultimate condition giving rise to those clashes of national economic interest which lead to international war is the existence of independent national sovereignties' (Robbins, 1939b: 99).

In this respect, Robbins maintains that classical liberalism is 'anarchic', as international relations are only tackled through national diplomatic efforts, without any superior coercive institution. But the existence of systems of power with an exclusive and absolute sovereignty is not coherent with the necessity to safeguard peaceful international relations nor with economic efficiency. The economy is in fact founded on the production and consumption of private and public goods. As concerns the former, they need to be produced and exchanged in a plurality of territorially concentric markets because each good and service is provided to satisfy the needs of more or less wide groups of individuals. Each market for each good needs to be backed and guaranteed by specific rules and juridical systems.[2] Similarly, there are collective and shared needs that require the production of public goods which are not to be provided necessarily at the national level. In both cases, the economy needs an institutional, political and juridical system which has to be structured from the local to the global dimension, following a principle which we would now call *subsidiarity*.

According to Robbins (1937a, 1937b, 1939a,1939b, 1940) the most adequate constitutional framework coherent with these urges is the federal one. Federalism provides an optimal constitutional equilibrium between decentralization and centralization, between local and global. 'Independent Sovereignty must be limited' (Robbins, 1939b: 104) and 'the national States must learn to regard themselves as the functions of international local government' (Robbins, 1939a: 105).

A mere confederative agreement among national States, as those who had characterized the several international conferences in the 1930s, would be unable to provide the collective public goods which are necessary to achieve a truly peaceful international framework and for the constructive operation of global market forces. What is required is a constitutional architecture based on a multilevel federal system which allows decentralized choices and, at the same time, central strategic unity: in Robbins' own words: 'There must be neither alliance nor complete unification, but Federation; neither *Staatenbund*, nor *Einheitsstaat*, but *Bundesstaat*' (Robbins, 1937a: 245).

For Robbins, the federal structure does not necessarily imply less government, in a negative-sum game as for Hayek. Federal authorities may decide whether or not to intervene in economics and to what extent (Robbins, 1940: 240–241). Of course, we are not suggesting that Robbins would have argued in favour of socialist policies, but simply that the political struggle (for example, between liberal and socialist policies) was to be framed within an appropriate constitutional set of rules and institutions where also supranational decisions are taken in a democratic way and not left to the law of the strongest which usually governs diplomatic conferences.

A federal structure is therefore a constitutional architecture where different ideological approaches can politically confront each other, not necessarily a means to reduce public intervention in the economy. Robbins' *constitutional federalism* is therefore the opposite of Hayek's *instrumental federalism*, presenting the provision of concentric collective goods not as a trade-off but as a constitutional question to be faced *ex ante* according to the assessment of their spillover effects.

## Early European integration and the rise of functionalism

Soon after the Second World War a vivid debate started on the ways to pursue European integration, banning forever conflicts and wars among its member States. In this debate, a major intellectual role was played by the federal solution envisaged by Einaudi and Robbins, which became a political agenda. The contributions of these two economists can be said to have shaped the early project for European integration in the 1940s and early 1950s. Spinelli, among the founding fathers of the EU, is doubtless the most important representative of this. But Adenauer, De Gasperi, Monnet, Schuman and Spaak were also convinced of the merits and final goal of a European federation.

The urge of economic and social recovery pressed in the direction of country-specific paths of development, although the Marshall Plan helped find collective solutions; the need to stabilize transatlantic relations prevailed over genuine European integration projects, which were instrumental to the goal of forming a political fence against the USSR. For these reasons, it took some time to agree on a concrete project of European integration, which was boosted only after the Schuman declaration of 9 May, 1950.

Schuman himself and Monnet started to struggle for a project to pool – at a supranational level – two strategic sources of military power: coal and steel. The *European Coal and Steel Community* was founded in Paris in April 1951 among France, Germany, Italy and the three Benelux countries. The control over the two resources was given to a High Authority, governing the collective decisions on coal and steel as a directorate with full powers.

The political goal behind the ECSC, i.e. to build a European federation, was manifest not only in the declarations that gave birth to it, but also in the attempt that was made in the following years to parallel it with a European Defence Community, meant as an instrument to provide a credible international autonomous status to Europe. After the death of Stalin in 1953, the European countries felt that the dangers coming from the Soviet Unions were no longer credible and the European Defence Community failed. In 1954 France did not ratify it, de facto implying the death of the project.

Irrespective of this result, what is worth underlying is that this strategy of integration *by small steps*, in the early 1950s, was explicitly intended to set in motion a process that would lead to the building of a new power at the supranational level, a European-wide public sphere. It was Robbins' constitutional federalism that inspired such attempts; certainly not Hayek's instrumental federalism.

Things changed after the failure of the EDC. Since then, any approach to European integration that implied giving up national sovereignties in crucial areas (such as defence), was put aside and a new strategy was launched, targeting a gradual economic integration. It is usually told that this marked the birth of functionalism: a political vision that was born as a strategy for international integration aiming at challenging the federal goal. On the contrary, the protagonists of the early functionalist view were actually aiming at the federal goal. What happened in the 1950s was simply that they had to accept the fact that national governments were not willing to give up part of their sovereignty to supranational institutions and the only possible compromise to pursue some kind of integration process was to allow for the creation of a step-by-step integrated system of (mainly) market regulations. This is how the market started to gain momentum over politics in European integration.

Indeed, during the 1960s the most important attempts to push the accelerator on European integration were pursued in the realm of monetary relations (Maes, 2006), thanks to the attempt of France to escape Triffin's dilemma and create a 'regional monetary system' to avoid the negative influences of the dollar-exchange standard. It was the *political* will of France to challenge dollar hegemony that gave new impetus to *monetary* integration. Even in this case, the attempt had nothing to do with instrumental federalism and Hayek, although it might seem that leaving aside any goal of political union might resemble Hayek's dream for less public intervention in the economy.

Also in that period, the role of economists in forging the compromises that would foster European integration was crucial. Robert Triffin, Raymond Barre, Robert Marjolin, but even Otto Emminger, Guido Carli, Alexandre Lamfalussy and many others (especially those who contributed to the drafting of the Werner Report in 1970) attempted to serve the cause of a genuine step forward in European monetary integration. In Triffin's view, for example, a European monetary authority should be given the power to fully manage the monetary aggregates, even in a Keynesian perspective. And, again, it was the changing of the historical context and the resistance of national sovereign governments to give up part of their power that made it impossible to implement the ambitious plans of the Werner Report.

As concerns the role of economic theory in policy debates on monetary integration, the main economic theory used to hinder the acceleration of the process was the theory of optimum currency areas in Mundell's (1961) approach: Europe was clearly not an economic space where asymmetric shocks could be absorbed through the mobility of labour or prices flexibility, especially in the late 1960s, when the trade unions were gathering power. Most of those who opposed monetary integration used this theory to support their theses. Since then, the use of OCA theories would become a recurrent feature of all further debates on economic and monetary union in Europe.

## The 1970s: the crisis and a timid monetary integration process

In the 1970s, due to the end of the Bretton Woods system and the first major oil shock, Europe is in need and in search of a tool to stabilize intra-European exchange rates. The crucial ingredients in the debate that led to the final result of such efforts, the European Monetary System (launched in March 1979), are usually told to be two: a) the shift of the dominant policy models towards the new classical macroeconomics; b) the compromise between the 'economists' and 'monetarists' approaches to the making of European monetary integration. In the 1970s, although the political will was crucial, we can claim that the contributions from academic economists were particularly important to assist the decision to start a process of European monetary integration.

As concerns the first point, given the stress of the new classical macroeconomics on the fallacy of the trade-off between unemployment and inflation, the convergence of inflation rates implied in a monetary union (or a system to stabilize exchange rates) among European countries has no impact on the real side and bears no costs in terms of employment and production. Rational expectations, implying no fiscal illusion among economic agents, suggest that the only way out of stagflation and to import the credibility which is necessary to convince the markets not to speculate against *vicious* countries, lies in *tying one's hands* against expansionary economic policies through the commitment to join a stable exchange rate regime (in case of European countries, with Germany). This idea, first exposed in the *All Saints' Day Manifesto for a European Monetary Union* (Basevi *et al.*, 1975), would shape the debate on European monetary integration in the following years. This is probably the period in which economic ideas seem to influence most political decisions. In fact, the point is that the political decision to foster monetary integration required to be assisted by theoretical considerations and the changing paradigm of economic theory and policy during the 1970s provided this.

The other fundamental contribution was the debate between the so-called *economists* (led by Germany, in particular in European institutions) and *monetarists* (led by France), as Maes (2009) suggests. The latter label has not much to do with monetarism, the distinction between the two lying in the fact that *economists* thought economic integration was to be secured before monetary integration, through converging macroeconomic indicators, in particular price stability; and the *monetarists* thought monetary integration would bring about also greater economic integration. In this debate the influence of an important part of the neo-liberal thought emerges: ordoliberalism. Born from a German branch of the neo-liberal thought collective, with only some minor Austrian influences (Nedergaard, 2013: 3), ordoliberalism acquired an overwhelming importance in German policy-making to forge its strong commitment to the role of constitutional rules, to the competition policy, but also to the extraordinary role of institutions in providing collective choices. Although the influence of ordoliberalism on European integration is questionable (Nedergaard, 2013), its varying importance can perhaps be attributed to the varying hegemonic role of Germany in European economic and political balances.

An interesting aspect of the debate between *economists* and *monetarists* is that both sides largely used the theory of optimum currency areas. The *economists* claimed that European countries matched none of the criteria of optimality singled out in the literature, from Mundell (1961) to McKinnon (1963) and Kenen (1969). The *monetarists* acknowledged the authoritative change of Mundell's view (McKinnon, 2004) on this matter and further explored the idea that the criteria of optimality should be tested *ex post*, suggesting an endogenous approach to the OCA criteria. In 1969 Mundell (1973a, 1973b) claimed in favour of European monetary integration, against his previous opinion. The idea is that monetary integration allows for a better portfolio diversification and that the decision itself to accelerate monetary integration brings about effects that contribute to the fulfilment of the criteria for optimality.

A third approach to European monetary integration should be underlined in those years because it exerted some influence on the final compromise. It is the approach put forward by some exponents of the European Federalist Movement, who – with the help of Werner and Triffin, among others – managed to organize public discussions on the agenda towards the European Monetary System and may be said to have directly influenced the MacDougall Report and even Jenkins' speech in Florence, both in 1977. Their point was quite straightforward: a European Monetary System is an unstable and provisional compromise which is nevertheless necessary to set European integration in motion towards a revision of its (economic and political) governing structures. Explicitly inspired by the literature on constitutional federalism, they conceived the ecu as a first step towards a single currency and a federal budget (e.g. see Majocchi, 1978; Montani, 1978).

Although the debate was mostly occupied by these approaches to monetary integration (Masini, 2004), some have suggested that, again, Hayek might have exerted some influence. In 1976 Hayek publishes *Denationalization of Money*, where he suggests a different solution to the stabilization of the money and currency market. His suggestion was to denationalize completely the power of issuing money, giving it to commercial banks. Each of them would be entitled to issue its own money, whose success or failure would then rest on the credibility of the issuing bank and on the expectations of the market agents about its future perspectives.

Part of Hayek's arguments were brought into the debate by those who favoured a parallel currency approach to European monetary integration (whose most authoritative author was Roland Vaubel). Nevertheless, the idea was not as radical as Hayek's. The only point of similarity was that money is not necessarily a public good; money is but an instrument to make the market operate in the most efficient way and can be provided by several agents. In the specific case of Europe, it was suggested that a new currency was to be issued by a European Monetary Fund, circulating parallel to the existing national currencies. This would allow for a market decision of the relative importance and future success of the new currency, without any top-down political decision.

This approach was successful, in a way. The ecu was a parallel currency, although intended as a basket of the existing currencies, so that it was unavoidably linked to them and not completely autonomous in its evolution. Nevertheless, also the increasing role of the ecu in the private markets in the 1980s testifies to the effect envisaged by Vaubel, i.e. the possibility that the market, rather than the governments, might eventually make the experiment a success or a failure. This radically changed with the project of Economic and Monetary Union, in the late 1980s, as we shall illustrate in the next section.

## From the Delors Report to the euro

During the 1980s the world changed dramatically, although in the previous decade the oil shocks had already ignited a worldwide redistribution of economic and political powers. The bipolar system collapsed and a new transition was opened towards a different balance in the world. The very first outcome was, not surprisingly, the establishment of a hegemonic stability ruled by the USA, the only surviving superpower. Through international institutions and think-tanks, a new (mainly US-based) financial elite tried to establish a new order of macroeconomic and political stability. The Washington Consensus is only a label to describe part of this process. Even the alleged rise of neo-liberalism is only an attempt of provide a simplified explanation of what was happening in that period.

The main objective was to secure the economic and political balance of power from the risk that the transition might challenge the US hegemony in ruling the financial and political order. The austerity stances and the increasing liberalization and deregulation of markets imposed by the IMF on debtors was a tool to widen the basis of US power in the world. The crucial questions are: why and how could this aggressive hegemonic strategy be pursued? Was it only the result of a specific will by the US government? Or was it also the result of a missing alternative way to the establishment of a new and reasonably stable economic and political world order? What happened in Europe may cast some light on these questions.

In 1984 the European Parliament passed a proposal, drafted by Spinelli, for the reform of the Treaties that explicitly aimed at the creation of an economic and political federation, in order to prepare the Old Continent to face the new global challenges as a credible, single actor. The opposition of Mrs Thatcher obliged to make a new attempt along economic integration only. In 1988 the Heads of State and Government asked the European Commission to establish a study-group to enquire into the conditions for a European economic and monetary union. The task was given to a group chaired by Jacques Delors and the report was presented in April 1989 and discussed in the Madrid Summit in June 1989, launching the process to the European economic and monetary union (EMU). A process that in the following months would be further accelerated by the fall of the Berlin Wall and the negotiations that would lead Germany to reunification.

Among the main protagonists of this process we should cite Delors (President of the EU Commission) and Tommaso Padoa-Schioppa (Co-Rapporteur of the Report). The first was the political leader who took up the responsibility to pioneer further steps in European integration. Padoa-Schioppa provided a fundamental intellectual and technical support, in particular with the idea of the *inconsistent quartet* that set the steps of European integration from the mid-1980s to the end of the 1990s. Indeed, after the decisions to promote factors mobility (1989) and to create a single market (1992), the increasing monetary integration should imply less national autonomy in economic policy.

Delors was a convinced federalist, although this claim is sometimes challenged, as Padoa-Schioppa was. They played different institutional roles and had different cultural backgrounds which differentiate between the ways they made their intensions manifest. They both shared the idea that only at the European level the concept of sovereignty, as the capacity of public authorities to satisfy the needs of the people, could have some meaning. And they thought that a genuine economic and monetary union was the first step towards the final goal of a supranational political union, not a goal in itself. They were both inspired by constitutional federalism and made it clear on several occasions, although Padoa-Schioppa (1992, 1997, 2001, 2004a, 2004b) was certainly more explicit on this.

The result was different from what they had imagined, for several reasons. The first point to be underlined is that they knew that a monetary union alone would be unsustainable in the long run without a special attention on growth, collective investments at the European level, stronger and more democratic institutions. And they worked hard for this, first of all Delors, with the *White Paper* on *Growth, Competitiveness, Employment* (Delors 1993). This should be considered the first strategic document of economic policy for the EU. As is known, the Heads of States and Governments ignored the document and concentrated on the technical transition towards the euro, designing constraints of national macroeconomic convergence rather than European-wide instruments for growth.

In those years, the institutional architecture was designed that would lead to the present unfinished project of European integration, with monetary authority given to a Central Bank with a narrow mandate over price stability, and national fiscal policies whose only common feature is the constraint over budget expansions. Although this resembles a neo-liberal approach to the redistribution of powers (a sort of instrumental federalism), even on this occasion Hayek had nothing to do with this. It is true that the only intellectual and policy counterpart to the Delors Report was attempted by the British government's proposal, following Hayek, for a parallel currency approach to monetary integration (Masini, 2010). As in the 1970s, the proposal aimed at a market approach to integration, based on a parallel (to the national ones) currency, issued by a European Monetary Fund that would have to gain credibility among operators. The proposal, contrary to what happened in the 1970s with the partial success of this strategy and the creation of the ecu, was quickly dismissed and disappeared from the economic and political debate in a few months.

The political agreement among all major countries (in particular France and Germany) made negotiations in the Summits and in the two Inter-Governmental Conferences on *Economic and Monetary Union* and on *Political*

*Union* direct towards the only credible proposal: the one for a single currency. After the political commitment was expressed, negotiations started on the conditions that each candidate to monetary union should satisfy for access. In the following years, after the Maastricht Treaty, any attempt to push further on European institutional and economic integration was abandoned: no country was ready to give up further parts of national sovereignty after accepting to give up monetary sovereignty. The resulting compromises, characterized by a European Central Bank aiming only at price stability and the *Stability and Growth Pact* designed to reduce the possibility to run budget deficits and accumulate debt, were not the expression of an intellectual supremacy of the neo-liberal paradigm (and not even of the ordoliberal component of such complex and multifaceted thought), but of the failure of national elites to fully understand that the greater interdependence worldwide and the opening of a transition to a new world order, was challenging the ability of all national public authorities in Europe to cope with them effectively. European governments were not ready to implement the institutional and redistributive measures that would allow the monetary union to survive in times of recession.

Hence the critique to the European economic governance to be a *federal* (meaning *supranational*) monetary structure that ties the hands of national governments, jeopardizing the possibility to finance the expansion and even the survival of the welfare state. This *misunderstood* coincidence between a *federal structure* and a *neo-liberal device* has brought about a general uneasiness towards enlarging the scope of supranational institutions in other domains of economic and political governance in Europe. European sovereignty is said to imply the reduction of national sovereignty, which is the only level democratically legitimated to decide how much welfare state should be financed. Nevertheless, the key point is that the capacity to satisfy the needs of European citizens does no longer depend on national exclusive sovereignty and a mere coordination of national budget policies but on a multilevel institutional architecture based on a federal constitution, as Einaudi and Robbins suggested, with a proper federal budget.

During the late 1990s, endogenous theories of optimum currency areas criteria (Frankel and Rose, 1998) helped gather support around the euro project, thus positively influencing academic and policy debates in the following years. And the first steps of the new European currency had allowed for optimism. The euro-sovereign debts crisis since 2010 reversed this trend and raised old and new critiques. But until a new distribution of powers among local, national and supranational authorities is given a constitutional relevance and credibility, the European Union and the eurozone will be the weak chains of a new world economic and political order that is quickly evolving and shaping.

## Conclusion

From what we have illustrated, it should be manifest that Hayek's neo-liberal approach to (instrumental) federalism has little if nothing to do with the

European integration project. Yet, the present EU architecture seems very similar to the neo-liberal vision, i.e. the creation of a system of economic governance completely detached from political legitimacy. As Hayek (but also Friedman and Buchanan, among many) hoped, it is a system where less public intervention in the economy has been achieved, reducing sovereignty at the single national level while not providing a democratic public sphere at the supranational one.

The ECB, politically independent and with a very narrow formal mandate, holds the monetary authority. Fiscal authorities are in the hands of national governments, but they are limited in their budgetary policies not only by monetary constraints but also by formal budget constraints imposed by treaties that were agreed by national governments and not by their peoples. This suggests the conclusion that neo-liberalism (through Hayek or via the more realistic, although overestimated, influence of ordoliberalism) shaped the EU, imposing the supremacy of the market and the interests of the financial elites over the citizens. Even the fact that the euro was shaped while the neo-liberal consensus emerged at the global level seems to point towards this conclusion.

It might also be argued that the present situation derives from the fact that Delors, Padoa-Schioppa and all those who held a *constitutional federalism* approach to European integration, lost their struggle to create an Economic and Monetary Union designed to provide European-wide collective goods aiming at an increasing political union towards a federation. As if their intellectual foundations were weaker than those of the counterpart. It is certainly true that the misunderstanding concerning the identity between federalism and neo-liberalism depends on the struggle that *constitutional federalism* lost, politically, against *instrumental federalism* in the last sixty years. This may also explain why Hayek, the most renowned representative of what we call *instrumental federalism*, is considered a very influential intellectual figure behind the present architecture of the European Union. Nevertheless, as we have shown, this is a wrong claim, which neglects and misunderstands completely the nature of the European failure.

A more robust conclusion we can draw from the picture we have provided is that the present ambiguous and inefficient architecture of economic and political governance of the eurozone and of the EU in general depends on the resistance that national governments systematically showed in sharing and transferring sovereignty from the national to a supranational institutional system. Or, to put it in a more problematic way, the resistance of national governments to give up their power has paved the way to an architecture of economic governance that is coherent with neo-liberal ideas. The present changing and ambiguous compromises characterizing European economic and political governance depend on the struggle between the final aims of those who support constitutional federalism and the resistance of national powers to give up their sovereignty.

We can wonder if this was the precise will of some powerful economic, political or intellectual lobby. More likely, it is just the result of the difficulty for national ruling classes to give up their myopic vision of power and of their struggle to keep it at the national level – although such power is shrinking due to the increasing complexity and interdependence worldwide – instead of transferring sovereignty to European institutions and prepare for a political fight at that level. If this is true, it means also that, as concerns the relationship between economic theories and policy-making, the intellectual role of the architects of the euro in designing a weak economic and political governance of Europe is overestimated. And that actually, only constitutional federalism has really shaped the way Europe looks today, because it has provided the only reference point really antithetical to the confederative system implied in the retention of sovereignty at the national level, thus obliging to find ever new compromises of increasing degrees of integration. Until this contradiction is solved with a genuine federal structure (instead of the return to national exclusive sovereignties), it is hardly credible that Europe may play a role in the new world order that has been shaped in the last thirty years.

## Notes

1 According to the official site of the European Union, they are (in alphabetical order): Konrad Adenauer, Joseph Bech, Johan Willem Beyen, Winston Churchill, Alcide De Gasperi, Walter Hallstein, Sicco Mansholt, Jean Monnet, Robert Schuman, Paul-Henri Spaak and Altiero Spinelli (http://europa.eu/about-eu/eu-history/founding-fathers/).
2 Robbins (1937a) several times recalls Edwin Cannan's *Wealth* (1928, Chapter IV) and Adam Smith's *Wealth of Nations* (the beginning of Book Four, Part Three) as his main sources for the extension of the externalities and spillover effects of human choices to the international planning as a whole and to a pyramidal institutional architecture.

## References

Basevi, G., M. Fratianni, H. Giersch *et al.* (1975). 'The All Saints Day Manifesto for European Monetary Union.' *The Economist*, 1 November.
Cannan, E. (1928). *Wealth*. London: Staple Press.
Cressati, C. (1992). *L'Europa necessaria. Il federalismo liberale di Luigi Einaudi*. Torino: Giappichelli.
De Grauwe, P. (2013). 'Designing Failures in the Eurozone. Can They Be Fixed?' *LES Europe in Question Discussion Paper Series*, 57.
Delors, J. (ed.) (1993). *Growth, Competitiveness, Employment. The Challenges and Ways Forward into the 21st Century*. COM 93/700, Bulletin of the European Communities, Supplement 6/93.
Einaudi, L. (1897). 'Un sacerdote della stampa e gli Stati Uniti europei.' *La Stampa*, 20 August, pp. 1–2.
[Einaudi, L.] Junius (1918a). 'La Società delle Nazioni è un ideale possibile?' *Corriere della Sera*, 5 January. In Idem (1920), pp. 79–94.
[Einaudi, L.] Junius (1918b). 'Il dogma della sovranità e l'idea della Società delle Nazioni.' *Corriere della Sera*, 28 December. In Idem (1920), pp. 143–156.
[Einaudi, L.] Junius (1919). 'Fiume, la società delle nazioni ed il dogma della sovranità.' *Corriere della Sera*, 6 May. In Idem (1920), pp. 157–168.

[Einaudi, L.] Junius (1920). *Lettere politiche di Junius*. Bari: Laterza.

Einaudi L. (1943). *Per una federazione economica europea*. Roma: Edizioni Clandestine Movimento Liberale Italiano. In Idem (1986), pp. 67–98.

Einaudi L. (1944). *I problemi economici della federazione europea*. Lugano: Nuove Edizioni di Capolago. In Idem (1986), pp. 99–161.

Einaudi L. (1947). 'La unificazione del mercato europeo.' In *Europa federata [Federated Europe]*. Milano: Edizioni di Comunità. In Idem (1986), pp. 163–169.

Einaudi L. (1948). 'Chi vuole la pace.' *Corriere della Sera*, 4 April. In Idem (1986), pp. 59–63.

Einaudi L. (1986). *La guerra e l'unità europea*. Bologna: Il Mulino.

Frankel, J. A. and A. K. Rose (1998). 'The Endogeneity of the Optimum Currency Area Criteria.' *Economic Journal*, 108 (449), pp. 1009–1025.

Friedman, M. (1962). *Capitalism and Freedom*. Chicago: Chicago University Press.

Gillingham, J. (2003). *European Integration 1950–2003. Superstate or New Market Economy?* Cambridge: Cambridge University Press.

Giordano, A. (2006). *Il pensiero politico di Luigi Einaudi*. Genova: Name Edizioni.

Harmes, A. (2012). 'The Rise of Neoliberal Nationalism.' *Review of International Political Economy*, 19 (1), pp. 59–86.

Hayek, F. A. von (1931). *Prices and Production*. London: Routledge and Kegan Paul.

Hayek, F. A. von (1932). 'Das Schicksal der Goldwärung. Der Deutsche Volkswirt', Berlin. 12 and 19 February. Reprinted as 'The Fate of the Gold Standard' in Hayek, F. A. von (1984). *Money, Capital and Fluctuations: Early Essays* (ed. R. McCloughry). London: Routledge & Kegan Paul, pp. 118–135.

Hayek, F. A. von (1933a). *Monetary Theory and Trade Cycle*. London; Toronto: Jonathan Cape.

Hayek, F. A. von (1933b). 'Über 'neutrales Geld.' *Zeitschrift für Nationalökonomie*, 4, pp. 659–661. Translated into English as 'On "Neutral Money"' in Hayek, F. A. von (1984). *Money, Capital & Fluctuations: Early Essays* (ed. R. McCloughry). London: Routledge & Kegan Paul, pp. 159–162.

Hayek, F. A. von (1937). *Monetary Nationalism and International Stability*. London: Longmans Green.

Hayek, F. A. von (1939). 'Economic Conditions of Inter-State Federalism.' *New Commonwealth Quarterly*, V (2 Sept.), pp. 131–149. Reprinted in Hayek, F. A. von (1948). *Individualism and Economic Order*. Chicago: University of Chicago Press, pp. 255–272.

Hermann, C. (2007). 'Neoliberalism in the European Union.' *Studies in Political Economy*, 79, pp. 61–89.

Kenen, P. (1969). 'The Theory of Optimum Currency Areas: An Eclectic View.' In Mundell, R. A. and. Swoboda, A. (eds.). *Monetary Problems in the International Economy*. Chicago: University of Chicago Press.

Kley, R. (1994). *Hayek's Social and Political Thought*. Oxford: Clarendon Press.

Maes, I. (2006). 'The Ascent of the European Commission as an Actor in the Monetary Integration Process in the 1960s.' *Scottish Journal of Political Economy*, 53 (2), pp. 222–241.

Maes, I. (2009). 'Economic Thought at the European Commission and the Creation of EMU (1957–191).' *La Sapienza Department of Economics Working Papers*, 2 (14 May).

Majocchi, A. (1978). 'Fluttuazione, aggiustamento della bilancia dei pagamenti e moneta europea.' In Movimento Europeo – Movimento Federalista Europeo (1978). *L'unione economica e il problema della moneta europea*. Milano: Franco Angeli, pp. 109–125.

Masini, F. (2004). *SMEmorie della lira. Gli economisti italiani e l'adesione al Sistema monetario europeo.* Milano: Angeli.

Masini, F. (2010). 'Alternative Routes to Monetary Integration in the British Economic and Political Debates (1989–1991).' *Storia del Pensiero Economico*, 1, pp. 71–98.

McKinnon, R. I. (1963). 'Optimum Currency Area.' *American Economic Review*, 4, pp. 717–725.

McKinnon, R. I. (2004). 'Optimum Currency Areas and Key Currencies: Mundell I versus Mundell II.' *Journal of Common Market Studies*, 42 (4), pp. 689–715.

Mitrany, D. (1933). *The Progress of International Government.* New Haven: Yale University Press.

Mitrany, D. (1943). *A Working Peace System: an Argument for the Functional Development of International Organization.* London: The Royal Institute of International Affairs.

Mirowski, P. and Plehwe, D. (eds.) (2009). *The Road from Mont Pelerin. The Making of the Neoliberal Thought Collective.* Cambridge (Mass.); London: Harvard University Press.

Mises, L. von (1919). *Nation, Staat, und Wirschaft.* English translation by Leland B. Yeager (1983). *Nation, State and Economy.* New York: New York University Press.

Mises, L. von (1927). *Liberalismus.* Jena: Gustav Fischer Verlag; English translation (1929). *Liberalism in The Classical Tradition.* New York: Foundation for Economic Education, reprinted 1996.

Montani, G. (1978). 'Le competenze dell'esecutivo europeo in materia di moneta e finanza.' In Movimento Europeo – Movimento Federalista Europeo (1978). *L'unione economica e il problema della moneta europea.* Milano: Franco Angeli, pp. 61–107.

Montani, G. (2008). *L'economia politica dell'integrazione europea.* Torino: UTET.

Morelli, U. (1990). *Contro il mito dello stato sovrano. Luigi Einaudi e l'unità europea.* Milano: Franco Angeli.

Mundell, R. A. (1961). 'A Theory of Optimum Currency Areas.' *American Economic Review*, 51 (Nov.), pp. 509–517.

Mundell, R. A. (1973a). 'Uncommon Arguments for Common Currencies.' In Johnson, H. G., and Swoboda, A. K. (1973) (eds.). *The Economics of Common Currencies.* London: Allen and Unwin, pp. 114–132.

Mundell, R. A. (1973b). 'A Plan for a European Currency'. In Johnson, H. G. and Swoboda, A. K. (1973) (eds.). *The Economics of Common Currencies.* London: Allen and Unwin, pp. 143–172.

Nedergaard, P. (2013). 'The Influence of Ordoliberalism in Eueropean Integration Processes. A Framework for Ideational Influence with Competition Policy and the Economic and Monetary Policy as Examples.' *MPRA Paper*, 52331.

Padoa-Schioppa, T. (1992). *L'Europa verso l'unione monetaria. Dallo Sme al trattato di Maastricht.* Torino: Giulio Einaudi.

Padoa-Schioppa, T. (1997). *Il governo dell'economia.* Bologna: Il Mulino.

Padoa-Schioppa, T. (2001). *Europa, forza gentile. Cosa ci ha insegnato l'avventura europea.* Bologna: Il Mulino.

Padoa-Schioppa, T. (2004a). *La lunga via per l'euro.* Bologna: Il Mulino.

Padoa-Schioppa, T. (2004b). *L'euro e la sua banca centrale. L'unione dopo l'unione.* Bologna: Il Mulino.

Palley, T. I. (2013). 'Europe's Crisis without End: The Consequences of Neoliberalism.' *Contributions to Political Economy*, 32 (1), pp. 29–50.

Robbins, L. C. (1937a). *Economic Planning and International Order*. London: Macmillan.

Robbins, L. C. (1937b). 'The Economics of Territorial Sovereignty.' In Woodward Manning, C. A. (ed.). *Peaceful Change*. London: Macmillan, pp. 41–60.

Robbins, L. C. (1939a). *The Economic Basis of Class Conflicts*. London: Macmillan.

Robbins, L. C. (1939b). *The Economic Causes of War*. London: Jonathan Cape.

Robbins, L. C. (1940). 'Economic Aspects of Federation.' In Chaning-Pearce, M. (ed.). *Federal Union. A Symposium*. London: Jonathan Cape, pp. 167–186.

Sally, R. (1998a). 'Classical Liberalism and International Economic Order: An Advance Sketch.' *Constitutional Political Economy*, 9 (1), pp. 19–44.

Sally, R. (1998b). *Classical Liberalism and International Economic Order. Studies in Theory and Intellectual History*. London: Routledge.

Sen, A. (1970). 'The Impossibility of a Paretian Liberal.' *The Journal of Political Economy*. 78 (1), pp. 152–157.

**Part II**

# Europe between confederalism and federalism

Part II

Europe as a 'federal' federation
and federation

# 3 Confederalism as a solution for Europe

*John McCormick*

Having mired the European Union (EU) in the greatest existential crisis in its history, the troubles of the eurozone have provided pause for deep thought regarding the future of European integration. For some, the crisis has sparked deepening resistance to the work of the EU, reflected in the increased vote for eurosceptic and populist political parties at the 2014 European Parliament elections. For others, it has made all the more urgent the need to pool more authority in the interests of efficient policy-making at the European level, thereby accelerating the federalizing tendencies of integration. Somewhere between these two positions, the fallout from the crisis has encouraged new demands for reform of the European Union, although the details of such reforms are contested. There is, in short, no broad consensus on how to proceed.

The EU can never be the same again, but whether this means a retreat, an advance or a lateral move remains to be seen. For now, at least, it is clear that levels of public trust in the European Union – and of optimism about its future – are in decline. But it must also be said that levels of public trust in national government are also in decline in a Europe still struggling to emerge from recession, where unemployment often remains stubbornly high, and where the public mood is often angry and mistrustful of political elites. What we are witnessing is not just a crisis for European integration but a crisis for government more generally. And this is not just a problem in Europe, but also in the United States, where public and political opinion is deeply divided over how to address the country's many economic and social problems.

It is worth noting that neither the European Union nor the European Economic Community before it have ever functioned to the general satisfaction of political and public opinion. Almost from the time of the signature of the 1951 Treaty of Paris there have been problems and crises, some more serious than others. Writing in 1980, Stern (1980: 873) concluded that 'Europe huddles in precarious prosperity, its economic vulnerability [is clear] … its political regimes are shaky, its sense of purpose is muted, [and] its youth disaffected', all sentiments that continue to apply today. Wallace noted in 1982 that the European Community had 'disappointed the hopes of the more idealistic of its founders, and failed to achieve the most ambitious of its objectives', sentiments which – once again – continue to apply today. But he also noted that such hopes 'were founded on two linked illusions: that politics could be tamed within the European enterprise, and that national governments would allow themselves to be bypassed and undermined' (Wallace, 1982: 57).

Writing in the early 1990s, somewhere between the signing of the Maastricht treaty and completion of the single market, Stanley Hoffman found little to celebrate in the state of European affairs. Maastricht, he lamented, had 'marked the beginning of a serious crisis' for Europe, every Western European economy was stagnant, European governments had turned inward, troubling questions were being asked about the relationship between the EU and its member states, there was little progress on the single currency, Italian politics faced an 'apocalyptic crisis', Britain was still in decline, Yugoslavia had been a 'disastrous tragedy' and Europe's ambitious plans were 'now falling apart'. Disheartened by what he saw, Hoffman concluded that it might be time to say 'goodbye to a united Europe' (Hoffman, 1993: 46).

Since then, the negative referendum votes in Ireland on the treaties of Nice and Lisbon, the negative votes in France and the Netherlands on the constitutional treaty, and developments in the eurozone have all been greeted as blows to the European project. And yet in spite of speculation that each of these events might lead to stagnation and/or retrenchment, the EU has survived, has generally learned from its mistakes and has moved on. In doing so, it appears to have fulfilled the prediction of Jean Monnet that 'Europe would be built through crises' and would be 'the sum of their solutions' (Monnet, 1978: 417). However, it has apparently not yet fully heeded his warning that in the building of Europe, 'nothing would be more dangerous than to regard difficulties as failures' (Monnet, 1982: 11).

The charge given to the authors of this collection of essays was to critically review the options available as we consider exits from the eurozone crisis. The three alternatives most commonly touted are a federal Europe, a strengthening of the intergovernmental qualities of Europe and a breakdown of Europe into a looser association of states, or indeed into the system of sovereign nation states that preceded European integration. To choose among these options in the face of the aura of permanent crisis that currently afflicts the European experiment is not easy. Never before has there been greater hostility to the notion of a federal Europe, and nor has there been greater uncertainty about its future, and yet large numbers of Europeans would be deeply disappointed if the region was to return to the era of the nation state. At the same time, we must not overlook the large number of Europeans who have never much engaged with the debate over European integration, and neither know nor much care how it works or what difference it makes to their lives. While Europe may exercise, fascinate and frustrate its scholars and political leaders, the absence of opinions within large parts of the electorate is as much a problem as their presence.

While all three options have their supporters and their critics, and none is likely to win broad acceptance, there is a more particular way of looking at the second of these options (a strengthening of the EU's intergovernmental qualities) to which surprisingly little attention has been paid, and yet which offers prospects of winning wide political support without significant institutional reform. This is to acknowledge the EU as a confederation of states that have pooled authority and resources in areas where it makes the most practical and political sense, that retain control over domestic matters where it makes the most practical and political sense, and that can thereby avoid either creating a supranational European government or returning to the era of the nation state. Such an arrangement – it will be argued in this chapter – is a compromise that would both preserve the best of what the EU today has to offer while assuaging the concerns of all but the most hardened eurosceptics.

This chapter goes beyond addressing the fallout from the crisis in the eurozone and looks more broadly at the prospects for reform in the European Union from a political perspective. It argues not just that the EU is best understood as a confederation (albeit with some federal qualities), but also that if it was more broadly acknowledged as such, the debate about the current dynamics and future direction of European integration would be more focused, informed and productive. The most fundamental handicap faced by that debate is the lack of agreement on how best to understand and characterize the European Union. In the absence of such an agreement, European publics are understandably confused about the reach and implications of integration, and much of the debate over the EU and its policies is both misinformed and clouded by myth and misconception. In the absence of an accurate frame of reference, it is near impossible to have a productive conversation about the future of integration, let alone its present.

Confederalism not only best explains the structural pattern within which most EU institutions are currently arranged, but is also a powerful response to many of the concerns of eurosceptics and to many of the criticisms of neo-liberalism. It is a channel through which approaches to free trade, deregulation and privatization can be re-considered in such a way as to preserve their strengths and control their weaknesses. It addresses many of the concerns that critics of neo-liberalism have about loss of self-determination, promotion of inequality and exploitation, increases in corporate power, and unregulated economic activity. Above all, it provides a valuable point of reference against which the personality of the European Union can be better understood without being distracted by worries about the federalization of Europe or the breakdown of the European experiment.

This chapter begins with an assessment of the role played by confederal ideas in the debate about Europe. It defines confederalism and speculates on the reasons why confederalism has so rarely appeared in discussions about the EU. It then looks at the state of public opinion on the EU, drawing on polling data to make three key points: faith in the EU is declining, public knowledge about the EU is limited, and the debate about Europe will continue to be handicapped until these two problems are addressed. It then reviews the evidence of the EU's confederal qualities and the value of confederalism as a means of understanding the EU and making informed decisions about its future. It concludes by arguing that exits from the eurozone crisis based on either more or less integration will not win broad political and public support, and that the combination of decentralized and joint decision-making offered by confederalism offers the strongest prospect for winning such support. Furthermore, the many doubts that exist about the use of confederalism in understanding the EU could be assuaged by the EU becoming the benchmark for confederalism, in much the same way as the United States has become the benchmark for federalism.

## Confederalism in the debate about Europe

Remarkably little attention has been paid to the notion of confederalism as a means for understanding the EU. In spite of the hostility it often generates, federalism is employed far more often in debates about the character of the EU, and while there is no question that many Europeans support the goal of a federal United States of Europe, there is also no question that many others vehemently oppose such a notion. This was made abundantly clear by the results of the 2014 European Parliament elections, in which a combination of low voter turnout and large wins for eurosceptic and populist political parties led for calls for reforms that would make the EU less remote and easier to understand. Opinion is so clearly divided over a federal Europe that any effort to move substantively in that direction in the wake of the eurozone crisis would result in an immediate bifurcation of public opinion, resulting inevitably in some member states moving towards deeper integration while others move in the opposite direction, and perhaps even leave the EU altogether.

In an effort to clarify the utility of confederalism as a means for understanding the European Union, a useful point of departure is to briefly discuss what the EU is not. To begin with, it is not a standard international organization, if this is defined as a body based on voluntary cooperation, communal management, shared interests, and institutions that are designed to manage and coordinate while enjoying few if any independent powers (Zweifel, 2005). The European Economic Community (EEC) in its earliest iteration may have been a fairly conventional international organization based primarily on intergovernmental decision-making, but those days are long gone. The EU today consists of institutions, political networks and legal obligations that have pushed it into new political territory, giving it many clearly supranational qualities and far greater ambitions than any other international organization.

Neither is the EU a federal European superstate, because to be as much would demand the existence of a fully fledged and elected European government with powers and responsibilities that were independent of those of the member states. To be sure, there is no universal template for federalism, and none of the world's two dozen or so federations look exactly the same (Watts, 2008). However, what they all have in common is a distinctive and clearly defined national government with independent powers, sharing authority with subsidiary state or provincial governments that each also have independent powers. The EU has some federal qualities, most clearly reflected in the work of the European Parliament and the European Central Bank, but most talk of a federal Europe is couched in terms of the future rather than the present. We cannot even talk accurately of a 'government' of the European Union, because to do so would be to imply that the EU institutions have the same kinds of independent powers as the governments of the member states to make and enforce law and policy. The most that we can say about EU institutions is that they constitute a process of governance, by which decisions, laws and policies are made without the existence of the conventional institutions of government. In other words, the EU is 'a political system but not a state' (Hix and Høyland, 2011: 2–5).

We must also remember that the European project is more than the network of EU institutions and agencies; it also includes the political, economic and cultural ties that European states (including those outside the EU) have built among themselves both formally and informally and outside the obligations of EU membership, the regional and local units of government that often have the most direct impact on the lives of Europeans, the growing sense among Europeans of being European, and the many other cross-border initiatives undertaken by cooperative bodies such as the Council of Europe and a complex network of European interest groups and think-tanks. 'Europe' is, in short, more than the institutions of the European Union.

As for confederalism, which might be regarded as a conceptual cousin of federalism, it is clear that the EU is not a *de jure* confederation (if for no other reason than it has not been formally declared as such in the treaties), but this does not mean that it is not – or cannot be – a *de facto* confederation. The latter is best understood as an administrative system in which independent states cooperate (usually for reasons of security, efficiency or mutual convenience), retaining the powers that they consider best reserved to themselves, and working together on matters best dealt with jointly, such as foreign trade and security policy. In order to allow this to happen, they create institutions designed to facilitate cooperative intergovernmental decision-making, into which citizens have only indirect input via the governments of member states, and whose character is primarily intergovernmental. The member states remain independent, and function independently in multiple significant areas of policy. As Lister puts it (1996: 106), if a federation is a union of peoples living within a single state, then a confederation is a union of states with a central authority deriving its authority from those states. This almost exactly describes the way in which the European Union works.

One of the rare supporters of the idea of the EU as a confederation is Majone (2006: 136), who argues that the term *confederation* describes 'precisely' the arrangement found in the EU and expresses his regret that confederalism has been 'practically banned from the discourse about the future and finality of the Union'. Elsewhere (Majone, 2009), he argues that while the model of a United States of Europe is bound to fail – both because it lacks popular support and because it finds itself unable to deliver the public goods which Europeans expect to receive from a fully fledged government – it could become an effective confederation built on the foundation of market integration. Meanwhile, Moravcsik (2007: 25) has argued that the EU is, 'despite a few federal elements, essentially a confederation of member-states'. *The Economist* (2009) agreed, albeit perhaps unwittingly, when it suggested that – in the wake of the final passage of the Treaty of Lisbon – the EU would 'continue as a mainly intergovernmental organization with supranational attributes'. Commission president José Manuel Barroso said much the same thing during his 2012 State of the Union address when he spoke of the need for the EU 'to move towards a federation of nation states' (Barroso, 2012), an analysis that could be construed to imply a European confederation.

One related alternative is to think of the EU as a hybrid, containing features of both federalism and confederalism, an idea which in turn depends upon how we understand federalism (McKay, 2001). Burgess (2006: 239) suggests that while the EU is

> not a federation in the conventional sense ... it is nonetheless a political union with strong federal and confederal elements .... [or] a new kind of federal-confederal union that we can classify as a 'new confederation' or a new federal model.

Blankart (2007) says much the same when he argues that the EU is neither a confederation nor a federation, but is instead an 'association of compound states', some policies being dealt with in a federal manner and others in a confederal manner. And Watts (2008: 56–8) describes the EU as a 'hybrid confederation-federation', identifying its confederal roots in the powers of the Council of Ministers, its small budget, its legal basis in a series of treaties, and the policy powers retained by the member states. He sees its federal qualities in the work of the European Commission and the European Court of Justice, although – curiously – not in the European Parliament.

One way of better understanding the confederal features of the EU is to contrast it with a federation. The latter is a unified state, within which power is divided between central and local levels of government, each of which has independent powers. There is a direct link between all levels of government and citizens in the sense that each of those levels of government exercises authority over citizens, and is answerable directly to those citizens. By contrast, a confederation is a group of sovereign states with a central authority deriving its powers from those states, and citizens are linked indirectly to the central authority via the governments of the states in which they live.

It is clear that the idea of a confederal Europe has failed to gain much traction in the academic world in general terms as well as in its application to the EU (for two of the few exceptions, see Forsyth, 1981; Lister, 1996). There are several possible reasons for this:

- Any entity that resembles a confederation can simply be described as a weak form of federation, a concept that has attracted considerably more study and attention. The links between the two ideas are illustrated by how often they have been confused with each other.
- It is an arrangement that falls short of the United States of Europe that most federalists would like to see, and hence they are unlikely to regard it with much favour. Indeed, they would likely regard the declaration of a confederal Europe not as a compromise, but as a surrender or an admission of failure.
- In an ironic counterpoint, it does not please those who are opposed to a federal Europe because most examples of confederations from history have evolved into federations, the United States being the prime case in point. In his classic study of politics, Henry Sidgwick argued (1891: 519) that confederations – assuming they stay together – have a 'tendency' to evolve into federations, although he conceded that differences in race, religion and historical traditions could 'indefinitely retard' the process. The notion of confederalism as a stage in a process rather than an end in itself was illustrated by Jean Monnet's 1960 plan for a European confederation, which he saw only as a pragmatic step towards an ultimate European federation (Winand, 1993: 257).
- It is not a concept with which most of those involved in the debate about Europe are familiar; that debate has mainly revolved around the binary option of the EU as either an international organization writ large or as a federal superstate, and relatively little attention has been paid to options that lie between these two. Federations are better understood at least in part because there are simply more of them in existence, while confederations are studied much less because – in their application to states – they are found only in history.
- Confederalism does not fit with the strong statist tradition in Europe; Majone (2006) argues that Europeans have lived with states since Westphalia, that a confederation is not a state, and thus that it is unsatisfactory to most Europeans as a political option.

Perhaps the most fundamental reason why confederalism has failed to gain much traction among scholars of the EU is because it has become more usual to think of the EU as an exercise in multi-level governance (MLG). This is best understood as an arrangement in which power is shared among the supranational, national, sub-national and local levels of government, with a high degree of interaction (Puchala, 1975; Marks, 1993; Hooghe and Marks, 2001). While interesting, its core problem is that it differs little from federalism, which comes in a such a wide variety of forms that it can easily be shown to overlap with MLG. The latter, in spite of its popularity, sheds little new light on the dynamics of the European Union, while at the same time allowing scholars to discuss federalism without using a term that is often unpopular.

It behooves political scientists to set aside these distractions and to think more carefully about confederalism as a tool both for better understanding the European Union and for making it more understandable to its often confused citizens. Wheare (1963: 10–11) noted the critical role played by the United States in helping define what we understand by the 'federal principle' of dividing powers between general and regional governments such that each are within independent and yet coordinated spheres. The federal principle, he argued, 'has come to mean what it does because the United States has come to be what it is'. Why then, could the EU not become the template for the 'confederal principle', and why could it not come to have new meaning as a result of the EU being both acknowledged and considered as a confederation?

Just because most earlier confederations have either failed or have evolved into federations does not mean that the EU could not become the world's first example of a sustainable or end-state confederation. Indeed, the unique historical, political and economic circumstances within which the EU has evolved have already prompted many observers to consider it *sui generis*, but this is an empty term; to argue that the EU is unique is to avoid explaining what it is. It could, instead, be both *sui generis* and confederal, thereby allowing us to both recognize the uniqueness of the EU while giving the EU model some substance. But before we can achieve the state of institutional stability that meaningful confederalism demands, we must first address what is perhaps the most fundamental problem facing Europe today: the variable quality of the debate about its past record and future possibilities.

## The troubled quality of the debate about Europe

The bulk of analyses of the problems faced today by the European Union focus on five major topics: addressing the needs of the eurozone, the costs and benefits of austerity, the implications of persistent high unemployment, the restrictions faced by worker mobility and the single market in services, and worries about Europe's ability to compete globally. In other words, the problems are couched in large part in economic terms, the questions posed about the future of the EU come largely from economists, and it is economists who are most often heard as we consider our options.

But predating such problems, certainly made worse by them, and containing potentially longer lasting effects, has been the problem of declining public faith and trust in the European experiment. In the pre-Maastricht era of the permissive consensus, when decisions on integration were taken in large part by political and bureaucratic elites, there was little input from ordinary citizens, and public opinion was rarely seriously taken into account. But the debate over Maastricht sparked a backlash against integration, which has grown steadily since then, as reflected in the rise of anti-EU political parties in many member states, and several votes against EU initiatives in national referendums. Recent Eurobarometer polls have revealed several notable trends in public opinion (European Commission, 2013: 58, 97, 101):

- The number of Europeans who feel that things are headed in the wrong direction at the European level grew from 23 per cent in 2007 to a high of 55 per cent in 2011 before tailing off slightly to 49 per cent in 2013.
- Trust in the EU fell from a high of 57 per cent in 2007 to a low of 31 per cent in 2013.
- The number of Europeans who have a positive image of the EU fell from 52 per cent in 2007 to 30 per cent in 2013.

No debate about Europe is today complete, it seems, without reference to euroscepticism, and no lasting decision on the exit from the eurozone crisis can be made without taking into consideration the balance of public opinion on integration. But three critical points need to be made as we review that consideration. First, euroscepticism must be fully and accurately understood. The term is often used in such a way as to imply that opposition to the EU stems from the same core sources and makes approximately the same arguments, when in fact it comes in several different shades ranging from support for reform to support for abolition and/or exit from the EU (see, for example, discussion in Kopecký and Mudde, 2002).

Second, it is not just the EU that has been the subject of declining trust and optimism; there has also been declining faith in government more generally, and there are growing numbers of people who feel that their country is headed in the wrong direction. While 60 per cent of residents of the EU had little or no trust in the EU in 2013 (a marked increase from 32 per cent in 2007), they held it in higher esteem than they held their own national governments, in which 71 per cent had little or no trust (European Commission, 2013: 55, 92). And while 49 per cent of residents of the EU felt that things were headed in the wrong direction in the EU in 2013, they have long felt that matters have been worse at home: 56 per cent felt that things were headed in the wrong direction in their country in 2013, an increase from 41 per cent in 2007. There is, meanwhile, little difference in levels of satisfaction in democracy (50 per cent dissatisfied at the national level and 46 per cent dissatisfied at the EU level (European Commission, 2013: 71, 73)) or in prospects for the economic situation at the national, European and global levels: about 18 per cent at all levels thought that it would improve, about 41–44 per cent thought that it would stay the same, and 27–34 per cent thought that it would worsen (European Commission, 2013: 29).

Finally, Eurobarometer polls show that large numbers of Europeans neither understand the EU nor much follow the news regarding developments in the EU. Between 1997 and 2006, Eurobarometer measured perceived knowledge of the EU by asking respondents to score themselves between 1 (signifying that they knew nothing at all about the EU) and 10 (signifying that they knew a great deal). The average for the EU-15 was in the range of 4.0–4.5, and changed little with eastern enlargement. Scores in the more knowledgeable member states (such as Austria, Denmark and Germany in 2002) were in the range of 5.2–5.4, and in the least knowledgeable member states (such as Spain, Portugal and the UK) were in the range of 3.2–3.8. No more than 23–29 per cent of respondents in each survey gave themselves a 'passing' score of 6 or higher, 68–76 per cent of respondents gave themselves failing scores of 5 or less, and 17–22 per cent of respondents admitted to knowing almost nothing about the EU.

More recent efforts to measure levels of knowledge have been framed differently, but have had similar results. Thus in 2007, respondents were asked about their knowledge of 'European political affairs', to which only 30 per cent responded that they considered themselves 'very' or 'fairly' well informed, while 68 per cent considered themselves 'not very' or 'not at all' informed (European Commission, 2007: 125). Europeans have also been asked in recent years to comment on the statement 'I understand how the European Union works': the Spring 2013 poll found that 51 per cent thought they understood the EU while 46 per cent thought they did not (percentage shares that have been approximately flipped since the breaking of the eurozone crisis). Meanwhile, only 16 per cent of Europeans had a strong interest in politics, with another 44 per cent having a moderate interest, and those interested in national politics outnumbered those interested in European politics by 75 to 62 per cent.

We thus have a public debate about the European Union coloured both by confusion and declining enthusiasm, with which large numbers of people remain unengaged, in which there is little agreement on the character and implications of the subject of the debate, but which must also be understood within the context of declining faith in government more generally. Little is likely to be achieved of a constructive nature under such circumstances. The only way to emerge from crisis in a constructive and sustainable fashion is to engage European citizens, and the only way to do this effectively is to help them better understand the qualities and the possibilities of integration. To describe the EU as *sui generis* is – as noted earlier – unhelpful, and we have already seen that it is neither an international organization writ large nor a federal European superstate. It does, however, reflect many of the qualities of a confederation, albeit with federal qualities, and it is with this in mind that we are most likely to identify constructive exits from the eurozone crisis.

## Confederalism as a way forward

If more Europeans are able to understand the EU, then they will be better equipped to decide for themselves how they regard it, and less likely to be swayed by the appeals of those partisan elites (such as political leaders, political parties, interest groups and the media) who are so adept at representing its work and powers in a manner that suits their preferences. In order to be sustainable, the EU must be acclaimed as a source of solutions to the problems of its member states, rather than as a source of the problems themselves. And the only way to do this effectively is to talk not about the prospects for a federal United States of Europe (a widely unpopular notion) but instead to explore ways in which a consensus can be reached on the kind of Europe that has the most appeal and the fewest prospects for being misunderstood. Confederalism offers such an option.

The EU reflects the core notion of a confederal system in the sense that it is an association of independent states that cooperate where it makes the most sense, retain those powers best reserved for themselves, and work together in cooperative institutions where the interests of citizens are mainly represented indirectly through national governments. These institutions have few if any truly independent powers or areas of policy responsibility; even in the five areas of policy for which the EU has been given competence by the treaties (competition, customs, fisheries conservation, monetary policy in the euro-zone, and trade), key decisions are still made at an intergovernmental level, even if it is the general EU interest that lies at the heart of those decisions.

The confederal qualities of the EU can be seen in three main areas. First, with the exception of the European Parliament, residents of the EU member states have a direct political relationship only with their home-state governments, who speak on behalf of the citizens of the member states in the meeting-rooms of the European Council and the Council of Ministers, and play a key role in appointments to the European Commission, the European Court of Justice and the European Central Bank. Meanwhile, the EU is lacking a fundamental feature of a conventional federal system: a European constitution adopted by the member states and capable of being amended and developed by proposals from the EU institutions and the approval of a majority of member states. Instead the EU is based on a series of treaties designed and developed by intergovernmental conferences. It is in this area in particular that the EU continues to reflect its origins as an international organization.

Second, there is – as we have seen – no EU government in the sense that there is a network of elected institutions with independent powers to enforce law and policy, but only a system of governance allowing for decision-making without the existence of the conventional institutions of government. The 'leaders' of the EU – particularly the presidents of the Council, the Commission and Parliament, the high representative for external relations, and the trade com-missioner – have powers to administer and to offer guidance and leadership, but they are still ultimately the servants of the member states and have fewer powers than their national counterparts.

Third, the member states of the EU are still distinct political units with sep-arate legal identities, which can enter into bilateral agreements with non-EU states in most areas of policy, and still maintain their own national defence forces and pursue independent security policies. The EU is a voluntary asso-ciation from which its members are free to leave, if they wish, without such a departure being considered secession. And there is no EU citizenship that could replace citizenship of the member states, and most of the citizens of the member states still have a higher sense of allegiance to their home states than they do to Europe.

While champions of a federal Europe might be reluctant to acknowledge the confederal qualities of the EU – because to do so would be to admit that a federal Europe might be out of reach – it is also essential to acknowledge that politics in democratic systems revolves around compromise, and confederalism offers a political compromise between the champions and the opponents of federalism. It ensures that critical policy powers remain in the hands of the government of the member states, but also acknowledges that there are areas in which it makes more sense for the member states to cooperate. It represents neither the federal option, at which so much criticism and concern has been directed, nor a return to the era of the nation state and the admission of failure that this would represent.

Confederalism also offers a compelling response to criticisms of the EU as an elitist construct that has involved the surrender of powers to Brussels. It would preserve the democratic structures of the member states and potentially make more clear to Europeans that the power remains in the hands of national governments. Certainly the lines of authority in a confederal EU would be more clearly demarcated than in the current arrangement that is neither one thing nor the other. With accountability lying more directly with national governments, the opportunities for publics and political leaders to shift the blame for domestic problems to a higher level of shared governance would be reduced, and both power and responsibility would be seen to lie more clearly with the member states. Confederalism would also place more pressure on governments to focus on agreeing which areas of policy were best dealt with in concert and which were not, thereby giving more emphasis to subsidiarity and proportionality in designing policy; that is, limiting the EU to taking action only in those policy areas where integration made the most sense, while ensuring that its actions did not go beyond the objectives of the treaties.

Confederalism also offers a powerful answer to many of the criticisms of neo-liberalism. Free trade, deregulation and privatization can all be reconsidered within a confederal framework in such a way as to preserve their strengths and control their weaknesses. Because it involves less pooling of power, confederalism does not threaten self-determination, or promote inequality and exploitation, or pave the way to increases in corporate power in the same way as federalism. The experience of federations suggests that even though there is a division of power between national and regional governments, the national level tends to accumulate authority at the expense of the units, creating a new level of 'big government' that is not always adept at understanding the needs of local communities. The EU case has revealed that the pooling of authority in a one-size-fits-all sense does not always work, the pressures that have been created by meeting the terms of membership of the euro being a case in point. Confederalism is based on the principle of power being retained by the units, and in the EU case would address concerns about the loss of such power to Brussels.

Finally, confederalism offers a powerful answer to those who worry that the federalizing pressures of European integration might be causing member states to lose their separate identities. As an alliance of independent states, a confederal EU would leave states free to cooperate without generating so many fears among those who worry about loss of state identity. Identity is wrapped up with political power, and a union of states promises to allow greater recognition of separate identities than would a federal union of people living within a single European state.

Of the options available to us as we consider exits from the trials and tribulations of the eurozone crisis – as well as the effects of the euroscepticism whose origins far pre-dated that crisis – confederalism offers the strongest prospects for protecting the achievements of the European Union while assuaging the concerns of those who worry about the effects of a federal Europe or a return to the era of the European nation state. It not only best explains the structural pattern within which most EU institutions are currently arranged, but is also a compelling compromise between the often starkly different futures proposed for the EU as it emerges from the eurozone crisis.

## References

Barroso, J. M. (2012). 'State of the Union Address.' Delivered to the European Parliament, 12 September.

Blankart, C. B. (2007). 'The European Union: Confederation, Federation or Association of Compound States?' *Constitutional Political Economy*, 18 (2), pp. 99–106.

Burgess, M. (2006). *Comparative Federalism: Theory and Practice*. London: Routledge.

*The Economist* (2009). 'Wake up Europe!' 16 October.

European Commission (2007). *Eurobarometer 67*. Spring.

European Commission (2013). *Eurobarometer 79*. Spring.

Forsyth, M. (1981). *Unions of States: The Theory and Practice of Confederation*. Leicester: Leicester University Press.

Hix, S. and Høyland, B. (2011). *The Political System of the European Union* (3rd edition). Basingstoke: Palgrave Macmillan.

Hoffman, S. (1993) 'Goodbye to a United Europe?' In *New York Review of Books*, 27 May. Reprinted in Hoffman, S. (1995). *The European Sisyphus: Essays on Europe 1964–1994*. Boulder, CO: Westview Press.

Hooghe, L. and Marks, G. (2001). *Multi-Level Governance and European Integration*. Lanham, MD: Rowman and Littlefield.

Kopecký, P. and Mudde, C. (2002). 'The Two Sides of Euroscepticism: Party Positions on European Integration in East Central Europe.' *European Union Politics*, 3 (September), pp. 297–326.

Lister, F. K. (1996). *The European Union, the United Nations, and the Revival of Confederal Governance*. Westport, CT: Greenwood.

Mahone, G. (2009). *Dilemmas of European Integration: The Ambiguities and Pitfalls of Integration by Stealth*. Oxford: Oxford University Press.

Majone, G. (2006). 'Federation, Confederation, and Mixed Government: An EU-US Comparison.' In Menon, A. and Schain, M. (eds.) *Comparative Federalism: The European Union and the United States in Comparative Perspective*. Oxford: Oxford University Press.

Marks, G. (1993). 'Structural Policy and Multi-level Governance in the EC.' In Cafruny, A. and Rosenthal, G. (eds.) *The State of the European Community*. Vol. 2. Boulder, CO: Lynne Rienner.

McKay, D. (2001). *Designing Europe: Comparative Lessons from the Federal Experience*. Oxford: Oxford University Press.

Monnet, J. (1978). *Memoirs*. Garden City, NY: Doubleday.

Monnet, J. (1982). Quoted in *The Economist*, 20 March.

Moravcsik, A. (2007). 'The European Constitutional Settlement.' In Meunier, S. and McNamara, K. R. (eds.) *Making History: European Integration and Institutional Change at Fifty*. Oxford: Oxford University Press.

Puchala, D. J. (1975). 'Domestic Politics and Regional Harmonization in the European Communities.' *World Politics*, 27 (4), pp. 496–520.

Sidgwick, H. (1891). *The Elements of Politics*. London: Macmillan and Company.

Stern, F. (1980). 'Germany in a Semi-Gaullist Europe.' *Foreign Affairs*, 58 (Spring), pp. 867–86.

Wallace, W. (1982). 'Europe as a Confederation: The Community and the Nation-State.' *Journal of Common Market Studies*, 21 (1), pp. 57–68.

Watts, R. J. (2008). *Comparing Federal Systems* (3rd edition). Montreal: Institute of Intergovernmental Relations.

Wheare, K. C. (1963). *Federal Government* (4th edition). Oxford: Oxford University Press.

Winand, P. (1993). *Eisenhower, Kennedy and the United States of Europe*. New York: St Martin's Press.

Zweifel, T. D. (2005). *International Organizations and Democracy: Accountability, Politics, and Power*. Boulder, CO: Lynne Rienner.

# 4 Beyond the 'ever closer union'

## National interests, institutional power shifts and threats to the 'permissive consensus' in Germany

*Roland Sturm*

The future of the European Union depends on its ability to coordinate its institutional capacities and on strategies to make these capacities compatible with the national interests of EU member states. A strategic approach is necessary, which can accommodate both the constitutional and the policy challenges caused by the diverging perceptions of the recent banking and currency crisis of the EU and the connected national discourses on EU politics. National interests have never been absent from decision-making on the European level, be it in the European Council, the Council of Ministers or even the Commission. So far, however, there has been no controversy with regard to the generally accepted way forward for Europeans, the 'ever closer union'. This controversy has slowly been taking root and for mostly domestic reasons has even reached Germany, a traditionally Europhile country. Germany has used its weight in the EU to contribute to an institutional power shift, which strengthens the decision-making process in the European Council. Supranational interests in the EU and those actors with integrationist preferences find it harder today to legitimize the goal of 'more Europe'.

To fathom the limits of the integration impetus today, this contribution first develops the logic of European economic and political integration. It then informs on what we know at present about the competing forces of supranational and intergovernmental politics in European institutions and their traditional balance. Finally, it uses the example of Germany for characterizing political change. The mass-elite gap in German EU politics erodes the country's 'permissive consensus' on the EU. Germany also has to come to grips with expectations difficult to control. An acceptance of its potential new role as benevolent hegemon and by implication of more intergovernmentalism in the EU conflicts with its self-image as a pro-integrationist country. German politicians do not want to give up their integrationist credentials in the long run, but are insecure about how they should act short-term when for domestic reasons national interests, which limit a deepening of EMU, determine their European agenda. They are not alone in this dilemma. All Euro-countries are hesitant to further compromise their national sovereignty in economic matters, not least for domestic reasons, because everywhere public opinion regarding European integration is at best ambivalent (de Vries, 2013).

Although ordinary citizens are sceptical, governments still prefer European solutions for example for the rescue of the euro to national ones (Pütter, 2012: 168). With the exception of a few member states such as the UK, the Netherlands or the Czech Republic, governments envisage more economic and political integration.

## Economic integration and political integration – two strategies to sideline the nation-state?

For the success of European integration, it has always been important that the new partnership of nation-states would be able to overcome the confines of a free trade zone, and that the integration process would institutionalize a political dimension capable of making decisions on behalf of Europe. The scope of political integration this implies, remained, however, controversial, more so than advances in economic integration (with the exception of the euro). On the one hand, there is the argument of the neo-functionalists. They believe that a deepening of political integration is the logical consequence of a deepening of economic cooperation. On the other hand, liberal intergovernmentalists would argue that governments are able and willing to determine the parameters of politics no matter how closely interconnected national economies in the EU are. In this perspective, the one-way-street called 'ever closer union' is a very limited view of the kind of structural 'mobility' the European Union allows, and it overlooks the important role of domestic political pressures in the EU member states.

The present status of the EU is more complicated than the juxtaposition of the relative importance of economic and political integration implies. Both elements of a united Europe have experienced frictions caused by the revival of national interests. The treaty on stability, coordination and governance in the economic and monetary union (fiscal compact) marks the culmination of a tendency to forge a coalition of the willing when it comes to the deepening of economic integration – a tendency that found earlier expressions for example in the creation of the euro or the Schengen agreement. Political integration has resulted in the development of a new political arrangement. This arrangement embodies 'two European Unions', one in which the Commission is in the driver's seat and which is responsible for routine business in the EU, and one in which the European Council shapes politics, takes responsibility for crisis management and for the ad hoc mediation of national interests. With the banking crisis and the sovereign debt crisis, the gulf between the Commission's Europe and the European Council's Europe has widened. Pütter (2012: 162) remarked that this observation

> poses a challenge to established concepts of intergovernmental relations within the EU. Apparently, policy-coordination as a method of collective decision-making in a system of decentralised political responsibilities has become enshrined as a core European 'method'. It now firmly exists

alongside the classical Community method and the latter's focus on 'integration by law'.

The German Chancellor Angela Merkel likes the distinction between the 'community method' of European integration, i.e. the Commission-led integration process, and the 'union method' of European integration, i.e. the European Council-led integration process. For her it was appropriate therefore – even if this brought her into conflict with views widely held in her own party – to withstand all suggestions that, as a consequence of the severe economic crises in the EU, the idea of a United States of Europe was back on the negotiation table. She even thought that the direct election of the President of the Commission would be a step too far (Merkel, 2013). In Chancellor Merkel's view, a treaty reform, which gives the President of the Commission more visibility and legitimacy, would strengthen the kind of Europe in which she as national representative is not involved. As she sees it, the representation of national interests in the EU should be strengthened not weakened.

## National interests in European politics

The fact that both the European Council and the Council of Ministers provide a forum for the articulation of national interests is no surprise, though the newly established influential position of the European Council vis-à-vis the Commission with regard to policy initiatives is important to note (Pütter, 2012). The Council of Ministers has traditionally avoided the kind of confrontational politics the European Council at times is able to produce. In both European decision-making bodies, informality and consensus building are the rule. The European Council has no choice. It needs unanimity for its decisions. In the Council of Ministers, decision-making seems to be easier, because the EU treaties have, over time, increased the number of policy fields in which qualified majority voting is possible. Empirical work has shown that this was only of marginal importance for the procedures in the Council. On the contrary, consensus is an unintended by-product of the formal rules, which allow qualified majority voting, as Häge (2012: 483) argues:

> member states form larger and larger coalitions until they reach the necessary numbers to constitute a blocking minority. If, at the end of this process, all member states are organized in blocking minority coalitions, then no policy can be adopted without unanimous consent.

Between 1994 and 2002 on average 81 per cent of Council decisions were made by consensus without voting (Heisenberg, 2005: 66). A preference for the smallest common denominator, which sets a higher hurdle for decision-making than the treaties did, may help to explain why, in times of crisis, the European Council, because of its 'forum qualities' became the more attractive arena for the articulation of national interests.

*Table 4.1*  Voting for national interests in the Council of Ministers (1996–2002, contested legislative acts)

| Country (by size of population) | Vote against as % of contested votes | Abstentions as % of contested votes |
|---|---|---|
| Germany | 17.93 | 8.76 |
| United Kingdom | 8.37 | 5.18 |
| France | 6.37 | 5.98 |
| Italy | 13.15 | 5.18 |
| Spain | 4.78 | 5.18 |
| Netherlands | 11.16 | 2.79 |
| Greece | 5.98 | 0.80 |
| Belgium | 5.98 | 4.78 |
| Portugal | 2.79 | 5.18 |
| Sweden | 10.36 | 1.99 |
| Austria | 4.78 | 2.39 |
| Denmark | 10.76 | 3.59 |
| Finland | 3.59 | 0.80 |
| Ireland | 3.59 | 0.40 |
| Luxembourg | 1.59 | 3.19 |

Source: Heisenberg (2005: 76).

What the decision-making processes in the European Council and the Council of Ministers have in common is the importance they attribute to informal agreements behind closed doors. One can only speculate, how and how often, national interests were expressed, and how influential national interests were for bargaining processes in the Council (Zimmer *et al.*, 2005: 403). In the literature we find the assumption that 'Council bargaining involves less "hard nosed bargaining"' and more 'setting aside national interests to move legislation forward' (Heisenberg, 2005: 67). This provokes two questions: Which issues caused 'hard nosed bargaining', and was there more 'hard nosed bargaining' as a consequence of the recent economic crises in the member states (for example a limit to vote trading)?

We do know that an essential element of the consensus oriented negotiation process is the role of Germany and France as 'engines of political integration' (Schild, 2010; Demesmay, 2013). We also know that it is easier to make deals in the Council if a less strongly defended national interest can be traded against a more strongly defended one. Vote trading and policy leadership smooth over conflicts. This does not imply, however, that national interests have disappeared or are of less importance. On the rare occasion when there are contested votes, it is possible to document national interests. It may be surprising that Germany, which claims to have a general integrationist preference, is on top of the list when it comes to abstentions and votes against legislation in the Council (Table 4.1). What may explain this apparent contradiction is the fact that the non-consensus decisions did not include major political decisions or new programmes. Still, German voting with regard to non-consensus decisions implies a more general aspiration to have a distinct voice when it comes to future EU policies (Heisenberg, 2005: 77).

Zimmer *et al.* (2005) have analysed interviews with 125 experts, most of whom belonged to the national delegations to the Council of Ministers, to find out what the general preferences of the delegations were that determined their decisions on more specific legislation. Here a much clearer picture emerges where individual red lines were drawn by member states when voting in Council decisions. Zimmer *et al.* identify 'a relatively stable conflict line within the Council of Ministers, namely the conflict between the north and the south, around which opposed voting blocs emerge over matters of subsidies and financial contributions, market regulation and protectionism' (Zimmer *et al.*, 2005: 413). Germany, for example, 'demands further regulation, more protectionism and subsidies, if these are in accord with its vital national economic and consumer interests' (Zimmer *et al.*, 2005: 412). Golub, who worked with the same data set, added a measure of salience to the issue preferences of individual countries. He found that 'national differences in legislative bargaining process are much more pronounced than previously recognized ... and the relative winners tend to be the small states rather than the large ones' (Golub, 2012: 1311). The empowerment of the European parliament, most recently by the Lisbon Treaty, has contributed to an increase of proactive politics of member states in the Council. In the case of controversial decisions of national importance, rather than relying on national officials in preparatory committees of the Council, ministers will take the initiative and stress national interests, because they know that public and political awareness for the issue grows once the co-decision procedure for European legislation is applied. It is easier for ministers to work behind closed doors than to cope with the challenge of widely publicized political conflict (Häge, 2011).

National interests should be completely absent from the Commission's decision-making process. The TEU in its Article 17 states explicitly: 'In carrying out its responsibilities, the Commission shall be completely independent. ... the members of the Commission shall neither seek nor take instructions from any Government or other institution, body, office or entity.' The member states have much more ambivalent views regarding the political neutrality of the Commission. For example, their decision to stick with the 'one country/ one commissioner' principle raises the question, whether the decision-making process in the Commission really remains outside the influence of national priorities. Research has shown that this is not always the case. Egeberg (2006) found that the Commissioners tend to champion interests inherently linked with their portfolio. In addition, they do not forget, however, their country of origin's interest, EU interests or party political interests. Much depends on the type of policy they have to deal with. Commission Officials are much more explicit. They frankly admit that their national backgrounds shape their views on European integration more than their professional backgrounds. This, however, does not imply that in the Commission intergovernmentalists are in the majority: 'No more than half of Commission officials take sides in the partisan battle between supranationalism and state-centrism. Supranationalists outnumber state-centrists more than two to one' (Hooghe, 2012: 104). For Commissioners there is no incentive, apart from his or her own convictions, to prefer national policy networks and by implication national interests. Now that their cabinets are 'denationalized' (Egeberg and Heskestad, 2010) and information and advice are available in networks composed of individuals with a cosmopolitan background (Suvarierol, 2008), Commissioners can much more easily keep their distance from national interests, if they wish to do so.

Among the European institutions, the Commission seems to be an important counterweight for political renationalization efforts of EU member states, which result from new domestic pressures. The neutraiity of the Commission is to a lesser degree endangered by the current institutional setting than by efforts to open up the election of the President of the Commission. A directly elected President would necessarily be a party politician who has to find votes, especially in the bigger member states. At present domestic pressure in the nation-states for 'less Europe' are influencing primarily the Council of Ministers and the European Council. New national interests, which developed as a reaction to EU rescue policies, have the potential to challenge the architecture of the EU, as the German example shows.

## The slow disappearance of the 'permissive consensus' in Germany

German post-war politics relied on European integration as a road to peace and freedom, and as the only alternative that allowed a reintegration of Germany into the community of democratic nations. The German political elite as well as the vast majority of at that time West Germans developed a positive, even emotional, attitude towards Europe. Efforts made to build bridges in the form of European institutions, but also in the form of bottom-up initiatives, e.g. town partnerships (*jumelages*), were widely popular. European integration was also a promising perspective for the united Germany after 1990. The EU's generous political and economic support for the integration of East Germany into the European Community, especially in the form of structural aid to develop East German regions, was very welcome. Chancellor Helmut Kohl regarded the deepening of European integration as the best strategy to convince the European partners that there was no need to fear an enlarged Germany. His idea was to anchor Germany firmly in Europe, even if this meant the end of the popular German Mark. It was not Germany that was supposed to shape Europe. The aim was not a German Europe, but a European Germany: 'Despite domestic concerns especially on EMU, neither the federal government nor the parliamentary opposition parties attempted to exploit Germany's potential against its traditional role of an important but "tamed power"' (Maurer, 2003: 116).

The political elite could rely on popular support for this kind of European integration policy, though since the 1980s this support has lacked enthusiasm. Since the 1990s an emotional distance to 'Europe' has developed, especially after the introduction of the euro (Risse, 2003). Until recently in German political discourse the European 'democratic deficit', which has provoked an ongoing debate EU-wide, remained, however, a problem of intellectuals only. The German political elite relied in matters concerning the EU on the 'permissive consensus' of the voters who were not interested in controversies on Europe. In Germany even for European elections, the EU was not a topic in its own right. What politicians interpreted as 'carte blanche' in European politics was in truth the result of widespread 'relaxed fatalism' (Köcher, 2012) among German citizens. A dangerous kind of neglect, which has the potential to develop into Euroscepticism, evolved in German public opinion and at the general election of 2013 almost gave a party, critical of the euro, access to the national parliament. The Alternative für Deutschland (AfD) missed the 5 per cent hurdle by only 0.3 per cent of the vote.

In German parliament, controversies on Europe were rare. Neither the enlargement of the EU to the East nor new European treaties or the currency union provoked political conflict. This was indirect proof of the fact that – as opinion polls showed – a wide gulf between the EU as a project of the national political elite and the ordinary citizens' perceptions of the EU had developed. EU politics was for 'experts' (Noelle-Neumann and Petersen, 1999: 597), a view shared by many members of parliament. Even the budgetary challenges implied by the efforts to strengthen European economic governance did not provoke the opposition parties to position themselves as opponents to the government in European affairs (Table 4.2). An exception was the Left Party, which has its origins in the Communist Party that ruled East Germany. Not that this party attacked Germany's commitment to defend the euro. It criticized, however, European crisis management for its alleged bias in favour of the banks and the interests of neoliberalism. The other parties had dissenters in their ranks, too. The support for initiatives to strengthen the euro area and to support member states with economic problems was weaker in the governing parties, the Christiandemocrats and the Liberals, than in the opposition parties. Dissent here concentrated on doubts whether it was wise to give German financial support to member states, which seemed to shy away from taking responsibility for their economic problems and therefore could develop into a permanent problem for the eurozone.

This dissent found some resonance in the German public, especially when TV reports showed protests on the streets of the nations in crisis with pictures of the German Chancellor dressed up as a Nazi. The underlying problem was summarized by a commentator in the *Financial Times*. He remarked when Germany decided to support Cyprus:

> The Germanophobia is unfair. Behind the shouting and wrangling, German taxpayers will once again be funding the biggest single share of yet another eurozone bailout. It seems a bit harsh that Germany is extending loans of billions of euros to its neighbours – only to be accused of neo-Nazism in return.
>
> (Rachman, 2013)

Table 4.2 Support of opposition parties in the German parliament (*Bundestag*) for legislation concerning the sovereign debt crisis in the eurozone

| | Voting results in parliament in % (government majority 53.3%) | Social democrats in % | Alliance 90/Green Party in % | The Left Party in % |
|---|---|---|---|---|
| 7.5. 2010 Financial support for Greece | 63.1 | 2.0 (the majority of the party abstained) | 82.3 | 0 |
| 21.5. 2010 ESM | 51.5 | 0 (the majority of the party abstained) | 0 (the majority of the party abstained) | 0 |
| 29.9. 2011 Additional Resources for ESM | 84.5 | 94.5 | 94.1 | 0 |
| 26.10. 2011 Additional resources for EFSF | 81,2 | 86,9 | 91.1 | 0 |
| 27.2. 2012 Second aid programme for Greece | 80.1 | 86.3 | 92.6 | 0 |
| 29.6. 2012 ESM | 79.8 | 87.6 | 95.5 | 0 |
| 29.6. 2012 Fiscal Compact | 78.8 | 78.7 | 79.4 | 0 |
| 19.7. 2012 Support for Spanish banks 18.4. 2013 | 76.4 | 80.1 | 79.4 | 0 |
| Aid programme for Cyprus | 81.0 | 85.9 | 98.4 | 0 |
| Aid programme for Cyprus: Agreement between ESM and Cyprus | 81.0 | 83.8 | 98.4 | 0 |
| Prolongation of the Irish EFSF credit | 81.0 | 93.6 | 100.0 | 0 |
| Prolongation of the Portuguese EFSF credit | 83.5 | 94.1 | 98.4 | 0 |

Source: Sturm (2014, in print).

The German government did not take note of the Nazi provocations. It concluded, however, that a change of the pro-European public mood in Germany was under way. This interpretation together with other developments in national politics encouraged the German government to rely more on the European Council as an arena for European decision-making and forward planning than on the Commission. The latter had come up with wide-ranging ideas such as Eurobonds and other elements of financial transfers from the better-off member states to those in crisis (COM, 2012: 777). Such ideas would have created additional support for the slowly growing number of Eurosceptics in Germany and, for that reason, were already no attractive option for the German government. For the first time the government saw itself confronted with doubts about the benefits of Europe.

In comparison with the approach to Europe most other members of the EU prefer, it is important to note that it is quite a new phenomenon to hear German politicians talk about German national interests in the EU context. Traditionally Germany's ambition has at best been to guide from the rear (*The Economist*, 15 June, 2013: 11). There were three developments in German politics that undermined the Europhile political consensus of Germany's political elite: (a) a new political discourse on the EU both on the mass and on the elite level of politics; (b) the 'domestification' (Bugdahn, 2005) of the EU conflict over Euro rescue policies; and (c) legal arguments, including last, but certainly not least, the rulings of the Federal Constitutional Court.

(a) In 2012 and 2013, the media confronted the German public with questions such as 'Will the euro survive?'; 'Will inflation destroy my savings?' or 'How much does Germany have to pay for member states in crisis?' The political discourse did not provide, and to some extent could not provide precise answers. This created an atmosphere of insecurity and a feeling of powerlessness on the mass level of politics. When Finance Minister Wolfgang Schäuble remarked that the national budget had no room for additional expenditure programmes such as higher pensions for women who had children, because of the financial resources needed for the rescue of Greece, this brought home to many Germans that a new conflict had begun to evolve. National interests can diverge from eurozone interests (Brössler, 2012).

On the elite level of politics, the permanent conflict of representatives of the Bundesbank, defending the Bundesbank's monetary policy tradition in the European Central Bank (ECB), with the majority of the members of the ECB board caused public estrangement in Germany and challenged the goal of a deepening of the economic and monetary union. In its policies, the ECB has left behind important features of the Bundesbank model, which it was supposed to imitate on the European level. Institutional isomorphism was the concession made to Germany when it gave up the European anchor currency, the German Mark. In the pre-crisis years, i.e. before the ECB distanced itself from the Bundesbank model, empirical research had shown that public support for EMU rested on the reputation of the euro and the ECB (Banducci *et al.*, 2009). In the crisis years, the reputation of the ECB suffered. In protest against the ECB's monetary policies both Axel Weber as president of the Bundesbank (2011) and Jürgen Stark (chief economist of the ECB until 2012) left the ECB. Axel Weber's successor in the office of president of the Bundesbank, Jens Weidmann, found himself most of the time in opposition to the policy priorities set by the ECB president Mario Draghi (Ruhkamp, 2012). So both on the mass and the elite level of politics in Germany critical attitudes towards European integration developed, and began to influence the strategic choices of the German government.

(b) The European debate on alternative strategies to protect the euro-area had domestic consequences. The German parties developed strategies to move the conflict from the European to the national political level, and to integrate it into the national level of party political competition – although avoiding a parliamentary confrontation. The Green Party and the Socialdemocrats identified themselves with some reservations – the Left party did this enthusiastically – with the anti-austerity movements in other Euro-countries. In October 2012 one of the chairpersons of the Left party even joined an anti-Merkel rally in Greece when the Chancellor visited the country. The christian democrats and the Liberals defended Germany's European rescue strategies and defined austerity as the price to pay for economic growth and the financial assistance of the better-off member states of the EU to the less fortunate ones. The Socialdemocrats took sides with the French Socialists and argued that budgetary discipline needs to be combined with state-financed incentives for economic growth. They even accepted the idea that Germany should contribute more to help member states in crisis. This political partnership found its most visible expression when the newly elected French President François Hollande met the SPD candidate for the German Chancellorship and the leading politicians of the party in the Élysée Palace on 5 April, 2013. Symbolic politics of European solidarity as demonstrated by both the Left party and the Socialdemocrats did not convince German voters at the 2013 election, but they remind us that the once undisputed domestic trust in the government's decisions on European affairs was no longer guaranteed.

During the 2014 European election campaign, the German parties for the first time in the history of European elections had to address controversies on European politics. The eurosceptical AfD challenged above all the Christiandemocrats. Their Bavarian branch, an independent party – the Christian Social Union – chose to be critical of the EU, but at the same time, the party stressed its pro-European convictions. The consensus on European integration remained the 'raison d'état' for all German parties, but doubts have been growing. Is Europe on the right track, should new enlargements really be imminent, and how to deal with the consequences of the free movement of people in the EU? These are only some of the questions that have come up in Germany, and they are important in a number of other EU member states, too.

(c) In Germany trust in the EU also eroded, because the European reactions to the crisis in the eurozone challenged Germany's legal(istic) culture.

The way the Treaty of Lisbon was ignored or interpreted to camouflage the fact that the Euro rescue operations broke European law (at least in the eyes of German critics of rescue policies) provoked a new wave of attacks on the deficits of the EU's legal culture by leading German professors of public law. Paul Kirchhof, a former judge at the German Constitutional Court argues, for example, that the no bail-out rule of Article 125 TFEU was broken. He sees this in a broader context, namely the tendency of decision-makers in the eurozone to prefer political rather than constitutional solutions for European problems. This has the consequence that the rule of law, which is essential for the legitimacy of the EU, has lost much of its former reputation (Kirchhof, 2012, 2014).

In the eyes of European partners, the German tradition may overestimate the need for legal guidance in policy-making, especially when, as it was the case, the German government cannot agree to transfers of competences to the EU as long as the Federal Constitutional Court has not ruled positively. For German politicians, many of them lawyers, it is self-evident that there are high hurdles to ad hoc institutional change. How difficult it is to translate political decisions into legal terms illustrates the surprising logic of the judgment that the European Court rendered in the Pringle case (the approval of the EMS in November 2012). As an observer noted:

> With the fate of the euro hanging in the balance, it had to approve the ESM. ... The Court managed to achieve this goal, but only by resorting to the strained reasoning that Member States have always had the ability to provide financial assistance via an instrument such as the ESM and that nothing has changed as a result of the debt crisis.
>
> (Borger, 2013: 113)

This is a good example of the clash of pragmatism and dogmatism when interpreting European law.

A number of German politicians, and especially Wolfgang Schäuble, the German Minister of Finance, is opposed to treaty change by generous interpretation of its content. Schäuble prefers a formal treaty change to accommodate new economic powers of the Commission. Most of the member states are reluctant, however, to support this strategy. They see the danger that once this process starts it will open up a wide range of issues, and that it is not predictable whether a new treaty could find sufficient support in all member states. The only ally German politicians have with regard to the idea of treaty reform is the British government, although for the wrong reasons. Whereas Wolfgang Schäuble, for example, wants more Europe (but based on rules, not on the volatile results of political negotiations), the British government would like to reduce the competences of the Commission, i.e. prefers less Europe (*The Economist*, 27 April, 2013: 26).

The German Federal Constitutional Court also contributed to an atmosphere favourable of a less positive attitude with regard to the vision of an 'ever closer union'. It investigated the long-term consequences of Germany's involvement in European rescue policies. In the Court's rulings of 2011 and 2012, it stipulated that the budgetary powers of the German parliament take precedence over decisions the government plans to make on the European political level (Hölscheidt, 2013). The parliament has to be able to control the budget now and in the future. This excludes the Europeanization of budgetary policy-making in the context of EU rescue policies (Pehle, 2011; Kranenpohl, 2013: 94). Parliament has to secure national interests. For the Federal Constitutional Court, a welcome side effect of its rulings is that the protection of national competences also strengthens the Court in its institutional competition with the Court of the European Union. In its ruling on the Lisbon Treaty, the Federal Constitutional Court stressed that there are core competences, which the German Constitution attributes exclusively to the German parliament. By implication, this means that the German Constitution guarantees the Federal Constitutional Court a permanent role in legal oversight. In 2014, in its decision to forward for the first time a court case to the Court of the EU (Bundesverfassungsgericht, 2014), the German Constitutional Court was very critical of the legality of the ECB's Outright Monetary Transactions and its Securities Market Programme. The section of the legal community that opposes the way the EU interprets the Lisbon Treaty, must have felt vindicated.

Long before the various economic crises and efforts to rescue EU member states in trouble had reached the headlines of the German press, political scientists compared the relationship between Germany and Europe with the shifting of tectonic plates (Jeffery and Paterson, 2003). There is slow change, but this change can be decisive. This image describes very well where we stand today. Generalized support for European integration continues to fall with important consequences for the elite consensus on Europe in Germany. The growing incongruence of national interests with important EU policies has led to a debate on Europe's future. Does a pro-European attitude imply these days more Europe, and if so under which conditions?

**Power shifts in the EU – do we have to live with a German hegemon?**

In the euro crisis, the Europeanization of decisions at first sight has led to a strengthening of EU institutions. Fiscal rules, surveillance and enforcement in the euro area are now the pillars of European economic governance. When one looks closer at the history of the new provisions and the controversies surrounding them, one comes to a less optimistic conclusion. Europeanization did not originate from the EU's supranational institutions, the Parliament and the Commission, but from the European Council. A new preference in EU politics has developed for intergovernmental bargaining following the traditional patterns of foreign policy, including geopolitical and balance of power arguments. One instrument in this bargaining process is, for example, coalition-building based on national interests. Germany has been joining this kind of power game reluctantly. One reason is that for geopolitical reasons there is always the danger that traditional foreign policy, independent of German policy preferences, sees in Germany an awkward power. Typical for this kind of thinking is the remark of Cambridge historian Brendan Simms that Germany 'sits uneasily at the heart of an EU that was conceived largely to constrain German power but which has served instead to increase it, and whose design flaws have unintentionally deprived many other Europeans of sovereignty' (*The Economist*, 13 April, 2013: 25).

It is obvious that in EU decision-making processes political coalition-building structures are already in place: there are – depending on the issue – coalitions of euro and of non-euro countries, of North and South European countries, of countries with a more and of countries with a less important financial segment of their economies, of economically competitive and less competitive countries, etc. Since 2012 a traditional coalition, the Franco-German pro-integration axis, has been going through a difficult time (Peel and Carnegy, 2013), although this may change in the future. The new pluralism of coalition-building in the EU has provoked the question of who takes the lead with regard to policy initiatives. The European Council seems to believe that its role vis-à-vis the Commission, which is supposed to initiate EU legislation, needs strengthening, at least when it comes to strategic problems of European integration. This makes the question 'who sets the agenda?' an intergovern-mental one. Because of its economic potential Germany was attributed a special responsibility. The fiscal compact, for example, has strong German support. Whether the fiscal pact is testimony to German dominance in the Eurogroup is open to controversy. There is no empirical evidence for this con-clusion, as has been shown by Schäfer (2013). Still, critics see Germany as the new hegemon in the EU. The German government rejects, however, the idea that Germany has developed into the dominant power in the EU. 'Germany's preferred self-image is a bigger version of Switzerland: economically success-ful but politically modest', as outside observers have noted (*The Economist*, 13 April, 2013: 6).

In 2011, the Polish Foreign Minister, Radek Sikorski, attracted a lot of attention when he remarked in his Berlin speech that he feared Germany's power less than Germany's inactivity in European affairs. Many seemed to agree, but still viewed Germany's role with scepticism. Germany looked like a hegemon in the EU context, and was therefore quasi-automatically in the role of a lead nation, but was it prepared to lead and was German leadership acceptable to others? Mark Mazower, a historian at Columbia University, observed: 'Neither the Germans themselves nor anyone else seem very com-fortable with this. Yet Berlin's primacy is a reality that cannot be wished away' (Mazower, 2013).

Meanwhile a controversy on German hegemony in the EU, on the defin-ition of hegemony and on the duties of a hegemon has developed. Social scientists in Germany tend to go back to a book of the 1930s by Heinrich Triepel (Triepel, 1938) where they find the standard definition of a hegemon.

Triepel makes the fine distinction between dominance and hegemony. For him a functioning hegemony needs the acceptance of the hegemon's political partners. The hegemon deserves acceptance, because whenever there is a conflict he does not simply follow his own interests, but knows and respects the interests of his partners. If the hegemon does not know what the interests of his partners are, he has to find them out in order to come to a consensus on political solutions. Hegemony, in this definition, serves a greater cause. The hegemon needs to convince his partners that the way he influences politics has nothing to do with command and control, but thrives on compromise and conviction.

Christoph Schönberger argued that Germany's role in a European Union, which is characterized by a preference for more intergovernmentalism, fits very well Triepel's definition. Germany may be unwilling to lead, but it has the duty now to act as a benevolent hegemon. This includes the duty to sacrifice its own interests for the common good of European integration. According to Schönberger the power shift, which resulted from European rescue strategies, does not produce German dominance in the EU, but an increased German responsibility to make the EU work, even at a price for the German taxpayer (Kundnani, 2012; Schönberger, 2012).

It is unrealistic that in EU politics the meaning of hegemony can be divorced from the much more negative terms dominance and power. Though German Chancellors have always stressed that they did not want a German Europe, but that they prefer instead a European Germany, accusations of a hidden German agenda have never ended. Schönberger (2012: 2) argued that it would therefore be wise to look for political alternatives to Germany's unwanted hegemony. His preference is a new political level in the EU, which has to be independent of national interests: a European federal government. A European federal government could provide a framework that prevents the stronger members of the EU from dominating the Union. This worked in the past as the example of the Union of States in the USA shows, where the bigger states were no longer able to put pressure on the smaller ones once the federation had come into existence. In other words, the alternative to the unpopular German hegemony is supposed to be the United States of Europe. This option currently has, however, few friends in the member states of the EU. There are a number of supporters of this idea in German politics and the social sciences (Habermas, 2013), but this small group of opinion leaders hardly has the potential to shape a political vision for the whole of Europe (Sturm, 2013).

## Conclusion

The EU remains in the paradoxical situation that although more cooperation would help to protect the euro, existing national interests have the consequence that individual strategies to protect member states from the consequences of rescue politics have gained acceptance. Even more paradoxical are the demands Germany is supposed to fulfil. Its partners expect Germany to accept a leading role in the eurozone when it comes to (financial) solidarity. At the same time, Germany is supposed to play a politically modest role in Europe and to acknowledge national interests of its partners without pursuing national interests of its own. For this complex set of expectations and demands, the former German foreign minister Guido Westerwelle found the political formula: Germany should not try to dominate the EU. Germany should lead by setting an example of best practice and should try to convince its partners (*Frankfurter Allgemeine Zeitung*, 10 April, 2013: 1). This may be nothing but a formula for Germany's 'leadership avoidance reflex' (Maurer, 2003: 115). Alternatively, it describes a dilemma. National interests are back, but it remains a puzzle how to accommodate them in a framework for which the deepening of European integration is a reference point of central importance.

## References

Banducci, S. A., Karp, J. A. and Loedel, P. H. (2009). 'Economic Interests and Public Support for the Euro.' *Journal of European Public Policy*, 16 (4), pp. 564–581.

Borger, V. (2013). 'The ESM and the European Court's Predicament.' In *Pringle German Law Journal*, 14 (1), pp. 113–139.

Brössler, D. (2012). 'Griechen gegen Mütter.' *Süddeutsche Zeitung*, 10 December, p. 4

Bugdahn, S. (2005). 'Of Europeanization and Domestication: The Implementation of the European Information Directive in Ireland.' *Journal of European Public Policy*, 12 (1), pp. 177–199.

Bundesverfassungsgericht (2014). 2 BvR 2728/13 vom 14.01.2014, Absatz-Nr. (1–105).

Demesmay, C. (2013). 'Hat der deutsch-französische Bilateralismus Zukunft?' *Aus Politik und Zeitgeschichte*, 1–3, pp. 37–42.

De Vries, C. E. (2013). 'Ambivalent Europeans? Public Support for European Integration in East and West.' *Government and Opposition*, 48 (3), pp. 434–461.

Egeberg, M. (2006). 'Executive Politics as Usual: Role Behavior and Conflict Dimensions in the College of European Commissioners.' *Journal of European Public Policy*, 13 (1), pp. 1–15.

Egeberg, M. and Heskestad, A. (2010). 'The Denationalization of *Cabinets* in the European Commission.' *Journal of Common Market Studies*, 48 (4), pp. 775–786.

Golub, J. (2012). 'How the European Union Does Not Work: National Bargaining Success in the Council of Ministers.' *Journal of European Public Policy*, 19 (9), pp. 1294–1315.

Habermas, J. (2013). 'Ein Fall von Elitenversagen.' *Der Spiegel*, 5 August, p. 27.

Häge, F. M. (2011). 'Politicising Council Decision-Making: The Effect of European Parliament Empowerment.' *West European Politics*, 34 (1), pp. 18–47.

Häge, F. M. (2012). 'Coalition Building and Consensus in the Council of the European Union.' *British Journal of Political Science*, 43, pp. 481–504.

Heisenberg, D. (2005). 'The Institution of "Consensus" in the European Union: Formal versus Informal Decision-making in the Council.' *European Journal of Political Research*, 44, pp. 65–90.

Hölscheidt, S. (2013). 'Parlamentarische Kontrolle in der Eurokrise.' In Eberbach-Born, B., Kropp, S., Stuchlik, A., and Zeh, W. (eds.) *Parlamentarische Kontrolle und Europäische Union.* Baden-Baden: Nomos, pp. 105–129.

Hooghe, L. (2012). 'Images of Europe: How Commission Officials Conceive Their Institution's Role.' *Journal of Common Market Studies*, 50 (1), pp. 87–111.

Jeffery, C. and Paterson, W. E. (2003). 'Germany and European Integration: A Shifting of Tectonic Plates.' *West European Politics*, 26 (4), pp. 59–75.

Kirchhof, P. (2012). 'Verfassungsnot!' *Frankfurter Allgemeine Zeitung*, 12 July, p. 25.

Kirchhof, P. (2014). 'Geldeigentum und Geldpolitik.' *Frankfurter Allgemeine Zeitung*, 13 January, p. 7.

Köcher, R. (2012). 'Entspannter Fatalismus.' *Frankfurter Allgemeine Zeitung*, 7 October, p. 8.

Kranenpohl, U. (2013). 'Ist Karlsruhe "Europa" ausgeliefert? Die Gestaltungsmacht des Bundesverfassungsgerichts und die europäischen Gerichtsbarkeiten.' *Zeitschrift für Politik*, 60 (1), pp. 90–103.

Kundnani, H. (2012). 'Was für ein Hegemon?' *Internationale Politik*, 3, pp. 21–25.

Maurer, A. (2003). 'Germany: Fragmented Structures in a Complex System.' In Wessels, W., Maurer, A., and Mittag, J. (eds.) *Fifteen into One? The European Union and its Member States.* Manchester: Manchester University Press, pp. 115–149.

Mazower, M. (2013). 'German Fear of History Jeopardises Europe's Future.' *Financial Times,* 19 July, p. 7.

Merkel, A. (2013). 'Interview.' *Der Spiegel*, 3 June, p. 30.

Noelle-Neumann, E. and Petersen, T. (1999). 'Die Bürger in Deutschland.' In Weidenfeld, W. (ed.) *Europa-Handbuch.* Gütersloh: Bertelsmann, pp. 585–602.

Peel, Q. and Carnegy, H. (2013). 'An Uneven Entente.' *Financial Times*, 21 January, p. 6.

Pehle, H. (2011). 'Das Urteil des Bundesverfassungsgerichts zur Griechenlandhilfe und zum Euro-Rettungsschirm – ein integrationspolitisches Grundsatzurteil.' *Gesellschaft – Wirtschaft – Politik*, 60 (4), pp. 415–422.

Pütter, U. (2012). 'Europe's Deliberative Intergovernmentalism: The Role of the Council and European Council in EU Economic Governance.' *Journal of European Public Policy*, 19 (2), pp. 161–178.

Rachman, G. (2013). 'The Crisis and the Making of a German Europe.' *Financial Times*, 26 March, p. 9.

Risse, T. (2003). 'The Euro between National and European Identity.' *Journal of European Public Policy*, 10 (4), pp. 487–505.

Ruhkamp, S. (2012). 'Der freundliche Bremser.' *Frankfurter Allgemeine Zeitung*, 28 April, p. 16.

Schäfer, D. (2013). 'Der Fiskalvertrag – ein Ausdruck deutscher Hegemonie in der Europäischen Union?' *Integration*, 36 (2), pp. 107–123.

Schild, J. (2010). 'Mission Impossible? The Potential for Franco-German Leadership in the Enlarged EU.' *Journal of Common Market Studies*, 48 (5), pp. 1367–1390.

Schönberger, C. (2012). 'Hegemon wider Willen. Zur Stellung Deutschlands in der Europäischen Union.' *Merkur*, 66 (1), pp. 752–763.

Sturm, R. (2013). 'Europa – Wunsch und Wirklichkeit.' *Gesellschaft-Wirtschaft-Politik*, 62 (3), pp. 311–314.

Sturm, R. (2014). 'Doch nicht alternativlos? Die EU-Krisenpolitik im Parteienwettbewerb.' In Jesse, E. and Sturm, R. (eds.) *Bilanz der Bundestagswahl 2013. Voraussetzungen, Ergebnisse, Folgen.* Baden-Baden: Nomos, pp. 511–530.

Suvarierol, S. (2008). 'Beyond the Myth of Nationality: Analysing Networks within the European Commission.' *West European Politics*, 31 (4), pp. 701–724.

The Economist (2013). 'Special Report on Germany: Europe's Reluctant Hegemon.' *The Economist*, 15 June, p. 11.

Triepel, H. (1938). *Die Hegemonie. Ein Buch von führenden Staaten.* Stuttgart: Kohlhammer.

Zimmer, C., Schneider, G., and Dobbins, M. (2005). 'The Contested Council: Conflict Dimensions of an Intergovernmental EU Institution.' *Political Studies*, 53, pp. 403–422.

# 5 The neo-liberal defeat of European integration and the need for a supranational political economy

*Zoltán Pogátsa*

One can compare the European Union (EU) to the so-called Rorschach test, the dark ink blot of the psychologist that conjures up widely diverse images in the minds of different observers. Unlike the ink stain, however, the EU has significance, albeit one that is mostly misinterpreted. Often the business community gets it right, but due to self-interest supports the purple fog that surrounds it for reasons of camouflage. Those on the political Left usually fail to see its real nature. They are devoted to the idea of a post-nationalist political Europe, a social Europe, a sustainable Europe or a Europe of regions. These are castles in the air. They are practically nowhere in the treaties, they exist only in the imaginations of euroenthusiasts who fail to see the wood of the free trade regime behind the tree of political symbolism.

In this chapter we revisit the history of European integration in an attempt to demonstrate how neo-liberalism derailed the European integration project. We shall also argue that a substantive supranational political entity is needed if we are to overcome the deep lack of purpose, legitimacy and support in which the EU finds itself.

## How free trade replaced federalism as the centrepiece of European integration

Introductory courses to European integration, no longer a popular subject across Europe, but once generously supported from Brussels, usually mention the 1951 Treaty of Paris, establishing the European Coal and Steel Community, as the starting point of the European project. The main heroes of this 'autobiography' are Jean Monnet and Robert Schuman, the two Frenchmen who initiated the setting up of this common organisation. Such a presentation of events serves a particular purpose. The history of European integration after the Second World War is arranged for naive students across the continent as a coherent, linear unfolding of events starting with the lessons learned from the trauma of the Great War and leading without detours to the creation of the European Union in 1992, and beyond. Yet in reality this history is anything but coherent, and far from linear. We shall argue that contrary to popular belief and the vehement propaganda of Brussels, the

European Union has not developed into a supranational political unit. It does not possess most of the attributes ordinary citizens tend to read into it. In fact it is little more than what the business pages of British newspapers often call it: a European trading system.

Without a doubt, the origins of the process can indeed be traced back to the experience of the Second World War. Although various ideas to unite parts or all of Europe had previously been put forward, it was only at the end of this tragic war that it really sank into the minds of Europeans that a radical departure was needed in order to leave behind the Westphalian rivalries that had plagued the continent for centuries. While other regions of the world, most notably the United States were advancing rapidly, uninvaded and intact, Europe periodically destroyed itself in senseless wars, and as a consequence fell behind its competitors in terms of economic might. The first calls for unity were therefore well and truly federalist. Most notable amongst these, as it is well documented in countless histories of post-WWII Europe, were Winston Churchill, who gave a now famous speech on the subject, the former Italian opposition figure Altiero Spinelli, who headed the European federalist movement towards the end of the war, and the first post-war German Chancellor, Konrad Adenauer, who steered his part of divided Germany firmly into the European integration movement. Thus all larger founding member states had their own heroes. The federalist ideal was to transfer sovereignty from the level of the competing nation states, which, given the experience of the Second World War, could not be trusted, to a supranational level. Yet in view of such ambitious goals, the actual political achievements in the late 1940s and in the 1950s must strike the student of European integration as being conspicuously modest.

A number of initiatives were launched after the end of the war to create the desired pan-European political institutions. Yet nothing came of them. The most significant defeat was the abandonment of the Pleven Plan (championed by French premier René Pleven, but like the Schuman Plan, also drafted by Monnet) for a supranational European army within a newly created European Defence Community in 1952. The initiative would also have created a European Political Community as a wider framework. A similar organisation, the Western European Union, had actually been set up in 1948, but it has been by and large dormant ever since. By the middle of the 1950s the continent looked more like a breaker's yard than a construction site, full of ruins of institutions that never took off the ground.

The one institution which did become a reality, however, was the European Coal and Steel Community (ECSC) of 1951, later curiously canonised as the origin of European integration. The agreement, a result of the famous Schuman Plan, named after the French foreign minister of the time, but drawn up by his advisor Jean Monnet, regulates the shared production of coal and steel between Germany and France. Although the Benelux countries joined their larger neighbours in the initiative, as did Italy in an attempt to break out of international isolation, the European Coal and Steel Community was a far cry away from any superstate. What it really was can be explained in a number of ways. In the hagiography of the European Commission the ECSC is usually spinned as a politically motivated venture, an attempt to monitor German production of coal and steel, the two resources most needed for war, in order to make sure the defeated country does not rearm. It can therefore be fitted in as a convenient, if somewhat strange, starting point of a long march towards a vision of a politically united Europe. The uncomfortable truth, however, is that the last thing worn-out and destroyed Germany, with its young men killed and its Eastern part occupied by the Soviet Union, would have wanted was a war with its only potential guarantors of independence. Since the Allies were in effect occupying powers in the Western part, they would have had other means of making sure Germany did not rearm anyway. In addition, there is the delicate parallel of the French occupation of the Ruhr after the First World War to secure reparations...

From the point of view of economic history, an alternative, more realistic interpretation of the ECSC would refer to the typically French concepts of *sectoralism* and *indicative planning* (Cohen, 1977; Zysman, 1977; Hall, 1990; Daley, 1996; Levy, 1999). The immediate reason for the introduction of these policies was the war, the necessity to manage the home economy, to turn civilian industrial capacities towards producing a gigantic amount of armaments in a very short period of time, and the need to stop prices from spiralling out of control due to steeply accelerating demand. As it is clear from retrospective analysis (Parker, 2005: 146–152), it was also an opportunity to try out state intervention of a Keynesian inspiration in real life. Jean Monnet had worked in America during the war years, first attached to the British mission there, then as the regulator of aid to the free French forces fighting against the Nazis. After liberation, Monnet was appointed to head the new national development plan, the *Plan de Modernisation et d'Équippement*. The principle of indicative planning was widely applied in post-war *statist* France, helped not insignificantly by the fact that Monnet managed to channel American aid and loans towards financing projects in the plan he directed (Gillingham, 2003: 21). Based on Monnet's intentions, the method was then also extensively used in the ECSC framework to control prices and production in the coal and steel sectors. These French-inspired dirigiste policies relied on sectoralism, a view of the economy that saw the economy as a set of industries, such as energy, transport, automobile, finance, and so on, each with their own logic and role within the entirety of a national economy. This was distinctly different from the Anglo-Saxon approach to economic policy, which viewed itself as applying uniform fiscal and monetary policy to a homogenous entirety of the economy, with no desire for state intervention in industries. With the European Coal and Steel Community, French-style sectoralism was raised to the European level.

Whichever explanation or description of the Coal and Steel Community we accept, we are still left perplexed why this rather limited, sectoralist, etatist organisation would eventually come to be identified and canonised as the point of departure of today's European Union. Without a doubt, it was the first organisation built on supranational principles, and it did establish the High Authority, the Common Assembly, the Special Council of Ministers and the Court of Justice, the seeds of today's defining institutional setup, but these bodies had extremely limited powers and served a completely different purpose. The underlying principles of these organisational forms had little overall effect on the eventual content of European integration, and after being merged into the European Communities in 1967, and into the European Union in 1992, the European Coal and Steel Community peacefully expired in oblivion on 22 July 2002.

The organisation that did in fact grow to dominate the European integrative process was the *European Economic Community (EEC)* created in 1957 with the Treaty of Rome, until today the most important international treaty in post-war Europe. This organisation had a very different logic to it than what Monnet had wished for or advocated. The creation of the EEC was preceded by the famous Messina conference in Southern Italy. It is interesting to trace back what exactly happened at that decisive meeting. The idea of the EEC, based on a free trade zone and a customs union, was actually proposed not by Monnet or the French delegation, but by the Benelux countries, who had had such cooperation since 1948. European leaders gathered at Messina then appointed the Belgian foreign minister Paul-Henri Spaak to prepare a report outlining the possibility of creating a Europe-wide customs union. The French were originally even opposed to the idea, as they felt a free trade zone built on liberal economic principles would be incompatible with their dirigiste and plan-based economic orientation. Monnet and his colleagues were focused instead on Euratom, once again a sectoral agency, overseeing the civilian use of nuclear power across borders. As much as they believed this area to be the key issue of the future, Euratom never really created any real excitement, and was later completely overshadowed by the Economic Community both in importance and visibility. Eventually both organisations were ratified in the Treaty of Rome in 1957 by exactly the same group of countries which had signed the Paris Treaty six years earlier. When the UK was kept out of the EEC by French President de Gaulle, it organised its own trading system, the European Free Trade Association (EFTA), with a membership of seven. Hindered by geographical discontinuity, this organisation never really developed any further.[1]

*Sine ira et studio*, it is hard to deny that it was the free trade area idea that really laid the foundations for future union as we know it. This approach was more of a break than a continuity with the statist and sectoralist logic of the Coal and Steel Community. As opposed to the ideas of planning and dirigism that dominated the ECSC and Euratom, the underlying logic of the European Economic Community was market based and liberal. Although deliberately blurred by official EU hagiography of Monnet and Schuman today, it is in fact the Benelux and the free trade ideal that is the real source of European integration as we know it today. The Paris Treaty and the two

Frenchmen, although clearly not without merits, have been made centrepieces of the Brussels orthodoxy for two important reasons. On the one hand their projected eminence helps portray France as being at the heart of European integration: 'the engine', as it was known for decades, more frequently than not along with Germany. On the other hand it allows for insistence on the façade of the EU as a supranational political institution originating in the High Authority and the Assembly, and in this way much more than a European trading system. In reality it is hardly more than a free trade regime even today. In the long run the ECSC and Euratom turned out to be mere inherited appendages to the Economic Community.

## The functionalist compromise with neo-liberalism

The federalist acceptance of the free trade Economic Community as the centrepiece of the European integration process was justified by a project that is usually referred to as *functionalism*, a general approach that has at its starting point the realisation that a political, federal Europe could not be forged directly in the 1950s. Such a radical departure was simply too much for politicians in the nation states immediately after the war, whatever their initial leanings had been. A United Europe therefore had to be created through other means: almost by stealth, based on the *aufklärist* counsel of a pioneer group of experts, without relying on popular support; in fact, often against the wishes of the populace, since it is frequently argued that had the European demos been consulted, we would never have reached the current level of integration. When citizens were eventually consulted in rare referenda about Europe, they mostly voted down initiatives such as the Maastricht and Nice Treaties, or the European Constitution. Astoundingly, this leads leading European politicians to condemn referenda in general as antidemocratic and populist. The lack of citizen participation in the European project is not an aberration of our times, a sign of deplorable ignorance and disinterest on the part of European citizens, but a long durée feature of the form of integration that has unfolded with the deliberate aim of keeping citizens out. The technical term invented in integration theory to describe this approach was functionalism. It was believed that if they could integrate states in areas which were less visible and less politically sensitive, most notably in trade, they would be joined together by a thousand invisible threads. At some point the acceptance might arise that participating states might as well unite politically, once there is little left to separate them in areas which matter, but are less symbolic than culture or outright political institutions. There was even the assumption that one area of integration would pull with it another one, almost like an automatism (Haas, 1958). This was labelled a *spillover* in integration theory, a mechanism through which it was believed a federal Europe would eventually come about. Functionalism was therefore not a complete alternative to federalism, only a roundabout way of achieving the same thing. Just like in the case of several other ill-fated ideologies, there was a strong conviction that the lack of popular support during the period of construction would later be justified by output legitimacy (peace, development, convergence, etc.) in the longer run. In essence, functionalism was a compromise between weakened federalism and liberal trade-based integration theory, often simplified to the maxim that countries that trade do not go to war with each other.

The real alternatives to federalism and functionalism were either *intergovernmentalism*, as the idea of a 'Europe of nation states' came to be called (Moravcsik, 1993), or radical nationalist isolationism, which meant total opposition to any kind of association between national states. This latter is sometimes referred to as euroscepticism. This is an extremely problematic term, since sceptics of something are usually critical supporters rather than enemies, yet 'euroscepticism' has come to be synonymous with enmity. Sceptics, as understood in the traditional sense of the word, might actually be for cooperation, but not in its existing form. A federal political system that views itself as democratic should reserve linguistic space for those who are sympathetic, but are searching for alternatives. Such views are presently pressed into the 'Eurosceptic equals anti-European' corner. At the same time, some of those who are altogether opposed to the idea of the EU (such as Le Pen, Haider, Jobbik, the BNP, UKIP, Golden Dawn, or indeed nationalists from any EU state) are so vehemently against it that scepticism seems a decidedly euphemistic term to describe their zeal.

As for political integration, the federalists have never given up. The debate between the free trade intergovernmentalists and the political federalists has never ceased to exist, but the actual evolution of the formal corpus of the EU makes it little more than an economic regime. This is something that very few realise, and even less dare to point out. A significant victory for supranationalism was achieved by the first President of the Commission, German law professor Walter Hallstein. His team, made up of dedicated federalists, created a confusing and complex labyrinth of bureaucracy to include areas in the work of the Commission that went far beyond its originally intended functions. This was justified by the already mentioned principle of spillover, the conviction that one area of integration would inevitably have intended and unintended consequences in other areas as well. Hallstein's period signalled the beginning of a rather problematic tradition in Europe of creating a large number of carton institutions, many of them empty behind the façade, generating intransparency and a sense of perplexity in the European populace as to who does what and who really does anything. (This habit was taken to new extremes later, after the creation of the Union in 1992.) Hallstein's main contribution, however, was not so much the expansion of the activities of the Commission, but achieving general acceptance for the idea of European community law, hierarchically above national legal systems. The basis of this globally unique system was found to originate in the Treaty of Rome, which turned the European Court of Justice (ECJ), set up at Paris six years earlier to issue rulings related to the coal and steel industries, into a veritable community institution. The Court asserted the existence of community law through a number of decisive precedent cases. In the landmark case of Van Gend en Loos in 1963, the ECJ ruled that the European Community, through the will of member states expressed in the Treaty of Rome, 'constitutes a new legal order of international law for the benefit of which the states have limited their sovereign rights albeit within limited fields' (Van Gend en Loos ECR1, 1963). The creation of a pan-European legal system with direct applicability in the member states is probably the single most important contribution towards a future Federal Europe. It secures irreversible rights to the community bodies, the Commission and the European Parliament to increase their influence over European matters. These legal competencies, together with the activism of the Commission in the Hallstein style have allowed the expansion of community decision making into areas which had originally not been intended to be supranational. These areas include most notably agriculture, but also regional policy, employment policy and the environment. Decades later, the community even ventured into areas such as justice and home affairs, and became rather successful at it. There are also a number of policy areas into which the federal level has stuck a foot, but has never quite managed to master it. These include a very wide range of subjects such as transport policy, energy, research, and even audiovisual policy. Monnet at some point even managed to convince the Commission that it should introduce indicative planning on a European scale. As a consequence, the so-called Medium Term Economic Policy was launched as a means of coordinating member states' policies, but by 1964 it was clear that it would fade away and not become one of the central aspects of European integration (Holland, 1982). However, the tendency to expand their competencies has inevitably locked the Commission and the Parliament into an ongoing struggle with the Council, the decision-making body of prime ministers and heads of states representing member states. The resulting compromise is a set of confusing decision-making processes that combine both community and intergovernmental decisions in ways that are extremely difficult to grasp and keep in mind for European voters. Not only is this setup intransparent, adding to the so-called 'democratic deficit' of the Union, but as we shall demonstrate, it also hides the fact that key decisions are in fact almost always made by the Council. In spite of the increasing power of the community institutions, even today's European Union is a dominantly intergovernmental organisation. Hallstein and his successors have been right in pointing to the famous opening passage in the Rome Treaty on 'ever closer union' in the sense that the powers of the federal level have indeed increased over time, but only to the degree and in solely in the areas where the member states have felt it convenient to let go of their privileges.

## Thatcher and the neo-liberal end to the functionalist dream

Unfortunately for the federalists, the political Right was captured by the neoliberal movement in the 1970s. With the entry of Britain into the Communities, Margaret Thatcher became a defining voice in European affairs. Having implemented the neo-liberal ideology of Friedrich Hayek and the Mont Pelerin Society into practice in Britain, she was now determined to take it to victory in Europe as well. The famous U-turn of Francois Mitterrand in 1983 eliminated France as a potential countervailing force. The towering figure of Jacques Delors[2] emerged for some time as her federalist counterweight, unmatched by any Commission president ever since, and the continent-wide reunification process ignited by Soviet leader Mikhail Gorbachev gave spiritual impetus to another wave of federalist enthusiasm.

A further boost to the essentially liberal economic nature of European integration came with the 1986 Single European Act (SEA), agreed to by member states with the view to eliminate obstacles to a single internal market by 1992. Although usually connected with the name of Commission President Jacques Delors, a former French Christian Socialist minister of finance, the drafting of the SEA was actually the work of the lesser known British internal market commissioner, Lord Arthur Cockfield. In fact the SEA was the rare element of European integration that Margaret Thatcher wholeheartedly endorsed, famously calling it 'the foundation upon which everything was to be built' (Thatcher, 2002: 372–373). The central aim of the SEA complemented very coherently the market-inspired domestic policies of Prime Minister Thatcher, of whom Lord Cockfield was a close associate. The SEA aimed at the removal of non-tariff barriers to trade, including domestic regulations, a move towards free trade in services, the elimination of customs procedures, harmonisation of industrial standards, the opening up of public procurement in member states to competition from within the community, as well as setting strict limitations to trade-distorting state aid. The Treaty also endorsed the principle of mutual recognition of products, first stated in the notable European Court ruling in the Cassis de Dijon case in 1979 (Cassis de Dijon ECR 649, 1979).

In contrast to the SEA, which was not in the focus of his vision for Europe, Delors did later score two successes that moved the community forward in the direction of a real federal superstate for a while. One of them was the Delors Packet, which increased the Commission's competencies, the other the Treaty of Maastricht in 1992, which created the European Union and took the federal level into new areas of involvement. The Packet was an attempt by Delors to restructure the community budget managed by the Commission, in order to spend less on the Common Agricultural Policy (CAP) and more on structural policy, including regional development and employment. This was a much welcome reform, unfortunately unparalleled ever since. Agriculture had grown to dominate the majority of overall community expenditure on a continent where farming was already of only marginal importance within the economy. The rechannelling of spending to the much more relevant problems of regional disparities and job creation was an encouraging development. Thanks to Delors, programming replaced the atomised project approach in these areas. The new approach was reminiscent of the state-centred, developmentalist French indicative planning model. (Delors had been socialised under Monnet.) Unfortunately the shifts initiated by Delors have since stalled, and in many cases have even reversed. CAP is still the biggest burden on the EU budget, and is incessantly criticised by small farmers and environmentalists for supporting large-scale, unsustainable agriculture (Smedshaug, 2010). Structural and regional policies have lost significance dramatically. They were overregulated, underfinanced and unable to adapt to the new realities of global competitiveness. The questionable track record of cohesion policy to achieve convergence in the South and the East of the Union has deteriorated the output legitimacy of the functionalist project itself. The financial perspectives after the departure of Delors failed to follow up the expansion of the Union, resulting in an erosion of the significance of EU transfers for less affluent member states. The spectacular blunder of a common competitiveness strategy without financial means and adequate coordination (the Lisbon strategy and Europe 2020) reinforced the impression of extreme diversity of economic models, as opposed to a 'sustainable' form of a 'European social model' that Delors pushed for but never achieved. Some member states remained welfare states (Scandinavia), others eroded their welfare models (Britain, then France, later Germany), while still others had never even had one (Southern and Eastern Europe) (Esping-Andersen, 1985; Misgeld *et al.*, 1992; Rothstein, 1996; Alestalo *et al.*, 2009; Sejersted, 2011). Delors' slogan of a European social model now sounds empty, however much citizens of the continent would wish for it. A rhetorical commitment to a 'European social model' never materialised in the acquis communautaire, and member states with the exception of the Scandinavians set about rolling back even their national welfare states.

The welfare state was an achievement of European civilisation. It was also highly successful not only in terms of social cohesion and mobility, but also in terms of employment and economic growth, especially compared to the decades of neo-liberalism that followed it. It was also a guarantee for democracy in that it secured a materially independent and well-educated block of voters who were well positioned to defend and maintain democratic institutions and values. Unfortunately the economic shocks of the 1970s (two oil shocks, the Nixon shock and the Volcker shock) shook the European economies. The propaganda machinery of the neo-liberal movement, generously financed by corporations (Burgin, 2012) that were increasingly transnational in scope and size, was well prepared to exploit these weaknesses. It convinced the middle classes who had grown affluent in the welfare state that they no longer needed to show solidarity towards the poor, and this would allow them to increase their affluence faster.

The neo-liberal movement first conquered the conservative parties in the 1970s, and then from the 1980s onwards increasingly made headways into the left-wing parties as well (Mitterrand, Blair, Schröder) (Toynbee and Walker, 2011). The ideological underpinnings were provided by Anthony Giddens' *Third Way* (Giddens, 1998). Social democratic parties moved in to the centre to occupy the 'cultural left – economic right' combination of the Liberal parties, which suffered severe electoral loss as result.

In spite of the rhetoric about a 'Social Europe', welfare states remained almost exclusively national regimes. The Anglo-Saxon economies moved radically towards a neo-liberal model, the Mediterraneans never developed full welfare states, and a large number of small member states from the former Eastern Bloc entered as neophyte converts to the Anglo-Saxon faith (Pogátsa, 2009a, 2009b; Greskovits and Bohle, 2012). Even Germany reduced its wage share in output radically, created a low wage underclass and an overpaid CEO class. The intergovernmental Union has become overwhelmed by member states moving away from the welfare state model, with only Scandinavia preserving it and extending it with a sustainability dimension. Significantly but not surprisingly it was the only region of the EU that was left standing after the Great Recession reached Europe after 2008. (Germany is generally believed to be another winner, and has certainly strengthened its European standing, but this was based on a 'beggar thy neighbour and thy lower class' basis, harvesting the eurozone by competing with lowering wages, which had dramatic consequences elsewhere in the eurozone.)

The free movement of capital, one of the basic tenets of the actually existing integration process, has allowed jobs to flow abroad. The Eastern enlargement further strengthened this process by boosting competition between social and labour market systems rather than harmonising these. This has had a negative effect in the East, where often as many as half of the population lives below or close to a subsistence minimum, with only rudimentary welfare provisions and very low job security. It has also had a negative effect in the North and the West, where Eastern competition has been used by political forces as a point of reference to push for an erosion of the welfare achievements. The principle of free movement of services and labour also contributed to undermining important national labour market provisions. Landmark rulings by the European Court of Justice, such as the Laval and Rüffert cases, have dealt enormous blows, the significance of which is unrecognised across Europe.

Simultaneously with these processes, several member states (primarily the UK, Luxembourg, Cyprus, Malta, but also partially Ireland, Austria and Latvia) and partner states (Switzerland) have developed themselves into quasi tax havens, as demonstrated by the International Tax Justice Network, a non-governmental organisation that did the homework of assessing the global impact of offshoring instead of the international institutions such as the IMF, the EU or the OECD (International Tax Justice Network, 2012). Offshore finance has grown from a peripheral phenomenon into a massive global system that drains resources from national budgets and welfare coffers (Shaxson, 2011; Zucman, 2013; Zucman and Johannesen, 2014). In a number of EU member states the pension system, for instance, would return to sustainability if resources were not diverted offshore. However, the above mentioned member states have blocked the resolution of this cross-border issue.

It must be added that generally accepted demographic arguments about welfare state unsustainability rest on shaky ground. With youth unemployment critically high in but a handful of states, and dramatically high in Spain,

Italy, Croatia and Greece, the argument that there are not enough babies born is preposterous. The reality is that private sector jobs have gone to low wage countries outside of Europe, and the public sector is unable to respond to the changing nature of social demand (away from technologically obsolete towards social services, care for the elderly, healthcare, etc.) by creating public sector jobs because it is underfinanced due to profit and wealth offshoring, as well as tax rate competition to the bottom.

Maastricht was even more of a success for federalists than the Delors Packet. First, it created the 'Union' itself. The term is clearly more political, more state like, more federal and potentially broader in content than 'communities', the previous label. It reminded people of the United States and the Soviet Union. All this in spite of the fact that the EU was not a state, and it has not gained that status in the international system ever since either. What it really has been is subject to debate amongst international lawyers and experts of international relations, since no similar elaborate supranational equivalent exists. Although the EU is still based on the member states' pooling of their sovereignty, the acceptance of the nomen was a huge success for euroenthusiasts of the supranational persuasion. It leaves citizens with the impression that their various states are embedded within a larger state, which will potentially grow to encompass all the usual fields of government life associated with a nation state. It also gives them the false idea, albeit receding, that this larger state somehow has the power to monitor and punish their national politicians, who are often detested simply by virtue of the fact that they are closer and more visible than EU leaders, who are frequently perceived and portrayed as their preferable alternative. This bogus dichotomy has its basis in the fact that amidst the royal blue smokescreen European citizens have very opaque ideas about what the community level does, and in what direction it pushes the continent.

The Maastricht Treaty laid out the famous three pillars structure, with all the previous achievements in the supranational first pillar (thereafter the European Community), plus two intergovernmental pillars, that of Common Foreign and Security Policy (pillar two) and Justice and Home Affairs (pillar three). This mental map never really caught on amongst citizens, and the origins of this enigmatic setup remained unknown outside the euro-profession. It owed its creation to a historic compromise between the intergovernmentalists and the federalists. The latter would have wanted to communitise both foreign policy and internal security, but national politicians would not have it. The outcome was the compromise of the pillar structure, which hid the differences from the layman's sight, but provided guarantees of the national prerogative to governments. It has to be added that pillar two, foreign policy, has since turned into an acknowledged blunder, whereas pillar three, justice and home affairs, has silently crept into the first, communitarian pillar. This latter development, broadly connected to the Schengen process of eliminating borders, has led to what is arguably the most successful aspect of the federal EU. It is probably also its most visible and most popular aspect for ordinary citizens.

The Maastricht Treaty had one additional achievement. It laid out the rules for the attainment of the single European currency. The euro is simultaneously a federalist political and a free trade economic project. On the one hand it symbolises the readiness of member states to give up a key aspect of their figurative sovereignty to create a world pioneer supranational currency unit. On the other hand it is a way of enhancing free trade between firms in the EU by eliminating conversion costs and risks emanating from exchange rate volatility. Unfortunately the monetary union came about with serious birth defects. It was introduced as a suboptimal currency area (Mundell, 1961; Lapavitsas *et al.*, 2010), which meant that inadequately low nominal interest rates caused an artificial asset boom in numerous high growth peripheral member states in the South and the East, which could have been avoided with autonomous monetary policy. The eurozone also failed to monitor wage policy, which enabled Germany to institute a strategy of wage suppression to counterbalance its slow productivity growth, and thereby to harvest the eurozone through becoming price competitive. Between 1995 and 2007 Germany lowered its household income to GDP ratio by almost ten percentage points. This neo-liberal 'beggar thy neighbour and thy lower classes' policy made many Germans richer, and pushed the eurozone into crisis (Flassbeck and Lapavitsas, 2013). Its side effect, the exposure of Northern European banks to the crisis countries, made austerity-based policies inevitable there, since neither devaluation nor debt inflation remained as alternatives (Blyth, 2013: 100–102). All in all, the monetary union that was originally seen as a major step forward towards symbolic political union eventually ended up eroding the output legitimacy of the functionalist project at a scale unprecedented in the history of European integration (Fiorentini and Montani, 2012; Pogátsa, 2014).

Various waves of expansion have portrayed the EC/EU as an anchor of modernisation and democratisation. The accession of less affluent Southern European countries in the 1980, coming out of right-wing dictatorships, and even poorer Eastern Europeans in the 1990s, leaving behind socialist regimes, has elevated the standing of 'Europe' as both means and end. This is not completely without reason, but as we shall attempt to prove, there is far less in democratic or modernising substance in the Brussels system than is commonly believed. Extremely crudely put, the EU today is essentially a free trade regime, with a huge agricultural transfer mechanism, and a federalistic façade of democratic credentials which it is unable to live up to or enforce. However, it is understood as something remotely different by Europeans in the East and the West. It is even more unclear what they would hope it would one day become.

## There is no political Europe

The most puzzling feature of the European Union is that it leaves open the most important questions about its goals, legitimacy and purpose, commonly known in Brussels speak as its *finalité*. How far does it want to expand? What functional areas does it seek to take over from member states? What is its purpose? Does it aim to be a proper state one day? Of course it is no accident that these elementary questions are left open and unanswered. Such is the very nature of functionalism. The moment an assertive answer would be provided one way or another, too many of the present day supporters of integration would walk out in protest.

The process of European integration was a struggle between narratives even before the enlargements. There was a fight between federalists who wanted a European superstate on the one hand, and intergovernmentalists on the other, who wished to retain the power of the nation state. There was a parallel but not unrelated struggle between adherents of the European social model (of a Scandinavian, Rhineland or French etatist kind) and the neo-liberal Anglo-Saxon model. The existence of the latter diversity, that of social models, meant that the extent of European cooperation was coded into the agreements. Even though the Treaty of Rome spoke of an 'ever closer union', which would theoretically enable a superstate as its finality, the prevailing system of intergovernmentalism meant that only those elements of the puzzle were put in place which enjoyed universal support from all governments. With the expansion of the organisation from the original six to nine and beyond, this became increasingly difficult. With the addition of Ireland and especially the UK in 1973 the community received its first members who were fundamentally opposed to the idea of going much beyond economic cooperation based on trade. Expansion into the Mediterranean in the 1980s added members who were not directly opposed to the idea of a more social Europe, but who were not clearly in support of it either, never having developed into fully fledged welfare states themselves. The next wave of enlargement, usually dubbed Nordic, added countries that were once again fully supportive of ideals such as a socially active state and sustainability. Thus Europe stood at the end of the millennium already deeply divided and unable to move on. Everyone felt that the last major push forward had been achieved at Maastricht in 1992, and since then the engines have stalled. There started a wrangling over institutions and decision making that still has not quite ended today. One reform proposal after another was put forward, alienating citizens and giving the EU an image of a pointless bureaucracy, while the most essential and sensible questions related to purpose, desired extent and competencies were still not answered. The EU gained an image that it spent its summit meetings discussing form rather than content. Of course those taking part in these struggles knew exactly that beneath form lay content. Behind debates that appeared to be focused on organs, positions and powers, there was hidden the question of the future of European integration. Those few in the know understood very well that preserving the never admitted privileges of the member state governments would limit the EU forever to a liberal trade regime with a few add-ons such as Schengen and environmental policy. Transferring decisive rights and meaningful budgets to supranational organs such as the Commission and Parliament would on the other hand enable the various majorities to move forward into areas such as legally enforceable social, environmental and political rights uniformly across the continent. These were the areas that were clearly identified by most analysts as the logical extensions of the already existing acquis, but the reasons for intransigence were also clear.

Regrettably, the EU today is for the most part a building block of the global Washington Consensus, and only infrequently its challenger. The reasons why this is not recognised by those opposed to neo-liberalism is that there are still alternative hopes attached to it – though less and less. Supporters of European federalism/supranationalism, the European social model, defenders of human rights and the environment feel that the EU is still just as much their project as the project of liberal free traders. This stems either from their lack of understanding of how the EU functions and what it does, or from their unwillingness to abandon a ship they once commanded, turn against it and launch another one.

The EU has in fact been hopelessly hijacked by neo-liberalism. Even with the Lisbon Treaty in force, the Council still has effective veto power in all forms of decision making, including the co-decision procedure, where the European Parliament has the strongest powers. In the Council itself, states reign. Some crucial areas are exempt from majority decision making altogether (e.g. taxation, foreign policy), while in others the internal culture of the EU prevents the majority principle from actually taking hold. In times when commitment to the Union is weak in most member states, and resentment towards it growing, it is unlikely that a majority of states are going to crowd upon a single member state (or a small group of member states) in a certain issue, risking to impose a decision that is strongly rejected by the population of that state, risking total alienation.

As a consequence, the governance of the Union is increasingly left in the hands of the member states. The Commission has slipped in significance since Delors, with Barroso voluntarily playing a subservient role, and the Parliament has never achieved real significance in spite of its continuous and gradual strengthening. There has never been a breakthrough for supranationalism, and it is unlikely to happen.

## The need for a supranational political economy

The doomed thrust for a European Constitution sealed the fate of the functionalist promise to the federalists. The EU remained a predominantly intergovernmental organisation, where the Council, representing governments, makes the most important decisions. The Commission is a pensioner of the Council in that its independent budgetary sources have been withdrawn, and commissioners depend on member states for re-election. Citizens have such indirect influence on the makeup of the Commission anyway that it amounts to little if anything. The other supposed counterweight, the Parliament, the only elected supranational institution of the world, representing Community interests, has continued to gain powers, but it is still essentially subdued by the Council. Within the Byzantine decision-making system of the Union, the Parliament has its strongest powers in the co-decision procedure, where it can veto the decisions of the Council. Unfortunately the reverse is also true, which means that there is not a single form of decision making where the Community interests could overrule the partial interests of the member states. As a consequence, the Parliament cannot play a ground-breaking role in the integration process. Though European citizens are not familiar with this institutional jungle, nor can they realistically be expected to be, they have enough experience to suggest that national rather than European parliamentary elections are decisive in terms of issues that they really care about. As a consequence they abstain from voting in EP elections, or use them to punish incumbent national governments.

The Council, which we can thus be identified as the platform where long-term decisions are made in the essentially intergovernmental EU, reproduces the deep divisions of the member states. The Lisbon Treaty essentially guarantees veto rights in fundamentally important issues such as taxation. In other areas the majority could theoretically vote down the minority, but in reality it is hard to imagine a majority group crowding up on a member state that has strong opposing interests in a given question. The support for the EU is already at such a low point in most member states that going against the perceived vital interests of a member state would push anti-European sentiments to a boiling point. In the world of package deals and horse trading governments therefore broker deals to uphold the status quo. As a consequence, arguably no treaty of historical importance has been signed since 1992 Maastricht. European integration has stalled.

European citizens had been explicitly and deliberately excluded from major decisions related to European integration for decades. When they were first asked in referenda, they mostly voted down the initiatives as a sign of protest that the European Union does not provide them with solutions to the issues they really care about. Eurobarometer regularly polls Europeans about such issues. Jobs, immigration, corruption, climate change and similar issues usually top the list. Citizens also opine that the Union is unable to answer these challenges for the most part. Member states have not transferred adequate competencies to the community level to enable it to act to meet these challenges.

Europe needs a constitutional basis that clearly defines its values,[3] and a dominantly federal rather than a dominantly intergovernmental political institutional setup. Real federalisation needs willing member states. Willing member states presuppose functioning democracies that would represent more than economic elites. Unfortunately, the quality of member state democracies has eroded to a degree where the mainstream cartel parties are more dependent on campaign financing from big business and high net worth individuals than on voters (Katz and Mair, 1995; Detterbeck, 2005). Citizens are mobilised by mass media not for progressive policies, but through the vilification of the other, especially in the cultural domain, while economically the two cartel parties converge in neo-liberal policies. Most member states are in essence captured democracies (Stigler, 1971). Thus the answer to Europe's problems lies at home, and it starts with banning business entities from campaign financing, and effectively limiting individual contributions as well.

Almost all of the economic, social, environmental and political problems of Europe require a strong supranational political economic actor. Those critics of the EU who complain about too much control from Brussels are very far from actual reality, except perhaps regulative over bureaucratisation in matters of lesser importance. In decisive issues, the political economy of the EU is fragmented and in the hands of member state governments captured by national elites. A long list of these has been enumerated in this study. The European construction must be renewed, and it must be renewed from the nation state up.

## Notes

1 It was later merged with its rival, the EC, formally creating the additional entity of the 'European Economic Area' to make life difficult for students of integration. Most of its members eventually ended up inside the EU.
2 Delors was a paradoxical political character himself. Before becoming Thatcher's European counterweight, he was in fact instrumental in Mitterand's U-turn as his finance minister. As a consequence, Thatcher's foreign secretary Howe thought Delors would implement 'our policies'. Thatcher vetoed a previous French candidate for Commission President, but not Delors (Campbell, 2004: 307).
3 The fact that the EU does not have a solid common 'constitutional' value basis even in the sense of an unwritten, 'spiritual constitution' is evidenced by the recent vote in the European Parliament on the so-called Tavares Report on Democracy in Hungary, where the Socialist, Liberal and Green factions endorsed the critical report, while the European People's Party endorsed the Government of Hungary.

## References

Alestalo, M., Hort, S. O. and Kuhnle, S. (2009). *The Nordic Model: Conditions, Origins, Outcomes, Lessons.* Berlin: Hertie School of Governance Working Papers.

Blyth, M. (2013). *Austerity: The History of a Dangerous Idea.* USA: Oxford University Press.

Burgin, A. (2012). *The Great Persuasion: Reinventing the Free Markets since the Depression.* London, England: Harvard University Press.

Campbell, J. (2004). *Margaret Thatcher. Volume Two: The Iron Lady.* London: Pimlico Random House.

Cohen, S. (1977). *Modern Capitalist Planning: The French Model.* Berkeley: University of California Press.

Daley, A. (1996). *Steel, State and Labor: Mobilization and Adjustment in France.* Pittsburg: University of Pittsburg Press.

Detterbeck, K. (2005). 'Cartel Parties in Western Europe?' *Party Politics*, 11(2) pp. 73–192.

Esping-Andersen, G. (1985). *Politics against Markets.* Princeton: Princeton University Press.

Fiorentini, R. and Montani, G. (2012). *The New Global Political Economy: From Crisis to Supranational Integration.* Cheltenham: Edward Elgar.

Flassbeck, H. and Lapavitsas, K. (2013). *The Systemic Crisis of the Euro – True Causes and Effective Therapies.* Berlin: Rosa Luxemburg Stiftung.

Giddens, A. (1998). *The Third Way – The Renewal of Social Democracy.* Cambridge: Polity.

Gillingham, J. (2003). *European Integration 1950–2003: Superstate or New Market Economy?* Cambridge: Cambridge University Press.

Greskovits, B. and Bohle, D. (2012). *Capitalist Diversity on Europe's Periphery.* New York: Cornell University Press.

Haas, E. B. (1958). *The Uniting of Europe; Political, Social, and Economic Forces, 1950–1957.* Stanford: Stanford University Press.

Hall, P. (1990). 'The State and the Market.' In Hall, P., Hayward, J. and Machin, H. (eds.) *Developments in French Politics.* London: MacMillan, pp. 171–187.

Holland, S. (1982). *The Uncommon Market.* London: Macmillan.

International Tax Justice Network (2012). *The Price of Offshore Revisited.* International Tax Justice Network.

Katz, R. S. and Mair, P. (1995). 'Changing Models of Party Organization and Party Democracy: The Emergence of the Cartel Party.' *Party Politics,* 1(1), pp. 5–31.

Lapavitsas, C., Kaltenbrunner, A., Lindo, D., Michell, J., Painceira, J., Pires, E., *et al.* (2010). *Eurozone Crisis: Beggar Thyself and Thy Neighbour.* London: Research on Money and Finance Occasional Report.

Levy, J. (1999). *Tocqueville's Revenge: State. Society and Economy in Contemporary France.* Cambridge: Harvard University Press.

Misgeld, K., Molin, K. and Amark, K. (1992). *Creating Social Democracy: A Century of the Social Democratic Labor Party in Sweden.* Pennsylvania: Pennsylvania State University Press.

Moravcsik, A. (1993). 'Preferences and Power in the European Community: A Liberal Intergovernmentalist Approach.' *Journal of Common Market Studies,* 31(4), pp. 473–524.

Mundell, R. (1961). 'A Theory of Optimum Currency Areas.' *American Economic Review,* 51, pp. 657–665.

Parker, R. (2005). *John Kenneth Galbraith: His Life, His Politics, His Economics.* Chicago: University of Chicago Press.

Pogátsa, Z. (2009a). 'Hungary: From Star Transition Student to Backsliding Member State.' *Journal of Contemporary European Research,* IV.

Pogátsa, Z. (2009b). 'Slovakia: Tatra Tiger or Belated Reconstruction?' *Acta Oeconomica,* 4.

Pogátsa, Z. (2014). *The Political Economy of the Greek Crisis.* Riga: Sit Lux Academic Publishers.

Rothstein, B. (1996). *The Swedish Model and the Bureaucratic Problem of Social Reforms.* Pittsburg: University of Pittsburgh.

Sejersted, F. (2011). *The Age of Social Democracy: Norway and Sweden in the Twentieth Century.* Princeton: Princeton University Press.

Shaxson, N. (2011). *Treasure Islands: Tax Havens and the Men Who Stole the World.* London: Bodley Head.

Smedshaug, C. A. (2010). *Feeding the World in the 21st Century: A Historical Analysis of Agriculture and Society*. London: Anthem Press.

Stigler, G. (1971). 'The Theory of Economic Regulation.' *Bell Journal of Economics and Management Science*, 3, pp. 3–18.

Thatcher, M. (2002). *Statecraft: Strategies for a Changing World*. London: Harper.

Toynbee, P. and Walker, D. (2011). *The Verdict: Did Labour Change Britain?* London: Granta Books.

Zucman, G. (2013). 'The Missing Wealth of Nations: Are Europe and the US Net Debtors or Net Creditors?' *The Quarterly Journal of Economics*, 128(3), pp. 1–44.

Zucman, G. and Johannesen, N. (2014). 'The End of Bank Secrecy? An Evaluation of the G20 Tax Haven Crackdown.' *American Economic Journal*, 6(1), pp. 65–91.

Zysman, J. (1977). *Political Strategies for Industrial Order: State, Market and Industry in France*. Berkeley: University of California Press.

# 6 Can the EU be democratised?

## A political economy analysis

*Heikki Patomäki*

The European Union's democratic deficit has been talked about for decades.[1] The metaphor 'democratic deficit' is, however, a somewhat deceptive basis for thinking about the future possibilities of democratising the EU. The term 'deficit' refers to a quantitative amount that is missing, to a shortage of something, or perhaps to a gap of some sort. It brings to mind a dish or container, that is only partially full. Pour a little bit more into it, and the deficit is gone. The English word 'deficit' is often used, moreover, in reference to amounts of money, such as in 'budget deficit'.

The concept of deficit also involves an implicit (sometimes explicit) comparison with liberal-democratic member states, which may be seen as 'full containers'. In this discourse, democracy in the member states is working just fine. The EU container can be filled by making the EU institutions more similar to those in its member states, or to some idealised version of them. Thus democracy emerges as an institutional model, towards which the EU is gradually moving.

> The Maastricht, Amsterdam, Nice and Lisbon Treaties contributed to improving the democratic legitimacy of the institutional system by reinforcing the powers of Parliament with regard to the appointment and control of the Commission and successively extending the scope of the co-decision procedure.[2]

The citizens' right of initiative and dialogue between the European institutions and civil society are also cited as signs of progress.

The point of this chapter is not to question the value of strengthening the role of the European Parliament or involving citizens and civil society actors in the EU processes. What I want to argue, however, is that a political economy analysis of the disparities and contradictions of the EMU points strongly towards alternative and more empowered EU-institutions. A problem is that establishing such institutions could further deepen the problem of democratic legitimacy, unless we can think of ways of democratising EU practices and institutions in a broader way.

What also matters, therefore, is how political possibilities and democracy are understood. My second argument is that the analysis of real political possibilities for democratisation together with a broader critical-reflexive conception of democracy, evokes sensitivity towards relations of power, hegemony and domination. A focus on power-relations in the wider political economy sense provides novel insights into the conditions and possibilities of democracy in the EU.

## Contradictions of the EMU

In 2009–12, many eurozone countries, and especially the deficit countries, faced an acute public debt crisis. The public debt problem continues to get worse, but the Outright Monetary Transactions' Programme (OMT) established by the European Central Bank in summer 2012, has succeeded in calming the bond markets. Although the underlying problem lies largely in private debt and in the long-term process of financialisation (van Treeck, 2009; Rasmus, 2010; Fouskas and Dimoulas, 2013: especially ch. 2; Patomäki, 2013: especially chs 3 and 4), usually the problem has been framed as a problem of excessive public expenditure.

Despite single market and common money, there is no European fiscal policy. By its very design, the euro is a foreign currency for all participating countries. Neither the supply of money nor the interest rate is under their control. If and when they run deficits, euro countries must turn to world financial markets and to investors who are indifferent to the fate of people and nations. Investors try to make quick profits whenever they can by anticipating short-term developments. Moreover, the longer-term current account imbalances within the eurozone have been possible due to the absence of a mechanism to balance current account surpluses and deficits.

When the debt to GDP ratio rises, especially for deficit countries, a vicious circle easily begins, as it has done time and again during the euro crisis. The demand for default swaps rises, contributing to a decline in credit ratings; thereby interest rates rise, leading to high interest payments worsening turning the debt problem into an acute crisis; and so on. The subsequent rescue loan packages to the crisis countries have followed the standard IMF model, warranting lower interest rates than in private markets, but only on the condition of strict measures of austerity and privatisation. Austerity tends to contract economies further and thus worsen the debt problem.

At the most general level, the problems of the EMU – many of which apply also to the world economy as a whole – can be understood in terms of the relationship between the parts and the whole in capitalist market economy.[3] Characteristically, the mutual dependency of the parts and whole works out through effective demand and the multiplier effect. For (post-)Keynesian economic theories, there is no automatic mechanism synchronising diverse temporal processes. Aggregate supply (the total productive capacity of the economy) does not usually equal aggregate effective demand (total spending capacity). Without mechanisms to ensure a sufficiently high level of effective demand for the goods and services produced, these developments will result in excess capacity and unemployment. Many developments are self-reinforcing due to positive feedback loops: lack of demand for goods translates into decline in investments, leading to more unemployment and less demand, and so on.

Demand is always monetised, so what matters is whether the interested consumers and investors can afford to buy the goods and services. As the propensity to consume tends to decrease with higher income, demand depends also on income distribution. Due to degrees of monopoly – always part and parcel of developments in capitalist market economy – and financial and other more or less fixed temporal commitments, prices do not easily decrease to match insufficient demand. And if prices do fall, a self-reinforcing deflationary spiral becomes rather likely.

Under these circumstances, it is the task of public authorities to ensure full employment and to stimulate and shape investments and growth. The problem is that the more globalized economic activities are, the more the effects of state policies will spread elsewhere. Moreover, particular state-actors see things only from their own limited point of view and thus tend to commit the fallacy of composition. This fallacy typically arises from the assumption that what is possible for one actor at a given moment must be possible for all (or many) of them simultaneously. If the economic policies of different states are contradictory, for instance if states simultaneously attempt to transfer their economic difficulties abroad by increasing their exports relative to imports, the end result can be bad for many countries, or for all.

When we look at things from the standpoint of all actors and countries at once, then for instance attempts to increase cost competitiveness through internal devaluation prove contradictory. Imagine a simplified world of only two countries. Both try to enhance their competitiveness by putting down wage-level or taxes and social benefits. As a result, neither country emerges as more cost-competitive than before, but both countries face smaller export markets. There will be less efficient demand in the system as a whole, thus a weaker basis also for economic growth (or worse, there will be a recession or even depression in both countries). The characteristically dire social consequences of this kind of policy turn out to be counterproductive from the viewpoint of its own publicly expressed rationale, namely growth.

## Declining support for the EU and a rational response to it

Our fates are irrevocably interconnected, but often in a contradictory and counterproductive manner. The disparities and contradictions of the world economy and especially the EMU have resulted in a long economic downturn. The orthodox policy responses have in turn tended to increase unemployment and inequalities, both causing in various social problems. Moreover, attempts to tighten budgetary discipline and control (and to a degree also the creation of the banking union) have transferred powers to the EU level, without introducing related new mechanisms of democratic participation or accountability. These developments have not left the popularity of the EU intact.

The developments of 2010–14 have been associated with a waning of confidence in the EU. In spring 2013, it was reported that 'public confidence in the European Union has fallen to historically low levels in the six biggest EU countries'.[4] The latest Eurobarometer from December 2013 tells a similar story. The proportion of Europeans who trust the EU has fallen from the peak of 57 per cent in 2007 to 31 per cent in 2013. In the first few years of the euro this trust stayed consistently at 44–50 per cent; with the euro crisis, it began to fall significantly (European Commission, 2013: 5).

When exactly does a quantitatively 'measured' decline in confidence constitute a legitimation crisis? This is difficult to judge. Surveys are contingent on respondents' perceptions of current events, as well as on framing the questions. Representation of the 'public opinion' is itself a political act, carried out for various ethico-political purposes. 'Public opinion' as measured by surveys (such as those of the Eurobarometer) is not a simple total sum of private opinions, neither is it an ideology or general will (Derrida, 1992: 87–8). 'Public opinion' tends to be fragmented. Its components can also be apathetic or indifferent; or hostile to being surveyed. While the reasons for a particular attitude towards an issue may vary, each line of reasoning follows an inner, more or less consistent logic of meanings. These meanings matter to people and are thus normatively laden and loaded (Sayer, 2011). From the standpoint of rational discourse of democratic citizens, the validity of claims concerning the EU and its future possibilities can be critically assessed.

To the extent that the economic troubles, rising social problems and new forms of budgetary surveillance and discipline have contributed significantly to the de-legitimation of the EU during the short euro era, normative evaluation should focus on the social structures and mechanisms that have causally generated these effects and developments. From a normatively oriented point of view, the question becomes whether it would be possible to accomplish a transformation 'from unneeded, unwanted and oppressive to needed, wanted and empowering sources of determination' (Bhaskar, 2011: 6). For instance, would it be possible to absent the absence of adequate mechanisms to balance current account surpluses and deficits in the EU, and perhaps globally? Would it be possible to subject the European supply of money and interest rate under political control, to aid fiscal policy? What new institutions are required for European fiscal policy, in terms of both public revenue and expenditure? Could also monetary policy support the aim of full employment? How could the process of financialisation itself be reversed?

These questions suggest a programme of major institutional transformations, implying new powers on a European and perhaps also on a global scale. Consider a scenario that I have developed elsewhere (Patomäki, 2013: ch. 6). The scenario of a 'social-democratic EU' includes European taxes and proper fiscal policy. The EU budget is comparable to public expenditure of the biggest member states, i.e. at least 7–8 times the 2014 budget. Economic policy is based first and foremost on fiscal means, seeking full employment and economically and ecologically sustainable growth. Monetary policy aims at supporting fiscal policy promoting investments and growth. If over-capacity and lack of sufficient demand develops, public budgets and thus efficient demand will be increased with central bank funding (this indicates also common Eurobonds, partly replacing national debt).

In this scenario, moreover, EU regional policies aim at reversing self-reinforcing processes of uneven developments and guaranteeing most even possible regional development level throughout the EU. Common income, wage and industrial policies are established and investments have been partially socialised, following the classical Keynesian line. The member states are allowed to follow similar economic policies.

In this post-Keynesian scenario common budget and laws are more significant than ever. This makes the question of democratic legitimacy of the EU institutions even more acute. For instance, the Council is a problematic institution from a democratic point of view.[5] Arguably it should be replaced with something more democratic. This suggests applying traditional parliamentary democratic principles[6] at the EU level: the Commission, or a new EU government, should be made directly responsible to the parliament, a parliament (possibly bicameral) deciding on budgets and on laws. Parliamentarians and citizens should get the right to put forward legal and budgetary motions. This is in line with the basic thrust of the 'democratic deficit' discourse.

However, as the European Central Bank (ECB) plays a key role in this scenario, the quest to democratise the ECB emerges too.[7] For instance, the ECB can be made answerable to a democratically elected council or to the European Parliament, perhaps to its second chamber. The federal Senate-principle can be employed, each euro country having the same amount of elected representatives (two or three).[8]

Apart from formal institutions, democratic legitimacy stems in important part also from well-functioning economic policy, from full employment and social justice, as well as from social rights and a sufficient level of guaranteed basic income for all EU citizens. These also enable citizens' equal participation in political processes. Furthermore, to make economic developments less prone to crises, the EU plays a role in coordinating and otherwise harmonising income and wage policies. At the most general level, the EU takes part in shaping the rate, composition and direction of economic growth through active public investment policies, also to make growth ecologically and socially sustainable.

Going beyond conservative versions of social democracy, this scenario may involve room also for direct, participatory and deliberative democracy. Hope for a better future – requiring at least some tentative understanding of the next level of the good society – could stem from promises to democratise social sub-systems and pluralise forms of property. These can be made subject to experiments and learning.

## On the political possibilities for change

Any plausible account of democratisation of the EU would have to include a careful analysis of the world historical context of transformative political actions. This analysis must take into account the relevant rules, resources, actor-identities, structures and mechanisms. What is the actual and potential political support for a reform proposal? What kinds of social forces could be expected to support a change? What kinds of circumstances might induce change-oriented activities? What are the prevailing structural constraints; and what are the established procedures of decision- and law-making? What would be the feedback and possibly cumulative effect of a reform? Could a particular reform enable, or preclude, other reforms?

EU institutions cannot be transformed without revising the basic treaties. In the past, treaty-revisions have been piecemeal, cumbersome and time-consuming. The Treaty establishing a Constitution for Europe (TCE) took two and a half years to negotiate but was never ratified (most member countries adopted it without referenda, but French and Dutch voters rejected the document in May and June 2005). The ruling parties and coalitions in the member states and in the European Parliament set limits as to the possible directions of changes. The newly elected European Parliament for 2014–19 is neither transformative (the leading EPP group supports the *status quo*; while the numerous Eurosceptic groups are against giving any new powers to the EU) nor especially legitimate (voter turnout in May 2014 was only 43.9 per cent). In 2014, hardly any member state is ruled by a party or coalition that would support a full-scale 'social-democratic model' of the EU. It is true that some governments prefer more economic stimulus under the circumstances of 2014–15; but even the left is divided on the big picture.

A deeper understanding of the prevailing political forces requires looking more closely at the hegemonic ideas and how they are being reproduced. As a systematic analysis is beyond the scope of this chapter, a few remarks will have to suffice. Michał Kalecki (1943) famously argued that the business leaders and capitalists wish to create circumstances (1) in which the level of investments and thus employment *depend on their confidence*, which gives them 'a powerful indirect control over Government policy' (ibid.: 325); (2) in which the *scope of* private and profit-oriented *markets is maximised*; and (3) in which the business leaders and capitalists do not cease to have measures to *discipline the workers* and their demand for equality and democracy. These 'wishes' are best seen as a transfactual tendency, constituted and rationalised by particular notions of efficiency, justice and freedom.[9]

There can be and also have been – especially during the Bretton Woods era – powerful countervailing tendencies, but economic globalisation has once more opened up possibilities for this tendency to thrive. Stephen Gill and David Law (1989) have developed an account of the structural power of transnational capital to clarify why this tendency has become, again, so strong since the 1970s and 1980s. Transnational corporations make investment decisions on a regional or global scale, thus conditioning states through their expectations of 'minimal political risks' and good 'business climate'. Under these circumstances, politicians and voters have learnt lessons from the past experiences of state policy. As interests and power tend to interfere in communication and learning processes, these lessons tend to be biased or contested. While ambiguous, typical lessons drawn from these experiences (e.g. Sweden in the mid-1970s, France in the early 1980s) have tended to favour the neo-liberal right: 'confidence', good 'business climate' and 'competitiveness' have come to be seen as prerequisites of successful economic policy. Social democratic and socialist parties in different countries have adapted not only to these ambiguous lessons but also to the changes in their potential electoral base, which has become increasingly middle-class, individualist and consumerist (partly due to the very success of the welfare state). Hence the shift to the right.

The ensuing perspective is individualist also in another sense. The 'international' too can be understood as consisting of *separate state-individuals*, the EU being *sui generis*, but for many purposes like a state. Even when state actors' awareness develop and they stop seeing the social context in mere parametric terms (as an 'external thing-like environment'), and when they become aware of the strategic interactions and game-like situations between individual actors (Elster, 1978: 159), they may still reify theirs and others' interests and options. For instance, governments may recognise that economic globalisation is a Prisoner's Dilemma game, where states compete in attracting investors by means of neo-liberal reforms, which may be seen as less than fully desirable because of their negative effects on democracy, social justice and security, well-being and indeed on economic growth. However, because of the reifications of interests and strategic options, the individual state-actors still do not know how to resolve the contradiction between individual and collective rationality – and this reification and incapability may also be a co-result of particular interests playing a role in the communication and learning processes.

Social processes, also when they originate from contradictory rules, principles and effects, are often self-reinforcing. After a critical turning or tipping point, the dynamics of self-reinforcing process, characterised by positive feedback to at least some actors, tends to support and institutionalise the original choice or choices. Thus reversals become increasingly difficult. Dynamics triggered by particular events and/or processes at one point in time may reproduce themselves or accelerate even in the absence of the recurrence of the original events or processes (Pierson, 2004). The mechanisms of learning, power and institutionalisation are particularly important in triggering and sustaining a self-reinforcing process. Actors respond to others' actions in a way that seems to give evidence for a generalised world view, or culture, which is reproduced also through systems of media and education. A slight change in relations of power may also imply more power to change the rules of the game within which political contestations take place (for instance, more room is opened up for the influence of private money and lobbying in politics). Finally institutionalisation can further reinforce a historical process and its direction, by creating new vested interests and by binding also political opponents and locking in the current policies.

Even when a particular geo-historical path turns out highly counterproductive, the political organisation may be no longer able to learn and change its course. Given how the EU has been constructed since the Maastricht Treaty, and given the hegemonic situation in European and in the global political economy more widely, the Euro-crisis has not been deep enough to induce real changes. The EU continues along its set path. It is a key characteristic of a rational democratic society that it learns and transforms itself easily. However, a non-learning society becomes, with no trouble at all, blind, and 'is driven, like bullet or torpedo, wholly by its past', to quote Karl Deutsch (1963: 111). This may indeed be the fate of the EU.

## Meanings of democracy and processes of democratisation

At this point it is important to clarify the meaning of democracy. What does it mean to say that humans are free, equal and autonomous and that they should themselves rule and determine their own future? What should democratic equality and will-formation mean, especially in a globalising context? Democracy is best conceived as a process of democratisation, within which the very idea of democracy itself is being contested, discussed and redefined (see Patomäki and Teivainen, 2004: 1–9). There is no model that would exhaust all democratic possibilities; and without any movement towards further democratisation, strong tendencies to corruption and accumulation of power can easily take over. In other words, within a supposedly stable state of democracy, de-democratising tendencies may become self-reinforcing and thereby also contribute to reducing political organisations' learning capacity.

John Dryzek (1996: 5 *et passim*) has argued that there are at least three different criteria to identify democratisation:

1 *Franchise*, i.e. the number of participants in any political setting.
2 *Scope*, i.e. the domains of life and social relations under democratic control.
3 *Authenticity*, i.e. the degree to which democratic control is substantive rather than symbolic, informed rather than ignorant, and competently engaged.

It is important to add also a fourth criterion, concerning the self-delimitation of democratic political action:

4 *The self-binding of democracy*, i.e. a democracy should not be allowed to destroy democratic practices and procedures of peaceful disagreement and conflict resolution; and a majority should not be allowed to destroy its own learning capacities or to deny others voice and equal access to the decision-making positions.

Any system or area of social life can be democratised. The larger the number of people allowed on an equal basis to participate in the political process, either directly or through their representatives, the more democratic they are.

According to the 'all-affected' principle, *everyone* who is affected by a decision, policy or law has a *prima facie* right to participate in the process of collective will-formation.[10] Plurality of voices and wide participation imply a thriving democracy. Authenticity of participation is also the key to understanding the learning capacities of the community or organisation. Not everyone can, of course, participate in all processes – hence the need for elected representatives and deliberative forums – but everyone can take part in some processes, and all processes should be open to everyone concerned either directly or via representatives.

Democracy refers also to specific qualities of the institutional setting within which political processes take place. Thus democracy involves principles such as the rule of law, principle of publicity and diverse principles of separation of powers (see Kuper, 2004, for an insightful discussion on many of these principles). The rule of law and principles of publicity are meant to guarantee legal equality and everyone's free access to all relevant information; and the point of power-separations is to minimise the risk of self-reinforcing tendencies of de-democratisation. With right modifications, these principles can be applied in any context, in the workplace as well as in central banks, in national parliaments as well as in multinational corporations.

A well-functioning democracy requires also fair and equal opportunities for free education; and guarantees for basic means of living under all circumstances. As the use of critical reason is essential for authentic and democratic will-formation, public universities and research institutes too have a vital role to play in a democracy.

## What does it take to democratise the EU?

What, then, can be done to democratise the Union? Political economy as a viewpoint draws attention to important mechanisms and processes other than those of formal parliamentary democracy. In large measure, democratic legitimacy wells from the outcomes of economic policy and from the way political economy institutions are organised, especially in terms of their democratic responsiveness and accountability. What makes things complicated is that political economy analysis of the European integration process reveals also a self-reinforcing process, stemming from economic globalisation, whereby the 'wishes' of business leaders and capitalists have become entrenched in the prevailing culture, vested interests and institutional arrangements, thus making changes difficult. Unionists, civic actors and political parties have reacted to this hegemony within the Union in diverse and often also contradictory ways (see e.g. Erne, 2008, for an analysis of labour organisations' responses).

What are the complex conditions of institutional changes towards a well-working and democratic EU? Real world constraints include the structural power of investors; the influence of the lobbyists; and the way education and media are being arranged. Also the rights and principles that are constitutive to relevant forms of agency – e.g. the private corporations, or citizens and their associations – shape power-relations. Each site of power can be democratised, with implications to the possibilities of changes in other sites and contexts. Also democratisation can become self-reinforcing, even if it is also true that each positive feedback always works only to a point.

The structural power of global investors can be alleviated and, over time, overridden by means of collective actions by the states, through fashioning new international law and creating new systems of global governance (or government). Aided by support from civil society organisations and movements, these collective actions can create new worldwide regulations and regimes and generate institutional innovations such as global taxes. This is an old idea: overcoming contradictions by collective actions.

The problem is that at least some states, which are constrained by the structural power of transnational capital, should be able to develop an autonomous will to overcome this power by means of joint actions with other likeminded states, by building 'coalitions of the willing'. The formation of will for changes can best be seen as a learning process, characteristically triggered and provoked by a crisis. So far the euro crisis has led to small concessions by the EU and some of its member states in this direction, most notably with the proposals of financial regulation and the transaction tax, but apparently a deeper crisis is required before something genuinely new can emerge. The more entrenched the prevailing ideas, the bigger the crisis or catastrophe must be for collective learning to take place.

The influence of the lobbyists is the second major constraint for adequate institutional changes. The power of lobbyists can be seen in the outcomes of many EU (Cronin, 2013) and global (Beder, 2006) processes. For instance, it has been argued that 'far from being a solution to avoid future public bailouts and austerity, Europe's new [2014] banking union rules look like a victory for the financial sector to continue business as usual'.[11] The business as usual includes locking-in the liberalisation of the financial markets. This outcome is in important part a result of the lobby groups of the banks having been part of the process of creating the banking union every step of the way (the European Banking Federation has even played a key part in forming the proposals of the Commission). This particular but important example exposes a general problem, characterising law- and policy-making in the EU. Lobbying in Brussels has become a billion-euro industry. The lobbying 'community' in Brussels consists of from 15,000 up to 30,000 lobbyists, two-thirds of whom are representing transnational corporations and banks. Lobbyists in Brussels are claimed to influence some 75 per cent of European legislation. Especially the corporate lobbyists follow carefully the 'wishes' of business leaders and capitalists and related ideas.[12]

The EU lobbying practices pose a major obstacle to any democratic change. As John Rawls (1973: 226) argues, if political 'funds need to be solicited from the more advantaged social and economic interests, the pleadings of these groups are bound to receive excessive attention'. Non-governmental organisations have too often been content to call for improved ethical codes of practice and making lobbying practices more transparent. Given the ideal of citizens' equality in political processes, the main democratic objective must be to keep the practices of lobbying heavily restricted or to cut them out entirely (only public consultations of various experts are needed, and by official invitation only). For exactly the same reason, also the role of private money in national and European elections should be strictly curtailed. The most simple and fair principle would be to allow only the same amount of public funding for all candidates and prohibit all forms of private funding.

The same holds true for public forums and space. In democratic systems, they must be free and open to all. 'The liberties protected by the principle of participation lose much of their value whenever those who have greater private means are permitted to use their advantages to control the course of public debate' (Rawls, 1973: 225). There are only rudiments of a European public debate. The public forums are still largely nationally based. From a political economy point of view, however, what is particularly striking is the commercialisation of media and the way national media have been integrated to global media corporations. Working parallel with the upsurge of new media technologies and mediatisation of politics, these processes have transformed the nature of public space (see Axford and Huggins, 2001; Meyer, 2002). The rise and concentration of advertisement-based commercial media and the weakening of public broadcasting systems worldwide have led to a logic of disseminating particular interpretations that may be less direct and more diverse than straightforward propaganda, yet bears resemblance to Orwellian newspeak (Herman and McChesney, 1997; Szántó, 2007). Truth-seeking investigative journalism, coupled with long-term educational intent, is replaced with infotainment in which everyone tries to get attention by whatever means, and in which the 'wishes' of the advertisers and corporate owners play a weighty and, over time, increasing role.

Commercial media power is largely based on advertising. This suggests that taxing advertising at a high rate, the game can be smoothed out and funds diverted towards supporting public media. The tax rate on mere image advertising could be set at 100 per cent and the tax on other forms of advertising at 50 per cent. The tax could be agreed within the Union or, more preferably, globally. National authorities would collect the tax. A part of the revenues collected in Europe should go to financing a public pan-European media company, which could operate via the satellites and the Internet, but may also be able to develop print outlets as well. Its explicit task would be to further democracy and cultivate principles and virtues of good public journalism.

Last but not least, also the privatisation and commercialisation of higher education and research can be seen as an ancillary obstacle to democratic changes. The rise of the corporate university (Patomäki, 2005; Washburn, 2006) assumes somewhat different forms in different local and national contexts, but overall the developments have been relatively uniform worldwide (Mittelman, forthcoming). The thrust of these developments has been to subsume universities and other organisations of higher education and research to immediate economic interests, understood in terms of commercially viable innovations and employment. New mechanisms of surveillance and control have been created in the interest of making academics and researchers as 'productive' as possible, understood through the lenses of 'new public management' and other theories modelled on corporate governance and competitive markets. These theories have been better at commodifying intellectual activities and expanding the role of managers and central administration than actually spurring innovations or employment. As a result, however, academic freedom has been compromised in various ways, most characteristically in terms of 'wishes' and the fashionable ideas of the business leaders and capitalists. This in turn has an effect on higher education, tending towards producing 'disciplined minds', i.e. salaried professionals lacking creativity or courage to use critical reason (Schmidt, 2001).

There is no simple measure to reverse these developments or to set universities and other relevant organisations to a new path. Given that the privatisation and commercialisation of higher education and research have been essentially linked to the concept of 'national competitiveness', the ideal solution would be a global or at least European agreement on the basic framework and principles of free, publicly funded and self-governing universities. Realising that the corporate university is in fact counterproductive in view of innovations or learning more generally, some national authorities may well conclude that they can and should adopt an alternative model, premised on classical republican theory about the virtues of public good. The alternative system would replace technocratic management by past results with a collegial system of free discussion and democratic decision-making, providing sufficient facilities for all researchers and teachers (external funding being only an auxiliary possibility). The education of citizens is seen as a key task of universities. A successful model is likely to spread rapidly, as has happened in the past.

## Conclusion

The democratisation of the EU means more than mere cautious and piecemeal expansion of the powers of the European Parliament or those of its citizens. The quantitatively 'measured' decline from 2010 to 2014 in confidence in the EU is already verging on a legitimation crisis. It seems clear that the economic troubles, rising social problems and new forms of budgetary surveillance and discipline have contributed significantly to the de-legitimation of the EU during the short euro era.

I have argued, first, that the euro crisis and related economic problems of the Union can be explained by post-Keynesian economic theories, implying the need for common fiscal policy, drastically revised central bank mandate and redistributive mechanisms in the Union. These kinds of reforms could, however, aggravate the legitimation problems of the Union, unless the union is further democratised. Proper parliamentary democratic principles can make a big difference, but it would also be critically important to democratise the ECB. In the post-Keynesian EU legitimation could also come from economic policy ensuring full employment and social justice, as well as, from new social rights and a sufficient level of guaranteed basic income for all EU citizens. Those policies would give legitimacy to the Union.

It is at this point that the trickiest part of my argument started. Any plausible account of democratisation of the EU would have to include a careful analysis of the world historical context of transformative political actions. What makes things complicated is that political economy analysis of the European integration process reveals also a self-reinforcing process, stemming from economic globalisation, whereby the 'wishes' of business leaders and capitalists have become entrenched in the prevailing culture, vested interests and institutional arrangements, thus making changes difficult. Moreover, EU institutions cannot be transformed without revising the basic treaties. In the past, treaty-revisions have been piecemeal, cumbersome and time-consuming.

Is it the fate of the EU to be blind and 'driven, like bullet or torpedo, wholly by its past' until the bitter end of some sort? Aided by the insight that any system or area of social life can be democratised, in the final part I focussed on the extrinsic and intrinsic conditions of changing the EU towards a post-Keynesian and democratic direction. Real world constraints on transformations include the structural power of transnational investors; the influence of the lobbyists in Brussels; and the way media research and education are being arranged across Europe and the world. The problem in each of these instances is corporate power, which can be countered by various measures: from global and European taxes and regulations to drastically curtailing the role of lobbyists and private funds in the process of opinion- and will-formation.

World history proceeds through nodal points. The rupture and breaking point may first occur also locally; a successful model is likely to spread rapidly. Any successful political strategy by a government or political party would have to combine attempts to shape the extrinsic and intrinsic conditions for acting otherwise, by building European or worldwide coalitions of the willing, with various economic and other policies that can succeed even under the rather constrained contemporary circumstances. It is true, of course, that learning may occur also within the current EU institutions, but this is unlikely to happen unless the crisis deepens even more.

## Notes

1 While widely accepted as the starting point of discussions, not everyone agrees that there is a democratic deficit in the EU. Christopher Lord (2008: 317) singles out three variants of the argument that 'EU democratic deficit' is a false problem: (1) the Union does not need to be democratic, because it does not and cannot allocate values in any efficient way; (2) the Union is already as democratic as it needs to be, perhaps even more democratic than its member states; or (3) a more democratic

Union is undesired or undesirable, since it would presuppose a bigger role for European-level majorities of voters or representatives in making decisions binding on all.

2 As stated in the official website of the European Union, at http://europa.eu/ legislation_summaries/glossary/democratic_deficit_en.htm.

3 For a summary of the key concepts and arguments of (post-)Keynesian economic theory, and why the whole is more than the sum of its parts, and how both should be seen in processual terms, see Patomäki (2013: ch. 2). For more detailed introductions, see King (2002) and Lavoie (2009). At a deeper level, the question is ontological and concerns how individual agents and social wholes are related (see e.g. Archer, 1995). The context of any given action by an individual or collective agent consists of a range of components and aspects of the whole in question; the question of the relationship between actions and their context is the agency/structure problem in social theory.

4 'Crisis for Europe as trust hits record low. Poll in European Union's six biggest countries finds Euroscepticism is soaring amid bailouts and spending cuts', *The Guardian*, Wednesday 24 April 2013, available at http://www.theguardian.com/world/2013/apr/24/trust-eu-falls-record-low.

5 The Germany–France axis has frequently set the agenda of the Council, but especially since the euro crisis, the German government has assumed leadership in steering the development of the Union. This is not justified and cannot be acceptable in the long run (for a critique of the current German leadership, see Beck, 2013). Moreover, the Council is generally regarded as the least open to the public. It has several problems from a democratic point of view. Ministers of the governments lead the negotiations, but their accountability is too indirect to be credible. 'Successful' negotiations require all too often that citizens do not even know what their government is seeking (or what the agenda is). There are also limits to how far individual control could ever add up to collective control. To what extent the control of individual governments in the Council can add up to control of the Council as a whole? From the point of view of individual voters, votes cast in national elections on European issues may be at the opportunity cost of voting for a preferred party on domestic issues; and from that of national representatives, the costly acquisition of expertise on EU issues may be time that has to be diverted from full scrutiny of domestic issues. Moreover, also the EP cannot check and balance the Council either, as its powers are ill-defined and enmeshed with those of the EU bureaucracy (Lord, 2008: 318).

6 Also the role of national parliaments can be strengthened in the EU, in spite of the issue of costly acquisition of EU expertise (see note 5). This might be a reasonable response to Jürgen Habermas' (2012: 36–7) conception according to which every citizen participates in the European opinion- and will-formation processes both as national and European citizen than that of preserving the role of the Council. It should also be stressed that according to the principle of subsidiarity, supranational decisions should not be made unless necessary. The principle of subsidiarity may be applied even against 'fair competition' within the common market, thus prioritising values other than 'free markets'.

7 The doctrine of central bank independence is based on two fears. The fear of political business cycles is not based on solid historical evidence (the case of Nixon in the early 1970s was an exception, not the rule); while the fear of inflation is grossly exaggerated and one-sided (it is in the interests of the owners of capital and especially financial capital to aim for the lower possible level of inflation, that is, for the maximum retention of the value of money and debts over time). Please note, however, that also a democratised ECB would be in some important ways independent from the Commission, Parliament and member states' governments, as its governing council is elected separately.

8  This would take a long step in countering the one-sided German leadership in the Union and especially the EMU. The Council of the ECB could also include representatives of other EU institutions, in particular the Parliament and the Commission (or whatever the successor of Commissions will be called). At any rate, the directly elected representatives would have a clear majority in the Council. The federal senate principle would ensure that the central bank reflects different regions and interests in a balanced manner and does not set monetary policy, for example, to support only a single large surplus country or in view of the short-sighted desires of the biggest member states.

9  The ethos of a capitalist market economy has always been based on the negative conception of freedom from state (or any forceful) interference, and on the scalar distribution model of justice – the more you contribute, the more you get. John Locke justified these with a labour theory of value. Everybody is entitled to their personhood and products of their own labour. Private property and its yields may accumulate over time. Contemporary theorists have redefined this in terms of supposedly *neutral market procedures*, claiming that what matters is procedural distribution, and, second, that playing by the competitive rules of the market ultimately *benefits all parties*. The standard message of mainstream neoclassical economics is similar. The two key notions of neoclassical economics are: (1) Pareto optimal equilibrium and (2) marginal productivity. Pareto-optimality means that no arrangement can improve the position of anyone without making worse the position of somebody else. This implies that redistribution is not allowed to increase overall well-being or justice. Pareto-optimality is used routinely by the economists as a normative standard in evaluating different possible institutional arrangements. Furthermore, according to the theory of marginal productivity, the contribution of a factor is defined to be the marginal product of that factor. If we make enough assumptions about rationality, nature of transactions, the substitutability of factors, diminishing returns, and so forth, then a mathematical theorem can be invoked to show that the sum of the contributions, thus defined, will be exactly the amount produced. If we make additional assumptions to ensure 'perfect competition', it can be shown that the market price of each factor will be equal to its contribution. In a famous, and also contested, interpretation of the ethical-political essence of marginalist economics, John B. Clark wrote in 1899:

> it is the purpose of this work to show that the distribution of income to society is controlled by a natural law, and that this law, if it worked without friction, would give to every agent of production the amount of wealth which that agent creates.
> (Clark, 1908: 1)

Assuming the scalar distribution model ('the more you contribute, the more you get'), this amounts to a theory of justice according to which in competitive markets everyone gets what they deserve. (Patomäki, 2006: 107–8; see also O'Neill, 1998, for a systematic and critical discussion of the alleged neutrality of markets).

10  Johan Karlsson (2006) is right to say that the all-affected principle generates problems immediately as soon as we try to use it to draw political boundaries. Political boundaries cannot be redrawn for each issue at stake. Yet it is often possible to include those outside in the process of opinion- and will-formation. Moreover, systematic patterns of discrepancy can also be used as an argument for redrawing the inside/outside boundaries and for creating new common institutional arrangements. Sofia Näsström (2011) argues that we should first distinguish between the all-subjected principle and the all-affected principle; and second allow for different meanings for the all-affected principle.

11  Corporate European Observatory (2014). 'A union for big banks', available at http://corporateeurope.org/financial-lobby/2014/01/union-big-banks.

12 See the 'Power of lobbies' page of Corporate European Observatory at http://corporateeurope.org/power-lobbies.

## References

Archer, M. S. (1995). *Realist Social Theory: The Morphogenetic Approach*. Cambridge: Cambridge University Press.

Axford, B. and Huggins, R. (eds.) (2001). *New Media and Politics*. London: Sage.

Beck, U. (2013). *German Europe*. Translation by Livingstone, R., Cambridge: Polity.

Beder, S. (2006). *Suiting Themselves: How Corporations Drive the Global Agenda*. London: Earthscan.

Bhaskar, R. (2011). *Reclaiming Reality: A Critical Introduction to Contemporary Philosophy*. London: Verso (originally published in 1989).

Clark, J. (1908). *The Distribution of Wealth: A Theory of Wages, Interest and Profits*. New York: MacMillan, available at http://www.econlib.org/library/Clark/clkDWtoc.html.

Corporate European Observatory (2014). 'A Union for Big Banks', available at http://corporateeurope.org/financial-lobby/2014/01/union-big-banks.

Cronin, D. (2013). *Corporate Europe: How Big Business Sets Policies on Food, Climate and War*. London: Pluto Press.

Derrida, J. (1992). *The Other Heading: Reflection on Today's Europe*. Trans. by Brault, P. A. and Naas, M. B., Bloomington: Indiana University Press.

Deutsch, K. W. (1963). *The Nerves of Government: Models of Political Communication and Control*. New York: The Free Press.

Dryzek, J. S. (1996). *Democracy in Capitalist Times: Ideals, Limits and Struggles*. Oxford: Oxford University Press.

Elster, J. (1978). *Logic and Society: Contradictions and Possible Worlds*. Chichester: John Wiley & Sons.

Erne, R. (2008). *European Unions Labor's Quest for a Transnational Democracy*. Ithaca, NY: Cornell University Press.

European Commission (2013). *Public Opinion in the European Union. Standard Eurobarometer 80 Autumn 2013 First Results*. Brussels: Directorate-General for Communication, available at http://ec.europa.eu/public_opinion/archives/eb/eb80/eb80_first_en.pdf.

Fouskas, V. K. and Dimoulas, C. (2013). *Greece, Financialization and the EU: The Political Economy of Debt and Destruction*. Houndmills, Basingstoke: Palgrave Macmillan.

Gill, S. and Law, D. (1989). 'Global Hegemony and the Structural Power of Capital.' *International Studies Quarterly*, 33, pp. 475–99.

The Guardian (2013). 'Crisis for Europe as trust hits record low. Poll in European Union's six biggest countries finds Euroscepticism is soaring amid bailouts and spending cuts', Wednesday 24 April, 2013, available at http://www.theguardian.com/world/2013/apr/24/trust-eu-falls-record-low.

Habermas, J. (2012). *The Crisis of the European Union: A Response*. Translation by Cronin, C., Cambridge: Polity.

Herman, E. S. and McChesney, R. W. (1997). *The Global Media: The New Missionaries of Corporate Capitalism*. London and Washington: Cassell.

Kalecki, M. (1943). 'Political Aspects of Full Employment.' *The Political Quarterly*, 14, pp. 322–330.

Karlsson, J. (2006). 'Affected and Subjected – The All-Affected Principle in Transnational Democratic Theory.' *Discussion Paper*, Social Science Research Center Berlin, Sp Iv 2006–304, available at http://papers.ssrn.com/sol3/papers.cfm?abstract_id=2274644.

King, J. E. (2002). *A History of Post Keynesian Economics since 1936*. Cheltenham: Edward Elgar.

Kuper, A. (2004). *Democracy Beyond Borders: Justice and Representation in Global Institutions*. Oxford: Oxford University Press.

Lavoie, M. (2009). *Introduction to Post-Keynesian Economics*. Houndmills, Basingstoke: Palgrave MacMillan.

Lord, C. (2008). 'Still in Democratic Deficit.' *Intereconomics*, 43, pp. 316–20.

Meyer, T. (2002). *Media Democracy: How the Media Colonize Politics*. Cambridge: Polity.

Mittelman, J. (forthcoming). *The Global Transformation of Universities*. Cornell: Cornell University Press.

Näsström, S. (2011). 'The Challenge of the All-Affected Principle.' *Political Studies*, 59, pp. 116–134.

O'Neill, J. (1998). *The Market: Ethics, Knowledge and Politics*. London: Routledge.

Patomäki, H. (2005). *Yliopisto Oyj. Tulosjohtamisen ongelmat – ja vaihtoehto* [University Inc. The Problems of the 'New Public Management' – and an Alternative], Helsinki: Gaudeamus.

Patomäki, H. (2006). 'Global Justice: A Democratic Perspective.' *Globalizations*, 3, pp. 99–120.

Patomäki, H. (2013). *The Great Eurozone Disaster: From Crisis to Global New Deal*. London: Zed Books.

Patomäki, H. and Teivainen, T. (2004). *A Possible World: Democratic Transformation of Global Institutions*. London: Zed Books.

Pierson, P. (2004). *Politics in Time: History, Institutions and Social Analysis*. Princeton: Princeton University Press.

Rasmus, J. (2010). *Epic Recession: Prelude to Global Depression*. London: Pluto Press.

Rawls, J. (1973). *A Theory of Justice*. Oxford: Oxford University Press.

Sayer, A. (2011). *Why Things Matter to People: Social Science, Values and Ethical Life*. Cambridge: Cambridge University Press.

Schmidt, J. (2001). *Disciplined Minds: A Critical Look at Salaried Professionals and the Soul-Battering System that Shapes Their Lives*. New York: Rowman & Littlefield.

Szántó, A. (ed.) (2007). *What Orwell Didn't Know: Propaganda and the New Face of American Politics*. New York: PublicAffairs.

van Treeck, T. (2009). 'The Macroeconomics of "Financialisation", and the Deeper Origins of the World Economic Crisis.' *IMK Working Paper*, 9/2009, available at http://www.boeckler.de/pdf/p_imk_wp_9_2009.pdf.

Washburn, J. (2006). *University, Inc.: The Corporate Corruption of Higher Education*. New York: Basic Books.

# 7 *Res Publica Europaea*

## A citizens-based concept to re-think political integration of Europe

*Ulrike Guérot[1]*

### Introduction: short history of European integration discourse

The history of political integration is long and libraries can be filled with books about political union (Hix and Hoyland, 1999, 2011; Wallace and Wallace, 1996; Rissen-Kappen, 2008), European federalism (Bogdandy, 1999) and the question of a European belonging and imagined communities (Anderson, 1991). The aspirations towards a constitution of the European Union (EU),[2] a process that failed in 2005 with the two negative referenda in both the Netherlands and France, have evoked, as much as many other issues, much academic debate and dispute. Especially in Germany the discourse was much shaped by juridical arguments and hence plunged for decades into manifold and detailed discussion about European federalism or *'Staatenbund'* vs *'Bundestaat'*.[3] The political sciences discourse on the other hand concentrated more on multi-level governance features, neo-functionalist theories of market integration as well as their respective spill-over effects (Jachtenfuchs, 1996, 2010; Scharpf, 2002). Until today, the common feature of both of these branches on how a future European Union could be and what it could look like is that most citizens of European member states have never heard of them.

It is only through the euro-crisis in 2008 that the institutional flaws of European integration became tangible to a broader audience. The awareness of European citizens then triggered a different political discussion about Europe: with growing Euro-populism becoming a main trend in several member countries, especially in Greece, France, Hungary, Italy, the Netherlands or Finland (Fieschi *et al.*, 2013; Grabow and Hartleb, 2013). In very simple words: the euro crisis was the moment of truth when the only half-finished Treaty of Maastricht proved to be too incomplete. It had designed a monetary union without political union and any kind of fiscal transfer mechanism. Already by 1992, everybody engaged in drafting the Maastricht Treaty knew about these flaws and where they could lead should they ever be put to the test.[4] It had to be the euro-crisis that peeled off the left-over wishful thinking to reveal the euro's crude reality as an 'orphan currency', a currency without democracy (Pisany-Ferry, 2008).

The post-crisis discussion then shifted away from a legal or political scientist perspective and focused essentially on the – missing – social and political dimension of Europe, more precisely the EU. Thus it was constructed *euro-governance*, which was institutionalized more or less outside of the existing treaties during the crisis years under the so-called 'Union Method'.[5] This led to a tangible democracy deficit (Guérot, 2013a) and a deficient democratic (Priester, 2014) and social structure of the current eurozone management (Tsoukala, 2013). Policy was seemingly left to the European Central Bank (ECB) and the crisis management of Mario Draghi who is famous for the sentence 'the ECB is ready to do whatever it takes to preserve the euro. And believe me, it will be enough.'[6] Applied to Carl Schmitt's notion that a sovereign is who decides in case of an emergency (Schmitt, 1923), the ECB was (and could still be seen as) literally the sovereign of Euroland. The unfortunate 'catch-22' of the euro-governance system became apparent in that it is incapable – in a political and legal way – of finding the needed democratic solutions and that its current condition is untenable.

This problem – together with the multi-fold origins of the euro crisis which is way beyond a simple problem of profligate Southern countries causing a debt crisis (Soros and Schmitz, 2014) – has been widely analysed and described in the literature.[7] Such analyses (Auer, 2013) have highlighted the various factors leading to the deplorable 'executive deficit' of the EU (Veron, 2012). Recent research has also underscored the intertwined character of a financial market and banking system crisis and the systemic euro crisis (Offe, 2013).

On the one hand, this is why most recent – and also more popular – literature has been largely exploring the political economy of Europe and the eurozone at large (Beck, 2012; Habermas, 2011c; Menasse, 2012). This literature goes beyond institutional design discussions only, and strongly attacks the technocratic structure of the EU and its flawed social and democratic dimension. On the other hand, growing literature exists which argues in favour of euro roll-back or maintains that the euro has failed in its current structure (Geppert, 2013; Heisbourg, 2013). Europe and the euro thus started to be criticized for their lack of democratic and social dimension, rather than only for their institutional design. Democracy as such became the topos of the crisis discussion, replacing the notion of European integration.

This chapter is not about tracing the various legal, political economist or political scientist's discussion about European integration and its flaws. It has the ambition to concentrate on current political trends, the dynamics of the broader public discussion about European integration and the need to reframe the discussion about European democracy. It develops the concept of a *Res Publica Europaea*, shifting the discussion away from the notion of a 'United States of Europe' towards the concept of a European Republic,[8] based on Ulrich Beck's statement that if states are given the ultimate authority about the integration process, the European project cannot succeed.

## The post-crisis momentum: European populism and 'more or less' Europe?

Post-crisis European integration seems to be in a deadlock. This is mainly due precisely to the perception of the EU as not democratic or social by an increasing number of citizens and so public dissatisfaction is growing. These observations have induced an unhealthy and polarized debate about 'more or less' Europe, with the 'less-Europe' arguments ostensibly on the winning side. From Le Pen in France to Syriza in Greece, the True Fins in Finland or Geert Wilders in the Netherlands: Euro-populism is on the rise. And even in Germany, where the absence of such extreme parties has long puzzled political analysts, the AfD (Alternative für Deutschland) is winning more and more votes. Whereas right wing movements focus on the notion of sovereignty and the nation states, left wing criticism focuses more on the unsocial nature of euro-governance. Northern Euro-populism reacts on the need of so-called 'transfer-union',[9] whereas Southern Euro-populism attacks the social consequences of austerity policy.[10] It is important to note that the pro-European argument is thus under pressure and attacked from two sides – left and right. The confrontational line of the discussion is thus more between a European mainstream argument, dependent on the existing system of the EU and its technocratic structure, and anti-system opposition rather than between countries or political parties.

What is more important to note is that the 'pro-Europe' argument nearly cannot win as it struggles to defend a flawed, undemocratic and unsocial system: defending the current euro-governance is, indeed, difficult in various respects. It means defending a system without a strong parliamentarian component as long as the European Parliament (EP) is without right of legal initiative and the role of national parliaments is inadequate. Within the system of Euro governance, only the German Bundestag is capable enough and therefore has recently taken on the role of 'Congress for the eurozone'. Furthermore, the role of the European Council is opaque and within it the steering capacity of the bigger countries such as Germany and France is doubtful. Not to mention that much of this comes at even bigger cost for smaller EU member states. Yet pro-European arguments are isolated in the sense that they try to defend a system without offering a classical opposition, meaning policy alternatives or the reversibility of policy decisions. The EP is all too often struggling to find a majority to outvote the Council, which leads to a suppression of traditional political division along party lines, whereas the Commission is the real agenda setter on most of the macro-economic policy shaping and it has the supremacy on the European semester. These, plus the role of the Troika, are the most important ingredients to a rather technocratic structure of the euro crisis management, resented by people as being non-democratic.

The euro crisis has de facto led to a situation in which supply-sided economic policies have been constituted on secondary European law level, and each and every following Commission – regardless of the majority of the

European Parliament – will be bound to execute the rules of the fiscal compact. Politics, however, is in principle about options and alternatives.

The EU governance setting in its *sui-generis* set-up and the triangular proceedings between Council, Commission and EP do thus intuitively not correspond to what citizens perceive as democratic and how they experience it in their national context. The EP, for instance, is mostly exhausting itself with 'grand-coalition' settings and votes in '70plus' majority settings to out-vote the Council (Maurer, 2013). Indeed, these structures and mechanisms are not undemocratic in a legal sense: after all, they are embedded in numerous European treaties which all have been signed by the member states and accordingly ratified. Still, these structures are far from a fully fledged democracy as defined by Montesquieu offering a clear division of power between a legislative and an executive body. The lack of 'politicization' of the EU and how it could be achieved is thus the key for solving the current euro crisis.

Needless to say that the above described techno-structure of the EU offers sufficient leeway for lobby groups, which manage to handle the system at their guise and are the real souffleurs for many European policies ranging from consumer protection to regulatory affairs and energy policy. Accordingly, the European governance system does often not so much suffer from opposing member states' positions on policy issues, but from organized lobby interests against unrepresented civil societies' interests. The latter is another structural problem as European citizens – and their social or other interests – are not well organized in a transnational setting and can thus not be voiced or enacted through representatives.[11] The additional language plurality and a missing European public sphere with European media remain the main handicap for this (Grimm Dieter, 1995; Guérot, 2012). It is because the *horizontal* policy making (and thus democracy) is imperfect in the European context, that the discussion about Europe ends up in a *vertical* confrontation between the EU level and the nation state. My argument here is that the techno-structure of the current EU system provides a breeding ground for Euro-populism. Citizens who are against the EU policy need to be de facto against the EU polity.

Rather consequently, bureaucracy and over-regulation from Brussels have been criticized regularly, whereas 'Brussels' *per se* is not the real initiator of regulation. It is rather national lobby groups and the respective companies.[12] The notoriously famous curved cucumber is the best example: The origin of the cucumber regulation was not a civil servant of the Commission, but the German association of fruit and vegetable producers. And only when, after much advisory effort from the likes of such interest groups, the Commission then publishes new regulatory guidelines does its work become visible to a greater public. However, national authorities often could have gone against the attempt of regulation during the whole process from green book to white book to Council decision but often they don't do it. Brussels bureaucracy is the perfect scapegoat, but seldom at the origin of the regulatory initiative. Still, it fuels the argument of an opaque European structure, which current Euro-populism is smartly picking up.

The ridiculousness of regulations like the one on cucumbers in turn is what Euro criticism has been waiting for and hence Brussels is blamed for its 'regulatory-mania'. The consequence of these biased and fogged discussions is that European citizens turned against Brussels. From cucumbers to oil cans, the bureaucratic Moloch in Brussels is the bestselling argument against the EU, fuelling the 'less-Europe' argument. A few moments after such EU criticism, one usually hears the second-best-selling code word against Brussels: 'subsidiarity'. This is problematic in two respects. First, the notion of subsidiarity is ill-chosen. In its German origins of the Catholic Social Sciences (Nell-Breunig, 1980), it was more a principle to define the relationship between the individual and society, rather than pointing to a multi-level governance structure. Second, and even more importantly, the principle of subsidiarity is becoming increasingly a notion to drop out of the European law context and to claim exceptions and further exemptions based on 'cultural difference'. In other words: with flaveo horizontal European democracy, subsidiarity becomes a rescue mode in which a country's interest is defined as self-interest only. Current discussions then quickly include drafts of national 'competence catalogues' for the EU, just so to define those areas that are at the very core of a given country's interest and that must therefore not be handled by any other.[13] Subsidiarity deserves the emotional argument of citizens to determine the way they live, more than it has a political meaning. When Normand schools recently argued for Normand apples to be in the fruit compote of school canteens in Normandy, their arguments referred back to the principle of subsidiarity. And so did the Dutch claims for Dutch milk and Dutch schools. Now, these are perfectly legitimate claims, especially if they correspond to people's expressed political preferences. Hence, the – juridical or legal – problem is not the lack of subsidiarity, which allegedly the EU treaties do not allow. The real problem is the lack of transparent and transnational policy making in the EU, conveying citizens' interests to the level of legislation: if Chilean apples end up in French school canteens, then probably the reason is that the EU (i.e. the Commission in a deliberative procedure with the Council and the EP) has at some point (i.e. through standard procedures and outside of public scrutiny) agreed to preferential trade agreement with Chile and hence making Chilean apples cheaper than Normand apples. Since Normand citizens have in practice no means to influence this procedure due to a dysfunctional European democracy, subsidiarity becomes the only cure against policies considered 'unfair' or where citizens rightly contest that they do not want them. More examples can be found but the pattern remains the same. Without transnational coalition building and majority finding, European democracy is flawed at the horizontal level. It is without a clear division of powers, with no opposition and almost no reversibility of policy decisions while citizens feel betrayed or overruled by Brussels, or both.

The only solution to end this unhealthy dichotomy of 'less or more' Europe would be to shift the public discussion towards questions about a 'different' Europe and to move the discussion out of its *vertical* structure towards a *horizontal* structure. Questions such as 'more for the EU or more for the member states', 'more EP decisions or more MP decisions', 'more EU competence or more subsidiarity' always point to the difficulties of the multi-level governance of the EU and the still lacking intertwinement of both the EP and national parliaments. But more importantly, they overlook that the nations and their electoral and administrative bodies are largely part of the EU decision-making system, so that the construction of a dichotomy between national state and European union is not truly constructive. The real question would be how to create a parliamentarian structure of 'crossed legitimacy' in a bi-cameral system, so that the decision about the collective priorities of the EU citizens – the aim for a common good of a *Res Publica Europaea* – could find expression through a strong legislative body.

The decisive question would then be how to shape a fully fledged, large-scale, multi-lingual European democracy – starting with the eurozone – with a distinct division of power, where citizens' interests can be voiced in a transnational setting and where national debates can be de-homogenized. Obviously, there is, if any, no easy answer to this question and it would be a tremendously challenging endeavour. As Wolfgang Streeck rightly points out (Streeck, 2013), in such a 'jacobinian-unitarian' European democracy, the dominance of the German people would be a huge problem and consequently the problem to secure minority rights, which would need to be out-balanced in an appropriate way, is why he rules this out as a solution. The question refers to the basic question of shifting the European Parliament – or at least a future eurozone Parliament – to a 'one man one vote' composition, or, in other words, to the question where the proportional element in the institutional set-up of a different and more legitimate European polity should come in. The very fact that the EP does not correspond in its current form to this principle was one of the most important arguments of the German Constitutional Court in its ruling on the Lisbon Treaty[14] when it stated that the EP is not yet fully democratic in a traditional sense and triggered the '*Integrationsverantwortungsgesetz*' ('Law about the Responsibility for Integration'), a German law putting the German Bundestag in a new legal responsibility for the European law-making process.

Moving out of a 'less or more Europe' matrix would equally suppose to consider concepts such as 'demoicracy' (Nikolaidis, 2013), trying to rethink a fully fledged democracy with several demos as the constitutive community that wants to organize in a democracy. The lack of single demos is one of the classical arguments put into field against the possibility of European federalization, with the demos tight to national borders and thus sovereignty in the current context. However, with a growing discussion on a *trans*national form of organization of Europe which reflects a transnational social and living context of an increasing number of European citizens, the concept of demoicracy could come close to trespassing the traditional borders in which democracy has been framed so far and open up the gate to a common form of managing the common European public good in a different kind of a pan-European parliamentarian democracy. Demoicracy would correspond to the concept of a democracy of more than one people, formally constructed around the notion of a nation; and rely on the conscience choice of forming a transnational political body together. Such thinking could give leeway to the decomposition of discourse, which is still often framed in country-to-country cleavages, whereas the coalitions of opinions are already cross-border. The de-homogenization of national policy discourses is thus a key element to promote European democracy, essentially by giving civil society a cross-border voice.

Most of the time, policy discussion in Europe, e.g. on energy policy, are not divided into *a* French position (e.g. nuclear energy) and *a* German position (e.g. renewable energy) or *a* Polish position (e.g. carbon). But many French citizens are in favour of renewable energy, some German energy companies would love to return to nuclear energy and many SMEs in Poland are engaged in windmills, but cross-border coalition building of civil society can hardly articulate appropriately in the political decision-making process. So the Rubicon question for the current political deadlock of European integration is if the EU can ever evolve into a system of fully fledged horizontal democracy, allowing its politicization and where transnational coalition building among European citizens could happen in a policy system that confronts legislative vs executive body and if so how? And could it be a way to overcome the rising populism in Europe? Or to what extent does one need to consider Ludwig Wittgenstein's word that the border of one's language is the border of one's world?

## The sketch-out of a *different* Europe and modern problems of democracy

The current problem of European democracy and the current populism going against a technocratic Europe refers obviously to the difficult task of thinking and creating a common European public and media sphere, which is however critical for every political community. Europe, more precisely the eurozone, thus struggles currently with a dysfunctional democracy and a variety of institutional, cultural and other backdrops. Hence, is Europe alone with this – or is Europe, the EU, just a particularly bad place to cope with a variety of meta-trends, which put democracy under strain on a global scale?

Assessing the EU's current sub-optimal institutional set-up might be only a first step in searching for the many reasons for anti-euro-populism. Modern democracy comes with many challenges and is currently under strain in other parts of the world too. Academic research about the very meaning of modern democracy – and the threats to it – has increased in recent years, discussing the principles of participatory democracy, its features of evaluation and scrutiny, and the problem of lacking efficiency (Keane, 2009). Furthermore, a huge amount of literature has been produced pointing to the problem of 'post-democracy' (Crouch, 2009; Habermas, 2011b) which is that, although participatory democracy in a formal structure is still alive, policy options, especially towards more social policies, seem reduced (Progressive Centre, 2012). In the words of Pierre Rosanvallon, we distinguish today 'between democracy as a regime of popular sovereignty and democracy as a society of equals' (Rosanvallon, 2013: 83) and thus have shifted to an only formal understanding of democracy, acknowledging ever less that democracy relies on 'a social body' (Rosanvallon, 2013: 48). Very roughly summarized data suggest that the poor no longer not vote, just because they no longer believe that their vote is changing policy for the better (Bühlmann *et al.*, 2008). Democracy is thus hollowed out or, in the words of Colin Crouch: 'You can always vote but you have no choice.' This is largely true for the EU where, for example, in April 2012, political force was mobilized to avoid a referendum in Greece because of the fear that voters could go against the austerity policy of the Troika (Habermas 2011a).

In essence, democracy is submitted today – in Europe and elsewhere – to various societal or other aspects, which may request a substantial change of the (institutional) reference frame for democracy. Five of them can be mentioned quickly (this chapter is not the place to go deeper into them):

- *Democracy and efficiency*: the efficiency axiom makes democracy appear inefficient and slow and renders democracy less efficient than non-democratic regimes. Democracy, in times of globalization, is thus globally under social strain, whereas it increases, on the surface, in its functional form as a regime of popular sovereignty (Neyer, 2013);
- *The impact of digitalization and the internet on representative democracy*: ('political economy of the internet') (Engemann, 2003): the internet may erode representative democracy (for better or worse) and we haven't figured out the long-term implications for the organizational mode of modern democracies (Engemann, 2003; Morozov, 2011);
- *Democracy and the social crisis:* the return of huge income spread in Western countries and societies is measured all over the place and the lasting negative impact on (or actually the threat to) the functioning of democracy is not yet known (Rosanvallon, 2013; Stiglitz, 2011; Wüllenweber, 2012). This discussion is related to the research on the role of capital in the twentieth century (Piketty, 2014);
- *Democracy and demography*: the structural 'disempowerment of youth' by demographic trends (especially in Germany) avoids change and leads to wrong policy choices (e.g. retirement instead of infrastructure spending) (Gründiger, 2014);
- *Democracy and robotics technology*: how to organize democracy in societies where – soon to come – some 60–80 per cent of citizens will no longer need to work, as innovation has replaced their work by machines, as innovation studies tend to predict.

As much of the latent and open populism in Europe and the broader malaise of societies can possibly be put on the account of one or more of these mega-trends – rather than exclusively on the deficiency of the EU's institutional system – the question is how the debate on European democracy could be opened up to integrate these meta-trend issues, rather than being stuck in an institutional reform discussion, which often does not touch upon the real underlying problem of modern democracy. In this context, a desirable development for the European democracy discussion at large would not only open up the horizon – and the questions – for discussion but also reflect on how Europe, a fundamentally reformed and transformed EU in the sense of a European *res publica* – could eventually become a solution to these problems, rather than being perceived as *the* problem.

## The idea of *Res Publica Europaea* and European democracy

The idea to organize the European Union based on the principle of a *Res Publica Europaea* rather than on the idea of a Union of Nation States is not new, but it is gaining momentum both in the academic and in the political debate. The core idea is to shift the EU from a concept of a United States of Europe to a European Republic. The central argument for this is to acknowledge that 'as long as nation states are given the authority about the process of integration' (Beck, 2012: 33), any federal structure cannot work. The European Council and its role in the system is de facto the biggest hurdle to deeper political integration.

The first academic work on Europe as a European Republic was launched by Stefan Collignon (Collignon, 2002), establishing the idea that Euroland needs to be considered as an aggregated economy, rather than designing economic policies in which the member states of the EU need to compete – on taxes, social welfare, export or labour law – against each other and pointing to the structural advantages of a sole eurozone economy. This political economy approach has been enriched by juridical studies about the legal dimension – and possibilities – to design the EU based on the principle of a European Republic and *res publica* in the midst of the constitutional convention of the EU. In a legal sense, as Armin von Bogdandy pointed out (Bogdandy, 2005), the notion of republic as used in the middle ages is a legal concept of cross national exercise of sovereign powers – exactly what the eurozone would need today. The quintessential problem of the eurozone governance today is that the principle of solidarity is still attached to the notion of sovereignty and thus national border (Guérot, 2013b). In other words: tax payers' money from one country can – for the time being – not be used for fiscal support (e.g. the rescue of banks) of other countries, without violating the principle of '*no taxation without representation*' (Kadelbach, 2006). All current discussions about Greek bailout packages, the ESM or the current OMT decision of the ECB, are determined by this legal 'no-go' argument. Even the more so in Germany, where the constitutional barriers set by the constitutional court in Karlsruhe are utmost present in public debate to a degree that have made them unimpeachable (Kundani, 2014). All current problems of banking union or the ongoing bailout discussions root within this single deadlock towards whatever system of debt mutualization: liability and accountability do not correspond within the eurozone. This logic is reflected in each OMT decision of Karlsruhe, from making the ECB a 'last lender of resort' on to creating a joint monetary and a fiscal backstop and finally including the newly agreed Single Resolution Fund (SRF) at the European Council meeting in March 2014.[15] The euro-zone lacks fully fledged horizontal democracy and division of power, thus a *common* use of the principle 'no taxation without representation', applied to the eurozone perceived as *one* aggregated economy and thus *one* democracy.

In more recent times, the concept of Europe as Republic has also gained momentum in political sciences, looking at the European integration process through the lens of democratic theory and concepts of liberal, communitarian or deliberative democracy theories (Thiel, 2012).

The discourse is about a new assessment of the legitimacy of European governance and the emergence of a political 'we' in Europe, which could be constitutive of a new form of European democracy. The hurdles to that 'we' and a collective identity as basis for democracy in the sense of reciprocal structure of problem solving are complex, and so is the discussion about the possible (or not) politicization of Europe.[16] Again, libraries have been filled with literature about the need of a homogenous society, different cultural traditions (and history) producing different ideas of what democracy is all about – or what its key features are, e.g. the importance of the role of a constitutional court, or even the importance of industrial fabrics of a country, which shape a country's socio-economic distribution pattern and the administrative procedure and structure which go with it (Habermas, 1999).

After all, statuary bodies dating from the early German nation state making in the nineteenth century, like the German '*Anstalt des öffentlichen Rechts*' – including local or regional banks – structure the economic life. They currently impact on the way a European banking union can be organized and which banks have to go under European authority. Democracy is thus much more than institutions or a polity; it is rather based on country-to-country specific principles, e.g. how social distribution is organized and processed and thus goes beyond an exclusive legal or juridical logic. Democracy is more about social bodies than about formal participation (Rosanvallon, 2013: 33).

The sheer idea that Europe could unite on one universal model for democracy being accepted as valid by all European citizens seems not in view. The European constitutional process failed in 2005 due to negative referenda in the Netherlands and in France and rendered the idea of an emerging European constitutional patriotism obsolete for the time being, with political discourses being rather re-nationalized post-crisis. To organize the transnational making of collectively shared opinions in Europe through a process of deliberated democracy seems not in reach and language is a big factor, when it comes to the often complained lack of the missing European public sphere.

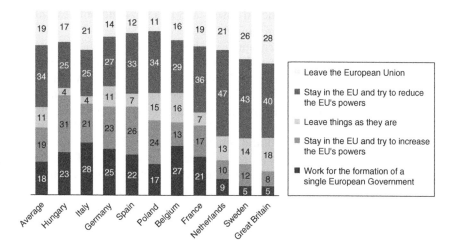

*Figure 7.1* The future of the EU – by country

European citizens do live in a dysfunctional democratic setting with the euro being an 'orphan currency' and resistance against this sub-optimal institutional structure is growing. However, there is still an aggregated (small) majority (exit UK, Netherlands and Sweden) of European citizens who either want to move towards a European federation, pledge for more integration or want at least Europe to stay on the current level of integration. In short, measured on a transnational level, European citizens are more or less split with respect to their common political future, with neither a large majority ready to give up on Europe nor a majority to move it any further (Figure 7.1):

The herewith-expressed 'catch-22' and the fracture of opinion in all EU countries could not be more tangible and perhaps, if a move towards a Europe as *res publica* or fully fledged democracy cannot be perceived, the real question is how long citizens in the various member states will accept such a legitimacy gap before they put their national governments under political and social strain fuelling populism – or whether the instable equilibrium of the current European institutions can last, provided that the social situation improves, especially in the South. With output legitimacy of the Euro-governance system coming back, input-legitimacy might be less required again soon.

Obviously, there are no easy answers on how the EU can pass the *Rubicon*, or as others have called it, the EU's 'Hamiltonian moment' (McCormick, 2012; *The Economist*, 2012), and how to move towards a 'citizens' Europe' and to overcome the nation state, especially the concept of national budgetary sovereignty for this, it would be sufficient to come to an individual, rather than collective understanding of sovereignty. The basis for sovereignty transfer would be citizens, not people (Somek, 2007). It would, indeed, require a new form of '*constitutante*' to constitute or forge this political entity called the

European Republic, e.g. a European wide referendum, where the result of the voting is not counted on a national basis – and this legal and political quantum leap is not likely to happen any time soon.

However, the political momentum for such ideas is growing. German president Joachim Gauck in his speech used the very words of a European *res publica* and also did not mention the United States of Europe.[17] A little later, a Manifesto for a European Republic was published in German first, but soon translated into several European languages (Menasse and Guérot, 2013). The legal concept of a European *res publica* was deepened in another article (Bogdandy and Guérot, 2013) and, finally, in January 2014, the European Movement Italy sent an open letter to Prime Minster Letta in favour of a European Republic. So the formula tallies, envisaging systemic rupture by default at some point and preparing for a European redesign.

In a nutshell, the concept of a European *res publica* for the eurozone could be based on the following features:

* *In a legal or institutional perspective*: a fully fledged parliamentarian system with a two-chamber structure, in which the European Parliament's full rights of initiative and legitimacy are 'combined' (Pernice, 2013) with the national parliaments, thereby overcoming the immanent power of the Council and shifting the system to a horizontal democracy with distinct division of power between the legislative and the executive body (Kadelbach, 2006). Legislative period and budgetary cycles would be connected, with accountability and liability thus on the same level. This new designed European parliament would have full budgetary sovereignty about the fiscal capacity of the EU, which would render joint monetary and fiscal backstops possible without the current legitimacy problems.
* *In an economic and social perspective*, the fiscal capacity of the eurozone would be increased and *common* automatic stabilizers such as a common unemployment assurance would be created. In social and tax matters, a *level-playing field* of rules would be established guaranteeing the same corporate taxes throughout Europe without race-to-the-bottom policies varying from member state to member state. The eurozone dimension would be enforced so as to guarantee the same rights and social access for all European citizens, including the portability of social benefits with respect to health or retirement, independently from the home country. Such a Euro-democracy would also require the right to tax and the right to borrow.

This would increase labour mobility while also avoiding cheap labour migration and abuse of one member state against another (Faist, 2013). Thus Europe would be more social. The idea of a European *res publica* is based on the idea that real wealth, income and competitiveness discrepancies within Europe are not essentially following national borders but are rather organized along a centre-periphery model, on the one hand, and a rural-urban structure on the other. Fiscal transfer would not be negotiated and bargained in a state-to-state setting – between *a* 'wealthy' Germany and *a* 'poor' Greece or Italy – at the Council level, but between growing regions and structurally weak regions – the latter being often rural areas in the periphery of the eurozone. Acknowledging that these two features unfold across national borders could lead to distinctly different policy mechanisms in economic policies of the EU Commissions and its tools, with respect to distribution and incentive schemes. The regional component of the EU's institutional set-up would be accentuated, which would also correspond to the tangible regional dynamics of today's Europe, hence not in a separatist way. Rather than focusing on regaining competitiveness for a *single* country, regardless of geographical and other possible structural shortcomings such as population density for instance, policies would be sensitive to distinguish between growing regions and structurally weak regions in Europe. Policies would then be adopted in accordance with such regional features: e.g. Greece will not become an export champion in engineering, but nor is Northern Brandenburg. This would also allow Europe to cluster industrial potential and to work on European champions in specific industrial segments, e.g. cyber, renewable energy, etc., rather than trying to re-industrialize rural regions as today. However, the mental pre-condition would be to step out of European policy discourses focused on creditor and debtor nations (Soros, 2013) or export-competition schemes, and to rather consider Euroland as an aggregated economy in which wealth would be distributed evenly through a newly designed market-state relationship including a *social contract* for the whole eurozone, which does not stop at national borders. It would mean to realize the symbiotic and highly intertwined relationship the European economies do already have, whereas – due to the trade imbalances – the aggregated wealth is very unevenly distributed (EuObserver, 2013; European Commission, 2014). In 2012, a McKinsey study found that the aggregated gain for the eurozone over the past ten years was around €300 billion, out of which one half went to Germany, a quarter to (Northern) Italy and only the remaining quarter to the other EU countries. It is not a surprise that Euroland is under social strain when gains and burdens have not been shared and even less evenly distributed because of both a dysfunctional state-market and capital-labour relationship within the eurozone. Here again, the lack of an executive body and of a strong common parliamentarian body flawed the democratic structure of the eurozone and guaranteed that no distributional structure in a transnational format could be put in place. The concept of a *Res Publica Europea*, the common management and common share of the public European good, trespassing national borders, would be the ultimate remedy to this situation.

## Core ideas for further political development of the eurozone

There is an idea for seizing the current crisis in Europe as an opportunity for reforms and positive change. The following will lay down what can be regarded a 'utopia for a democratic and social Europe' – 'utopia' referring to the classical understanding by Thomas More,[18] as a political lead idea which cannot be realized, but which serves as an unaltered concept, nonetheless striving to realize the biggest possible parts in the classical sense of political cybernetics. This utopia is a reality yet-to-be and an idea that mainly considers the eurozone its subject – a factor in making it a realistic one.

Such a eurozone will have a joint fiscal capacity, a eurozone budget way beyond the existing structure and cohesion fund on which transfers are based presently. Fiscal redistribution would work through a European unemployment insurance, which will simultaneously function as an automatic stabilizing instrument. The current European Stabilizing Mechanism (ESM) hence would be an embryo for the future European finance ministry, whose decisions would be deliberatively complemented by a eurozone parliament, equipped with legislative right of initiative and full budget privilege. Such a eurozone parliament will itself be connected to national parliaments in creative and innovative (yet to be defined) ways, raising its legitimacy through interconnected and entangled consultations and feedback structures between national and European levels.

This way, democracy within the eurozone would be strengthened: a strong European legislative body would be completed by at least the skeleton of a European executive body. This would mean developing European democracy towards a division of powers as envisioned by Montesquieu.

In turn, the current President of the Euro Group could become the future European Treasury, a real European Minister of Finance. Now, these ideas may seem adventurous but given the recent initiatives of the German *Glienicker Gruppe* (2013) and the French *Groupe Eiffel* (2014) as well as papers from both the French and German finance ministries,[19] the argument of a French-German engine for political change within Europe and the eurozone is still a sound one and may even be more powerful than ever.

Changing the institutional set-up within the eurozone as described would further have the advantage of overcoming the cumbersome term 'eurozone *governance*' and its technocratic approach during the crisis into something closer to European *government*. The eurozone governance of the past years was essentially nothing short of 'ownership of the many but responsibly of nobody' which is strikingly apparent in view of the Euro-Plus pacts, 'two pack', 'six pack' and the fiscal pact on top: the European Council cannot be voted out of office. Thus, euro-*governance* intrinsically conceptualizes democracy without opposition as well as irreversible decision making without democratic legitimacy. European policies therefore lack the possibility for corrections, which usually go hand in hand with parliamentary systems. The suggested changes aim to overcome these deficits of the political system of the eurozone.

The shell sketched out here arranges European democracy *horizontally* (European legislative vs European executive bodies), rather than *vertically*. Debating vertically arranged institutions and structures for Europe is outdated and misleading: asking which parliament(s) (the European parliament or any national parliament) should be given more rights entirely disregards the costs of playing the European parliament *against* national parliaments – legislation would become even more difficult. Connecting the European Parliament with national institutions of democratic representation in a horizontal manner vaccinates all against conflicts of interests.

Another important element of the utopia for a democratic and social Europe is the banking union, including a European bank resolution mechanism (SRM) where a European authority would have the final decision competency based on a joint European bank safeguarding fund. The March 2014 EU Council took still hesitant but visible steps towards this direction.[20] The eurozone would unilaterally become responsible for its banks and would re-capitalize them transnationally; the vicious circle of state and bank debts would finally be overcome. With such an entirely supranational European bank resolution mechanism, Euroland would finally have an executive or authority that transnationally decides on and implements European bank resolutions, similar to the decisions taken in the US in 2009. Market speculations would succumb. The Euro-System – respectively Euro-democracy – could in further steps raise a Euro tax, such a financial transaction tax that has been partially already been put in place, as additional income.

Lastly, the Commission might be divided into ministries, as a politicized European Union – or at least a politicized eurozone in the sense of a fully fledged parliamentarian democracy as sketched out above – could not combine the function of a neutral competition agency with more political functions, depending on – or being accountable to – majorities of a eurozone parliament. This might pave the way to a reduction of Commissioners, which would be another breakthrough in the principle of a nation state based system. For quite some time, the Commission has no longer been behaving like a 'Guardian of the Treaties', but rather like a company Board, where the President is balancing interests. As a body, in recent times also the Commission has been succumbing to a trend of re-nationalization. The Commission could be decomposed e.g. into a foreign ministry, emerging from the External Action Service, a trade ministry, a cyber ministry, an energy ministry, etc., and thus should also be reduced to the policy fields in which the EU/eurozone needs to be presented united on the international scene.

## What a two-tier Europe could look like

Much has been written on a two-tier Europe, considering that the eurozone definitely needs a different speed of political and fiscal integration. Literature usually distinguishes between the eurozone as a core circle, surrounded by 'pre-ins' (countries with the ambition, but also the legal obligation to join the euro, such as most prominently Poland, but all other EU countries with the exception of the UK and Denmark) as a second circle; and then a third circle composed of accession candidates (Balkan countries, Turkey or even Ukraine). It would obviously be important to tie the 'pre-ins' into the deeper political and fiscal integration process of the euro right from the beginning, e.g. by offering a legally binding frame to join the eurozone within a clear time horizon, so as to associate them e.g. to the contractual agreements or the European semester process.

The use of the common institution could obviously become a problem in a two-tier scenario and doubling of the institutions is certainly not an option. All legal solutions are obviously tricky and would probably need some bypassing of the existing treaties, at least in the beginning. But the recent euro-crisis management, which has hollowed out the community method and circumvented the existing treaties, has already broken the treaty paradigm. Yet, the eurozone members could agree on deeper integration within the current institutional set-up, e.g. on creating a different fiscal capacity, sub-voting mechanisms within the EP on a eurozone level or a eurozone tax, managed by the ESM, finding temporary solutions which would then be opened up to all. If the eurozone parliament should start off as a sub-entity of voting of the current EP (rather than a newly created body) and if the ESM – as spelled out in the Franco-German paper of May 2013 – takes over a large amount of the economic and fiscal policy coordination and programming imposed by the euro – and also parts of the new economic policy integration, e.g. in the field of labour policy – all other EU institutions would remain largely unaffected. The decomposition of the Commission would not impact on the 'pre-ins'. The moment they join the euro, they would acquire voting rights in the sub-entity of the eurozone parliament in a 'crossed legitimacy' with their national parliaments.

However – or hopefully – what would essentially change is the reform energy needed to overcome the current gridlock. The eurozone members would no longer make their political integration dependent on a vote of the EU 28: this would probably trigger a different energy. With the eurozone successfully able to overcome its systemic flaws pushing for deeper fiscal, budgetary and political integration, chances are high that the eurozone turns over time into an attractive magnet, capable of pulling the 'pre-ins' successively in. If Poland joined in a foreseeable future, this would mean critical mass for a couple of other countries in the North (Denmark) and East (Czech Republic) to join the eurozone and to participate in the by then created mechanism of deeper integration: Eurozone parliament and fully fledged democracy based on a new eurozone bi-cameralism, fiscal capacity, euro-tax, etc.

Most likely the countries remaining outside for an unforeseeable future would be the UK, due to its legal opt-out first but also to a very problematic political discussion about Europe and the lack of appetite to join the euro; Hungary, for a problematic domestic situation too; and, finally, Bulgaria, Rumania and Croatia, which are substantially less developed in economic terms than most of the EU 28 countries. As long as the EU finds an appropriate mechanism to bind these countries to the euro-core, it could still be a satisfying perspective for these countries to be members of a second tier of a powerful and reinvigorated euro-core rather than being one out of twenty-eight countries in an institutional catch-22 and in the progress of rapid systemic disintegration anyway. The same would apply to the third circle, where the flexibility of these countries to decide first, whether they want to join the EU/eurozone and thus become a 'pre-in' of the Euro-core; or stay in a loser relationship based mainly on trade on foreign policy ties, could even be bigger.

The real question seems to be whether such a European reform process can be envisaged on purpose and by choice or whether the historical process is rather 'by default', meaning that the current EU polity system will at some point suffocate from its own complexity (or be victim of European populism) and only then leave the place to a *different* Europe, a Europe of a *Res Publica Europaea*.

## Notes

1 This chapter was written with the precious and indispensable help of Victoria Kupsch, who took care of research, footnotes and the cleaning-up of the language.
2 See European Constitutional Group (1993) and Action Committee for European Democracy (2007).
3 See debate regarding the prospects of European (Integration) Studies: Diez (1996) and the response of Börzel (1996).
4 See Schwarz (2012) and the related discussion on the 'Krönungstheorie' (coronation theory).
5 Speech of Chancellor Angela Merkel in Bruges on 3 November, 2011.
6 Speech by Mario Draghi at the Global Investment Conference in London on 26 July, 2012. Verbatim available from European Central Bank at https://www.ecb.europa.eu/press/key/date/2012/html/sp120726.en.html.
7 In Germany, most prominently by Streeck (2013) and Schwarzer and Wolff (2013).
8 In this sense, the article does not aim to deliver a fully academic or theoretical contribution.
9 AfD Party Program for the Elections of the European Parliament, Ch. 5 'Courage for Germany!' as agreed on 22 March, 2014. https://www.alternativefuer.de/wp-content/uploads/2014/03/Europaprogramm-der-AfD.pdf (in German).
10 Speech by President of the parliamentary group of SYRIZA-USF, Alexis Tsipras. 'Europe is on the edge' in London on 15 March, 2013. http://www.syn.gr/gr/keimeno.php?id=31419.

It is widely accepted that the strategy of European Elites and the Greek government cannot provide a viable prospect of exit from the crisis. The only thing that austerity has accomplished is to plunge Europe into economic depression and to throw Greece in an unprecedented humanitarian crisis. Austerity is leading the Greek economy and society down a catastrophic path.

11 One of the very few transnational examples is the right to water campaign of a conglomerate of national citizens' initiatives: http://www.right2water.eu/.
12 For more details see this study about Lobbying in the EU: http://corporateeurope.org/sites/default/files/attachments/financial_lobby_report.pdf.
13 See Competence Catalogues of Dutch and British governments.
14 BVerfG Karlsruhe (Constitutional Court) in Lisbon: http://www.bundesverfassungsgericht.de/entscheidungen/es20090630_2bve000208.html.

15  European Council, Conclusions. 21 March, 2014. Available at http://www.consil-ium.europa.eu/uedocs/cms_data/docs/pressdata/en/ec/141749.pdf.
16  Out of the many publications: Meyer (2004).
17  J. Gauck, Speech on the prospects for the European idea, February 2013. Available at http://www.bundespraesident.de/SharedDocs/Reden/EN/JoachimGauck/Reden/2013/130222-Europe.html;jsessionid=6D36AA095CD36559E9DEB306A4F3 E644.2_cid379?nn=1891680.
18  Thomas More, Utopia. Book II. Available through Jon Roland of the Constitution Society http://www.constitution.org/tm/utop2.pdf.
19  See for instance 'Un budget pour la zone euro', www.tresor.economie.gouv.fr/8197_tresor-eco-n-120-un-budget-pour-la-zone-euro.
20  EU-Council Conclusions, March 2014, p. 16ff. http://www.consilium.europa.eu/uedocs/cms_data/docs/pressdata/en/ec/141749.pdf.

## References

Action Committee for European Democracy (2007). 'A New Treaty and Supplementary Protocols.' *Explanatory Memorandum*, 4–06–2007.

Anderson, B. (1991). *Imagined Communities: Reflections on the Origin and Spread of Nationalism*. London: Verso Edition.

Auer, S. (2013). 'The End of the European Dream.' *Eurozine*, 22 February. http://www.eurozine.com/articles/2013-02-22-auer-en.html.

Beck, U. (2012). *Das deutsche Europa*. Berlin: Suhrkamp Verlag.

Bogdandy von, A. (1999). 'Supranationaler Föderalismus als Wirklichkeit und Idee einer neuen Herrschaftsform.' *Zur Gestalt der Europäischen Union nach Amsterdam*. Baden-Baden, 30 (1), pp. 65–92.

Bogdandy von, A. (2005). 'Die Europäische Republik.' *APuZ*, 36, pp. 21–27.

Bogdandy von, A. and Guérot, U. (2013). 'Eine neue Leitidee – die europäische Republik.' *Frankfurter Allgemeine Zeitung*, 219, 20 September. http://www.faz.net/aktuell/politik/staat-und-recht/europaeische-union-und-deutschland-eine-neue-leitidee-die-europaeische-republik-12581462.html.

Börzel, T. A. (1996). 'Zur (Ir-)Relevanz der "Postmoderne" für die Integrationsforschung Eine Replik auf Thomas Diez' Beitrag "Postmoderne und europäische Integration" Zeitschrift für Internationale Beziehungen.' *Heft*, 2 (S).

Bühlmann, M., Merkel, W., Weßels, B. and Müller, L. (2008). 'The Quality of Democracy. Democracy Barometer for Established Democracies.' *Zürich: National Centre of Competence in Research Democracy of the Swiss National Science Foundation*, Working Paper 10a.

Collignon, S. (2002). *The European Republic*. London: Bartelsman Foundation.

Crouch, C. (2009). *Post-Democracy*. Cambridge: Polity Press.

Diez, T. (1996). 'Postmoderne und europäische Integration Die Dominanz des Staatsmodells, die Verantwortung gegenüber dem Anderen und die Konstruktion eines alternativen Horizonts Zeitschrift für Internationale Beziehungen.' *Heft*, 2 (S), pp. 255–281.

Engemann, C. (2003). 'Electronic Government. Vom User zum Bürger. Zur kritischen Theories des Internets.' *Bielefeld*.

EuObserver (2013). 'Germany to Face EU Trade Surplus Probe.' 13 November. http://euobserver.com/news/122093.

European Commission (2014). 'Exportstärke ist gut, Binnenkonjunktur zu schwach.' 6 March. http://ec.europa.eu/deutschland/press/pr_releases/12152_de.htm.

European Constitutional Group (1993). *A Proposal for a European Constitution.* London.

Faist, T. (2013). 'Soziale Ungleichheiten durch soziale Sicherung in Europa.' *Leviathan*, 41 (4), pp. 574–598.

Fieschi, C., Morris, M. and Caballero, L. (2013) (eds.). *Populist Fantasies: European Revolts in Context.* UK: Counterpoint.

Geppert, D. (2013). *Ein Europa das es nicht gibt- die fatale Sprengkraft des Euro.* Berlin: Europa Verlag.

Glienicker Gruppe (2013). 'Aufbruch in die Euro-Union.' *Zeit Online*, October. http://www.glienickergruppe.eu/.

Grabow, K. and Hartleb, F. (2013). 'Europa- nein danke? Studie zum Aufstieg recht- und nationalpopulistischer Parteien in Europa. Konrad Adenauer Stiftung e.V., Sankt Augustin.' http://www.kas.de/wf/doc/kas_36200–544–1-30.pdf.

Grimm Dieter, D. (1995). 'Braucht Europa eine Verfassung?' *Juristenzeitung*, 50 (12), pp. 581–591.

Groupe Eiffel (2014). 'Pour une communauté politique de l'Euro.' February, http://www.groupe-eiffel.eu/.

Gründiger, W. (2014). 'Renten für die Babyboomer.' *ZEIT Online*, 7 April. http://www.zeit.de/politik/deutschland/2014–04/rente-mit-63-teuer-unsozial

Guérot, U. (2012). 'Is Europe the New Babel? The Role of Language in Building a Transnational Democracy.' Lecture at the New York University, 18 May, 2012.

Guérot, U. (2013a). 'Europa zwischen Demokratie und Legitimationsdefizit.' *ApuZ*, 6–7 February. http://www.bpb.de/apuz/154376/zur-zukunft-der-europaeischen-demokratie?p=all.

Guérot, U. (2013b). 'Zwischen Haushalts- und Legitimationsdefizit: Zur Zukunft der europäischen Demokratie.' *APuZ*, 6–7, pp. 3–10.

Habermas, J. (1999). 'The European Nation State and the Pressure of Globalization.' *New Left Review*, 235, pp. 46–59.

Habermas, J. (2011a). 'Rettet die Würde der Demokratie.' *Frankfurter Allgemeine Zeitung*, 4 November.

Habermas, J. (2011b). 'Europe's Post-democratic Era.' *Guardian,* 10 November.

Habermas, J. (2011c). *Zur Verfassunge Europas.* Berlin: Suhrkamp Verlag.

Heisbourg, F. (2013). *La fin du rêve européen.* Paris: Stock.

Hix, S. and Hoyland. B. (1999 and 2011). *The Political System of the European Union.* London: Palgrave.

Jachtenfuchs, M. (1996). 'Conceptualizing European Governance.' In Jørgensen, K. E. (ed.), *Reflective Approaches to European Governance.* London: Macmillan, pp. 39–50.

Jachtenfuchs, M. (2010). 'Der Wandel des regulativen Mehrebenensystems in der EU.' *Der moderne Staat*, 3 (1), pp. 109–124.

Kadelbach, S. (2006). 'Vorrang und Verfassung: Das Recht der Europäischen Union im innerstaatlichen Bereich.' In Gaitanides, C., Kadelbach, S. and Rodriguez, G. C. (eds.) *Europa und seine Verfassung.* Baden-Baden: Nomos, pp. 219–234.

Keane, J. (2009). *Death and Life of Democracy.* London: Simon and Schuster.

Kundani, H. (2014). 'Even Germany's Intellectual Elite is Falling Out of Love with the EU.' *The World Today*, 70 (3).

Maurer, A. (2013). 'The Costs of Power'. *FAZ*, 20 October. http://www.faz.net/aktuell/politik/die-gegenwart/europa-der-preis-der-staerke-12625868.html (in German).

McCormick, D. (2012). 'Europe Needs its Own Fiscal Union Moment.' *Financial Times*, 20 June. http://www.ft.com/cms/s/0/40c037ea-baf3-11e1-b445-00144feabdc0.html.

Menasse, R. (2012). *Der Europäische Landbote*. München: Carl Hanser Verlag,
Menasse, R. and Guérot, U. (2013) 'Es lebe die europäische Republik!' *Frankfurter Allgemeine Zeitung*, 28 March. http://www.faz.net/aktuell/wirtschaft/eurokrise/zukunft-europas-es-lebe-die-europaeische-republik-12126084.html.
Meyer, T. (2004). *Die Identität Europas*. Frankfurt am Main: Suhrkamp.
Morozov, E. (2011). 'The Net Delusion: How Not to Liberate the World.' *The Guardian*, 9 January.
Nell-Breunig van, O. (1980). *Gerechtigkeit und Freiheit. Grundzüge katholischer Soziallehre*. München: Europa Verlag.
Neyer, J. (2013). 'Gobale Demokratie.' *Nomos*.
Nikolaidis, K. (2013). 'European Demoicracy and its Crisis.' *JCMS*, 51 (2). http://www.sant.ox.ac.uk/people/knicolaidis/00NicolaidisJCMS-2013Demoicracy.pdf.
Offe, C. (2013). 'Two-and-a-half Theories. Post-democracy in the Age of Global Financial Markets.' *Eurozine*, first published in German in *Transit*, 44 (109).
Pernice, I. (2013). 'The Autonomy of the EU Legal Order – Fifty Years After Van Gend.' *Walter Hallstein-Institut*, WHI-Paper 08/2013.
Piketty, T. (2014). *Capital in the 20th Century*. Harvard: Harvard University Press.
Piris, J. C. (2013). *The Future of Europe: Towards a Two-Speed EU?* Cambridge: Cambridge University Press.
Pisany-Ferry, J. (2008). 'Une Monnai orpheline.' *Le Monde*, 27 May. http://www.lemonde.fr/idees/article/2008/05/27/la-monnaie-orpheline-par-jean-pisani-ferry_1050264_3232.html.
Priester, K. (2014). 'Governance in Europa: Auf dem Weg in die Postdemokratie?' *Blätter*, 4 (14), pp. 99–110.
Progressive Centre (2012) *Why Social Democratic Parties Can No Longer Cater to their Electorate?* London, July.
Risse-Kappen, T. (2008). 'Exploring the Nature of the Beast: International Relations Theory and Comparative Policy Analysis Meet the European Union.' *Journal of Common Market Studies*, 34 (1), pp. 53–80.
Rosanvallon, P. (2013). *The Society of Equals*. Harvard: Harvard University Press.
Scharpf, F. W. (2002). Regieren im europäischen Mehrebenensystem – Ansätze zu einer Theorie. *Leviathan*.
Schmitt, C. (1923). *Soziologie des Souveränitätsbegriffs und politische Theologie, Hauptprobleme der Soziologie (Hg) Melchior Palyi*. München und Leipzig: Erinnerungsgabe für Max Weber.
Schwarz, H. P. (2012). *Helmut Kohl. Eine politische Biografie*. Munich: DVA.
Schwarzer, D. and Wolff, G. B. (2013). 'Memo to Merkel: Post-election Germany and Europe.' *Bruegel Policy Brief*, 2013/05. http://www.bruegel.org/publications/publication-detail/publication/794-memo-to-merkel-post-election-germany-and-europe/.
Somek, A. (2007). 'Kelsem Lives'. *European Journal of International Law*, 3 pp. 409–451.
Soros, G. (2013). 'How to Save the European Union from the Euro Crisis.' Speech delivered at the Center for Financial Studies, Goethe University in Frankfurt, Germany. 9 April. http://www.georgesoros.com/interviews-speeches/entry/how_to_save_the_european_union_from_the_euro_crisis/.
Soros, G. and. Schmitz, G. P. (2014). *The Tragedy of the European Union: Why Germany Has to Save the Euro in Order to Save Itself*. Munich: DVA.

Stiglitz, J. (2011) *The Price of Inequality: How Today's Divided Society Endangers Our Future*. New York: Norton and Company.

Streeck, W. (2013). *Gekaufte Zeit*. Berlin: Suhrkamp Verlag.

The Economist (2012). 'The Future of the EU (2). Don't Count on a Hamilitonian Moment.' 28 May.

Thiel, T. (2012). *Republikanismus und die Europäische Union. Eine Neubestimmung des Diskurses um die Legitimität europäischen Regierens*. Baden-Baden: Nomos.

Tsoukala, P. (2013). 'Euro Zone Crisis Management and the New Social Europe.' *Columbia Journal of European Law*, 20, pp. 31–76.

Veron, N. (2012). 'The Challenges of Europe's Fourfold Union.' *Bruegel Policy Contribution*, 2012/13. http://www.bruegel.org/publications/publication-detail/publication/741-the-challenges-of-europes-fourfold-union/.

Wallace, H. and Wallace, W. (eds.) (1996). *Policy Making in the European Union*. Oxford: Oxford University Press.

Wüllenweber, W. (2012). *Die Asozialen. Wie Ober- und Unterschicht unser Land ruinieren- und wir davon profitieren*. München: DVA.

# Part III

# Policy issues

# 8 Analysis and measurement of the state of integration and supranational prospects in the EU[1]

*Tibor Palánkai*

## Global economy and integration

The world economy has undergone fundamental changes in about the past 50 years; the main force behind these changes has been international integration. New circumstances have arisen for national economies, and their development and operation are now determined by global conditions. The analysis of these new trends should serve as the foundation of any contemporary global political economy.

In the past decades dozens of regional integration organisations have appeared, ranging from free trade areas to economic unions. With only a few exceptions (e.g. North Korea or Cuba) all the ca. 200 countries of the world participate in at least one such organisation or agreement. At the same time, integration has taken increasingly global dimensions. While the process of global integration is structured by regional integrations, the global and regional integrations build on each other. Not only are they in mutual interaction, but they also counterbalance one another. The global and regional integrations together represent international integration. Consequently, international integration can be defined as a new quality of international cooperation which creates new frameworks and structures of organisation and the functioning of the economy.

A distinction should be made between globalisation and global integration. The former is a long and complex process, while the latter is only one but important dimension of globalisation. Global integration is a phenomenon only of recent decades.

> Economic globalization constitutes integration of national economies into the international economy through trade, direct investment (by corporations and multinationals), short-term capital flows, international flow of workers and humanity generally, and flows of technology.
>
> (Bhagwati, 2004: 3)

Global integration is basically market integration, but its impacts and contexts are related to all sectors of social life.

Globalization is defined in what follows as integration of economic activities, via markets. The driving forces are technological and policy changes – falling costs of transport and communication and greater reliance on market forces. The economic globalization discussed here has cultural, social and political consequences (and preconditions).

(Wolf, 2005: 19)

By many standards, then economic integration had become a hallmark of globalization, deliberately promoted by governments, corporations, and international organizations alike.

(Lechner and Boli, 2005: 158)

Global integration entails fundamental changes in the character and structure of the international division of labour and cooperation.

The world economy experienced a profound realignment: the exchange of manufactures for raw materials that had underpinned the modern phase of globalization was replaced by a pattern of integration based on inter-industry trade. The geographical ties established in the nineteenth century became relatively less important; links between advanced economies, notably the triad of United States, Europe and Japan, became stronger. The new economy gave increasing prominence to trans-national corporations in general, and to finance, and commercial and information services in particular.

(Hopkins, 2002: 7–8)

A general semantic interpretation of integration itself presents no special difficulties. Expressed in the most general terms, integration is a process of unification, the merging of parts into a whole, becoming a unit, fitting together, melting into one another, linking up. It can be understood as the cooperation of parts, the harmonisation of their operation, their reciprocal influence and their becoming interconnected. According to F. Perroux, 'integration is the uniting of two or more economic units into a certain whole' (Perroux, 1954: 419). Integration in the general sense is the adaptation and interweaving of parts into a larger whole (Predöhl and Jürgensen, 1961: 371).

Many believe that the concept of integration as unification or merging is superficial and represents a quantitative approach. From a qualitative perspective, integration means the creation of more developed, efficient and high-quality organisations. This is considered as the organic concept of integration.

In the development of mankind, the process of the organisation of its activities into communities has had a decisive role; this has formed the basis for what we call 'social development'. These communities can be of a biological, ethnical, economic, political or security-based character. In a general term, I define integration as an organic process of community building, which is an important dimension of human history. According to this concept, the basic actors and starting points of any integration process are the individuals who are organised into different types of social organisms, and their metabolism is always decisive from the point of view of the operation, growth and welfare of the society and economy.

Integration is in this respect a historical process, which cannot be limited to its present global and regional dimensions. Integration is a historical tendency accompanying mankind, all the way from primitive families or tribes through empires up to the globally integrated societies of the present.

Industrial societies were accompanied with the *emergence of modern nation states*, which played an important role in the organisation of society and economy, and from the beginning they fulfilled fundamental political and authoritative functions. In our age, we experience the emergence and rapid growth of globally operating production organisations (TNCs), while the sovereignty of nation states is partially and gradually transferred onto regional and global (sometimes local) integration institutions. The latter ones constitute the basic regulatory frameworks of integration processes.

International integration is a multi-level process. Concerning international integration, I made a distinction between micro- and macro-integration as early as the 1970s.

> We conceive micro-integration as a unification process among the individual producers in forms of international production, trade, technological and development co-operations or common production units. The macro-integration emerges among the spheres of national economy and society. The two are closely related. The integration of masses of individual producers leads finally to the gradual integration of national economies, which we can define as interconnection of social reproduction processes. On the other hand, the macro-integration creates market and economic policy frameworks for the process of micro-integration (economic union).
>
> (Palánkai, 1976: 254)

The main bearers of micro-integration are the transnational networks, while macro-integration is organised into different global and regional institutions.

Integration is implemented in different stages. The most general distinction that can be made is between market and policy integration. The former is primarily conceived as the opening and unification of national markets, which is then followed by different forms of integrated economic policies.

The difference between the removal of 'artificial barriers' (liberalisation) and the integration of economic policies is expressed by Jan Tinbergen through the introduction of the concept of negative and positive integration.

> It appears useful to make a distinction between negative and positive integration. By the former we mean measures consisting of the abolition of a number of impediments to the proper operation of an integrated area. By the latter we mean the creation of new institutions and their instruments or modification of existing instruments.
>
> (Tinbergen, 1965: 76)

Thus, 'negative' integration is simply liberalisation, whereas 'positive integration' is institution building: partly the development of new institutions and mechanisms, and partly the modification of existing mechanisms. The approach of Willem Mole is similar.

> We make a basic distinction between integration of markets and of policy. The former relates to the taking away of barriers to movement of products and production factors between member states, the latter to setting up of common policies for the union.
>
> (Molle, 1994: 7)

International integration is a democratic process. It is the voluntary and free political and economic unification of sovereign nation states. It has nothing to do with former colonial 'integrations' that were based on aggressive conquests and subordinations.

Despite the 'novelty' of integration theory, it must be remembered that the idea of the European Union and within this, for example, a 'United States of Europe', was by no means anything new. From the sixteenth century onwards, the idea of uniting Europe, and efforts that aimed at this, had occupied the minds of many of the continent's great thinkers (Erasmus of Rotterdam, Jan Amos Comenius, William Penn, François-Marie Voltaire, Charles-Louis de Secondat Montesquieu and Immanuel Kant), and kept on reappearing among the main thinkers and statesmen throughout the next centuries, as they saw it as a way of avoiding war among European nations.

After two world wars the question of a European union arose with renewed force, and in contrast to earlier periods the integration initiatives of the leading European politicians (Winston Churchill, Jean Monnet, Robert Schuman, Konrad Adenauer and Alcide De Gasperi) did not merely attract attention but began to achieve practical results from the 1950s (with the creation of the ECSC, the Council of Europe and, more importantly, the European Communities). The question necessarily arises why previous attempts at uniting Europe had failed, while it seems to have evolved rather successfully after the Second World War. The answer is simple. The explanation is the emergence of international integration. Accordingly, the unification of Europe could become from the dreams and visions of great thinkers and statesmen a reality. The coherent theoretical basis and the directions of integration, and within it, European integration, thus gradually took shape.

## Possibilities of the measurement of integration

Beyond the theoretical definitions, the measurement of integration processes is equally important. Measurement of the state and process of integration (where we stand and where should we go) helps theoretical clarification and can provide guidance for practical actions. Measurement can happen in every dimension, which can extend the horizons of a theoretical analysis, and can also provide opportunities for policy resolutions.

1. When defining and measuring the content of integration we will concentrate here on real integration processes. The question is based on two schools of theory of integration: the theory of the division of labour and the theory of interdependence. According to these, integration is a new quality of international cooperation, meaning highly intensive, durable and complex relations which bring the participants into interdependence. This level of cooperation already calls for institutional and regulatory frameworks. Intensity and interdependence can be measured, therefore, both as a state and a process.

Interdependence can be defined as a new quality of international relations, whereby, as a result of the expansion of cooperation, the status of countries changes significantly toward one another, and at a certain point their policies and actions become mutually dependent. The question remains, however, what this critical point might be. What is the level of intensity when simple relations acquire a new quality and lead to an interdependence among nations? In order to answer this question a minimum dependency threshold needs to be set, beyond which it can be said that economic relations place countries in an interdependent position. This threshold is assumed to be somewhere around 10 per cent which means that if the proportion of foreign trade of a country in its GDP goes above that level, then, the given country has become dependent on foreign trade. In a similar vein, if for example the share of one oil supplier is more than 10 per cent of the oil import of a country, then that country is dependent on the given source. This threshold has been used as an indicator of dependence in cases of energy policy decisions of the International Energy Agency and the EC/EU. In transnational companies a more than 10 per cent share of external activities is assumed.

Theorising about interdependence started as early as the 1950s and 1960s, but in international relations interdependence became a core concept only during the 1970s[2] (Keohane and Nye, 1977). Interdependence and integration are often considered as synonyms, or at least as very close concepts.

2. Concerning the basic forms of integration, the list of Bela Balassa (1961) is still a reference point. Accordingly, he distinguishes the free trade area, the customs union, the common market and the economic and political union, which represent certain stages of integration (which are not necessarily hierarchical). The single market is not listed, but this is nothing else than the common market in its full and complete implementation. The parameters of each form are clearly set, and their progress can be easily measured.

3. In case of regulation and governance, the major concerns are their scope, competence, efficiency and democratic character. A number of studies have ventured into the analysis of the extension, intensity and efficiency of regulation. Efforts were also made to quantify them (such as applied forms and their extension; norms and prescriptions; their application and compliance with them; the extension of free trade, institutions and their competences; policy

harmonisation and coordination and their depth; the fields of common policies and their efficiency, etc.).

4. Undoubtedly, from the viewpoint of the analysis of the costs and benefits of integration, the customs union theories still serve as basic starting points. With the help of 'classical' customs union theories (e.g. trade creation and division, extension and contraction), these can be quantified with relatively simple equations in terms of efficiency and welfare. One of the advantages is that based on the calculation of tariff equivalences the analysis can be extended to the impacts of other trade obstacles (non-tariff barriers). The same applies to monetary union with the 'tariffication' of the conversion costs or exchange risks. For example, the 'trade creation' impacts of monetary union can be calculated accordingly. However, one of the limits of the theory is that the comparative advantages of integration are identified in a static approach, while it is clear that the gains are more substantial.

Later on the emphasis shifted to 'dynamic' customs union theories, which extended their analysis onto scale economy, impacts of intensification of competition and technical progress (innovations). It became clear that upon this basis the possible gains from integration were much greater, while their calculation got more complicated. According to dynamic theories, the impacts of integration condense into a more rapid or slower economic growth.

The present analysis attempts to define and measure only the content and institutional-regulatory processes of integration, while the measurement of the costs and benefits either on the regional or on the global levels goes beyond this study.

There have been several attempts to measure the extent and the state of global integration. World economic processes have been measured with various indices. The most popular ones include the Competitiveness, the Corruption, the Global Confidence or Connectedness (UNIDO) indices, just to name a few. Among them, the Globalisation Indices (A. T. Kearney/Foreign Policy, KOF, MGI, Ernst & Young, etc.) should be particularly mentioned; these aim at ranking the different countries of the world according to their progress in global integration.

In order to measure global and regional integration, we propose and introduce the concept of the integration profile, which is an extended method for analysing integration processes. Several indicators have been used to draw an integration profile; these are similar to those applied in the case of globalisation indices. The fields that are covered are more narrow, however, as only economic aspects are concentrated on. At the same time, the profile of the analysis is extended in certain directions. Apart from relations and their intensity, the structural, performance, dependence, equilibrium and convergence aspects are taken into account as well, which help to go beyond the quantitative characteristics, and therefore provide an indication of the quality and indirectly of the efficiency of integration process.

The creation of an integration profile gives us a picture that is composed of several mosaics. Needless to say, by putting the mosaics together, a final – complex and coherent – picture emerges. The main parameters and dimensions of the profile analysis can be summarised in the following:

1  Real-economic integration (integratedness);
2  Institutional and regulatory integration;
3  Comparative performances;
4  Convergence and divergence.

The present chapter analyses only the first two dimensions; performance and convergence matters are outside the scope of the research.

Real-economic integration (integratedness):

- Trade integration: flows, stocks, intensities;
- Structure of trade relations;
- Sub-regional concentration and interconnectedness;
- Intra-sector trade, place in value chains;
- Factor integration: flows, stocks, intensities;
- State and characteristics of financial integration;
- Transnationalisation of company sectors.

Institutional and regulatory integration:

- Participation in global institutional and policy structures, and regulatory processes;
- Compliance with EU institutions and policies (acquis communautaire).

Concerning integratedness, the chapter will try to give an overall picture of global integration processes, and EU integration will be summarised in a score board based on six parameters. In regulatory terms, this will be an attempt to summarise the present state of EU integration. Although this is a limited analysis, it will try to summarise some of the basic patterns of present-day international integration.

In order to measure trade and capital integration intensity, the following simple parameters are used:

1  Share of export and import to GDP, which can be related to total or intra-regional trade. The former indicates the intensity of global integration (integratedness), while the latter demonstrates the intensity of regional trade integration. The indices, besides intensities, also indicate openness and dependencies. The higher the indices, the greater is a country's openness and its dependence on external factors and processes.
2  Share of regional trade to total. This measures regional trade intensity, but at the same time conclusions can be drawn on the role of external relations. It can indicate regional concentration and the interconnectedness of relations.

*Table 8.1* Scaling of the level of intensity (dependence) of cooperation

| 0 | | 10% | | 25% | | 40% | | 60% | | 100 |
|---|---|---|---|---|---|---|---|---|---|---|
| I | No | I | Low | I | Medium | I | High | I | Very High | I |

3   The export and import of capital (Cx and Cm) shows the dynamics of integration, and their share in the GDP at a given moment is an indicator of the intensity of integration.
4   The relations of capital export and capital import are also important from the point of view of the level of development and balancedness.

In any given country, a high level of foreign investments can express a high intensity of global or regional integration. However, if its capital export is minimal or is lacking, it indicates unilateral dependences and an asymmetry in its integration. In highly developed countries, these indicators are balanced; most of them are net capital exporters.

When the intensity of cooperation is analysed in terms of trade and GDP relations, we propose five different categories (clusters) (Table 8.1).

Any trade share in GDP below 10 per cent can be considered as the indication of no external dependence, a structurally closed economy, and a lack of intensity. Low intensity is considered here between 10 and 25 per cent, medium intensity between 25 and 40 per cent, high intensity between 40 and 60 per cent, with very high intensity (dependence and openness) above 60 per cent. These ranges can be disputed, but in accordance with the literature, we accept 10 per cent as a minimum dependency threshold, and 40 per cent as a threshold of high dependence. The scaling is relative, in absolute terms, as 30 per cent of the share of trade in GDP is already a sign of high openness and dependence. This analysis can be carried out for goods or goods and services, for export and import, and for internal export. As export reflects competitiveness, export data is preferred. A similar, but slightly modified scaling is used for capital relation intensities.

## Some characteristics and patterns of international integration

Following the war, the emergence of integration meant a return to the intensification of relations, and the growth of international trade was 1.5–2.0 times higher than that of world production (see Table 8.2). The crisis years somewhat broke that trend, but in most cases the slowing down was proportional rather than diverging.

In the long run, rapid internationalisation created a new situation and qualitatively new dependences. In fact, what it has meant has been an emergence of growing interdependence that can be called integration. In the 1950s, the relation of world trade (export and import) to the aggregate world GDP was around 5–6 per cent. In recent times this share has increased to

*Table 8.2* Relations of growth of world trade and production

|  | *1870–1900* | *1901–1913* | *1914–1950* | *1951–1973* | *1974–1999* | *2000–2007* | *2008–2012* |
|---|---|---|---|---|---|---|---|
| World production | 2.9 | 2.5 | 2.0 | 4.8 | 2.9 | 4.3 | 2.5 |
| World trade | 3.8 | 4.3 | 0.6 | 7.6 | 7.0 | 5.5 | 2.9 |
| Proportion of the two | 1: 1.4 | 1: 1.7 | 1: 0.3 | 1: 1.7 | 1: 2.4 | 1: 1.3 | 1: 1.2 |

Source: Simai (2007: 240); UNCTAD (2013).
2000–2007:http://www.zanran.com/q/Volume_of_world_merchandise_trade_by_selected_region

around 20 per cent. This can be taken as an indicator of the emergence of a state of global interdependence that has developed in the last 50 years, and which has brought the actors of the world economy into a qualitatively new situation.

> Around 20 percent of world output is traded and a much larger proportion is potentially subject to international competition: trade has now reached unprecedented levels, both absolutely and proportionate to world output. Trade is key mechanism for moving goods, and increasing services, around the globe, and it is also central to technology transfer. At the very least it connects domestic markets to international markets, while historically opening up national markets to trade has often had radical effects in unleashing new competitive forces and transforming domestic economies.
>
> (Held *et al.*, 2005: 149)

In the last decades, the EU has developed into a state of high level of real-integration, which means a high intensity of relations, interconnectedness and interdependences.

In the last couple of decades, the trade of the EC/EU (both total and internal) has expanded rapidly, and the growth of the total export of goods and services was around twice more rapid than that of the GDP (see Table 8.3). In the past 50 years, the economy of the member states has strongly internationalised and integrated.

Due to these processes, the intensity of integration increased substantially (from about 8 per cent to nearly 25 per cent in terms of the internal trade share in GDP); structural openness, particularly for some smaller countries, reached a particularly high level.

As far as mutual trade is considered, the member countries passed the threshold of interdependence by the 1970s, and 40 years later, by the 2000s, the integratedness of the EU countries more than doubled. It is remarkable how the position of large economies (USA, Japan or China) has changed.

Transnational corporations (TNCs) are one of the most important actors of globalisation.

*Table 8.3*  Development of external trade in GDP, 1960–2008 (in % of GDP)

|  | 1960 | 1970 | 1980 | 1990 | 2000 | 2004 | 2008 |
|---|---|---|---|---|---|---|---|
| Total export (EU15) | 19.6 | 21.8 | 27.2 | 28.1 | 37.4 | 36.9 | 42.0 |
| Total import (EU15) | 19.2 | 21.4 | 28.6 | 27.5 | 36.9 | 35.4 | 41.2 |
| Internal export | 7.7 | 9.9 | 13.2 | 14.4 | 20.3 | 19.8 | 21.5 |
| Internal import | 7.9 | 11.0 | 13.2 | 14.6 | 21.8 | 22.2 | 22.3 |
| USA – total export | 5.2 | 5.8 | 10 | 9.6 | 11 | 10 | 13 |
| Japan – total export | 10.7 | 10.6 | 13.4 | 10.3 | 10.9 | 13.2 | 17.7 |
| China – total export | – | 2.6 | 10.6 | 16.1 | 23.3 | 34 | 35 |
| Developed c. export* | 8 | 18 | 23 | – | – | – | – |

Source: European Commission (2001); Eurostat (2009, 2010).
* The data are for developed countries in the years of 1950–1973–1985 (Held *et al.*, 2005: 171).

The international capital flows and the development of world economy is led by transnational companies. The international division of labour is more and more the internal affair of these company giants and substantial part of international trade is conducted between transnational companies, their mother and daughter companies.

(Mikroszkóp, Ecostat, 2005)

No doubt that the multinationals count. They represent the channel, through which the globalisation is realised.

(*The Economist*, 22 November, 1997: 108)

The global enterprises represent a complex system where the cooperating small- and medium-sized enterprises (SMEs), the banks and other service institutions also play an important role. In some sense, it is probably more appropriate to speak about transnational company structures or networks.

Today, the globalization of production is organized in large measure by MNCs. Their pre-eminence in world output, trade, investment and technology transfer is unprecedented. Even when MNCs have a clear national base, their interest is in global profitability above all. MNCs have grown from national firms to global concerns using international investment to exploit their competitive advantages. Increasingly, however, they are using joint ventures and strategic alliances to develop and exploit their advantages or share the costs of technological innovation. But the growing globalization of production is not limited to MNC activity, for over the last three decades there has been a significant growth in producer-driven and buyer-driven global production and distribution networks. The globalization of business is thus no longer confined to the MNC but also embraces SMEs.

(Held *et al.*, 2005: 282)

According to the UNCTAD analysis, these networks have been more and more institutionalised, and have taken legal and organised forms.

> While there has been a significant expansion of transnational production in the last three decades it has also become more institutionalized, as strategic alliances, subcontracting, joint ventures and other forms of contractual arrangements regularize inter-firm networks and arrangements.
>
> (Held *et al.*, 2005: 274)

The extension and intensity of relations have grown especially remarkably in the financial spheres.

Transnational networking can be analysed with the development of global value chains (GVCs). These

> consist of trade in intermediate goods and services that are incorporated at various stages in production process of goods and services for final consumption. The fragmentation of production processes and the international dispersion of tasks and activities within them have led to emergence of borderless production systems – which may have be sequential chains or complex networks, and which may be global, regional or span only two countries. These systems are commonly referred to as global value chains (GVCs).
>
> (UNCTAD, 2013: 122)

These global chains account for 28 per cent of world trade; however, this proportion is 38 per cent in the case of the EU (UNCTAD, 2013: 127), which is the highest percentage in comparison to any other region of the world economy. This indicates a very high level of global integration among the EU's economies.

The greatest weakness and deficiency of global integration lies in the underdevelopment of its institutional and regulatory frameworks. Undoubtedly, globalisation calls for an efficient regulation and democratic control. The appropriate legal and institutional frameworks for the normal functioning of markets are lacking, as well as a stable functioning of democracy. The main deficit is the weakness of the global dimensions of multi-level governance. Globalisation has not lessened the importance of governance; more rather, governance has taken on new dimensions. Beyond the national framework, these could be partly supplemented by regional institutional regulations.

Debates concerning the reform of the policies of the IMF, the World Bank and other international organisations have been going on for many years. The efficiency and democracy deficit in these respects is extremely serious. Nevertheless, with regard to the latter, there have been some promising developments at the level of civil society.

## Some general features of the structure and pattern of EU integration

The 28 EU members cannot be considered as a monolithic and uniform group. In fact, their diversity has further increased as a result of several waves of enlargements. Based on their sub-regional characteristics (supported by a later analysis), the 27 (28) members can be placed into different groups. As far as the Western European members are concerned, a distinction between Northwestern (Austria, Belgium, Netherlands, Luxembourg, Germany and Ireland) and Southwestern Europe (France, Italy and the UK) is easily justified based on certain parameters of performance and connectedness. Under certain parameters, the UK can be placed into either group. Ireland has been on the Western periphery of Europe, but at least in terms of per capita GDP it overtook several developed partners. In a more strictly defined Northern Europe, the Scandinavian EU (Denmark, Sweden and Finland) should be distinguished. These three groups constitute the Northern Centre of the Union.

Although the Southern EU members joined the EU as early as the 1980s, the two new Mediterranean members (Cyprus and Malta) are also considered here as part of the Southern EU.

The new Eastern members can be placed into three groups. There are clear differences between Central Europe (the Czech Republic, Hungary, Poland, Slovakia, Slovenia and Croatia) and the Eastern Balkans (Bulgaria and Romania). The latter group also claims a Central European status for itself, but on the basis of historical and cultural traditions (Catholic–Protestant versus Orthodox–Islamic), the distinction remains justifiable (although Romania is a special case). On the basis of their very different characteristics, the Baltic EU (Estonia, Latvia and Lithuania) can also be distinguished.

Although our focus here is on Central Europe, the above countries should be referred to as 'East-Central Europe', and based on historical, geographical and economic factors and ties, the Western extension of this sub-region should not be neglected. West-Central Europe is defined here as being composed of Austria, Germany and Italy. In a narrower sense, only Southern Germany (Bavaria or Baden-Württemberg) and North Italy (Venice or Lombardy) belong to this region (parts of the former Habsburg Empire), but the separation would be too complicated. Historically, Germany often defines itself as Central Europe (Mittel-Europa).

In the following, an attempt will be made to draw a synthetic real-integration profile of the EU. Six parameters have been chosen for a synthetic evaluation and measurement of the real-integration performance of EU members:

I   Place in KOF Index.
II   Intensity of trade integration.
III   Sub-regional interconnectedness.
IV   Intensity of capital relations (capital import in GDP).

*Table 8.4* Globalisation indices (ranking of selected countries)

| Country** | KOF (187)* | KOF. Economic (147) | MGI (117) | Kearney (62) | E&Y (60) |
|---|---|---|---|---|---|
| | 2012 | 2012 | 2008 | 2006 | 2011 |
| Belgium | 1 | 5 | 2 | – | 4 |
| Ireland | 2 | 3 | 4 | 4 | 3 |
| Netherlands | 3 | 6 | 5 | 7 | 6 |
| Austria | 4 | 14 | 3 | 9 | 19 |
| Singapore | 5 | 1 | – | 1 | 1 |
| Sweden | 6 | 8 | 9 | 10 | 7 |
| Denmark | 7 | 13 | 13 | 5 | 8 |
| Hungary | 8 | 7 | 10 | 20 | 9 |
| Portugal | 9 | 17 | 18 | 24 | 28 |
| Switzerland | 10 | 25 | 1 | 2 | 5 |
| Czech Republic | 13 | 12 | 7 | 16 | 18 |
| UK | 14 | 26 | 6 | 12 | 10 |
| Spain | 16 | 24 | 12 | 25 | 20 |
| Finland | 17 | 18 | 21 | 13 | 13 |
| France | 18 | 45 | 8 | 23 | 14 |
| Slovakia | 19 | 16 | 17 | 26 | – |
| Germany | 22 | 44 | 11 | 18 | 11 |
| Greece | 23 | 39 | 24 | 32 | 35 |
| Italy | 24 | 37 | 20 | 27 | 29 |
| Poland | 25 | 40 | 29 | 33 | 27 |
| Estonia | 26 | 11 | 27 | – | – |
| Slovenia | 28 | 27 | 32 | 17 | 12 |
| Romania | 34 | 51 | 34 | 30 | 31 |
| USA | 35 | 79 | 22 | 3 | 25 |
| Bulgaria | 38 | 38 | 30 | – | 22 |
| Turkey | 41 | 89 | 50 | 57 | 46 |
| Russia | 47 | 98 | 98 | 47 | 48 |
| South Africa | 53 | 64 | 44 | 49 | 52 |
| Japan | 55 | 120 | 45 | 28 | 43 |
| China | 73 | 107 | 57 | 51 | 44 |
| Brazil | 74 | 100 | 81 | 52 | 45 |
| India | 110 | 129 | 66 | 61 | 54 |

Source: Dreher *et al.* (2010); Ernst &Young (2012).

* Brackets: number of countries in the survey.

** In columns: the ranking of the country is indicated in the different indices. The full lists are not provided here.

  V  Balancedness of capital relations (capital import to capital export).
 VI  Structural convergence.

Needless to say, the analysis can be extended to other parameters as well (e.g. transnationalisation of company sectors), but probably these would not modify the picture substantially. Only the performances have been graded, and no rankings have been provided (see below). Performance is summarised on a one to five scale. A higher score indicates a higher level of integration.

## I.    Place in KOF Index

Among the Globalisation Indices (A. T. Kearney/Foreign Policy, KOF, MGI, Ernst &Young, etc.), the KOF Swiss Economic Institute Globalisation Index is considered as one of the most quoted and sophisticated of them all. The index follows the globalisation process of different countries from 2002 onwards, but it is calculated retrospectively from 1970.

The Index operates with 24 variables and it is extended to 187 countries of the world. The variables cover three main fields; they try to measure the economic, social and political aspects of globalisation processes. The Economic Globalisation Index in 2013 was prepared for 150 countries.

In the general index of 2012, all the EU countries were among the first 40 countries (see Table 8.4); only Latvia was ranked at the 44th place, as last among the EU members. The following scaling is proposed regarding a country's place in the KOF Index: 5: 1–20; 4: 21–40; 3: 41–60; 2: 61–80.

## II.    Intensity of trade integration

The intensity of the trade integration of EU members shows large differences.

The synthetic table was compiled on the basis of the trade date in percentage of GDP. For the synthetic scoring the following five-scale ranking was used:

5: <60%; 4: 40–59%; 3: 25–39%; 2: 11–24%; 1: >10%.

In terms of goods trade (export), Slovakia (73.5 per cent) and Belgium (73.4 per cent) are very high intensity countries, with Hungary (68.3 per cent) and the Czech Republic (66.5 per cent) following closely behind. Out of all the other countries, only the Netherlands is above 60 per cent. At the other extreme, Cyprus and Greece, with their ca. 8 per cent, are characterised by a lack of intensity. Nearly a dozen countries are in the medium intensity group (Austria, Bulgaria, Denmark, Germany, Finland, Ireland, Luxembourg, Malta, Poland and Sweden), and most of the larger countries (France, Italy, Spain, Romania or the UK) fall into the low intensity group. We tried to make certain corrections by taking the size of the countries into account, but none of the methods were justifiable.

If we look at the export of goods and services, the picture changes somewhat (see Table 8.5). The services trade gives around 12–15 per cent of the GDP. The Belgian ceiling of trade intensity in relation to goods was 73 per cent, which, coupled with services, increases to 91 per cent; nevertheless, this is still far from the record 168 per cent of Luxembourg. Bulgaria, the Czech Republic, Estonia, Hungary, Ireland, Malta and Slovenia (with Lithuania on the periphery) are also members of the very high intensity group. A particularly big jump (i.e. across two groups) is made by Luxembourg, Ireland,

*Table 8.5* Share of trade of goods and services in GDP in the EU (2008 in %)

| Country | Export of goods | Export of goods and services | Import of goods | Import of goods and services | Internal export in total | Internal export in GDP |
|---|---|---|---|---|---|---|
| Western European core countries | | | | | | |
| Belgium | 73.4 | 91.0 | 76.5 | 92.9 | 75.9 | 69.1 |
| Netherlands | 60.7 | 72.7 | 54.3 | 64.8 | 78.9 | 57.3 |
| Germany | 40.7 | 47.4 | 33.6 | 41.4 | 63.3 | 30.0 |
| Ireland | 43.9 | 81.2 | 31.1 | 71.3 | 62.8 | 50.0 |
| France | 20.9 | 26.5 | 24.0 | 28.9 | 63.9 | 17.0 |
| Italy | 23.6 | 28.9 | 23.6 | 29.4 | 58.9 | 17.0 |
| Luxembourg | 39.7 | 167.9 | 51.4 | 126.8 | 88.9 | 147.0 |
| Austria | 45.1 | 60.2 | 45.2 | 55.5 | 67.5 | 40.7 |
| UK | 17.4 | 28.1 | 23.8 | 31.4 | 57.0 | 16.0 |
| Scandinavian EU | | | | | | |
| Denmark | 33.6 | 54.7 | 34.0 | 52.3 | 69.8 | 23.5 |
| Finland | 35.5 | 46.0 | 32.3 | 42.0 | 55.9 | 19.8 |
| Sweden | 38.5 | 53.5 | 34.7 | 46.1 | 60.1 | 23.1 |
| Southern EU | | | | | | |
| Greece | 8.2 | 22.2 | 26.3 | 33.3 | 62.5 | 13.9 |
| Spain | 17.7 | 26.6 | 25.7 | 32.2 | 69.6 | 18.1 |
| Cyprus | 7.7 | 49.8 | 42.3 | 62.1 | 69.3 | 34.5 |
| Malta | 36.1 | 80.2 | 57.0 | 83.9 | 46.8 | 37.5 |
| Portugal | 23.0 | 33.8 | 35.8 | 42.6 | 74.4 | 25.1 |
| Baltic countries | | | | | | |
| Estonia | 53.8 | 76.1 | 65.7 | 80.4 | 70.1 | 53.3 |
| Latvia | 28.0 | 41.4 | 45.0 | 54.4 | 68.6 | 28.4 |
| Lithuania | 49.8 | 60.0 | 61.4 | 70.6 | 60.3 | 36.2 |
| Central Europe (East) | | | | | | |
| Hungary | 68.3 | 81.2 | 68.2 | 80.3 | 78.2 | 63.5 |
| Czech Rep. | 66.5 | 76.7 | 63.7 | 75.7 | 84.9 | 64.7 |
| Slovakia | 73.5 | 82.4 | 74.6 | 84.3 | 85.4 | 70.4 |
| Poland | 33.2 | 39.9 | 37.8 | 43.5 | 77.8 | 34.4 |
| Slovenia | 54.0 | 68.0 | 61.0 | 70.2 | 68.1 | 46.3 |
| East Balkans | | | | | | |
| Bulgaria | 44.8 | 70.5 | 70.4 | 83.7 | 60.0 | 42.3 |
| Romania | 24.5 | 30.9 | 37.9 | 43.7 | 70.5 | 21.7 |
| EU27 | | | | | 67.5 | |
| Japan | 38.0 | 48.0 | 18.8 | 28.6 | – | – |
| USA | 15.3 | 18.4 | 14.5 | 18.0 | – | – |

Source: Eurostat (2009).

Malta, Cyprus and Bulgaria. Most of the large countries do not change categories, but Austria, the Netherlands, Denmark, Lithuania, Latvia, Portugal and Romania fall into a higher group. In case of import, most of the countries remain in the same categories; only Cyprus, Greece and Malta (on account of services) are upgraded substantially.

What is important to note is that besides the highly developed small countries (Belgium, the Netherlands and Ireland) of the Core, the East Central European countries (Czech Republic, Hungary, Slovakia), as well as Bulgaria and Estonia, fall into the very high intensity group. Slovenia is not far from this category, either.

### III.   Sub-regional connectedness in EU integration

The strengthening of integration relations has meant an increase of the share of intra-trade among the member countries. The growth of cooperation, however, was not proportional, as the process was characterised with sub-regional concentrations, particularly among the neighbouring countries. This is a general characteristic of European integration, and the process was further strengthened by the various enlargements.

When measuring sub-regional concentrations or connectedness, we can depart from the proportions of external and internal trade. These proportions are roughly 65–35 per cent, as far as internal and external trade are concerned. A figure of 65 per cent has been chosen as the benchmark, above which there is high interconnectedness (with very high levels above 75 per cent). Between 45 and 65 per cent, interconnectedness is at a moderate level, while 10–45 per cent is an indication of a low level.

We also wish to introduce the notion of strategic partnership; that is, the proportion of another country is more than 10 per cent in a country's or region's trade. If these proportions are mutual, then, in spite of certain dependence asymmetries, we can speak about a relatively balanced interdependence.

In 1989, the proportion of the future associated Eastern partners in the trade of the EU was only around 2.7–2.8 per cent, which means that they were marginal partners. In parallel to their high individual trade shares and structural weaknesses, they had a unilateral dependence on the EU economy. Following a rapid increase of trade shares (from a third to two-thirds by the early 2000s), that dependence grew further, but the EU has also become 'dependent' on these countries in the process, as the share of the ten associated members in EU trade reached about 11–13 per cent. Therefore, from its originally marginal position, East-Central Europe has become a strategic partner of the EU, which had an impact on the enlargement process as well.

The EU internal trade is highly concentrated sub-regionally. The Western European EU members, besides the high intensity of their trade, are characterised by a high level of connectedness (which is above 65 per cent) as well. In the case of Belgium and Ireland, about 85–86 per cent of their intra-export goes to the sub-regional partners, but this proportion is close to 65 per cent in the case of the UK. About 75 per cent of the intra-trade takes place within the Western European core countries.

Inside the core, Germany is a central and strategic partner. On average, 23.2 per cent of the EU total trade is provided by Germany. The two extremes in this respect are Ireland with 11.4 per cent and Austria with 43.1 per cent of

*Table 8.6* Intensity of interconnectedness in internal export in the main sub-regions of the EU in 2009

| Region | Share export in total in % | Share of population in total in % | Interconnectedness quotient |
|---|---|---|---|
| EU 27s | 100 | 100 | 1 |
| Western Europe | 74.8 | 60.1 | 1.25 |
| Scand. EU | 6.0 | 5.0 | 1.20 |
| East-Cent. E. | 10.5 | 10.3 | 1.02 |
| Baltic c. | 0.7 | 0.8 | 0.93 |
| Southern EU | 6.6 | 13.8 | 0.47 |
| Latin EU* | 23.9 | 36.2 | 0.66 |

* FR, IT, ES, PT.

Source: Eurostat (2011).

the German share. In spite of the high German participation, the countries of the region are also strategic partners of Germany, as their share is above 10 per cent in the export trade of Germany. In terms of internal export, this is the case with France, Italy, the Netherlands and the UK, with Belgium and Austria close to this position. Consequently, despite the German preponderance, the core countries' relations are characterised by a balanced interdependence. Nevertheless, the distinction between North and Southwestern Europe needs to be once again emphasised, mostly because of their different positions in terms of trade balances.

The other main region that is highly connected with the Western European core is East-Central Europe (66–73 per cent). Only Slovakia differs, but its lower connectedness can be explained by its special relations with the Czech Republic. The share of Germany is striking (accounting for about one-third of trade); only Slovakia differs in this respect with its ca. 23 per cent. With its close to 15 per cent in German trade, the region serves as a strategic partner for Germany as well. In a similar vein, Central Europe is also a strategic partner for Austria (20 per cent) and Italy (11 per cent).

The intensity of interconnectedness can be measured by confronting the rates of trade and population, i.e. by comparing the share of the various sub-regions in internal trade and the total population (see Table 8.6). After filtering out the differences that arise from the size of the regions, the quotient of the two indicates the interconnectedness of the respective regions. However, differences arising from the levels of development do still remain.

The data reflect an interconnectedness minimally above average for East-Central Europe. If we take into account the differences in the levels of development, this interconnectedness can be considered as intensive, as compared to Western Europe and Scandinavia. The low interconnectedness of the Southern EU is striking. The picture does not change if we consider only the 'Latin' countries of the sub-region.

As the sub-regional trade relations indicate, the distance or the geographic proximity of the countries is a significant factor. This is further strengthened by traditions, historical ties or cultural or linguistic similarities.

The level of connectedness is influenced by several special bilateral relations, based on geographical or cultural proximity, or historical-political factors (the relations of successor states of former federations after 1990). These are demonstrated by a high degree of bilateral trade shares, which in some cases can reach 20–35 per cent. Such an example is the 36.5 per cent share of Greece in Cyprus' EU export, the 35.1 per cent share of Spain in the case of Portugal, the 26.3 per cent share of the UK in the case of Ireland, the 26.7 per cent share of France in the case of Spain, or the 15 per cent share of the Czech Republic in the case of Slovakia. In the Baltic region, there are especially high levels of bilateral connections between Finland and Estonia (26.3 per cent), Lithuania and Latvia (22.4 per cent) and Latvia and Estonia (20.1 per cent), the latter being an inheritance of the Soviet past.

### IV.   Intensity of capital relations ( capital import in GDP )

Factor market integration plays an important role from the points of view of the efficient allocation of resources and the exploitation of the benefits offered by integration. It is measured with labour and capital movements, with the inclusion of flows and stocks. The export and import of capital (Cx and Cm) indicates the dynamics of integration, and their share in the GDP at a given moment is an indicator of the intensity of integration (see Table 8.7).

In order to measure the intensity of capital relations, we propose the same scale as in the case of trade. The only difference is that the boundary between moderate and high intensity is 45 per cent, which is the EU average.

According to synthetic scoring, the countries are ranked on the basis of the following scale:

5: <60%; 4: 45–59%; 3: 30–44%; 2: 11–29%; 1: >10%.

About half of the EU countries are characterised by a very high (nine countries) or a high level of capital intensity (four countries), while only two countries (Italy and Greece) fall into the low intensity category. Germany is a special case, as it falls just within the 'border', and it is also the largest country of the union.

### V.   Balancedness of capital relations ( relation of capital import and capital export )

In any given country, a high level of foreign investments can express a high level of intensity of global or regional integration. However, if a country's capital export is minimal or is lacking, it indicates unilateral dependences and an asymmetry in its integration. In highly developed countries, these indicators

*Table 8.7* FDI in EU countries in 2009 and in 2011

| Country | Internal stock in 2009 ($bn) | Internal stock in 2009 in % of GDP | External stock in 2009 ($bn) | External stock in 2009 in % of GDP | External stock in % of internal stock in 2009 | Internal stock in 2011 in % of GDP |
|---|---|---|---|---|---|---|
| Western European countries | | | | | | |
| Belgium | 947 | 200 | 892 | 188 | 94 | 195 |
| Ireland | 248 | 111 | 289 | 130 | 117 | 116 |
| Netherlands | 644 | 81 | 953 | 120 | 149 | 68 |
| UK | 1 104 | 51 | 1 580 | 73 | 124 | 50 |
| Austria | 173 | 45 | 163 | 43 | 95 | 38 |
| France | 985 | 38 | 1 493 | 57 | 150 | 34 |
| Germany | 945 | 29 | 1 250 | 41 | 141 | 25 |
| Italy | 364 | 17 | 486 | 23 | 135 | 15 |
| Scandinavian EU | | | | | | |
| Sweden | 332 | 82 | 353 | 87 | 106 | 63 |
| Denmark | 154 | 50 | 198 | 64 | 128 | 44 |
| Finland | 85 | 36 | 130 | 54 | 150 | 32 |
| Southern EU | | | | | | |
| Portugal | 115 | 49 | 69 | 29 | 59 | 46 |
| Spain | 632 | 43 | 626 | 43 | 99 | 42 |
| Greece | 42 | 13 | 39 | 12 | 93 | 10 |
| East-Central Europe | | | | | | |
| Hungary | 100 | 78 | 20 | 16 | 21 | 60 |
| Czech Rep. | 126 | 64 | 15 | 8 | 12 | 58 |
| Slovakia | 53 | 60 | 3 | 4 | 7 | 53 |
| Poland | 185 | 43 | 29 | 7 | 16 | 38 |
| Slovenia | 15 | 31 | 9 | 19 | 60 | 31 |
| Estonia | 16 | 84 | 6 | 33 | 40 | 75 |
| Eastern Balkans | | | | | | |
| Bulgaria* | – | 63 | – | 1 | 1.5 | – |
| Romania* | – | 35 | – | 1 | 2 | – |
| EU27 | 7 598 | 46.6 | 8 888 | 54.5 | 118 | 42.8 |

\* Eurostat data.

Sources: OECD International Direct Investment Database, Eurostat, IMF. OECD/DAF –
INVESTMENT: DIVISION. October 2012.

are in a surplus, which means that on average the capital export exceeds capital import by 20–50 per cent. This can be considered as balanced, and this balance is on a high level of intensity in both dimensions. Although capital import has appeared in the new members, they are still far from the pattern of the developed countries, and there are still substantial differences among them.

## VI. *Structural convergence*

Structural convergence, which compares the commodity structures of internal export of the EU countries, is one of the most important parameters of an integration profile (see Table 8.8).

*Table 8.8*   Commodity structure of internal export of EU countries in 2010 (in %)

| Internal export | I. | II. | III. | IV. | V. | VI. |
|---|---|---|---|---|---|---|
| EU27 | 9.7 | 3.6 | 6.8 | 16.4 | 34.9 | 28.6 |
| Western Europe | | | | | | |
| Austria | 7.6 | 3.8 | 4.1 | 10.7 | 36.5 | 37.2 |
| Belgium | 10.0 | 3.0 | 8.8 | 30.3 | 21.1 | 26.7 |
| France | 15.8 | 3.5 | 3.8 | 18.7 | 35.5 | 22.6 |
| Germany | 6.9 | 2.7 | 2.8 | 16.6 | 42.4 | 28.6 |
| Italy | 9.2 | 1.7 | 3.7 | 12.4 | 33.4 | 39.6 |
| Scandinavian EU | | | | | | |
| Denmark | 20.4 | 3.9 | 12.9 | 13.2 | 21.1 | 28.3 |
| Finland | 2.2 | 6.6 | 11.6 | 9.1 | 23.9 | 46.7 |
| Sweden | 5.9 | 7.9 | 8.3 | 12.4 | 32.1 | 33.3 |
| Central Europe | | | | | | |
| Czech Republic | 4.0 | 3.4 | 4.3 | 5.8 | 53.9 | 28.6 |
| Poland | 10.6 | 2.7 | 4.5 | 7.6 | 40.8 | 33.8 |
| Hungary | 7.3 | 2.8 | 2.5 | 8.4 | 59.2 | 19.8 |
| Slovakia | 4.2 | 3.2 | 5.6 | 4.8 | 51.1 | 31.1 |
| Slovenia | 5.0 | 4.1 | 3.0 | 11.2 | 44.0 | 32.7 |
| Eastern Balkans | | | | | | |
| Bulgaria | 14.8 | 9.3 | 5.4 | 5.2 | 19.7 | 45.6 |
| Romania | 6.2 | 4.5 | 3.0 | 4.9 | 44.2 | 37.1 |
| Southern EU | | | | | | |
| Greece | 25.6 | 5.2 | 7.1 | 17.1 | 10.2 | 34.8 |
| Portugal | 10.4 | 5.9 | 3.8 | 8.5 | 27.9 | 43.5 |
| Spain | 16.2 | 3.5 | 3.5 | 13.5 | 36.1 | 27.3 |
| EU total export (in €m) | 245.405 | 92.494 | 172.243 | 414.866 | 883.958 | 686.588 |

Source: External and intra-EU trade, Annual statistical yearbook (Data 1958–2010).
SITC: 100.
I. 0–1 Food, drinks and tobacco
II. 2+4 Raw materials
III. 3 Energy
IV. 5–6–8 Chemicals and manufactured goods
V. 7 Machines and transport equipments
VI. 9 Other

The following section focuses on the differences among the EU member countries in terms of the structure of their internal EU trade (export).

The shares of manufacturing, and particularly that of machines and transport equipments, say a lot about the level of internal integration. Needless to say, the proportions are relative and, therefore, their comparison might be misleading. What is striking, however, is that compared to the average proportions of the Western Core (except Belgium), Central Europe is above that average, indicating that in the last decade the European manufacturing base has shifted to the region. With regard to the other manufacturing goods, they are also somewhat above average, and of course there are certain trade-offs between the two product groups (as in the case of Hungary).

While Spain is a little above the average in these sectors, the low level of the Southern EU is also striking. That is particularly the case with Greece, concerning machines and transport equipments (10 per cent). The Greek share of total internal manufacturing export (45 per cent) is almost half of that of Central Europe (Czech Republic and Slovakia: 82 per cent; Poland, Hungary and Slovenia: 77–79 per cent). As far as agricultural export is concerned, the Greek share is more than 25 per cent, while it is 11 per cent for Poland and 7 per cent for Hungary.

We can calculate synthetic score from the mathematical average of the six parameters. Thus, performance is summarized on a 1 to 5 scale. A higher score indicates a higher level of integration.

1   Extremely highly integrated countries: 5–4.01
    There are five small and developed core countries and two East-Central Europe countries in this group: BE, NL, LU, IE, AT, LU, HU and CZ.
2   Highly integrated countries: 4–3.01
    This group includes the large and developed (DE, FR, UK, IT) countries and the Scandinavian countries (FL, DK, SE), most of the Southern countries (PT, ES, CY), the Baltic countries (EE, LV), as well as Poland, Slovakia and Slovenia.
3   Moderately integrated countries: 3–2.01
    Greece, Malta, the two Eastern Balkan countries (BG and RO) and Lithuania belong to this group.
4   Low integrated countries: 2–1.01
5   No integration: 1 >

Although there are five formal groups, the countries can be placed into three of them. In some cases, the performance can be low or marginal (such as the trade integration of Cyprus or Greece), but the minimum moderate level of integration has been met by every single country.

In general, the EU is characterised by a high level of global and regional integration, which creates a unique position for the Union in the global economy. It should be noted that taking into account every parameter (and not just the KOF index but our analysis as well), Hungary and the Czech Republic, along with Benelux, Ireland and Austria, belong to the seven most highly integrated countries of the European Union.

## Some features of the regulatory integration of the EU

With its single market and economic and monetary union, the European Union is a unique regional integration organisation in the world economy. The basic forms, mechanisms and policies of integration are not uniformly and simultaneously introduced and applied by the member states. The past decades have increasingly demonstrated that EU integration corresponds to the notion of 'variable geometry' or 'multi-speed' Europe.

While basic market integration forms, including the single market, assume a relatively uniform and comprehensive implementation, the case is quite different in the case of an economic and monetary union. It was clear from the very beginning that the different countries were not equally prepared or mature, and the future stability and satisfactory operation of the project were already at stake. Furthermore, there were substantial differences in the interests among the countries. It is not surprising that so far the euro has been introduced only in 18 countries, while the inclusion of the other countries has been delayed by formal opting out agreements, or by different types of policy choices, which have placed their joining in the uncertain future. One typical case of staying out is the Schengen Agreement, but the same applies to some of the reform packages, particularly those which were created to improve the governance of the eurozone.

In the following, we will summarise the participation of different member countries in the main frameworks. While all the members participate in the single market, several countries have remained outside the Schengen Agreement. All the eurozone members participate in the euro reform projects (Euro Plus, Fiscal Compacts, Bank Union or ESM). The Euro Plus Pact has been joined by many non-eurozone countries as well, in fact, only four countries (UK, Sweden, Czech Republic and Hungary) have remained outside. Hungary, formally, was mainly against the company tax harmonisation. With regard to the Fiscal Compact and Bank Union, only the UK has rejected it, while the other non-eurozone countries either joined or conditioned their participation (Sweden, Czech Republic and Hungary, and concerning the Fiscal Compact Latvia and Lithuania).

When it comes to measuring institutional integration, quantified evaluation is not a possibility. Instead, the performance of the member countries is placed into three categories:

I   Very highly integrated countries;
II  Highly integrated countries; and
III Moderately integrated countries.

I. The 18 eurozone countries can be listed among the very highly integrated countries. These countries practically apply all of the policies and the legal and regulatory systems of the EU (acquis communautaire). The only exception is Ireland, but its staying out of Schengen can be explained by special geographical and political reasons. The 'very high' qualification of these countries is justified by the fact that these are the only countries which have a full single market and a single currency in the world economy.

II. Three countries can be placed into the highly integrated states (Denmark, Poland and Lithuania). They are not members of the eurozone, but they do take part in Schengen and participate in the monetary reforms. Poland is not a member of the ERM yet, but, along with Lithuania, they might become eurozone members in the foreseeable future. The relations of Denmark are very close to the eurozone membership.

III. Six members (United Kingdom, Sweden, Czech Republic, Hungary, Bulgaria and Romania) belong to the moderately integrated countries. Beyond the fact that they are not eurozone members, they do not participate in the ERM, and they stay out – either fully or partially – of the euro reform mechanisms. Bulgaria and Romania are still outside of Schengen and derogations are still in force against them. The future eurozone membership of these countries is uncertain, for which the reasons vary. The UK is definitely opting out, while in the case of the other countries either the political will is missing, or it is not yet clear when they will be able to meet the Maastricht conditions (e.g. Bulgaria and Romania).

It needs to be stressed that based on the levels and intensity of integration into the institutions and policies into EU structures, there is no member of the Union which can be classified as integrated at a lower than moderate level.

In sum, the EU is the most advanced regional integration in the present global economy. 1) It is the only integration organisation that has created a complex single internal market and 2) which has reached the level of a real economic union by creating a single currency (the 18 Eurozone members provide nearly 80 per cent of the EU's total GDP). 3) It has extended the principle of cohesion and solidarity to the level of the Union, and 4) it has gradually gained a *political identity* (become a 'polity'), and its institutional system has several elements of supranationality. The EU is a regional supranational integration model (democracy, environment, welfare state or integration). It is much more than a simple international organisation, but still much less than a classical federation.

Certain parallelisms can be observed between the high level of real-integratedness and institutional integration, which support the neo-functionalist notion of spill-over. Accordingly, the present level of institutional integration has strong economic bases, and any speculation about the collapse of the integration project (the eurozone disbanding) has no real foundation. At the present level of integratedness (the intensity of relations and the transnationalisation of company structures), the introduction and existence of the single currency implies large savings in transaction costs, which is an important factor of the competitiveness of the European economy. Some countries (such as Hungary or the Czech Republic) contradict these connections (i.e. very high integratedness and moderate institutional integration), but they pay a price in terms of their modest performance. Hungary is losing ground in convergence (producing a relatively slow growth), and pays a high price in financial terms (such as high debt service, bond yields, risk premiums and downgrading in credit rating).

On the other hand, the relatively high level of EU integration does not mean that it is satisfactory in its extension and its structure. It is without doubt that the economic union follows from the present high levels of intensity, interconnectedness and interdependence of the economies of the member countries. However, the EMU and the construction of the euro is an half-done structure and it is burdened with high deficits. These deficits are partly institutional-regulatory and partly political. From an institutional perspective, more federal structure would be needed, from a political point of view the democracy deficit should be addressed.

In the EU, the present crisis has encouraged and enforced several important reform steps, particularly in the area of Euro governance (European Semester, Fiscal Compound, European Stability Mechanism or Banking Union). These measures have greatly contributed to the consolidation of the eurozone, and averted the threat of a deeper economic crisis. In the longer run however, further steps would be needed. I fully share those views that propose the development of a real common budget for the Union.

The present budget should be reformed in terms of its size, its revenue resources (own resources) and in its powers to exert real macroeconomic regulatory functions. Many argue that with the establishment of a properly working economic and monetary union, the future integration of budgetary policies is unavoidable, and in order to deal with asymmetric shocks and to secure stability and prosperity, progress towards fiscal federalism is a necessary development.

The EC/EU budget can be regarded only as an 'embryo centre of a federal system' (referred to by A. M. El-Agraa (2004)), and so far only slow and contradictory steps have been taken towards a federal budget. In fact, one can rightly ask whether we can speak about any such progress, inasmuch as the federal union is not yet a declared objective that is also accepted by the member states.

The issues of a federal budget were raised by the MacDougall Report as far back as 1977, but owing to the far-reaching political implications, these recommendations lapsed into oblivion.

The MacDougall Report envisaged three stages of federal budget integration:

- Pre-federal integration with Community public expenditures, amounting to 2–2.5 per cent of Community GDP.
- Federation with small public sectors, with expenditures of 5–7 per cent of GDP.
- Union with large Community expenditures, reaching 20–25 per cent of aggregate GDP.

The European Union, transferring only about 1 percent of its total GDP among the member countries, is only about halfway even to a 'pre-federal budget', and the disputes about the budget reforms suggest no spectacular breakthrough in the foreseeable future.

National budgets (both at the federal and the local state level) generally rely on income from taxes or tax-like revenues and these vary in size but tend to amount to 40–50 per cent of a given country's GDP. Taxes are paid directly by citizens and legal persons, and we can define these as national budgets that have their 'own resources'.

A real common budget of the EU would assume revenue structures similar to the traditional 'national' budgets. The proposals for special own revenues (hydro-carbon tax, Tobin tax, etc.) are interesting, but are contradictory and offer limited solutions.

In order to exert the real regulatory functions, it is hard to avoid income taxes or the VAT. The obstacles are more psychological or political than real. People, generally, do not know which proportion of their income tax goes to the local or the 'national' budget. In fact, they do not care much about it, as they are more concerned about the general amount that they have to pay. Therefore, they would probably not care if a proportion of their income tax went to the EU budget, except if the media suggested each morning how disastrous that was. And they probably would not care too much if this change would be connected with a general reduction of the income taxes. Realistically speaking this process would need a long time, but the first steps should be taken. The company taxes would be obvious sources of the common budget, as the company structures of the Union are highly transnationalised.

The MacDougall Report had decisively formulated as early as 1977 the basic principles of the Community budget (MacDougall Report, 1977). According to the report, the Community budget must also fulfil the main stabilisation, allocation and redistribution functions of macroeconomic policy. It must ensure the promotion of price stability, the expansion of economic activities, employment and the efficient use of resources. As the common currency was created, these functions should have been extended. But these are still far behind what would be needed in reality.

## Notes

1 This study was supported in the framework of TÁMOP4.2.4.A/2–11–1-2012–0001. 'National Excellence Program – Elaborating and operating an inland student and researcher personal support system' key project. The project was subsidised by the European Union and by The European Social Fund.
2 The term 'interdependence' was first mentioned in the 'Communist Manifesto' of Marx and Engels, published in 1848.

## References

El-Agraa, Ali M. (2004). *The European Union. Economics and Policies.* Upper Saddle River, NJ: Prentice Hall.
Balassa, B. (1961). *The Theory of Economic Integration.* Homewood, IL: Irwin.

182   T. Palánkai

Bhagwati, J. (2004). *In Defence of Globalization*. Oxford: Oxford University Press and Council on Foreign Relations.

Dreher, A., Gaston, N., Marteins, P. and Van Boxem, L. (2010). 'Measuring Globalization – Opening the Black Box: A Critical Analysis of Globalization Indices.' *Journal of Globalization Studies*, 1 (1), May.

Ernst&Young (2012). *The World Is Bumpy. Globalization and the New Strategies for Growth*. London: EYGM Ltd.

European Commission (2001). *2001 Broad Economic Policy Guidelines*. Brussels.

Eurostat (2009). *Europe in Figures: Eurostat Yearbook 2009*. Brussels.

Eurostat (2010). *Europe in Figures: Eurostat Yearbook 2010*. Brussels.

Held, D., McGrew, A. G., Goldblatt, D. and Perraton, J. (2005). *Global Transformations*. Cambridge: Polity Press.

Hopkins, A. G. (ed.) (2002). *Globalization in World History*. London: Pimlico.

Keohane, R. O. and Nye, J. S. (1977). *Power and Independence*. Boston; Toronto: Little, Brown and Company.

KOF Index of Globalization (2010). Press Release, Friday, 22 January 2010. KOF (Konjunkturforschung), Swiss Economic Institute, Swiss Federal Institute of Technology, Zürich.

Lechner, F. J. and Boli, J. (eds.) (2005). *The Globalization Reader*. Malden: Blackwell.

MacDougall Report (1977). *Report of the Study Group on the Role of Public Finances in European Integration*. Brussels: Commission of the European Communities, Vol. 1.

Mikorszkóp, Ecostat (2005). 23 September, No. 89.

Molle, W. (1994). *The Economics of European Integration*. Dartmouth: Aldershot.

Palánkai, T. (1976). *A nyugat-európai integráció* (Western European Integration). Budapest: KJK.

Perroux, F. (1954). *L'Europe sans rivages*. Paris: Presses Universitaires.

Predöhl, A. and Jürgensen, H. (1961). 'Europäische Integration.' In Keller, R., Hirseland, A., Schneider, W. and Viehöver, W. (eds.). *Handbuch der Sozialwissenschaften, Bd.1*. Vienna: Springer-Verlag.

Simai, M. (2007). *A világgazdaság a XXI. század forgatagában* (World Economy in the Drift of 21st Century). Budapest: Akademiai Kiado.

Tinbergen, J. (1965). *International Economic Integration*. Amsterdam: Elsevier.

UNCTAD (2013). *World Investment Report*. New York: United Nations.

UNIDO Report (2011). *Networks for Prosperity*. Summary. Vienna, 14 November.

Wolf, M. (2005). *Why Globalization Works*. New Haven: Yale University Press.

# 9 From an 'austere' monetary union to a federal union

## More solidarity among European citizens

*Riccardo Fiorentini*

### Introduction

The creation of the Economic and Monetary Union (EMU) was a major step in the history of the European integration process. For decades after the Second World War, the European Community (EC) favoured economic integration with positive effects on growth, trade and welfare in Europe. However, the end of the Bretton Woods era and the international monetary and economic turbulence that dominated the 1970s made it clear that Europe should have gone further in the direction of tighter monetary, economic and political integration. At the end of the 1980s, the disintegration of the eastern European bloc and the transition of the former socialist states toward a market economy made the need for such a quantum leap even more compelling.

In the 1980s, the debate about the future of the European integration process culminated in the Delors Report (1989), containing proposals for an Economic and Monetary Union, an important step in the direction of European political union. It is useful to recall that in the Delors Report, EMU was not an independent goal but was part of a general process with social and political aspects aimed at removing the remaining macroeconomic obstacles to full European integration.

The Delors Report had a formidable political impact and its proposals were partially incorporated into the Maastricht Treaty, signed in December 1991 by the governments of EC member states. As is well known, the Maastricht Treaty led to the creation of the European Union (EU) whose main goals, among others, are:

> … to promote peace, its values and the well-being of its peoples … work for the sustainable development of Europe based on balanced economic growth and price stability, a highly competitive social market economy, aiming at full employment and social progress … promote economic, social and territorial cohesion, and solidarity among Member States.

In order to pursue its goals,

> The Union shall establish an economic and monetary union whose currency is the euro [and] shall pursue its objectives by appropriate means

commensurate with the competences which are conferred upon it in the Treaties.

(Art. 3 of the Consolidated Version of the Treaty of
the European Union)

Twenty-three years on, only the monetary part of the Treaty has been fully implemented with the establishment of the EMU and the creation of the European Central Bank (ECB). Other important goals have yet to be met. Unemployment in the Euro area, 7.4 per cent in 2007, reached the unprecedented levels of 12 per cent at the end of 2013 (Eurostat), and the recessive effects of austerity policies are eroding social cohesion and weakening solidarity among member states.

Undoubtedly, the current social and economic problems of the EU are in part due to the impact of the financial crisis which from the USA spread throughout the world in 2008. However, it is also true that the negative effects of the global financial crisis have been amplified by the institutional flaws of the EMU in which a 'restrictive policy bias' existed well before the European sovereign debt crisis and the introduction of fiscal austerity policies.

The origin of the present day troubles of the EU lies in the fact that the Maastricht Treaty established monetary but not fiscal union. Furthermore, the political mandate of the ECB is narrower than in other monetary unions so that the ECB cannot fully exert the stabilizing role normally fulfilled by other central banks (De Grauwe, 2013).

The EMU is unique in the history of monetary unions because, unlike in other experiments, it is neither a national monetary union, such as the USA, Italy or Germany which unified their domestic monetary markets after completing political unification, nor is it an international monetary union, such as the Latin or Scandinavian unions, where member states maintained their political independence (Bordo and Capie, 1993; Kindleberger, 1993; Fratianni and Spinelli, 1997; Bae and Bailey, 2011). In the case of the eurozone, independent states voluntarily transferred their monetary sovereignty to a supranational institution, the ECB, while retaining national responsibility for the management of fiscal policy. In other words, the EMU has a supranational monetary policy but not a supranational fiscal policy.

The problem of fiscal coordination in a monetary union in which a central monetary authority exists but fiscal policy is decentralized and left in the hands of national governments is of paramount importance. In fact, persistent divergences in fiscal balances among member states may place the existence of the union itself at risk. According to the classic analysis of time inconsistency in monetary policy (Kydland and Prescott, 1977; Barro and Gordon, 1983), in a monetary union the commitment of the central bank to maintaining price stability is not entirely credible if public debt in a member country spins out of control. In such an event, the monetary authorities of the union may be forced to intervene by bailing out the defaulting country through the direct purchase of sovereign bonds, but this kind of action undermines the commitment to price stability. If capital transfers from other members of the union became necessary, then these member states would bear the cost of the bail-out, a measure that is politically unfeasible. Finally, if the troubled state actually defaulted, the risk of contagion and general collapse would be very high.

In national monetary unions, the existence of a central (federal) government is the solution to the problem of fiscal coordination because the federal government can isolate and eliminate public finance problems arising at the local government level before they threaten the stability of the entire system. Furthermore, the transfer of funds from one region to another in a national monetary union is a standard practice and raises fewer political problems than the transfer of funds between independent countries in a common currency area.

In the case of the EMU, an attempt was made to solve the problem of fiscal coordination in 1997 with the Stability and Growth Pact (SGP), which requires members of the EMU to maintain government deficit/GDP and debt/GDP ratios below the well-known limits of 3 and 60 per cent. In the absence of a supranational European fiscal policy (the 'European Treasury'), the expectation was that the fiscal rules of the SGP and the threat of the 'excess deficit' procedure against non-compliant countries would provide sufficient *ex ante* coordination among domestic fiscal policies to prevent instability in the eurozone arising from public finance (Issing, 2008).

Despite the institutional flaws of the EMU and the objections of many economists that the eurozone failed to meet optimum currency area criteria[1] (Bayoumi and Eichengreen, 1993; De Grauwe and Vanheverbeke, 1993; Torres and Giavazzi, 1993; Feldstein, 1997), the EMU worked smoothly until 2008. In the 1999–2008 period, inflation and interest rates in Europe converged at a stable low level, the euro was increasingly used in international trade, becoming the second international reserve currency (Fiorentini, 2005; ECB, 2013). Furthermore, trust in the EMU was high so investors did not differentiate the risk profiles of sovereign bonds issued by various governments with traditionally very different reputations in relation to fiscal discipline. As a consequence, highly indebted EMU member countries like Italy benefited from the fact that low interest rates on their sovereign bonds reduced the cost of re-financing their large sovereign debt. Finally, the entry into the EU of Central-Eastern European countries was seen as a sign of the political success of the EU project.

After the outbreak of the global financial crisis in 2008, for a short period of time, the monetary and financial stability of the EU and the eurozone seemed to hold, until 2010 when the Greek sovereign debt crisis eventually revealed the limits and institutional flaws of the EMU. Suddenly, it became clear that monetary and financial convergence in the EU concealed processes of real divergence among European economies and that EU *ex ante* rules for dealing with the threat of default of a member country were not sufficient to prevent the fiscal crisis of one member spilling over into the whole area. The problems deriving from the 'original sin' of a monetary union not matched by a companion federal fiscal union became evident. As a consequence, the debate over the prospects of fiscal union in Europe gained momentum with contributions from a variety of quarters, including international institutions and independent European think tanks (European Commission, 2012; Tommaso Padoa-Schioppa Group, 2012; Allard *et al.*, 2013; Fernandes and Maslauskaite, 2013).

As far as EU institutions are concerned, an important step was taken with the publication in 2012 by the European Commission of the Blueprint for a Deep and Genuine Economic and Monetary Union. The Blueprint contained a list of short-term and long-term proposals aimed at introducing some degree of fiscal union in the EMU but it stuck to the current official view that national austerity, rigid rules and country-by-country fiscal consolidation are the right answers to the present-day problems of the EU.

However, in our opinion, austerity has actually prolonged the economic crisis rather than solving it, is unable to reach its goals and is responsible for the growing popularity of nationalistic and euro-sceptical movements in EU countries. Instead of promoting European solidarity, one of the official EU goals, austerity is straining the social fabric of European societies, stressing welfare systems and eroding support for the European integration project itself. In our belief, the EU needs to change direction towards greater solidarity among its countries and citizens. The change is both necessary and urgent but cannot be achieved without establishing a supranational fiscal union. The remaining part of this chapter explains why.

## Before austerity: the latent deflationary bias of the EMU

Why austerity policies, the Fiscal Compact and other emergency measures were adopted as the EU response to the Greek and sovereign debt crises cannot be fully understood except in light of the institutional asymmetry of a supranational monetary union lacking a supranational fiscal union, which gave the EMU a latent deflationary bias from the outset. This bias derives from both the monetary and fiscal provisions of the EMU treaties.

With the establishment of the EMU, European member states voluntarily transferred their monetary sovereignty to a new supranational authority, the ECB, and in doing so lost one important instrument of national economic policy. However, the loss of monetary sovereignty was largely formal. In fact, a close look at the experience of the European Monetary System (EMS) in the 1980s shows that in the EU, Germany determined monetary policy. As is well known, the EMS was an asymmetric system in which Germany played the role of leader. Fixed or quasi-fixed exchange rate systems suffer from the 'residual country' problem. Given $n$ countries, there are $n$-1 exchange rates to be determined. Therefore, there is one degree of freedom left, which means that only one country can pursue an independent monetary policy. The 'residual country' also has the advantage of being able to use its own monetary policies to address domestic problems. This occurred both in the Bretton Woods system, where the USA was the leader, and in the EMS, where Germany led the game. When the economic policy of the leader country conflicts with the needs of the other $n$-1 countries, tensions and conflicts arise that may lead to the breakdown of the exchange rate agreement. This was the case of the EMS after German reunification at the beginning of the 1990s. To prevent a rise in inflation due to the high cost of reunification, the Bundesbank adopted a tight monetary policy stance which pushed German interest rates up. In order to avoid the depreciation of their currencies, other members of the EMS also raised their interest rates, when the opposite would have been more appropriate, given the high unemployment levels at the time. As we know now, this resulted in the international currency crisis of September 1992 and the collapse of the EMS itself.

The problem of the asymmetric monetary policy of the EMS disappeared with the EMU along with national currencies and exchange rates. Today, monetary policy in the eurozone is determined by the Board of the ECB and not by the Bundesbank alone and monetary policy decisions are taken with a view to the monetary stability of the whole eurozone rather than the stability of any specific national monetary market.

The supranational monetary policy of the EMU suffers from the fact that the political mandate of the ECB is too narrow, confined as it is to providing price stability. The exchange rate and employment levels are not explicit targets of the ECB and Treaties prohibit the direct financing of government deficits. These institutional limits can be put in a nutshell by saying that the ECB is not and cannot be a true lender of last resort for the eurozone. Hence the ECB is a strange central bank compared to the Fed or the Bank of England which have wider political mandates including unemployment levels and recourse to a much larger array of monetary policy instruments.

Until the recent approval of the EU banking union by the European Parliament in April 2013, another institutional flaw of the EMU was the fact that the surveillance of the banking system was at the national level. Given the high degree of integration of European banking and financial sectors, entrusting surveillance to nations was an error leading to high costs in the management of the sovereign debt crisis. While any European bank can purchase bonds issued by another EMU member state, a national surveillance authority cannot control the whole range of investment activities of banks based in other EMU states. A supranational surveillance authority would have been required to do this. The asymmetry increased the systemic banking risk in the EMU and paved the way, throughout Europe, to excessive interdependence between sovereign debt and private banks, which in turn played an important role in the development of the sovereign debt crisis. This subject is dealt with in more detail in the next section.

Let us now focus on the sole institutional task of the ECB, price stability, and its implications for economic policies in the EMU. The ECB seeks to maintain inflation below but close to 2 per cent in the medium term over the entire eurozone. Obviously, this is an average value which may be too low for some countries and too high for others. Since monetary policy in the EMU cannot be tailored for any specific member state, a country which is negatively impacted on its own by the monetary policy adopted cannot count on the ECB to solve its difficulties. In the case of general symmetric shocks, such as the recent events in the EMU, expansive monetary policies are not adopted if they lead to inflation rates above 2 per cent. A potential conflict between fiscal policy and monetary policy also exists. Let us suppose that in a recession, the state of public finance allowed a coordinated expansion of government expenditure in order to raise aggregate demand in the eurozone but this policy drives inflation over the 2 per cent mark. According to its own mandate, the ECB would react with monetary restriction, driving up interest rates. The higher interest rate would probably generate an appreciation of the euro foreign exchange rate which in turn would negatively affect European exports, neutralizing the initially positive effect of fiscal expansion on aggregate demand. This example shows that, in quite plausible circumstances, monetary policy in the EMU has a built-in restrictive bias.

In relation to fiscal policy, as stated earlier, the SGP was created without European Federal Fiscal Union and introduced an *ex ante* coordination mechanism in order to prevent conflicts between national fiscal policies and euro-wide monetary policy. In relation to the 3 per cent and 60 per cent limits on deficit/GDP and debt/GDP ratios, these not only limit the scope for national fiscal policy in the case of asymmetric shocks in one country, they also create an unnecessary restrictive bias when real growth is positive but nominal growth is below 5 per cent. This can be seen from the following budget accounting equation, where $b$ represents the debt/GDP ratio, $d$ the deficit/GDP ratio and $gn$ the nominal rate of GDP growth.

$$b_t = \frac{1}{1+gn} b_{t-1} + d_t \tag{1}$$

In a steady equilibrium where $b$ stays constant, the deficit and debt criteria are mutually consistent only when nominal GDP grows at a 5 per cent rate. Lower rates of growth mean that the 60 per cent debt/GDP ratio limit can only be met if the deficit/GDP ratio falls below 3 per cent. Therefore, even if a country satisfies the deficit criteria, it may not satisfy the debt criteria. A smaller deficit or even a surplus becomes necessary. In this regard Otmar Issing, former member of the Board of the Deutsche Bundesbank and founder member of the executive Board of the ECB, has been explicit, noting that the main message of the SGP is that 'in normal economic conditions a country's budgetary position should be in (or close to) balance – or even in surplus if, in particular, the level of government debt is high' (Issing, 2008: 198). It is not a surprise that now the Fiscal Compact explicitly sets the obligation of a balanced structural fiscal position in all EMU member countries.

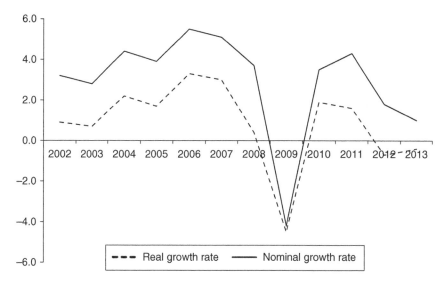

*Figure 9.1* Nominal and real GDP growth rate in the eurozone

A look at the Eurostat data for nominal and real growth rates (Figure 9.1) shows that in the period 2002–2013 the average nominal growth rate in the eurozone was above 5 per cent in just two years (2006 and 2007). It was below in the previous years, and collapsed to −4.1 per cent in 2009, remaining below 5 per cent thereafter. This simple debt arithmetic shows that in periods of positive real growth even so-called 'virtuous' countries like Germany may find it difficult to reduce and/or keep their debt/GDP ratio at 60 per cent. In Germany, the ratio has actually been continuously increasing since 2002, reaching 81 per cent in 2012; for five years running, from 2001 to 2005, Germany broke the SGP 3 per cent limit for the deficit/GDP ratio. France did the same from 2002 to 2004 and Italy from 2001 to 2006 (Table 9.1 and 9.2). Despite these violations, Germany – backed by France and Italy – used its prominent economic and political position inside the EU to block the excess deficit procedure against it as put forward by the EU Commission in November 2003. The credibility of the SGP suffered from that policy decision. Issing commented as follows:

> It was depressing to see how the German and French governments in particular flouted the Pact … Following in the slipstream of Germany and French fiscal policy, as it were, Italy too broke the rules. Greece was not long in joining them. In doing so, the three largest EMU countries, including the country that originally pushed the Stability and Growth Pact through against stiff resistance, took an axe to one of the pillars of monetary union.
>
> (Issing, 2008: 199)

Table 9.1 Government debt/GDP ratios

| | 2001 | 2002 | 2003 | 2004 | 2005 | 2006 | 2007 | 2008 | 2009 | 2010 | 2011 | 2012 |
|---|---|---|---|---|---|---|---|---|---|---|---|---|
| Euro area | 68.2 | 68 | 69.2 | 69.6 | 70.3 | 68.6 | 66.4 | 70.2 | 80 | 85.4 | 87.3 | 90.6 |
| Ireland | 34.5 | 31.8 | 31 | 29.4 | 27.2 | 24.6 | 24.9 | 44.2 | 64.4 | 91.2 | 104.1 | 117.4 |
| Germany | 59.1 | 60.7 | 64.4 | 66.2 | 68.6 | 68 | 65.2 | 66.8 | 74.5 | 82.5 | 80 | 81 |
| Greece | 103.7 | 101.7 | 97.4 | 98.6 | 100 | 106.1 | 107.4 | 112.9 | 129.7 | 148.3 | 170.3 | 156.9 |
| Spain | 55.6 | 52.6 | 48.8 | 46.3 | 43.2 | 39.7 | 36.3 | 40.2 | 54 | 61.7 | 70.5 | 86 |
| France | 56.9 | 58.8 | 62.9 | 64.9 | 66.4 | 63.7 | 64.2 | 68.2 | 79.2 | 82.4 | 85.8 | 90.2 |
| Italy | 108.3 | 105.4 | 104.1 | 103.7 | 105.7 | 106.3 | 103.3 | 106.1 | 116.4 | 119.3 | 120.7 | 127 |
| Portugal | 53.8 | 56.8 | 59.4 | 61.9 | 67.7 | 69.4 | 68.4 | 71.7 | 83.7 | 94 | 108.2 | 124.1 |

Source: Eurostat (table tsdde410).

Table 9.2 Government surplus-deficit/GDP ratios

| | 2001 | 2002 | 2003 | 2004 | 2005 | 2006 | 2007 | 2008 | 2009 | 2010 | 2011 | 2012 |
|---|---|---|---|---|---|---|---|---|---|---|---|---|
| Euro area | −1.9 | −2.7 | −3.1 | −2.9 | −2.5 | −1.3 | −0.7 | −2.1 | −6.4 | −6.2 | −4.2 | −3.7 |
| Germany | −3.1 | −3.8 | −4.2 | −3.8 | −3.3 | −1.6 | 0.2 | −0.1 | −3.1 | −4.2 | −0.8 | 0.1 |
| Ireland | 0.9 | −0.4 | 0.4 | 1.4 | 1.6 | 2.9 | 0.2 | −7.4 | −13.7 | −30.6 | −13.1 | −8.2 |
| Greece | −4.5 | −4.8 | −5.6 | −7.5 | −5.2 | −5.7 | −6.5 | −9.8 | −15.7 | −10.7 | −9.5 | −9 |
| Spain | −0.5 | −0.3 | −0.3 | −0.1 | 1.3 | 2.4 | 2 | −4.5 | −11.1 | −9.6 | −9.6 | −10.6 |
| France | −1.5 | −3.1 | −4.1 | −3.6 | −2.9 | −2.3 | −2.7 | −3.3 | −7.5 | −7.1 | −5.3 | −4.8 |
| Italy | −3.1 | −3.1 | −3.6 | −3.5 | −4.4 | −3.4 | −1.6 | −2.7 | −5.5 | −4.5 | −3.8 | −3 |
| Portugal | −4.8 | −3.4 | −3.7 | −4 | −6.5 | −4.6 | −3.1 | −3.6 | −10.2 | −9.8 | −4.3 | −6.4 |

Source: Eurostat (table tec00127).

The self-indulgence of the German government in that episode is in clear contrast with the harsh punitive position the Merkel government adopted over the Greek crisis. Historical memory seems to be very short in politics.

Returning to SGP fiscal criteria, when the nominal growth rate is below 5 per cent but growth is negative, the situation may become dramatic for countries whose debt/GDP ratio exceeds 60 per cent, because a deficit/GDP ratio of 3 per cent is not sufficient to reduce it. The deficit must be smaller or even negative (a surplus). From government budget accounting, we know that a budget deficit is the sum of the primary deficit plus the interest paid on public debt and that the dynamics of the primary deficit/GDP ratio depends on the real interest rate and the real rate of growth so that, as long as real interest rates are greater than real growth rates, the debt/GDP ratio dynamics is unstable and a static (constant) level of debt/GDP ratio exists only if the primary surplus/GDP ratio is sufficiently high.[2]

Consider now the case of a real growth rate that is greater than the real interest rate. In such a case it can be shown that the debt/GDP ratio is always under control and may be compatible with different primary deficits so that the 3 per cent limit on the overall government budget may be excessively restrictive. In general, therefore, in periods of economic expansion, or 'good times', the original fiscal rules of the EMU are very likely to impose fiscal policy that is more restrictive than necessary to keep public finance under control. It goes without saying, that the new rules embodied in the recent Fiscal Compact have worsened the situation.

Let us now examine weak growth or recession. In both cases, attempts to simultaneously meet the two fiscal criteria on deficit and debt necessarily end up in policies that are so restrictive as to generate a recessive vicious circle (Holland and Portes, 2012). To reduce debt, the fiscal authorities need to create a primary budget surplus by cutting public expenditure and/or raising taxes. This compresses aggregate demand, and weak or falling aggregate demand reduces production and growth, which in turn makes the burden of public debt even heavier. Furthermore, expenditure is likely to increase due to rising unemployment benefits, putting more pressure on public finances. The result is that the effort to meet the required fiscal criteria makes that goal more and more difficult to achieve and condemns the economy to persistent unemployment and stagnation (Calcagno, 2012). In addition, prolonged periods of fiscal restraint and unemployment may cause social unrest and disenchant European citizens in relation to the EMU, particularly when social expenditure is treated as an 'adjustment variable' to improve public budgets as is all too often the case (Fernandes and Maslauskaite, 2013).

### Is fiscal austerity in recession the answer to Europe's problems?

Since the onset of the Greek crisis in 2010, the political answer of EU leaders and institutions to the sovereign debt crisis in peripheral European countries has been country-by-country fiscal austerity and inter-governmental agreements on more rigid fiscal rules and mutual surveillance (Two Pact, Six Pact, Fiscal Compact) in line with the logic of the SGP discussed in the previous section. However, an important difference compared to previous rules exists, because the focus of fiscal policies is now on both deficit and debt dynamics, rather than on deficits alone, as before the sovereign debt crisis. In fact, the Fiscal Compact sets a clear and stringent path of debt reduction obliging governments to bring down the part of debt exceeding 60 per cent of GDP at a steady rate of 5 per cent per year and budgets, corrected for the economic cycle, also have to be balanced.

The strategy of fiscal austerity would have been correct if excessive profligacy, particularly in Southern Europe, were the cause of the increase in the eurozone debt/GDP ratio. Before 2008, this was true of Greece, and partially of Portugal, but not for other peripheral countries such as Ireland and Spain, where the debt/GDP ratio was low and decreasing (Table 9.1). Conversely, in France, the debt/GDP ratio increased throughout the period, as it did in Germany until 2007. In Italy, the ratio remained above 100 per cent, but slightly decreasing. Before 2008, in the EU, private rather than public debt increased considerably (De Grauwe, 2013). According to a study by the European Credit Research Institute, between 1995 and 2007 in the EU overall household debt increased by 300 per cent, and even more so in countries with a booming real estate sector, such as Ireland and Spain, where it underwent a six-fold increase (Chmelar, 2013). Public debt began rising after the onset of the global financial crisis because of recession and government bail-outs of the private banking sector. Higher public expenditure and the fall in tax revenues hit government budgets, and the ensuing larger deficits increased public debt. When the denominator of a ratio (GDP) decreases and the numerator (debt) increases, the outcome is a larger ratio. The case of Ireland is striking: the bail-out of the national banking system switched the government budget from surplus to a huge negative position in 2010 (Table 9.2) so that the Irish debt/GDP ratio moved from 24.9 per cent in 2007 to 117.4 per cent in 2012.

What caused the excessive accumulation of private debt in peripheral EMU countries? In a monetary union comprising countries with different economic structures and rates of inflation, the interest rates set by the ECB may be too high for some and too low for others. In countries where inflation is higher than the average, real interest rates are lower than in countries where inflation is low. Low real interest rates foster investments and aggregate demand, which in turn cause a negative balance of payments. Data for intra-EU trade show that after the introduction of the euro, Germany developed a trade surplus with Southern and peripheral Europe, while Spain, Portugal, Italy, Greece and Ireland ran a trade deficit (Dettman *et al.*, 2012; Boitani and Hamaui, 2013; Cour-Thimann, 2013). The counterpart of trade imbalances is capital outflows from surplus countries toward deficit countries. German banks financed the boom in demand (mainly housing) in Southern and peripheral Europe until the onset of the European sovereign debt crisis when investors lost confidence in the solvency of those countries and intra-EU capital flows reverted.

At that point, the close link between private banks and sovereign debt reared its head. Banks are the main holders of sovereign debt and government liquidity problems immediately translate into balance sheet problems for the banks. On the other hand, governments do not want domestic banking systems to fall into systemic crisis so bail-outs of important troubled banks are common (the 'too big to fail' syndrome). In the recent European financial and sovereign debt crisis, both sides of the relationship, government and banks, played an active role. In the absence of a banking union and lacking a supranational institution in charge of the surveillance of the eurozone banking system, the bursting of the private credit bubble and deterioration of the balance sheets of banks led to bail-outs by national governments; these impacted on government budgets; the fall of confidence in public finance caused capital outflows, a growing difficulty in rolling over the existing stock of government debt, a sharp rise in interest rate spreads, a fall in sovereign debt value and a further deterioration of the balance sheets of banks. The outcome was a self-fulfilling liquidity crisis and contagion over the periphery of the eurozone, coming close to threatening the survival of the EMU itself.

What could have prevented such a self-fulfilling liquidity crisis from developing? A fiscal and banking union alongside the immediate reaction of a lender of last resort able to create and inject into the economy the amount of liquidity needed to prevent speculation against sovereign debt. A lender of last resort must be a central bank and, indeed, one of the main historical reasons for establishing central banks was the need to create an institution able to correct the instability of financial markets and smooth over boom-and-bust credit cycles, which are unavoidable in modern market-capitalist societies (Minsky, 1982, 1986; Reinhart and Rogoff, 2009; Kindleberger and Aliber, 2011). However, in the EMU a true lender of last resort does not exist because the institutional mandate of the ECB prohibits the direct funding of government debt. Furthermore, within the ECB Board, German representatives have also strongly opposed intervention in the secondary market for sovereign bonds. The institutional mandate of the ECB and the political opposition of Germany explain why in 2011 the limited intervention of the ECB was insufficient to stop speculation. It was only after 6 September, 2012 when the ECB Governor Mario Draghi eventually announced the Outright Monetary Transaction programme (OMT) promising to buy unlimited amount of sovereign bonds, if necessary, to restore the proper functioning of monetary policy in the eurozone, that financial markets finally calmed down. With that decision, the ECB stretched the limits of its own mandate, moving in the right direction towards becoming a 'de facto' lender of last resort for the eurozone. However, the strings attached to the implementation of the OMT programme and the continuing opposition of the Bundesbank, which argued against the OMT programme before the German Constitutional Court, cast doubts about its future efficacy in the event of another major financial crisis in the EMU (De Grauwe, 2013).

If this diagnosis of the EMU crisis is correct, the focus on austerity as the cure for the EMU disease is obviously misplaced. The crisis in the eurozone was not caused by government overspending but by institutional flaws in the design of the EMU (lack of fiscal union and banking union, a too narrow mandate to the ECB), the development of intra-EU imbalances and the growth of a private credit bubble (Pisani-Ferry, 2012).

Undeniably, several countries in the EMU need to adjust their fiscal position before it becomes unsustainable in the long run, and, in some cases, to shrink an overblown (Tanzi, 2013). What we disagree with is the idea that generalized country-by-country fiscal austerity (the 'house in order approach') during a recession can be the source of stable growth in the EMU and EU, as the expansionary fiscal contraction view suggests (Giavazzi and Pagano, 1996; Alesina and Ardagna, 2010). Support for this position comes from Reinhart and Rogoff who, in a famous article, suggested that debt/GDP ratios above 90 per cent hamper average growth rates (Reinhart and Rogoff, 2010). However, their conclusions are flawed by the arbitrary exclusion of available data, coding and calculation errors (Herdnon *et al.*, 2014). In relation to the expansionary fiscal contraction hypothesis, it works only if fiscal multipliers are very low or close to zero and economic agents are rational and expect that a cut in current government expenditure will be matched by lower taxes and higher disposable income in the future. The extreme rationality of 'Ricardian equivalence' (Barro, 1974) is highly questionable (Ricciuti, 2003); several recent studies have convincingly shown that the true value of the fiscal multiplier is much higher than expected by EU officials and supporters of country-by-country austerity, with a mean estimated value of 1.5 (Auerbach and Gorodnichenko, 2012; Batini *et al.*, 2012; Coenen *et al.*, 2012 ; Blanchard and Leigh, 2013). Hence fiscal restraints have a very negative impact on GDP and the simultaneous adoption of restrictive fiscal policy in the eurozone very likely prolonged the recession, making the goal of a lower debt/GDP ratio difficult to achieve. In this scenario austerity is self-defeating (Calcagno, 2012; Zezza, 2012). Eurostat data show that the number of EU countries that cut public expenditure in mid recession rose from eight in 2009 to twenty-one in 2011 (Fiorentini and Montani, 2014). Can we reasonably expect simultaneous Europe-wide pro-cyclical economic policies to smoothe the economic cycle and promote growth in highly integrated EU countries?

The division of the eurozone into two groups, the indebted and deficit-ridden Southern peripheral area and the 'virtuous' surplus, creditor core in Northern Europe, clustered around Germany reveals a new type of asymmetry inside the EMU. This consists in the fact that deficit countries bear the entire cost of adjustments in intra-EMU trade imbalances. Imbalances are twofold because for every deficit position a surplus position exists; after all every debtor receives money from a lender. Excessive deficits are therefore possible only if creditors are willing to lend. In principle, trade imbalances among countries belonging to a monetary union in which a common currency circulates may be eliminated either by a contraction of expenditure in the deficit country or an expansion in the surplus country, or both. In practice, however, deficit countries are forced to deleverage and deflate domestic demand, while surplus countries can simply match their trade surplus increasing their stock of foreign assets. This happened in the EMU (De Grauwe, 2013). The trade balances of Greece, Spain, Italy and Ireland have recently improved mainly because of a decrease in domestic demand and a fall in imports (Dettman *et al.*, 2012). Without the ability to devalue a domestic currency, and with fiscal policy severely constrained by austerity and the new fiscal rules coded in the Two Pact, Six Pact and Fiscal Compact, the only way EMU Peripheral countries have to improve the competitiveness of their economy is to engage in internal real depreciation. This involves the compression of real wages and labour costs, a process that – where the EU inflation rate is below 1 per cent – is difficult to achieve and socially very painful. Expansionary policies in the EMU surplus country, Germany, would make the elimination of intra-EU trade imbalances much easier and less socially costly. The fact that this is not happening shows once again that solidarity in the EU is currently very limited.

Another worrisome aspect of the austerity policy in a time of recession is that its costs are very high for the population. An assessment of Troika (ECB, IMF and European Commission) financial assistance programmes commissioned by the European Parliament (Sapir *et al.*, 2014) concludes that in Greece, Portugal, Ireland and Cyprus the actual fall in domestic demand and GDP was sharper than anticipated and that unemployment arose much more than expected by the Troika itself. Financial assistance programmes have partially succeeded in restoring positive financial conditions in those countries but their social costs – overlooked and underestimated – have been very high, In this regard, the same report contains a textual analysis of the financial assistance programmes negotiated by the Troika after the onset of the financial crisis, which shows that they ignored issues of poverty, inequality and unfairness. All of this contrasts with the promises of full employment, social progress, solidarity and cohesion made at the time of the creation of the EU, enshrined in Art. 3 of the Consolidated Version of the Treaty of the European Union and in Art. 9 of the Consolidated Version of the Treaty on the Functioning of the European Union, known as the 'Horizontal Social Clause'. The latter states that

> In defining and implementing its policies and activities, the Union shall take into account requirements linked to the promotion of a high level of employment, the guarantee of adequate social protection, the fight against social exclusion, and a high level of education, training and protection of human health.

This is not what happened in the case of Greece where, for example, the effects on the population's health of budget cuts imposed by the Troika have been dramatic. A study published in the *Lancet* review reports that in order to meet the cut of 6 per cent of GDP in public expenditure, as agreed by the Greek government with the Troika in exchange for financial assistance, public expenditure in health care is now below the pre-2004 level of any EU member (Kentikelenis *et al.*, 2014). After such a radical reform and heavy expenditure cut, in 2013 the incidence of tuberculosis among the population has more than doubled on the previous year, malaria returned for the first time in forty years, delays in reimbursement have made some medicines unavailable and, in general, the cost of health care shifted onto patients who, in many cases, are unable to pay. In Greece only the employed have access to health insurance, so the rapid rise of unemployment has denied access to health care to an increasing number of people. The *Lancet* rightly concludes that 'alternative responses to the crisis would have allowed Greece to pursue difficult structural reforms, while preventing devastating social consequences' (Kentikelenis *et al.*, 2014: 751). But what are those alternatives?

## Fiscal union and solidarity: the right answer

In 2010, EU institutions and governments were clearly not well equipped to face the challenges raised by the sovereign debt crisis. The reaction to the Greek crisis was initially slow and hesitant and future historians will ask how EU institutions allowed the troubles of a country representing less than 2 per cent of EU GDP to become a crisis of the eurozone so severe as to threaten the survival of the EMU. The answer, of course, is bad institutional design, the lack of a fiscal union and no solidarity.

So far the response to the EMU crisis has been based on a 'sense of survival' rather than a 'sense of common purpose' (Fernandes and Maslauskaite, 2013; Pisani-Ferry, 2013). The 'sense of survival' is important to manage a crisis in the short run, but without a 'long-term' vision of what the EU should finally become, the viability of the EMU is not certain. After the completion of the EMU and the last enlargement rounds, EU governments seem to have lost a 'sense of common purpose' and, because of the social and economic costs of austerity, European citizens are increasingly asking themselves what benefits they have obtained from the EU and the EMU. The growth of euro-sceptical and anti-euro parties and movements is a clear sign of disaffection and discontent with current EU policies. In our view, a new 'sense of common purpose' should be based on the long-term project of a prosperous Europe in which economic growth is the basis for the preservation of the main features of national welfare systems which made the EU unique in the world.[3] This goal is not new, but so far the EU has been unable to pursue it on the basis of the 'open method of coordination' in which member states are individually responsible for the implementation of common tasks. We believe that both closer cooperation among EU governments and the strengthening of the role of EU supranational institutions are necessary. In the economic field, more effective and growth-oriented fiscal coordination requires supranational fiscal union along with some form of debt sharing and anti-cyclical collective insurance mechanisms. As to monetary policy, the ECB mandate should change to include more general macroeconomic stabilization targets.

The social effects of common economic policy decisions should always be evaluated before their adoption, after consultation from the outset with the European Parliament, representing European citizens, and its involvement in the decision-making process.

As far as fiscal union is concerned, as stated in the introduction, the sovereign debt crisis gave rise to a debate about the establishment of a 'true' fiscal union. The lesson of the crisis is certainly that the EMU needs to change and many now admit that creating a monetary union without a parallel fiscal union was a mistake. However, the label 'fiscal union' may include very different ideas and projects. For some, fiscal union means a full political and federal union with a federal government and a federal budget. For others, fiscal union is simply a synonym for stricter mutual control and surveillance over national fiscal and economic policies under the current institutional set-up of the EU. In our opinion, the only way to complete the European integration project in the long run is to move towards a full federal union. Clearly this is a very ambitious goal, requiring major reforms of EU Treaties (European Commission, 2012; Tommaso Padoa-Schioppa Group, 2012; Allard *et al.*, 2013; De Grauwe, 2013). Nonetheless, even if this is the goal, intermediate steps can be taken to reinforce cohesion and introduce greater co-responsibility and solidarity into the EMU. Before giving some examples, a preliminary discussion of solidarity, responsibility and co-responsibility in the EMU would be useful in order to avoid any misunderstandings.

First of all, solidarity in the EMU does not mean the unidirectional and permanent transfer of funds from 'virtuous' core countries to indebted 'peripheral' nations. The familiar argument of opponents of supranational federal union is that they do not want to pay others' debts. Generally they add that these debts are the fault of the countries that have practiced a loose fiscal policy and overspent. What we mean by European solidarity is something entirely different, such as the creation of a supranational mutual insurance mechanism which each country may resort to at times of economic difficulties.

Solidarity among EU governments is important but solidarity among European citizens even more so. The European integration project cannot survive without widespread citizen support, which is difficult to obtain if the perception is that membership costs outweigh its benefits and when the national political discourse focuses on the 'us against them'. If in Germany more and more citizens believe they are paying for the debts of 'lazy' southern Europeans and elsewhere many think that, via the euro, Germany is pursuing its own national interests at the expense of others, the EU has no future. Had a mutual insurance mechanism been in place at the beginning of the 2000s, Germany would already have benefited from it and today many German citizens and policymakers would probably have been less reluctant to help the GIIPS countries (see discussion below).

In order to restore solidarity among European citizens and revive popular support for the European integration process, the focus of EU policies needs to change from fiscal austerity to growth and must include the social dimension and not only the economy and finance. Policies targeted at social and territorial cohesion already exist in the EU (e.g. European Globalisation Adjustment Fund, European Social Fund, European Regional Development Fund, Cohesion Fund, Youth Employment Initiative) but their scope should be widened if 'the EU is not only concerned with economic growth, but also with social progress' (Fernandes and Maslauskaite, 2013: 22).

With regard to responsibility and co-responsibility, undoubtedly in a community of nation states sharing a common destiny, solidarity cannot exist without individual responsibility. Every country has to do its best to address and solve domestic structural problems: this is a prerequisite for creating reciprocal trust, the basis for solidarity. Therefore no EU member state can be exempted from agreed common rules and policies just because of a mutual assistance programme. However, rescue packages, where needed, must not be 'punitive' as they were in the case of Greece. Finally, individual responsibility and mutual solidarity make co-responsibility in the management of economic and social policies possible and desirable. If this can be achieved and the support of citizens can be renewed, then full fiscal union may eventually become a welcome and feasible goal of EU policy.

A major issue on the way toward fiscal union is the definition of the proper dimension of the EU federal budget. In 1977, the MacDougall Report estimated that in a pre-federal stage the budget of the EU should be around 2 per cent of GDP and 5–7 per cent if the EU became a full federal union with a small federal public sector. Currently, the last EU multi-annual budget amounted to just 1 per cent of EU GDP, down from the already small 1.24 per cent, a figure some consider insufficient for use as a tool of European economic policy. However, the sovereign debt crisis revealed that economic stability in the eurozone is a supranational public good that EU institutions must seek to provide (Trésor-éco, 2013). In our opinion the EU budget does not need to reach the dimensions suggested by the MacDougall report in order to stabilize the EU economy. In another paper we showed that by exploiting innovative financial tools, such as project-bonds (EIB, 2012), supranational aggregate demand can be boosted in Europe by 2 per cent, thanks to investment in supranational infrastructure and social projects, increasing the EU budget by just 0.19 per cent (Fiorentini and Montani, 2014).[4] Such an increase in the EU budget is possible under the current Treaties and would convey the message that the EU budget can be used as a useful instrument of European economic policies well beyond what is generally supposed.

As previously recalled, critics of the proposal of a fiscal union based on the pooling of common resources believe that it risks becoming a 'transfer union' characterized by the permanent transfer of funds from one state to another, creating problems of moral hazard. In other words, the fear is that in the presence of permanent transfers, highly indebted countries have no incentive to follow 'sound' budgetary policies. However, it is not necessary to create a 'transfer union' in order to have a good supranational stabilization tool in the eurozone. For example, a 'collective insurance fund' could work by countries with a positive output gap depositing a certain percentage of the difference between their actual and potential output into a common fund, and countries with a negative output gap being allowed to freely withdraw funds up to a given threshold. Withdrawals beyond that amount would be subject to the approval of other EMU governments and, in this case, made conditional on the adoption of appropriate economic policies. Persistent not compliance with the agreed policies would cost a loss of sovereignty over the management of domestic economic policy. Since, in general, the economic cycles of member states are not synchronized, the benefit of such a scheme is that every country knows that, sooner or later, it can count on the insurance fund in the case of idiosyncratic negative shocks, so none could complain that it is the 'net lender'. In fact, when the economic cycle picks up, the former borrower contributes to the insurance fund, becoming a lender (Tommaso Padoa-Schioppa Group, 2012). With this type of mutual insurance scheme, moral hazard would be minimized, solidarity among EMU member states would be enhanced and citizens would have a positive perception of European institutions.

Turning now to the social dimension of the EMU, one unpleasant feature of recent austerity policies is that they have used social and welfare expenditure as an adjustment variable. A more efficient use of funds in this field would be useful and is very often necessary but if the bail-out of the financial system occurs at the expense of welfare and public health while growth remains very weak and unemployment keeps rising, disaffection with the EU cannot but get stronger and stronger. To preserve social cohesion and stabilize the economy, a cyclical adjustment fund, such as the European Employment Stabilization Fund (EESF) aimed at helping European workers could be set up (Fiorentini and Montani, 2014). An interesting feature of such a proposal is that it would be directly targeted at individual European citizens and would require the temporary rather than permanent transfer of resources among EU countries. It is feasible in the short run if based on the expansion of the existing European Globalisation Adjustment Fund along the lines discussed in Fiorentini and Montani (2014).

The Common Unemployment Insurance System (CUIS) (Dullen and Ficthner, 2013) is another interesting proposal very close to the EESF and targeted at directly helping individual European workers in the case they lose their job without creating permanent transfer of funds from one European country to another. According to this proposal, workers would directly pay a part of their wages into the common European fund without incurring additional burdens because the new insurance would partly substitute for contributions to existing national systems. Of course, national government could always offer additional level of protection beyond the one granted by the CUIS. The common insurance fund would pay in case of short-term unemployment (up to one year) and according to the proponents it would have significant stabilization effects on the EU economy because it would result in income transfer to households which usually have a high propensity to consume.

A move in the direction of the establishment of a social pillar in the EU could be the exclusion of public social investment from budget targets, which would also help to reduce the pressure on national welfare systems (Vanderbroucke *et al.*, 2011). Also important are measures to facilitate labour mobility in the EU, the increasing transfer of pension rights and the improved dissemination of information about job opportunities in European countries (Fernandes and Maslauskaite, 2013).

Mutualization and co-management of sovereign debt is another hotly debated issue. In our opinion, several factors argue in favour of creating a large common market for sovereign debt in the eurozone. The first is that it would help the management and transmission of monetary policy in the EMU, improving the effectiveness of open market operations by the ECB. The second is that it would be a decisive step in the establishment of a large and liquid continental financial market under the co-responsibility of all member countries, and this would make any new speculative attack on sovereign debt in the EMU very costly (and unlikely).

Several proposals move in this direction, from Blue Bonds and Eurobonds (Delpla and von Weizsacker, 2010; Jones, 2010, 2012) to the European Redemption Pact proposed by the German Council of Economic Experts (Doluca *et al.*, 2012). What they share is the strong opposition of the German government, officially because of moral hazard. Yet, it is hard to imagine a federal fiscal union in a large monetary area such as the EMU without some form of Eurobonds. How moral hazard can be minimized by mutual insurance schemes has already been explained. Financial stability is an important public good which the EMU should provide; a Eurobond market would be a very useful tool for that goal. True, initially the yield on Eurobonds would be higher than on similar German bonds but even Germany, which currently pays very low interest rates on its debt, would greatly benefit from stronger financial stability of the eurozone in the medium and long run. Financial stability in a stronger and tougher EMU would make healthy economic growth easier for everybody to achieve.

The list could go on with other feasible supranational policies able to stabilize the EMU without imposing unnecessary austerity and destroying the main features of European welfare states, while at the same time increasing solidarity in Europe. Our hope is that national governments and EU institutions (Commission and Parliament) understand that the time for a radical change in EU policies has come and that a new 'sense of common purpose' based on co-responsibility and solidarity among European countries and citizens is possible.

## Notes

1   According to the standard optimum currency area theory (OCA), countries joining a currency area with a single currency or with several currencies which are irrevocably pegged, form an optimal area if the following economic condition are satisfied: price and wage flexibility; mobility of labour and other factors of production;

fiscal union which entails the possibility of supranational fiscal transfer among member countries. Those conditions assure that asymmetric shocks impacting on individual members of the currency union do not lead to a general crisis of the currency area (Mundell, 1961; McKinnon, 1963; Kenen, 1969). Clearly, the EMU fails to meet the standard OCA criteria, nor was the EMU project based on them (Mogelli, 2008).

2 Another implication, less obvious, is the following: if a country with a debt/GDP ratio above 60 per cent has a positive primary surplus, it still has to increase its primary surplus in order to reach and maintain the 60 per cent debt/GDP level (Tamborini, 1997). In practice, as long as real interest rates are greater than real growth rates, the fiscal rules of the EMU mean that a country has to adopt a more restrictive fiscal policy than would be necessary to stabilize and decrease the debt/GDP ratio.

3 Actually, one single European social model does not exist; there are at least four different welfare systems (Anglo-Saxon, Mediterranean, Continental, Scandinavian). However, comparing European social policies with other parts of the world, some common elements are evident. In general, in Europe, the access of citizens to welfare provisions is more universal and the level of expenditure is higher than in North America or Asian countries.

4 The Project Bonds Initiative in a joint project by the European Investment Bank and the European Commission aimed at stimulating capital market funding for large-scale infrastructure investment in transport, energy, communications and information technology. The initiative relies on public-private partnerships to attract additional funds from institutional investors.

## References

Alesina, A. and Ardagna, S. (2010). 'The Design of Fiscal Adjustment.' *NBER Working Paper Series*, W18423.

Allard, C., Brooks, P. K., Bluedorn, J. C. *et al.* (2013). 'Toward a Fiscal Union for the Euro Area.' *IMF Staff Discussion Note*, SDN/13/09.

Auerbach, A. J. and Gorodnichenko, Y. (2012). 'Measuring the Output Responses to Fiscal Policy.' *American Economic Journal: Economic Policy*, 4 (2), pp. 1–27.

Bae, K. and Bailey, W. (2011). 'The Latin Monetary Union: Some Evidence on Europe's Failed Common Currency.' *Review of Development Finance*, 1 (2), pp. 131–149.

Barro, R. (1974). 'Are Government Bonds Net Wealth?' *Journal of Political Economy*, 82, pp. 1095–1117.

Barro, R. and Gordon, D. (1983). 'Rules, Discretion and Reputation in a Model of Monetary Policy.' *Journal of Monetary Economics*, 12, pp. 101–121.

Batini, N., Callegari, G. and Melina, G. (2012). 'Successful Austerity in the United States, Europe and Japan.' *IMF Working Papers*, WP/12/90.

Bayoumi, T. and Eichengreen, B. (1993). 'Shocking Aspects of European Monetary Integration.' In Torres, F. and Giavazzi, F. (eds.) *Adjustment and Growth in the European Monetary Union*. Cambridge: Cambridge University Press.

Blanchard, O. and Leigh, D. (2013). 'Growth Forecast Errors and Fiscal Multipliers.' *IMF Working Papers*, WP/13/1.

Boitani, A. and Hamaui, R. (2013). 'L'Europa in Bilico fra Unione Monetaria e Stato Federale.' In Nardozzi, G. and Silva, F. (eds.) *La globalizzazione dopo la Crisi*. Milano: Francesco Brioschi Editore.

Bordo, M. and Capie, F. (eds.) (1993). *Monetary Regimes in Transition*. Cambridge: Cambridge University Press.

Calcagno, A. (2012). 'Can Austerity Work?' *Review of Keynesian Economics*, Inaugural Issue, pp. 24–36.

Chmelar, A. (2013). 'Household Debt and the European Crisis.' *Research Report European Credit Research Institute*, 13.

Coenen, G., Ergec, C. J., Freedman, C. *et al.* (2012). 'Effects of Fiscal Stimulus in Structural Models.' *American Economic Journal: Macroeconomics*, 4 (1), pp. 22–68.

Cour-Thimann, P. (2013). 'Target Balances and the Crisis in the Euro Area.' *CSEifo Forum*, 14 (April).

De Grauwe, P. (2013). 'Design Failures in the Eurozone: Can They Be Fixed?' *LSE 'Europe in Question' Discussion Paper Series*, 57/2013.

De Grauwe, P. and Vanheverbeke, W. (1993). 'Is Europe an Optimum Currency Area?' In Masson, P. R. and Taylor, M. (eds.) *Policy Issue in the Operation of Currency Unions*. Cambridge: Cambridge University Press.

Delpla, J. and von Weizsacker, J. (2010). 'The Blue Bond Proposal.' *Bruegel Policy Brief*, 3 (May).

Dettman, G., Mobert, J. and Weistroffer, C. (2012). 'Bilateral Current Account Rebalancing in the EMU.' *Intereconomics*, 47 (4), pp. 257–264.

Doluca, H., Hubner, M., Rumpf, D. and Weigert, B. (2012). 'The European Redemption Pact: An Illustrative Guide.' *German Council of Economic Experts Working Paper 2/2012*.

Dullen, S. and Ficthner, F. (2013). 'A Common Unemployment Insurance System for the Euro Area.' *DIW Economic Bulletin*, 3 (1), pp. 9–14.

ECB (2013). 'The International Role of the Euro.' *European Central Bank*, July.

EIB (2012). *An Outline Guide to Project Bond Credit Enhancement and the Project Bond Initiative*. Luxembourg: European Investment Bank.

European Commission (2012). 'A Blueprint for a Deep and Genuine Economic and Monetary Union: Launching a European Debate', p. 51.

Feldstein, M. (1997). 'EMU and International Conflict.' *Foreign Affairs*, November/December, pp. 60–73.

Fernandes, S. and Maslauskaite, K. (2013). 'Deepening the EMU: How to Maintain and Develop the European Social Model?' *Notre Europe-Jacques Delors Institute*, p. 162.

Fiorentini, R. (2005). 'The International Role of the Euro and the Relationship between Europe and the International Monetary Fund.' *Il Politico*, LXX (1), pp. 35–55.

Fiorentini, R. and Montani, G. (2014). 'A Keynesian Recovery Policy for the European Union.' *Bulletin of Political Economy*, 8 (2).

Fratianni, M. and Spinelli, F. (1997). *A Monetary History of Italy*. Cambridge: Cambridge University Press.

Giavazzi, F. and Pagano, M. (1996). 'Non Keynesian Effects of Fiscal Policy Changes: International Evidence and Swedish Experience.' *Swedish Economic Policy Review*, 3, pp. 67–103.

Herdnon, T., Ash, M. and Pollin, R. (2014). 'Does High Public Debt Consistently Stifle Economic Growth? A Critique of Reinhart and Rogoff.' *Cambridge Journal of Economics*, 38 (2), pp. 257–279.

Holland, D. and Portes, J. (2012). 'Self Defeating Austerity?' *National Institute Economic Review*, 222 (October).

Issing, O. (2008). *The Birth of the Euro*. Cambridge: Cambridge University Press.

Jones, E. (2010). 'A Eurobond Proposal to Promote Stability and Liquidity while Preventing Moral Hazard.' *ISPI Policy Brief*, 180 (March).

Jones, E. (2012). 'Eurobonds, Flight to Quality and TARGET2 Imbalances.' *European Policy Analysis*, 4, pp. 1–10.

Kenen, P. (1969). 'The Optimum Currency Area: An Eclectic View.' In Mundell, R. and Swoboda, A. (eds.) *Monetary Problems of the International Economics*. Chicago: Chicago University Press.

Kentikelenis, A., Karanikolos, M., Reeves, A. *et al.* (2014). 'Greece's Health Crisis: From Austerity to Denialism.' *Lancet*, 383 (22 February), pp. 748–753.

Kindleberger, C. (1993). *A Financial History of Western Europe*. Oxford: Oxford University Press.

Kindleberger, C. and Aliber, R. (2011). *Manias, Panics and Crashes: A History of Financial Crisis*. Gordonsville, VA: Palgrave Macmillan.

Kydland, F. and Prescott, E. (1977). 'Rules Rather than Discretion: The Inconsistency of Opriman Plan.' *Journal of Political Economy*, 85, pp. 473–491.

McKinnon, R. I. (1963). 'Optimum Currency Areas.' *American Economic Review*, 52, pp. 717–725.

Minsky, H. (1982). *Can 'It' Happen Again?* Armonk, NY: M. E. Sharpe Incorporated.

Minsky, H. (1986). *Stabilizing an Unstable Economy*. New York: McGraw-Hill.

Mogelli, F. P. (2008). 'European Economic and Monetary Integration and the Optimum Currency Area Theory.' *European Commission Economic Papers*, 302, pp. 1–58.

Mundell, R. (1961). 'A Theory of Optimum Currency Areas.' *American Economic Review*, 51, pp. 657–665.

Pisani-Ferry, J. (2012). 'The Euro Crisis and the New Impossible Trinity.' *Briegel Policy Contribution*, 2012/01, pp. 16.

Pisani-Ferry, J. (2013). 'Is the Euro Crisis Over?' *Project Syndicate*, 1 February.

Reinhart, C. M. and Rogoff, K. S. (2009). *This Time is Different*. Princeton: Princeton University Press.

Reinhart, C. M. and Rogoff, K. S. (2010). 'Growth in Time of Debt.' *American Economic Review: Papers & Proceedings*, 100.

Ricciuti, R. (2003). 'Assessing Ricardian Equivalence.' *Journal of Economic Survey*, 17, pp. 55–78.

Sapir, A., Wolff, G. B., de Sousa, C. and Terzi, A. (2014) *The Troika and Financial Assistance in the Euro Area: Successes and Failures*. Brussels: European Parliament.

Tamborini, R. (1997). 'Living in the EMU: The Dynamics of the Maastrict Treaty Fiscal Rules.' *Rivista Italiana degli Economisti*, 2, pp. 335–360.

Tanzi, V. (2013). *Dollars, Euros and Debt*. Houndmills, Basingstoke: Palgrave Macmillan.

Tommaso Padoa-Schioppa Group (2012). 'Completing the Euro: A Road Map toward Fiscal Union in Europe.' *Notre Europe-Jacques Delors Institute*, pp. 50.

Torres, F. and Giavazzi, F. (eds.) (1993). *Adjustment and Growth in the European Monetary Union*. Cambridge: Cambridge University Press.

Trésor-éco (2013) Un budget pour la zone euro. Lettre No 120. Paris.

Vanderbroucke, F., Hemerijck, A. and Palier, B. (2011). 'The EU Needs a Social Investment Pact.' *OSE Paper Series*, 5 (May).

Zezza, G. (2012). 'The Impact of Fiscal Austerity in the Eurozone.' *Review of Keynesian Economics*, Inaugural Issue, pp. 37–54.

# 10 Game changer? The transformation of global gas markets and the future of the EU–Russia energy relationship

*Richard Connolly*

## Introduction

Over the past decade, energy security has become one of the most important areas of EU energy and foreign policy. The increasing prominence of energy security as an issue of concern to policy makers is due to a number of inter-related factors. First, the rapid growth of developing economies, especially China, caused an epochal shift in global energy demand patterns. Global energy demand has ceased to be dominated solely by high-income countries, such as the USA, Japan and the Member States of the European Union. Instead, the faster growing populations and economies of China, India and elsewhere are beginning to shape the global energy landscape in new and sometimes unsettling ways (see Bradshaw, 2013). Second, European countries have become increasingly cognizant of the need to reduce a perceived over-dependence on energy supplies from Russia, the single largest supplier of energy to Europe. The shock of the 2006 and 2009 disruptions to gas supplies from Russia via Ukraine, as well as the advent of a more assertive Russian foreign policy since 2000 (e.g. Goldman, 2008; Hill, 2008; Perovic *et al.*, 2009; Aalto, 2012) have contrived to engender a feeling of collective anxiety over the vital role that Russian energy supplies play in sustaining economic activity in Europe. Third, the Lisbon Treaty of 2009 offered new possibilities to forge a common energy security policy founded on interconnecting national gas and electricity markets, the promotion of a competitive, rules-based energy trade both in Europe and its wider neighbourhood, and the diversification of sources of energy supply (see Treaty of Lisbon, Article 194).

The development of a common energy security policy, as articulated in the Lisbon Treaty, is aimed at reducing the strategic dependence of individual Member States on single external sources of supply, and to ensure that energy markets are liquid, open and functioning according to market-based rules. According to the Commission, achieving these aims would help secure the ultimate objective of ensuring 'the physical availability of energy products and services on the market, at a price which is affordable for all consumers (private and industrial), while contributing to the EU's wider social and climate goals' (Commission, 2010: 2). This statement hints at the multiple goals hoped to be achieved by a common energy policy, encompassing social, economic and environmental objectives.

The development of a common energy policy, however, has not taken place in a vacuum. Instead, global pressures, such as the growth in importance of developing economies and the resurgence of Russia as a foreign policy actor have hastened the need for Europe to formulate a single policy to represent the interests of its 28 Member States. Alongside the structural shifts in the global political economy described above, a revolutionary transformation in the global gas market has and continues to take place. Gas, a key component of the European energy mix, and one that has hitherto tied Europe to Russia, has undergone tumultuous changes in the way in which it can be extracted and transported across the world. The consequences of these changes will likely be felt for decades to come.

This chapter examines how the deep, rapid and still ongoing transformation of the global gas market is shaping European energy security, whether these changes are likely to result in a reconfiguration of the gas trade relationship between Europe and Russia, and whether Europe will be able to leverage global changes in the gas market to help it achieve its energy policy objectives. The chapter is organized as follows. The next section outlines the main contours of Europe's energy landscape, with attention paid to the role that Russia plays as a key supplier of gas to Europe. The third section describes the main features of the transformation of global gas markets, focusing on the role of shale gas and the growth in the trade of liquefied natural gas (LNG). The fourth section considers the role that gas market changes might play in reducing Europe's sense of supply risk from its current dependence on supplies of natural gas from Russia. The fifth section briefly considers the role that developments in global gas markets might have in helping Europe achieve its other energy policy objectives.

## The European energy landscape: main trends and policies

Over the last three decades there has been a gradual but highly significant change in the relationship between energy consumption and economic activity in Europe (Bradshaw, 2013: 52). Prompted by the energy crisis of the 1970s, European economies, on aggregate, experienced a dual process of economic restructuring and de-industrialization (Eichengreen, 2007; Berend, 2008). Faced with higher costs, European economies became more energy efficient. After the end of the Cold War, many European manufacturers also began to shift the labour-intensive stages of many industrial activities (e.g. final stage assembly) to countries with lower unit labour costs, usually East Asia (e.g. China), but also within Europe itself as, for example, stages of the production process were switched from western Europe to the ex-socialist countries of central and eastern Europe (see Connolly, 2008, 2012a, 2012b).

These trends in economic restructuring across Europe, along with modest population growth (Magnus, 2009), caused overall energy consumption to

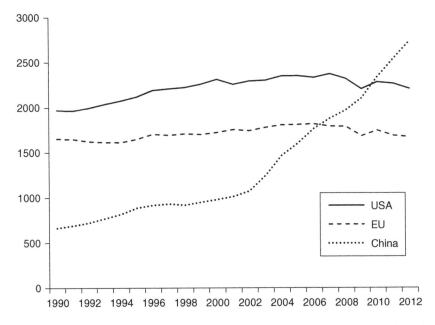

*Figure 10.1* Total energy consumption in the EU, USA and China, 1990–2012 (Mtoe)

decline from the peak reached in around the mid-2000s (Figure 10.1). As is evident, rapid economic growth in China, partially based on the relocation of industrial processes from Europe to China, has pushed China to become the world's largest consumer of energy. Nevertheless, if the overall EU level of energy consumption has started to decline, it is true that some countries use their energy more efficiently than others, with the average level of consumption concealing significant variation in energy intensity. As Table 10.1 illustrates, there is a clear divide between the richer economies of western Europe, which generate much higher levels of GDP per unit of energy used, and the ex-socialist countries of central and eastern Europe. Despite having experienced over two decades of economic restructuring and market reform, the legacy of wasteful and energy intensive planned economies continues to be felt. Indeed, despite the ex-socialist economies having experienced the most rapid growth in energy efficiency – with most generating over twice as much GDP per unit of energy used as they did in 1990 – absolute levels of energy intensity remain well below the EU average.

In addition to the huge disparities in energy intensity observed across Europe, it is also important to note that the economies of the region rely on a widely differing range of sources of energy supply. A function of geography, past investment decisions, energy policy and political considerations, the variation in energy mixes evident across Europe causes Member States to perceive different threats and opportunities to energy security. As Table 10.2 shows, oil

*Table 10.1* GDP per unit of energy use in the European Union, 2011 (constant 2011 PPP $ per kg of oil equivalent)

| Country | 1990 | 2000 | 2011 | Change 1990–2011 |
|---|---|---|---|---|
| Austria | 9.3 | 10.6 | 10.9 | 0.17 |
| Belgium | 6.3 | 6.4 | 7.4 | 0.19 |
| Bulgaria | 3.0 | 4.0 | 5.9 | 0.98 |
| Croatia | – | 8.8 | 10.3 | – |
| Cyprus | 9.7 | 9.3 | 11.2 | 0.15 |
| Czech Republic | 3.8 | 4.9 | 6.5 | 0.71 |
| Denmark | 9.7 | 11.7 | 12.9 | 0.34 |
| Estonia | – | 4.2 | 5.5 | – |
| Finland | 4.9 | 5.3 | 6.0 | 0.22 |
| France | 7.6 | 8.2 | 9.4 | 0.23 |
| Germany | 6.9 | 8.8 | 10.8 | 0.55 |
| Greece | 9.8 | 9.8 | 11.3 | 0.15 |
| Hungary | 6.1 | 7.2 | 9.0 | 0.46 |
| Ireland | 7.5 | 11.1 | 14.9 | 0.99 |
| Italy | 11.5 | 11.5 | 12.3 | 0.07 |
| Latvia | 4.6 | 7.1 | 9.4 | 1.04 |
| Lithuania | 3.6 | 5.9 | 9.3 | 1.58 |
| Luxembourg | 6.3 | 10.5 | 11.0 | 0.74 |
| Malta | 8.5 | 14.7 | 13.8 | 0.61 |
| Netherlands | 7.0 | 8.5 | 9.3 | 0.34 |
| Poland | 3.7 | 6.1 | 8.3 | 1.26 |
| Portugal | 11.5 | 10.5 | 11.8 | 0.03 |
| Romania | 4.2 | 6.1 | 9.6 | 1.29 |
| Slovak Republic | 3.8 | 4.7 | 7.8 | 1.06 |
| Slovenia | 6.4 | 6.9 | 8.0 | 0.24 |
| Spain | 10.2 | 9.9 | 11.8 | 0.16 |
| Sweden | 5.3 | 6.5 | 8.0 | 0.51 |
| United Kingdom | 6.7 | 8.3 | 11.7 | 0.76 |
| European Union | 7.1 | 8.5 | 10.2 | 0.44 |

Source: World Bank Development Indicators (World Bank, 2013).

accounts for 36.5 per cent of the EU's total energy supply, natural gas for 23.9 per cent, coal for 17.6 per cent, nuclear energy for 11.9 per cent, hydroelectric power for 4.4. per cent and renewables – despite years of brisk growth, for just 5.7 per cent. There are big differences between countries in the structure of their energy consumption. Hydroelectric power is a vital component of the energy mix in Austria (26.9 per cent of total primary energy) and Sweden (33.6 per cent), while nuclear energy is the single most important source of power in France (39.2 per cent). Renewables have grown in most countries, but have gained important shares of total primary energy supply in Denmark (20 per cent), Portugal (13.7 per cent) and Spain (10.3 per cent).

Fossil fuels, which account for 78 per cent of the European Union's energy consumption, remain the dominant source of energy. The importance of each fossil fuel varies. In Greece, oil is the dominant source of energy, accounting for 53.5 per cent of total primary energy consumption. Oil is also the

*Table 10.2*  Sources of primary energy consumption in selected European economies, 2012 (per cent of total primary energy consumption)

|  | Oil | Natural gas | Coal | Nuclear | Hydro-electric | Renewables | Total |
|---|---|---|---|---|---|---|---|
| Austria | 37.5 | 24.5 | 6.0 | – | 26.9 | 4.8 | 100 |
| Belgium | 50.5 | 25.1 | 5.0 | 15.0 | 0.2 | 4.3 | 100 |
| Bulgaria | 21.2 | 14.0 | 39.1 | 20.1 | 3.9 | 1.7 | 100 |
| Czech Republic | 21.7 | 17.7 | 39.6 | 16.5 | 1.7 | 3.1 | 100 |
| Denmark | 44.7 | 20.6 | 14.7 | – | – | 20.0 | 100 |
| Finland | 34.5 | 10.6 | 11.0 | 20.1 | 14.4 | 9.8 | 100 |
| France | 33.0 | 15.6 | 4.6 | 39.2 | 5.4 | 2.2 | 100 |
| Germany | 35.8 | 21.7 | 25.4 | 7.2 | 1.5 | 8.3 | 100 |
| Greece | 53.5 | 13.2 | 26.0 | – | 3.5 | 3.8 | 100 |
| Hungary | 27.4 | 40.2 | 13.7 | 16.4 | – | 2.7 | 100 |
| Italy | 39.5 | 38.0 | 10.0 | – | 5.8 | 6.7 | 100 |
| Lithuania | 43.3 | 50.0 | 3.3 | – | 1.7 | 3.3 | 100 |
| Netherlands | 49.5 | 36.8 | 9.5 | 1.0 | – | 3.0 | 100 |
| Poland | 25.7 | 15.3 | 55.3 | – | 0.5 | 3.2 | 100 |
| Portugal | 48.0 | 18.5 | 12.8 | – | 6.6 | 13.7 | 100 |
| Republic of Ireland | 47.7 | 30.8 | 11.5 | – | 1.5 | 7.7 | 100 |
| Romania | 26.2 | 36.0 | 19.9 | 7.7 | 8.3 | 1.8 | 100 |
| Slovakia | 20.7 | 32.0 | 18.9 | 20.7 | 5.9 | 1.8 | 100 |
| Spain | 44.1 | 19.5 | 13.3 | 9.6 | 3.2 | 10.3 | 100 |
| Sweden | 26.1 | 1.9 | 2.8 | 27.6 | 33.6 | 7.9 | 100 |
| United Kingdom | 33.6 | 34.6 | 19.2 | 7.8 | 0.6 | 4.1 | 100 |
| European Union | 36.5 | 23.9 | 17.6 | 11.9 | 4.4 | 5.7 | 100 |

Source: BP *Statistical Review of World Energy for 2012* (BP, 2013).

dominant fuel in Belgium (50.5 per cent) and Holland (49.5 per cent). Coal, considered the 'dirtiest' of the fossil fuels because of its relatively high carbon intensity, still accounts for 55.3 per cent of Poland's total energy mix, and is an important source of power in other central and eastern European countries. Perhaps most surprisingly, coal remains an important part of the energy mix in several high-income countries. In Germany, coal accounts for 25.4 per cent of total primary energy consumption, making it the second most important source of power. Moreover, in absolute terms, Germany's coal consumption of 79.2 Mtoe in 2012 made it the largest consumer of coal in Europe, and the seventh largest consumer in the world. Similarly, coal consumption of 39.1 Mtoe in 2012, made the UK the third largest consumer of coal in the European Union.

Of particular pertinence to this chapter is the importance of natural gas as a key component of nearly all energy mixes across Europe, with gas consumption growing almost relentlessly since 1965 (Figure 10.2). The important role played by natural gas in Europe has deep historical roots, based on the exploitation of North Sea gas fields, imports from North Africa, and perhaps most importantly the growth of dense gas supply relationships between the

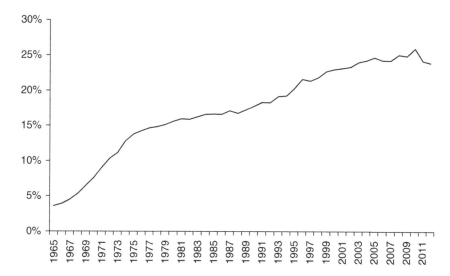

*Figure 10.2* Gas share of total primary energy consumption in the EU, 1965–2012 (per cent)

Soviet Union, on the one hand, and Austria, Germany and Italy, on the other, from the 1960s onwards (Hogselius, 2013), as well as by the legacy of Soviet gas links with the former planned economies of central and eastern Europe (Connolly, 2012b; Bradshaw, 2013). While path dependencies in energy mixes are important in explaining the importance of gas to the European economy, it is also true that many consider natural gas to be a relatively clean solution to meeting climate change goals due to it possessing a lower carbon intensity than oil and coal (Smil, 2010). As a result, the International Energy Agency (IEA) forecasts a rise in European gas consumption over the next 20 years (IEA, 2013, p. 128), especially as Germany attempts its *Energywiende* (roughly translated as 'energy transition'), which will be likely to place increased gas consumption – to supplant coal in power generation – high on the energy policy agenda (Buchan, 2012; Dickel, 2014). In short, gas looks likely only to grow in importance to Europe over the next few decades (Melling, 2010).

From an energy security perspective, Europe's weakness is that it does not produce sufficient gas to supply its own consumption requirements. While the countries of the Europe Union consumed 443.9 billion cubic metres (bcm) of gas in 2012, only 149.6 bcm was derived from domestic (i.e. EU) sources. The difference – 294.2 bcm, or 66 per cent of total EU consumption – was imported. This makes Europe the largest importer of natural gas in the world. Most of these gas imports were delivered through pipelines, with only around a fifth of imported gas arriving in the form of LNG, mostly from Qatar, Algeria and Nigeria. Of the gas that is delivered to Europe through pipelines, the largest single supplier is Russia (132.9 bcm in 2013; Gazprom, 2014), accounting for around a quarter of total European natural gas consumption, and around a third of European gas imports, although this is down from around half in the 1980s (Sutela, 2012: 113). It is important to note, however, that although Russia's role as a gas supplier is important to Europe as a whole, its influence varies across countries. Countries located in central and eastern Europe, such as Estonia and Bulgaria, are heavily reliant on Russian gas, while countries like Portugal do not import any gas from Russia. In this sense, it is not useful to speak of EU imports of Russian gas, but instead of individual Member States' imports of Russian gas (Solanko and Sutela, 2009).

The gas relationship between Member States and Russia is discussed in the fourth section. For now it is sufficient to state that Russia is clearly the most important actor in the European gas market, supplying nearly as much gas as Europe produces itself. As a result, it plays, and will continue to play, a key role in determining whether Europe will achieve its energy objectives. But what are Europe's energy policy objectives? And is there a big difference between EU objectives and those of Member States?

Europe's energy policy objectives are best summarized as the three 'E's': energy security, economic competitiveness and environmental sustainability (Commission, 2008; Bradshaw, 2013: 75). Energy security, defined by Daniel Yergin (1991) as 'assur[ing] adequate, reliable supplies of energy at reasonable prices' requires the 'reduction of risks to energy systems, both internal and external, and to build resilience to those risks that remain' (Dreyer and Stang, 2014: 11). The means to reducing these risks include: ensuring the efficient functioning of markets so that supply and demand can meet; the provision of production and transportation infrastructure; the development of risk management systems; maintaining a diverse range of suppliers; and demand reduction (energy efficiency).

Achieving energy security in a way that maintains economic competitiveness and in an environmentally sustainable fashion is fraught with tension, both between the three objectives themselves (e.g. does the environmental sustainability of renewables trump economic competitiveness if renewables are significantly more expensive?), and between the EU and its Member States (e.g. will a state such as Poland attempt to reduce its reliance on coal if it means relying on Russia for gas, even though this would represent a more environmentally sustainable course of action?). The latter tension is especially significant if only because energy policy remains primarily an area of national competence, even though the Commission has attempted to impose its energy vision on Member States through its role in creating the Single Market and coordinating climate change policy (Bradshaw, 2013: 74).

Russia's role as a key supplier of natural gas for many states represents the most obvious challenge to energy security (Perovic *et al.*, 2009; Aalto, 2012; Feklyunina, 2012; Le Coq and Paltseva, 2012). The perception of Russia as an unreliable gas supplier was exacerbated by the disputes between Russia and several 'transit' states (Belarus, Moldova, Ukraine), with the most notable disruption being the gas disputes between Russia and Ukraine in 2006 and 2009 (Yafimava, 2011; Smith Stegen, 2011; Feklyunina, 2012). The ex-socialist countries of central and eastern Europe tend to have a heightened perception of overdependence on Russian gas precisely because they rely on Russia for a much higher proportion of their gas and total primary energy needs (Noël, 2009). Estonia and Bulgaria, for example, both import all or nearly all their gas from Russia. This sense of vulnerability is not so acute among the larger economies of western Europe. Austria, Italy and Germany, for example, have more diverse primary energy mixes, and source their natural gas from a variety of suppliers.

To sum up so far, the economies of Europe use enormous amounts of natural gas to power their societies. Much of this gas is imported, with Russia the single biggest supplier. For some states, Russia's privileged position represents a threat to energy security (e.g. Poland, the Baltic states). For others (e.g. Germany, Italy, Hungary), Russia's relatively cheap gas offers an environmentally sustainable way to maintain economic competiveness. For some countries, gas is an important component of the overall energy mix, yet they do not rely on Russia for much or any gas (e.g. Spain, the UK). These tensions are felt unevenly across Europe, depending on whether Russia is in a key position as a supplier of gas. This has prevented the emergence of a single energy policy, especially in the area of natural gas imports. However, recent technological developments in the global gas market might offer the prospect of a massive increase in the supply and availability (liquidity) of gas on global markets, which in turn may allow the EU to formulate a common energy policy that meets its three energy policy objectives and reduces the risk that Russia might pose to energy security. The nature of the global gas 'revolution' is the subject of the next section.

### The global gas 'revolution': what could it mean for Europe?

It is the convergence of two distinct but related processes that makes up the global gas 'revolution': first, the extraction of unconventional gas, primarily shale gas; and second, the increase in traded liquefied natural gas (LNG).

The shale gas 'revolution' refers to a phenomenon that is primarily taking place in the United States. Shale gas, one of three types of unconventional gas, is, according to the United States Geological Survey, 'gas sourced from discrete fields or pools localized in structural stratigraphical traps by the boundary of gas and water'. Or, as Paul Stevens points out in simpler terms, 'a conventional gas well is drilled and the gas flows in commercial quantities. For unconventional gas, drilling is not enough to generate a commercial flow. Some other artificial stimulus and special recovery processes are required' (Stevens, 2012: 2). These special recovery processes include two key technologies: horizontal drilling and hydraulic fracturing, or 'fracking', a process which involves the injection of sand, chemicals and water into shale rock to release trapped hydrocarbons. Neither of the two technologies is new, with both having been employed for a number of decades, but in recent years they have been used to increasingly spectacular effect in US gas fields (Yergin, 2011).

As a result of the shale gas revolution, the Energy Information Administration (EIA) forecasts natural gas production in North America to grow by 56 per cent between 2010 and 2040 (EIA, 2013), with the US alone accounting for two-thirds of this growth. Shale gas rose from less than 1 per cent of domestic gas production in the United States in 2000 to over 20 per cent by 2010. The EIA projected that it will account for around half of the United States total gas supply by 2035. The impact of the shale gas revolution has been significant. The increased supply led to a sharp drop in US domestic gas prices. In 2012, average prices at Henry Hub were $2.76 per million British thermal units (mmBtu), down from $8.85 per mmBtu in 2008. This meant that in 2012 US gas prices were around 25 per cent of the price paid by German importers, and 16 per cent of the price paid for Japanese LNG imports (BP, 2013).

As well as boosting US production and estimates of recoverable reserves, the boom in shale gas led to a radical reassessment of global gas resources, although expectations about the rapid and economic exploitation of these resources remain cautious (see IEA, 2012; EIA, 2013). The EIA expects shale gas production to expand to countries with large technically recoverable resources, such as China, Australia, Mexico and parts of Europe (e.g. the UK, Poland and possibly Ukraine; see Pearson *et al.*, 2012), but the timing and rate of production growth in individual countries remains uncertain (Gény, 2010).

The convergence of the favourable geological, institutional (e.g. tax incentives, public R&D spending, etc.), political and infrastructural conditions that made the US shale gas revolution possible is not easy to repeat (see Stevens, 2012: 9). Nevertheless, it is certainly true that technically recoverable reserves have risen enormously as a result of the shale gas boom. For example, in the US alone, the BP estimate of gas reserves grew from 5 trillion cubic metres (tcm) in 2000 to 8.5 tcm in 2012. Upward estimates of a similar magnitude have been made in other gas producing states (BP, 2013).

As the US shale gas revolution played out, another important development that would result in the globalization of what were previously very much regional markets for gas was taking place. Like the technology used to extract shale gas, the technology to liquefy natural gas for transportation has been around for decades. However, in the last decade LNG technology costs have gradually come down, with LNG trade now accounting for around 10 per cent of all gas produced globally. Gas deficient countries such as Spain, South Korea and Japan, are especially reliant on LNG imports. Despite temporary setbacks in LNG trade in 2012 due to supply problems on certain markets (IEA, 2013), the planned development of new gas fields and the construction of LNG export facilities in countries such as Qatar, Australia, Russia and in eastern Africa has raised expectations that the LNG trade will continue to grow significantly in the years to come. The EIA expects world LNG trade to double from about 283 bcm in 2010 to 566 bcm in 2040 (EIA, 2013).

Despite technological developments, LNG remains expensive when compared to gas that is delivered through pipelines (compare the average LNG import price for Japan of $16.75 per mmBtu to the US Henry Hub price of $2.76 per mmBtu.) However, its great advantage is that it can be transported by tankers rather than pipelines, effectively globalizing gas markets. The growing global LNG trade is allowing gas exporters to sell to the highest bidders – currently located in East Asia – thus permitting gas importers to diversify their imports. This has facilitated the emergence of 'spot' prices on short-term capacity markets. Qatar has become, and will likely remain, the global leader in LNG exports. A number of other exporters, including Australia, eastern African countries, Russia and possibly the US, are expected to contribute to increasing liquidity in global gas markets.

In 2010, shale gas developments in the United States were having a significant impact on global gas markets, creating an oversupply of liquefied natural gas (LNG) and downward pressure on gas prices. The US, which had constructed significant LNG import infrastructure capacity in the 2000s, no longer required imported LNG due to the growth in cheaper, domestically produced shale gas. This caused a glut of LNG on global markets, with LNG diverted from its intended destinations in the US to new destinations in Asia and Europe (Stevens, 2012: 3).

The future of the global gas market is, as ever, unclear. What is certain, however, is that recent developments have opened up new possibilities for energy policy across the world, not least in Europe. The global gas revolution briefly described above has important implications for the EU's energy policy objectives as summarized as the three 'E's'.

First, as far as energy security is concerned, the global gas revolution offers the tantalizing prospect of a diversification of sources of supply. LNG makes it possible, at least in principle, for Europe to import gas from suppliers as far away as Mozambique and Australia. The shale gas revolution, and the presence of significant shale gas deposits in Europe, makes it possible for Europe to expand indigenous production.

Second, if indigenous sources of shale gas can be exploited, there is a chance that Europe could benefit from the boom of cheap natural gas as has happened on the other side of the Atlantic. Although a number of countries have prohibited shale gas extraction (e.g. France and Bulgaria), the presence of significant reserves in Denmark, the UK and Poland, offers the EU as a whole the chance to reduce its import dependency. If shale gas could be exploited at prices lower than the current prices paid for gas imported through pipelines or LNG terminals, then European economic competitiveness could be boosted.

Finally, increased production and/or consumption of natural gas (i.e. as a proportion of the primary energy mix) in Europe also offers an opportunity to utilize a relatively clean (i.e. less carbon intensive) fuel to help European economies meet the climate change policy targets articulated in the '20/20/20' vision (Commission, 2008). The Energy and Climate Package, adopted by the

European Parliament in 2008, states its objectives as being to achieve three goals by 2020: (1) reduce greenhouse gas emissions to 20 per cent below 1990s levels; (2) increase the share of renewables in total energy consumption to 20 per cent; and (3) to reduce total primary energy use by 20 per cent. Increased gas consumption in place of coal in particular would help Europe achieve the first of these three objectives.

To sum up, this section has shown how the global gas revolution has the potential to help European economies meet the EU's energy policy object-ives of security, competitiveness and sustainability. The next section examines Russia's role as the most important supplier of gas to Europe, focusing on why Russian gas is considered by some to represent a threat to energy security.

## Russia as gas supplier: why is it considered a threat to energy security?

In 2012, Russia produced 592.3 bcm of natural gas, making it the world's second largest producer behind the United States (681.4 bcm; BP, 2013). Russia also has the world's second largest reserves of natural gas (32.9 tcm), slightly behind Iran (33.6 tcm), and is the largest exporter of gas (200.7 bcm in 2012), well ahead of Qatar (124.7 bcm) and Norway (111.4 bcm). Of the 220.7 bcm of gas exported in 2012, 105.5 bcm was sent via pipeline to EU countries (BP, 2013). Given that nearly half of the gas exported from Russia ends up in EU countries, it should be clear that the relationship is one of mutual dependence: Russia depends just as much on European demand as Europe depends on Russian supply. However, a number of features of the Russian gas industry pose challenges to Russia's future export capacity.

First, domestically, the Russian gas industry is dominated by the state-controlled company, Gazprom (the state owns a controlling share of 50.001 per cent), which has a quasi-monopoly over production as well as full con-trol over transmission (gas pipelines) and exports to Europe. However, Gazprom's privileged position within the Russian gas industry has eroded. On the domestic front, Gazprom has been exposed to increasing competition in recent years (see Henderson, 2010). By 2012, Gazprom accounted for just under 75 per cent of total gas production, compared to 94 per cent in 1996 (Gazprom, 2014). Gazprom also possessed, until recently, a full export mon-opoly. However, in 2013, the Russian President, Vladimir Putin, announced a gradual weakening of Gazprom's export monopoly, with both Novatek's Yamal LNG and Rosneft-ExxonMobil's Sakhalin 1 project to build LNG ter-minals for export (Shadrina and Bradshaw, 2013). Uncertainty over the pre-cise institutional arrangements governing gas production and export is thus far from assured (see Locatelli, 2014).

Second, as well as being exposed to greater competition, Gazprom's produc-tion and transportation costs have risen and look likely to rise further in the future. Much of Russia's gas production already comes from Arctic onshore locations (the Yamal Peninsula and Archangelsk region) where environmen-tal and technical challenges are rising.[1] Dealing with these demands requires know-how and technological capabilities that are often only available from foreign, usually Western, companies. To this end, European energy companies, such as Total and Wintershall, play an integral role in Russian gas production. The involvement of foreign companies, and the technical demands imposed by production in harsh conditions, all means that costs have risen and profit margins have narrowed. Moreover, ensuring adequate production and transportation infrastructure is in place will demand enormous amounts of investment (IEA, 2011). Without this investment production and export capacity is subject to significant uncertainty.

Third, it is also uncertain as to whether domestic demand for Russian gas will grow at similar or higher rates than export growth. After all, the Russian economy has grown at an average rate of over 5 per cent per year since 1999. If robust economic growth is maintained in the future, domestic use of natural gas could grow beyond expectations (Solanko and Sutela, 2009).

Fourth, Russian government officials have increasingly spoken of an Asian 'pivot', with energy supplies at the heart of this turn to the east (see Lo, 2009; Lo and Hill, 2013). Indeed, in May 2014, a landmark 30-year deal was signed, estimated to be worth US$400 billion for Russia to deliver gas to China (Topalov and Falyakhov, 2014). It has been suggested that this might threaten future European supplies. Whether the significance of this deal has been overstated or not, it is true that even if the Sino-Russian gas deal is fully implemented, Russia will be supplying 38 bcm of gas through pipelines to China, with additional, smaller flows of LNG to follow. Compared to present gas exports to Europe of well over 100 bcm, the role of China is Russian gas exports is likely to remain much smaller than Europe.[2] Perhaps more importantly, there is little reason to think that supplies to China and Europe are mutually exclusive. European gas is supplied from regions in Russia's Arctic, while gas fields in Eastern Siberia will supply China (Henderson, 2014). The only question is whether Gazprom can secure the necessary investment to ensure that production continues in both areas.

Finally, and perhaps most importantly, Gazprom occupies a special role in Russia's system of political economy. The prevailing system of political system can be best described as an example of a *limited access order* (LAO; North *et al.*, 2012). LAOs are societies in which organizations limit market entry and competition to ensure that individuals or organizations (whether it be the state or firms) with market power can accrue rents. The creation of rents by states in LAOs is a consequence of the purposeful creation of differential access for individuals or organizations to the goods and services that the state can provide, such as enforcement of property rights and contracts, legal systems, etc. LAOs tend to exhibit relatively low levels of governance and democratic control, weak standards for the rule of law, and higher levels of corruption. The state, because of its role in the creation and distribution of rents, tends to be active in controlling or influencing significant portions of the economy.

Within this system of preferential access to and distribution of rents, Gazprom plays an important role. As Catherine Locatelli points out, 'the

"Gazprom model" is the organizational and institutional form that enables non-monetary relations and low energy prices to be best managed' (Locatelli, 2014: 55). This ensures that the Russian state, through Gazprom *inter alia*, is able to ensure that commercial imperatives, such as profitability, are secondary to political objectives that include the continued operation of large swathes of Russian industry that are otherwise insolvent (Gaddy and Ickes, 1998, 2010; Woodruff, 1999). In effect, the Russian state operates as the coordinating mechanism for a rent management system in which rents are transferred from rent-producing sectors of the economy (oil, gas) to rent-dependent sectors of the economy (large swathes of the military industrial complex, for example).

It is precisely the subjugation of Gazprom's commercial behaviour to political objectives that concerns many European consumers of Russian gas. Some countries see Gazprom as a potential 'energy weapon' that could be wielded in the event of geopolitical tensions between Russia and European countries (Monaghan, 2007).[3] The crises over gas supplies to Ukraine in 2006 and 2009 are usually cited as cases in point (Perovic *et al.*, 2009; Pirani *et al.*, 2009; Aalto, 2012), while the existence of large differences between prices charged to customers across Europe is also seen as evidence of the politicization of gas export policy. In addition, the construction of two new pipelines (Nord Stream and South Stream) that take gas direct to Europe's largest importers (e.g. Germany and Austria) while circumventing smaller eastern European countries (Poland, the Baltic states) has also been cited as a threat to energy security.

Taken together, the features of the Russian gas market described above can be seen as presenting a threat to European energy policy because: (1) it is not clear that the structure of the Russian gas industry will result in the necessary efficiency or investment required to assure future production and export capacity; (2) Russia may wish to 'pivot' to Asia and concentrate its resources on supplying the growing and seemingly more dynamic Asian markets; and (3) some European countries are worried that Gazprom will be used by the Russian state to achieve foreign policy objectives, despite the evidence so far suggesting that Russia is a reliable gas supplier.

It has been suggested in some quarters that the global gas revolution offers European economies the opportunity to restructure their relationship with Russia by reducing import costs from Gazprom and further diversifying their sources of supply (Sutela, 2012; Dreyer and Stang, 2014). The next section of this chapter examines whether it is likely that these objectives can be achieved.

## Can Europe wean itself off Russian gas and achieve its energy policy objectives?

This final section brings together the different threads of the argument presented so far. It examines whether the global gas revolution is likely to (1) increase its energy security by altering the European gas relationship with

Russia in Europe's favour; and (2) help Europe achieve its other energy policy objectives.

### The gas relationship with Russia and European energy security

So how might the global gas revolution change the EU's gas relationship with Russia? The most obvious area in which the EU might benefit is in accessing a much wider range of potential suppliers. Increasing the volume of supply as well as the range of suppliers offers the prospect of cheaper gas and increased energy security. If LNG import capacity is increased substantially, then European economies could, in principle, import gas from Africa, the Middle East and potentially even the United States. In 2012, LNG comprised around 20 per cent of the EU's natural gas imports. If this share were to increase, EU countries would have more leverage vis-à-vis Gazprom over gas trade. Indeed, the shale gas bonanza in the United States caused an influx of relatively cheap LNG in 2011–12, causing a sharp reduction (subsequently reversed) of gas imports from Russia. This reduction in imports was accompanied by the initiation of legal action by the Commission against Gazprom on competition grounds (Riley, 2012), suggesting that the EU felt emboldened by the opening of new supply opportunities to challenge its largest supplier of gas.

However, there are currently a number of practical constraints on how far EU countries might benefit from the global gas revolution. While under best case scenarios EU countries might increase domestic production of gas while also benefitting from increased supply elsewhere, changes to the global supply of gas do not necessarily favour European economies.

First, attempts to exploit domestic deposits of shale gas have so far met with disappointment as geological and political challenges hinder progress in this area.

Second, most of the world's existing LNG production is tied to long-term supply contracts, primarily for Asian economies which are prepared to pay a much higher price than the EU currently pays for Russian pipeline gas. Although there has been speculation that the US might turn into a globally important exporter of natural gas, there are a number of economic and political obstacles to this becoming reality. Even if US gas exports do flow in the future, the likelihood is that they will flow to Asia and not Europe (see Henderson, 2014).

Third, one EU response to concerns over Europe's dependence on Russian natural gas supplies is what has become known as the Southern strategy, or the Southern Corridor, to transport natural gas from the Caspian region and Central Asia. This, however, has encountered numerous problems (Yergin, 2011). The proposed Nabucco natural gas pipeline, the core component of the Southern Corridor, is no longer considered a commercially viable project, and has been replaced by the planned smaller-scale Trans-Anatolian natural gas pipeline (TANAP), which would connect to the Trans Adriatic Pipeline (TAP). The delays in fully developing the Southern strategy corridor natural gas pipelines to Europe, including trans-Caspian links, have forced Central Asian countries to look east (to China) rather than west to bypass Russia and open new markets. As a result, any significant increase in supply from Caspian and Central Asian sources looks unlikely to occur in the foreseeable future.

Fourth, while Europe currently possesses significant unused LNG regasification capacity, the majority of plants are located in southern Europe and the UK, and not in the central and east European countries that perceive Russia as the most important source of energy insecurity.

Fifth, it is by no means clear that gas supplies from Central Asia, the Caucasus, the Middle East or North Africa will be any more secure than supplies from Russia. Algeria, for example, has proven to be a much less reliable supplier of gas to the EU than Russia (Hogselius, 2013).

Finally, the EU has also taken steps to reform its own fragmented internal energy market. Although not directly related to the global gas revolution, its energy market reform does offer an additional tool to mitigate any perceived dependence on Russian gas (or that of any other supplier for that matter). In February 2011, European leaders pledged to complete the integration and liberalization of the internal European energy market by 2014, to ensure all European Member States are connected to a Europe-wide energy supply grid by 2015, to increase energy efficiency throughout Europe, and to improve the coordination of external energy policies. It is hoped that market liberalization and interconnection of electricity grids and pipelines will allow Member States to share and trade energy more flexibly than in the past. This could, in turn, reduce the impact of supply interruptions and overdependence on a single supplier. So far, attempts to improve the functioning of the internal market have made slow but steady progress. If successful, the EU will improve its energy security in relation to all suppliers, and not just Russia. After all, other important suppliers include Algeria, Libya and Nigeria, all countries in which political risk is considered considerably higher than, say, Norway. Ultimately, improving the functioning of the internal energy market will not by itself solve European fears of energy insecurity.

Overall, the global gas revolution and internal energy market reform all offer important possibilities to improve the EU's energy security in the future. However, their importance should not be overestimated. The large-scale gas relationship with Russia, based on a dense network of infrastructure and business relations at all stages of the supply and distribution process, has been constructed over the course of decades (see Hogselius, 2013). Consequently, any transition to alternative sources of supply is likely to take a long period of time, and come at considerable cost. Moreover, with supply from the EU's other large supplier – Norway – forecast to decline as EU consumption of gas rises, Russia's share in European gas consumption is more likely to increase than decline (IEA, 2013). Thus, the advantages offered by the global gas revolution in relation to Europe's gas trade with Russia are of marginal rather than fundamental importance. Consequently, European countries may benefit from paying more attention to maintaining a constructive and mutually profitable gas trade with Russia than with focusing on exploiting other alternatives that may or may not bear fruit.

### The global gas revolution and the EU's other energy policy objectives

If the gas relationship with Russia isn't likely to change significantly in the near future, what about the effects that the global gas revolution might have on the EU's other energy policy objectives?

The second 'E' of European energy policy is economic competitiveness.[4] Unfortunately, this objective has, if anything, been compromised by the global gas revolution. US gas consuming sectors (e.g. plastics, chemicals, etc.) have benefitted from a fall in gas prices (Henry Hub) of around 70 per cent between 2008 and 2012 (BP, 2013). By contrast, European prices have stayed roughly the same. While excess LNG supplies were priced relatively favourably in 2010–11 as suppliers sought new customers after the US turned to domestically produced shale gas, any switch to LNG supplies from the Middle East, Africa or elsewhere would likely see import prices rise towards the levels paid by Asian customers (around five times the US price), which is considerably higher than both the US price and the price paid by European countries (around three times higher than the US price) for Russian pipeline gas (as well as Norwegian and Algerian gas).

This means that if European countries were to embark on a deliberate policy of switching to alternative gas suppliers, primarily on global LNG markets, they would be likely to experience a decrease in economic competitiveness as gas-intensive industries would be forced to accept much higher overheads than their competitors in the US (IEA, 2014: 273). The only obvious way in which the global gas revolution could benefit European competitiveness would be for it to develop its own reserves of shale gas, something that so far appears to be precluded on political grounds. Because final gas consumption prices are also affected by other variables (e.g. national taxation regimes), it is possible for European countries to mitigate some of the loss in energy competitiveness.[5] Nevertheless, the main point to note in the context of this chapter is that the global revolution in gas looks unlikely to offer European economies a boost to their economic competitiveness. Moreover, the most cost-effective natural gas supply will remain Russian gas for some time to come, due to the fact that expensive infrastructure is already in place (for the most part).

The other 'E' of European energy policy refers to environmental sustainability. Initially, hopes surrounding the global gas revolution were that the availability of reasonably priced natural gas (compared to alternative fuels) in larger quantities would allow European commercial and household users to switch to a fuel that is less carbon intensive than oil and coal. In this scenario, the global gas revolution would see the natural gas share of final energy consumption rise at the expense of coal and oil. However, the share of natural gas in total energy consumption in several major European economies has fallen in recent years, not risen. In Germany, for example, gas consumption has fallen by nearly 15 per cent since 2007. Moreover, coal – the 'dirtiest' of the fossil fuels – consumption in Germany rose by 10 per cent between 2010 and 2012 (BP, 2013). Similar patterns were observed in the UK and Ireland, the Iberian Peninsula and France. What is perhaps most surprising is that this surge in coal consumption was a direct result of the global gas revolution. As US shale gas production rose and prices fell in the US, increasing numbers of power generation companies switched from coal to gas, in turn causing US coal prices to fall. European companies then imported the cheaper US coal. Thus, even though the direct European involvement in the global gas revolution has been rather limited, the consequences have been significant and in some cases inimical to EU energy policy objectives. For EU countries to meet environmental sustainability targets there will need to be a reduction in coal consumption and an increase in the use of gas. If this gas is to be supplied at a price that does not threaten European economic competitiveness, Russian gas is likely to be of crucial importance.

## Conclusion: plus ça change

The second section of the chapter described how the economies of Europe use enormous amounts of natural gas to power their societies. Much of this gas is imported, with Russia the single biggest supplier. The fact that Russia is of greater importance to some countries of the EU, such as central and eastern Europe, has prevented the emergence of a single energy policy, especially in the area of natural gas imports. The third section considered how recent technological developments in the global gas market might offer the prospect of a massive increase in the supply and availability (liquidity) of gas on global markets, which in turn may allow the EU to formulate a common energy policy that meets its three energy policy objectives and reduces the risk that Russia might pose to energy security. The fourth section examined Russia's role as the key supplier of gas to Europe. It was argued that Russia is often considered a threat to energy security because: (1) it is not clear that the structure of the Russian gas industry will result in the necessary efficiency or investment required to assure future production and export capacity; (2) Russia may wish to 'pivot' to Asia and concentrate its resources on supplying the growing and seemingly more dynamic Asian markets; and (3) some European countries are worried that Gazprom will be used by the Russian state to achieve foreign policy objectives, despite the evidence so far suggesting that Russia is a reliable gas supplier. However, as was argued in the fifth section, the global gas revolution has so far offered European economies very little opportunity to restructure their relationship with Russia by reducing import costs from Gazprom and further diversifying their sources of supply. Instead, the global gas revolution has threatened the economic competitiveness of some sectors within the European economy, and has caused an increase in the use of carbon-intensive coal. Unless European economies are prepared to pay much higher prices for imported LNG, the range of EU gas suppliers is also unlikely to increase markedly. As a result, while the global gas revolution has changed many things, the EU's dependence on Russian gas looks likely to remain the same. In this respect, it is worth stating that because Russia's role as the key supplier of gas is unlikely to change, a core objective of EU energy policy should be to *manage* dependence rather than *reduce* dependence. For this to occur, a unified and coherent EU energy policy is essential.

## Notes

1 Similar problems are also being encountered in the Russian oil industry. See Gustafson (2012).
2 Although the details of the price to be paid were made secret, estimates suggest that the profit margins on exports to China will be much lower than those to Europe for the simple reason that Gazprom still needs to construct the necessary infrastructure to transport gas from gas fields in Eastern Siberia to China. See Vedomosti (22 May, 2014) http://www.vedomosti.ru/opinion/news/26810471/rossiya-nachala-process-uskorennogo-sblizheniya-s-kitaem/.
3 It should be noted that there is no evidence of the use of gas supplies as a weapon to achieve political aims in Europe (i.e. not in relation to disputes with former Soviet states, such as Belarus, Moldova and Ukraine). Even in disputes with former Soviet states, it has been suggested that the nature of disputes was overwhelmingly commercial (Stern, 2006: 16). However, while there were certainly commercial justifications for cutting supplies to Ukraine, the fact that Gazprom fails to adhere to commercial principles in many other of its activities does suggest that political objectives were an important factor. In this respect, the issue is not so much that Gazprom was simply applying 'fair' rules to its dealings with Ukraine, but that it was very haphazard in implementing similar rules universally (i.e. without discrimination).
4 Economic competitiveness is a function of several variables, one of which is energy competitiveness. The IEA (2014: 261) defines energy competitiveness as 'the cost of providing energy services in one economy relative to other economies'.
5 It is also the case that the share of industry in the consumption of natural gas is, at 39 per cent, considerably lower than many other regions of the global economy, including Asia, the Middle East and Latin America (IEA, 2014: 264).

## References

Aalto, P. (ed.) (2012). *Russia's Energy Policies: National, Interregional and Global Levels*. Aldershot: Edward Elgar.
Berend, I. (2008). *Europe Since 1980*. Cambridge: Cambridge University Press.
BP (2013). *Statistical Review of World Energy for 2012*. London: BP.
Bradshaw, M. (2013). *Global Energy Dilemmas*. Polity Press.
Buchan, D. (2012). *The Energiewende – Germany's Gamble*. Oxford: Oxford Energy Institute for Energy Studies.
Commission of the European Communities (2008). *20 20 by 2020: Europe's Climate Change Opportunity*. Brussels: CEC.
Commission of the European Communities (2010). *Energy 2020: A Strategy for Competitive, Sustainable and Secure Energy*. Brussels: CEC.

Connolly, R. (2008). 'The Structure of Russian Industrial Exports in Comparative Perspective.' *Eurasian Geography and Economics*, 49 (5), pp. 586–603.

Connolly, R. (2012a). 'Climbing the Ladder? High-Technology Industrial Exports in Emerging Europe.' *Eurasian Geography and Economics*, 53 (3), pp. 356–379.

Connolly, R. (2012b). *Economic Structure and Social Order Development in Post-Socialist Eastern Europe*. London and New York: Routledge.

Dickel, R. (2014). *The New German Energy Policy: What Role for Gas in a De-carbonization Policy?* Oxford: Oxford Energy Institute for Energy Studies.

Dreyer, I. and Stang, G. (2014). *Energy Moves and Power Shifts EU Foreign Policy and Global Energy Security*. Paris: EU-ISS.

Eichengreen, B. (2007). *The European Economy Since 1945: Coordinated Capitalism and Beyond*. Princeton: Princeton University Press.

Energy Information Administration (2013). *International Energy Outlook 2013*. Washington, D.C: EIA.

Feklyunina, V. (2012). 'Russia's International Images and its Energy Policy: An Unreliable Supplier?' *Europe-Asia Studies*, 64 (3), pp. 449–469.

Gaddy, C. and Ickes, B. (1998). 'Russia's Virtual Economy.' *Foreign Affairs*, 53–67.

Gaddy, C. and Ickes, B. (2005). 'Resource Rents and the Russian Economy.' *Eurasian Geography and Economics*, 46 (8), pp. 559–583.

Gaddy, C. and Ickes, B. (2010). 'Russia after the Global Financial Crisis.' *Eurasian Geography and Economics*, 51 (3), pp. 281–311.

Gazprom (2014). Energy supplies to Europe data. http://www.gazpromexport.ru/en/statistics/.

Gény, F. (2010). *Can Unconventional Gas be a Game Changer in European Gas Markets?* Oxford: Oxford Institute for Energy Studies.

Goldman, M. (2008). *Petrostate: Putin, Power, and the New Russia*. Oxford: Oxford University Press.

Gustafson, T. (2012). *Wheel of Fortune: The Battle for Oil and Power in Russia*. Cambridge: Harvard University Press.

Henderson, J. (2010). *Non-Gazprom Gas Producers in Russia*. Oxford: Oxford Institute for Energy Studies.

Henderson, J. (2014). 'Russian Energy Policy – The Shift East and its Implications for Europe.' In Dreyer, I. and Stang, G. (eds.) *Energy Moves and Power Shifts: EU Foreign Policy and Global Energy Security*. Paris: EU-ISS.

Hill, F. (2004). *Energy Empire: Oil, Gas and Russia's Revival*. London: Foreign Policy Centre.

Hogselius, P. (2013). *Red Gas: Russia and the Origins of European Energy Dependence*. New York: Palgrave MacMillan.

International Energy Agency (2011). *World Energy Outlook 2011*. Paris: IEA.

International Energy Agency (2012). *World Energy Outlook 2012*. Paris: IEA.

International Energy Agency (2013). *World Energy Outlook 2013*. Paris: IEA.

International Energy Agency (2014). *World Energy Outlook 2014*. Paris: IEA.

Le Coq, C. and Paltseva, E. (2012). 'Assessing Gas Transit Risks: Russia vs. the EU?' *Energy Policy*, 42, pp. 642–650.

Lo, B. (2009). *Axis of Convenience: Moscow, Beijing, and the New Geopolitics*. Washington, D.C: Brookings Institution Press.

Lo, B. and Hill, F. (2013). 'Putin's Pivot.' *Foreign Affairs*. http://www.foreignaffairs.com/articles/139617/fiona-hill-and-bobo-lo/putins-pivot.

Locatelli, C. (2014). 'The Russian Gas Industry: Challenges to the "Gazprom model"?' *Post-Communist Economies*, 26 (1), pp. 56–69.

Magnus, G. (2009). *The Age of Ageing*. Singapore: Wiley and Sons.

Melling, A. (2010). 'Natural Gas Pricing and Its Future: Europe as the Battleground.' Washington, DC: Carnegie Endowment for International Peace. http://carnegieendowment.org/files/gas_pricing_europe.pdf.

Monaghan, A. (2007). *Russia and the Security of Europe's Energy Supplies: Security in Diversity?* Defence Academy of the United Kingdom, Conflict Studies Research Centre.

Noël, P. (2009). 'A Market Between Us: Reducing the Political Cost of Europe's Dependence on Russian Gas?' *Electricity Policy Research Group (EPRG). University of Cambridge, EPRG Working Paper* 916.

North, D., Wallis, J., Webb, S. and Weingast, B. (2012). *In the Shadow of Violence: Politics, Economics and the Problems of Development*. Cambridge: Cambridge University Press.

Pearson, I., Zeniewski, P., Gracceva, F., Zastera, P., McGlade, C., Sorrell, S. and Thonhauser, G. (2012). *Unconventional Gas: Potential Energy Market Impacts in the European Union*. Luxembourg: European Commission Joint Research Centre.

Perovic, J., Orttung, R. and Wenger, A. (2009). *Russian Energy Power and Foreign Relations: Implications for Conflict and Cooperation*. London and New York: Routledge.

Pirani, S., Stern, J. P. and Yafimava, K. (2009). *The Russo-Ukrainian Gas Dispute of January 2009: a Comprehensive Assessment*. Oxford: Oxford Institute for Energy Studies.

Riley, A. (2012). 'Commission v. Gazprom: The Antitrust Clash of the Decade?' *CEPS Policy Brief No. 285*, 31 October 2012.

Shadrina, E. and Bradshaw, M. (2013). 'Russia's Energy Governance Transitions and Implications for Enhanced Cooperation with China, Japan, and South Korea.' *Post-Soviet Affairs*, 29 (6), pp. 461–499.

Smil, V. (2010). *Energy Transitions: History, Requirements, Prospects*. Westport, CT: Praeger.

Smith Stegen, K. (2011). 'Deconstructing the "Energy Weapon": Russia's Threat to Europe as Case Study.' *Energy Policy*, 39 (10), pp. 6505–6513.

Solanko, L. and P. Sutela (2009). 'Too Much or Too Little Russian Gas to Europe?' *Eurasian Geography and Economics*, 50 (1), pp. 58–74.

Stern, J. (2006). 'The Russian-Ukrainian Gas Crisis of January 2006.' *Oxford Institute for Energy Studies*, 16, pp. 5–12.

Stevens, P. (2012). 'The "Shale Gas Revolution": Developments and Changes.' *Chatham House Briefing Paper*. London: Royal Institute for International Affairs.

Sutela, P. (2012). *The Political Economy of Putin's Russia*. London and New York: Routledge.

Topalov, A. and Falyakhov, R. (2014). 'Putin Prodiktoval Kitayu Tsenu' (Putin Dictated the Price to China). Gazeta.ru, 21 May 2014. http://www.gazeta.ru/business/2014/05/21/6042329.shtml.

Woodruff, D. (1999). 'It's Value that's Virtual: Bartles, Rubles, and the Place of Gazprom in the Russian Economy.' *Post-Soviet Affairs*, 15 (2), pp. 130–148.

World Bank (2013). *World Development Indicators Database*. http://data.worldbank.org/.

Yafimava, K. (2011). *The Transit Dimension of EU Energy Security*. Oxford: Oxford University Press.

Yergin, D. (1991). *The Prize: The Epic Quest for Oil, Money, and Power*. New York: Simon & Schuster.

Yergin, D. (2011). *The Quest: Energy, Security, and the Remaking of the Modern World*. London: Penguin.

# Part IV

# Political economy

From internationalism to supranationalism

# 11 Neo-liberalism, federalism and supranational political economy

*Guido Montani*

## Which multipolar world order?

Many policy-makers and scholars viewed the end of the Cold War as the beginning of the American century: the collapse of the Soviet empire paved the way for a unipolar world. The United States, as the lone superpower, was considered indispensable for a more peaceful, stable, thriving world order. Two decades on views have changed. Nobody can now deny that China, India, Brazil, Russia, Indonesia, South Africa and the European Union are striving for a new, autonomous role in international politics. Some scholars speak openly of *The End of the American Era* (Kupchan, 2002). The United States is less of a superpower and more of a major power, on the same footing as other partners. Even a convinced unipolarist admits: 'The United States must adjust and accommodate itself to this order and not simply run it as an imperial state.' Moreover it must 'accept some restrictions on how it can use its power' (Ikenberry, 2004: 87, 105).

In this chapter we examine the jerky transition from the old international order, founded by the United States after World War Two, to the new multipolar world order. The outcome of this process will not necessarily be a harmonious and peaceful world. Multilateral institutions built by the USA after World War Two ensured a forum for conflict resolution and a fairly stable international economy. Their success was confirmed at the end of the Cold War when all the new countries, Russia and China included, asked to be admitted to the UN and the WTO. The UN was founded by 46 states; it now numbers 193. The nations of the world are now linked by a dense network of international organizations, yet in spite of this, various crucial global problems – such as international terrorism, failed states, monetary and financial stability, climate change – appear unsolvable. Sometimes this dense network looks more like a giant trap than a vehicle for cooperation.

The present impasse in world politics has been perceptively analysed by Hale *et al.* (2013) in *Gridlock: Why Global Cooperation is Failing when We Need it Most*. In their words: 'The postwar institutions helped to create the new world, but they were not built for it' (p. 34). Moreover they recognize that: 'the 1945 paradigm of multilateralism, that was so effective in shaping the postwar era, can be replaced by another fit to meet the demands of the twenty-first century' (p. 311). Our task begins here. We want to propose a new paradigm: we believe that a shift from internationalism to supranationalism is necessary not only because the perils facing humankind are steadily increasing, but also because there is another hurdle to overcome, beyond those examined in *Gridlock*. In the last few decades the neo-liberal ideology has acquired increasing weight in international politics, conditioning national and international policies. A combination of neo-liberalism and nationalism now stands in the way of bold reforms to world institutions.

The core of neo-liberal ideology is generally considered to be a limited state at the service of a free market (for an overview see Blyth, 2013; Schmidt and Thatcher, 2013), but its relationship with internationalism is seldom examined. This relationship requires in-depth analysis. Here we refer mainly to a number of leading exponents of the Austrian School (von Mises, Röpke and Hayek), the Chicago School (Friedman and classical macroeconomists) and various scholars of international relations (for a survey, see Stein, 2010 and Moravcsik, 2010). All political processes, be they national or international, are immersed in the ideological ocean. Ideologies 'map the political and social worlds for us. We simply cannot do without them because we cannot act without making sense of the worlds we inhabit' (Freeden, 2003: 2). Studies of ideologies usually focus on traditional political thinking: liberalism, democracy, socialism and conservatism (Freeden, 1996). Here we will try to explore the complex field of internationalism, which can be viewed as the ideology of the international system of nation states. This task is a difficult one not only because ideologies always comprise a mixture of rational and non-rational arguments, but also because, since the beginning of the modern era, nationalism and internationalism have been the general framework within which traditional ideologies of liberalism, democracy and socialism developed. From that point of view, our approach differs from Freeden's, who considers nationalism a thin ideology whose role is mainly to emphasize the superiority of one nation over others. This is true, but it is necessary to recognize that nationalism was also the political mindset behind imperialism and war in the last century. It therefore seems reasonable to consider nationalism as the ideology of the nation state, the institutional container which facilitated the development of human rights, universal suffrage and the welfare state within its borders in the nineteenth century, but also – on occasion of the two world wars – stifled the cosmopolitan contents of liberalism, democracy and socialism (Montani, 2012).

We need an Ariadne's thread to guide us through this complex field. As a frame of reference we can take Hamilton's problem. Alexander Hamilton, one of the founding fathers of the American federal state, was the first to tackle the problem of the relationship between the federal government and the market, both in theory (in *The Federalist Papers*), and in practice (as Secretary of the Treasury in the Washington government). The state-market relationship is one of the most hotly discussed issues in economics and politics. The federal government played a crucial role in terms of creating an integrated continental market, and the thriving market was crucial for strengthening the new federal democracy. This relationship is also crucial in more general debate (where many philosophers weigh in) in terms of the dividing line between public and private goods. The question has already been studied from the point of view of market-preserving federalism since the federal constitution – a multi-level system of government – credibly commits the state to preserving the market. The credibility of the federal system is based on the existence of several competing public powers so that federalism 'greatly diminishes the level of pervasiveness of economic rent-seeking and the formation of distributional coalitions' (Weingast, 1995: 6). However, after the 2008 world financial crisis, we must consider the other side of the coin: excessive market power can undermine the stability of the democratic state, as happened in the USA and especially in the EU, where the EMU came under attack by international finance. Today we can say that a democracy-preserving market is no less necessary than its opposite. In this chapter we will attempt to study the state-market problem, which is usually discussed within a national framework, from an international and supra-national viewpoint. In the era of globalization the Hamilton problem has acquired a global dimension: no nation state can solve its own Hamilton's problem without a proper centre of gravity based on a balanced (state-market) global order.[1]

In the next section we examine how the state/market division can lead to a precarious balance between public and private values in modern societies. In the third section we examine the main features of the international order which came into being after World War Two and how it changed after the end of the Cold War, while in the fourth section we will consider the process of European integration made possible thanks to the creation of supranational institutions. Lastly, in the fifth section, we focus on issues of international security, economic integration, and the ecological challenge, showing why a supranational approach is required to tackle the main global problems of the twenty-first century.

## Market and state: the separation and the pendulum

The aim of this section is to demonstrate how one of the main tenets of neo-liberalism, namely that the market is a spontaneous order – the unintended by-product of the interaction of millions of individuals, as Hayek theorizes (Hayek, 1982: vol. 1, ch. 2; Sally, 1998: 184) – is historically groundless.

The birth of the market as an institution that is relatively independent from the state is the result of a very long historical process which began in the Middle Ages with the rise of long distance trade. The separation of the market from the state is a fundamental feature of modern society: it gives individuals the opportunity to choose their lifestyles in both the private and the public sphere. Yet it was a separation that carried a serious social cost.

In the book *The Great Transformation* (Polanyi, 1944), written during World War Two, the historian Karl Polanyi carefully describes the separation between economic and political society as the main cause of the collapse of nineteenth century civilization. Polanyi is well aware of the general, complex framework in question: the balance of power system 'which for a century prevented the occurrence of any long and devastating war between great powers', the international gold standard, the ideology of the self-regulating market and, finally the liberal state (Polanyi, 1944: 3). Polanyi rightly underlines the link between political and economic factors, such as the system of *haute finance*, which 'supplied the instruments for an international peace system, which was worked with the help of the powers, but which the powers themselves could neither have established nor maintained' (p. 10).

The core of Polanyi's analysis is the formation of the market economy, which

> is an economic system controlled, regulated and directed by the market alone; order in the production and distribution of goods is entrusted to this self-regulating mechanism. An economy of this kind derives from the expectation that human beings behave in such a way as to achieve maximum money gains.
>
> (p. 68)

A large part of Polanyi's book is devoted to describing the historical transition from the medieval system to the modern one, which required the transformation of labour, land and money into commodities, something they originally were not. 'None of them is produced for sale. The commodity description of labour, land and money is entirely fictitious' (p. 72). But this artificial cultural environment was necessary to pave the way for mercantilism and the formation of national markets in the sixteenth and seventeenth centuries, with the creation of national currencies, and the parallel labour and land market. All these developments were prerequisites for the dawn of the industrial revolution. Workers acquired freedom in the eyes of the law but were forced to abandon their villages in the country and go and work in the factories. In England in the nineteenth century,

> huge masses of the labouring population resembled more the spectres that might haunt a nightmare than human beings. But if the workers were physically dehumanized the owning classes were morally degraded. The traditional unity of a Christian society was giving place to a denial of responsibility on the part of the well-to-do for the conditions of their fellows.
>
> (p. 102)

After this very short summary of Polanyi's analysis of the origins of modern society, we would like to critique his underestimation of the role played by the international system of states in the collapse of nineteenth century civilization. The great value of Polanyi's work lies in its clear vision of the European system of great powers as the origin of the ideology of the self-regulating market. The free market was by no means a spontaneous order. Polanyi states quite clearly that 'a self-regulating market demands nothing less than the institutional separation of society into an economic and political sphere' (p. 71). And further on he says: 'there was nothing natural about *laissez-faire*; free markets could never have come into being merely by allowing things to take their course. ... *laissez-faire* itself was enforced by the state' (p. 139), and in the concluding chapter: 'the market has been the outcome of a conscious and often violent intervention on the part of government' (p. 250).

Polanyi rightly emphasizes the importance of the 'hundred years' peace' for the birth and dissemination of the liberal project in Britain. This peace was the result of a political equilibrium between the great European powers. However, during the nineteenth century all the national governments strove not to fall behind and, if possible, to increase their economic and military clout. The wealth of the people also meant more power for the state. Without this political background it is difficult to explain the rapid spread of the industrial revolution throughout Europe and the world. One economic historian says:

> The eradication of the power of feudal institutions (land tenures, guilds, etc.) in revolutionary France, the abolition of internal tariffs in France and Germany, the maintenance of an orderly system of law in Britain, the political unification of Germany and Italy – all depended on state action, and all moulded the framework of enterprise in ways which increased entrepreneurial security and helped the free flow of resources and men.
>
> (Supple, 1973: 307–308)

While the hundred years' peace lasted, the international movement for building a self-regulating market not only changed the living conditions of thousands of people in the nation states but also the relationships among them. Custom barriers were dismantled or drastically reduced and an international currency, for the first time in the history of mankind, united all the world's continents and states. The gold standard and international free-trade can be considered a spontaneous order, because no government planned them. During the belle époque Hamilton's problem appeared to have been solved. But a spontaneous order is not a market. Its stability was based on the precarious balance of power of the nineteenth century. The age of the gold standard can hardly be considered a successful outcome of the international liberal project.

Indeed the free-trade order was a very precarious one. After the unification of Italy and Germany cracks began to show in the European system of states, before it eventually crumbled and dragged all the social, economic and political achievements of the liberal age into the trenches of World War One. In all the warring nations governments were obliged to restrict individual rights and the free market was pressed into the service of political power. This trend continued after the end of the conflict, because the Treaty of Versailles did not succeed in restoring the conditions for cooperation and peace among the European nations. Mussolini's rise to power in Italy and Hitler in Germany showed that the constitutional framework of the liberal and democratic state was unable to deal with violence at home when war was a constant threat in the international context.

During this period we can observe the reversal and, in some cases, the complete failure of the liberal movement, which has seemed so strongly rooted in Western civilization. The Bolshevik revolution and the construction of the Soviet Union were explicitly conceived as a reaction to capitalist societies. The core of the Communist project was the abolition of private property and the labour market and their replacement with a centrally planned economy. Something similar also happened in Italy and Germany, though neither private property nor the labour market were formally abolished. The Nazi regime greatly restricted individual liberties, such as freedom of domicile and employment and, in the space of a few years, thanks to the development of the military industry, managed to attain full employment. This economic achievement

> was possible because, without following a preconceived plan, over the years [the Nazis] had transformed what still existed of the German market system little by little into a thoroughly regulated economy ... The Nazis were enabled to create an increasingly governmentally guided economy, where state directives rather than market rules affected production and consumption, through the availability of well-trained and loyal civil servants.
>
> (Hardach, 1976: 202)

The history of the state-market relationship shows that the drive for a self-regulating market ran out of steam at the end of the nineteenth century and was fully defeated by the rise of the totalitarian state. Several factors are implicated in this dramatic outcome. For instance, the working class, which had no political and social impact within the institutional framework of the liberal state, ruled by conservative and bourgeois elites, claimed more democratic power and called for radical reforms of the economic system. These internal changes also impacted international relations, but cannot be seen as a cause of war. The main factor behind the collapse of the international order was power politics between European sovereign states. Nation states both caused and fell victim to the arms race and the imperial partitioning of the world. The great illusion of the nineteenth century was believing that an enduring international liberal order was possible without a supranational institution to govern it. As we shall see in the next section, after World War Two, the great powers looked for a balance – Hamilton's centre of gravity – between a self-regulating market and a world government. But the result was only a provisional equilibrium.

## International integration: enforcement by military action

The aim of this section is not to summarize the main post-war events in international politics, but to clarify the principles on which the main international institutions were built and how they evolved.

We will focus on the United Nations (UN), the Bretton Woods system – the International Monetary Fund (IMF) and the World Bank (WB) – and the General Agreement on Tariffs and Trade (GATT), now World Trade Organization (WTO), because they are the main symbols of this international order, mainly thanks to the initiative of the United States and the agreement, or tolerance, of the Soviet Union. When, during the war, all these institutions were up for discussion, the general perspective was that they had to become an integrated whole. But even before the end of the war, it became clear that the Soviet Union would not accept to be part of institutions designed for monetary and trade exchanges among open or mixed economies. The Soviet Union preferred bilateralism to multilateralism. Therefore Stalin denounced the Bretton Woods institutions as a Western system dominated by the United States and prevented the socialist countries from joining them (Mayall, 1988: 55).

To evaluate the impact the UN had on the world community of sovereign states, we should first highlight the organization's internal contradictions. While the preamble states: 'We the people of the United Nations', article 2 declares that 'the Organization is based on the principle of the sovereign equality of all its Members'. Therefore it is not the people, i.e. the citizens, who are the founders and members of the UN, but the states. The second contradiction is that the touted 'sovereign equality' of all member states is breached by the veto right of the Big Five in the Security Council, which means that some states are more 'equal' than others. Indeed it is the Westphalian system of sovereign states in a new guise. 'State sovereignty' means that each nation state, unilaterally, can always decide to wage war on another member state even if the Security Council – which according to article 26 has 'the primary responsibility for the maintenance of international peace and security' – opposes this decision. In such a case the only way of obliging the defiant state to respect the decision of the Security Council is by – all or some of the members of the Security Council – going to war against the defiant state. Ultimately, war is not outlawed at all by the international community of sovereign nations.

These shortcomings were well known by the representatives of the nation states who convened in San Francisco. Nevertheless they approved the UN Charter for several reasons. The Soviet Union was willing to join the UN because, with its permanent seat on the Security Council, its superpower status was legitimized in the eyes of the world community, facilitating its hegemony over Eastern European countries. The smaller states saw the UN as a means for strengthening their collective influence on big power politics. Lastly, the United States were eager to create a safer, more stable world order, in order to avoid a Third World War.

> Americans agreed that it was important to encourage democracy and greater equality everywhere, but the impetus was not Wilsonian idealism. Basically, it was the felt need to create a world in which American values – and thus America – could survive and prosper.
>
> (Hoopes and Brinkley, 1997: 206)

Let's take a look at some elements which can offer an insight into the role of the UN in the international order and its development. First, the ideological aspect. The UN is a convenient juridical screen that justifies and preserves the status quo among the winners of World War Two. It is clear that at Yalta the hegemonies of West and East were carefully designated and the Cold War was no surprise for the American and Soviet governments. In order to keep political control over their respective hegemonies the two superpowers fostered two military alliances, NATO and the Warsaw Treaty. In perfect agreement with the old balance of power doctrine, the two superpowers, with their nuclear might, established a bipolar governance of the world: this edifice was the real guarantee of peace for the American people, the Soviet people and Europe, cut in two by the Iron curtain.

The second consideration is that despite the Cold War, the United States succeeded in implementing a policy in the Western hemisphere, from the Atlantic to the Pacific, that fostered the creation of a world market. When, just after the end of World War Two, it became clear that the Bretton Woods institutions would not suffice to reconstruct European countries and develop their economies, the US government launched the Marshall Plan. The US government was also in favour of European integration and, with the GATT, introduced a series of tariff cuts which greatly contributed to the growth of the world economy. The Bretton Woods system of fixed exchange rates worked fairly well until 1971, when Nixon cancelled the convertibility of the US dollar into gold. The collapse of the Bretton Woods system was the first serious evidence of the decline of America's international leadership. The new dollar standard, a system of floating exchange rates, managed mainly by the G7, caused a wave of international inflation, but was not a serious obstacle to the development of the world economy until the major financial crisis of 2008.

The third observation is that it is impossible to say that there was no Third World War thanks to the UN. But we can say that the UN contributed to a gradual change in international relations. The UN was not only a forum for international diplomacy; it also helped mould the contents and modus operandi of nation states' relationships. For instance, concerning security, the concept of preventive diplomacy and peacekeeping were crucial in ending conflicts in Africa and Middle East, when nation states' institutions were still fragile. The reference to human rights was disputed, especially by the Soviet

Union, because of possible violations of internal affairs. Indeed the enforcement of individual rights would have changed the nature of the UN. But the existence of the UN Charter gave many NGOs the opportunity to denounce violations of human rights, forcing national governments to respect the rights of their citizens. On the occasion of mass violations of human rights – such as genocide, massacres, ethnic cleansing, international terrorism – the possibility of peace enforcement was evoked. But, since the UN is not 'a world organization for the enforcement of peace', contrary to what President Truman declared in San Francisco in 1945, it can only organize coalitions of national military forces. Lastly, among the new concepts created before the end of the Cold War was that of the common heritage of mankind: namely that some material and immaterial good should be considered a public good for all humankind, not just for the people of one particular nation: a concept that challenges national sovereignty.

Before the fall of the Berlin Wall, two scholars of the realist school recognized that 'international organizations can facilitate the informal transgovernmental networks that are required for managing interdependence. International organizations are by no means a substitute for leadership, but they may contribute to its development and nurturing' (Keohane and Nye, 1989: 234). Moreover they observed that the UN system is part 'of the complex set of rules and institutions that affect how states manage their interdependent relationship. … Regimes are institutions in the broader sense: recognized patterns of practice that define the rules of the game' (pp. 270–271).

The end of the Cold War changed the international landscape again. New issues emerged. Global security became less a question of conflict among nation states and more a matter of protecting individuals from abuses perpetrated by their governments or other organized groups. In 1998 in Rome, the statute of the International Criminal Court (ICC) was approved. The court was established in The Hague and its task was to prosecute genocide, crimes against humanity, war crimes and crimes of aggression. In 1999 Kofi Annan, the UN Secretary-General, said that it was necessary to protect two sovereignties, that of states and that of individuals. A debate began on 'the responsibility to protect', with the idea of establishing criteria and rules to protect citizens when their human rights are threatened. The notion of human security became a principle of global governance. With regard to economic relationships, the financial crisis of 2008, originating in the United States, showed that the IMF, with its policies based on the Washington consensus, was unable to play a significant role in stopping the international spread of the crisis. For this reason, the G20, a new international institution where the emerging powers of China, India, Brazil and South Africa were represented, became the forum for organizing global cooperation. Lastly environmental issues, which were considered a minor problem internationally until the 1970s, were becoming a key challenge for the future of humanity.

The world of the twenty-first century is completely different from the postwar order. International relations can no longer be observed and managed using a state-centric model. We must concede that 'states share the stage with a multitude of other actors, and trends in global politics are shaped not only by states but also by a variety of other actors and forces' (Barnett and Sikkink, 2010: 62). In the new global society the role of international organizations has changed: states create and delegate critical tasks to international institutions to provide public goods. In short, 'we have moved well beyond a global society composed only of sovereign states' and therefore we can understand why 'the concept of governance has been emerging as a worthy alternative to [international] anarchy ... Governance is about how actors work together to maintain order and achieve collective goals' (Barnett and Sikkink, 2010: 78). The concept of global governance contains the idea of power (who governs), legitimacy (who is legitimate to govern) and compliance (who can enforce the decisions taken by the government). We will examine these questions in the last section.

We can conclude this section with some remarks on the doctrine of international neo-liberalism, including the modern understanding of Wilhelm Röpke and Friedrich Hayek's original formulation. In an overview of their ideas, Röpke is presented as the theorist of 'liberalism from below', in other words: 'in common with other German neo-liberals and the classical liberal tradition in general, Röpke emphasises the *national preconditions of international order* [original emphasis]', and similarly: 'Hayek describes the spontaneous order mostly in terms of market activities within nation-states. Nevertheless, the general features of the spontaneous order apply equally at the international level.' And, more clearly: 'in lieu of world government, an international Rule of Law and a world society, liberal values can only take root in the morals, customs and traditions of established and 'grown' national civil society'. As Röpke contends, 'more important than international institutions and legal documents are the moral-political forces behind the market that are only really effective within nations' (Sally, 1998: 147, 188, 193).

It is difficult, not to say impossible, to reconcile this conception of international neo-liberalism with the emerging notion of global governance. Of course there is something true in the idea that it is easier to organize international relations among states which have adopted an internal free-market regime. But today these 'national preconditions of international order' cannot explain the move towards international institutions capable of guaranteeing individual human rights even before their governments. Nor can this precondition explain why the present global financial market, which is likely a product of a spontaneous international order, provoked a worldwide crisis in 2008, which caused a drastic fall in global production, income and employment. Nor can it explain why three decades of UN conferences on climate change and sustainable development have not managed to come to a reasonable agreement on how the global economy should be ruled in order to prevent an ecological catastrophe. The market pan of Hamilton's weighing scale is undoubtedly becoming too heavy to be ruled by international institutions.

## Supranational integration: enforcement by law

The historical roots of European integration are clearly explained by the German historian Ludwig Dehio in an essay written in 1953. Pondering the state of Europe after two internecine conflicts he concludes: 'All these complex phenomena can be included within a single concept: the concept of the dying European system [of nation states]. That system is lying in ruins, but its spirit lives on.' To understand the European political crisis we can draw an analogy with the Hellenic system of the *poleis:* 'overshadowed by great powers outside Greece – first Macedon and then Rome – it died a slow death over many centuries. In both cases we find the tenacious but sterile survival of obsolete instincts.' Political death throes are a miserable and dangerous situation because a dying system of states whose spirit survives 'threatens to poison the creation of new [political systems]' (Dehio, 1960, 140–142). Dehio's image is crucial to gaining an understanding of the ambiguous panorama of European integration in the present, which combines a search for unity with the persistence of national divisions.

In this section our aim is to discuss three crucial features of the process of European integration: the significance of the creation of the Community; the single market and Economic and Monetary Union as two crucial European public goods, and lastly, an overview of the debate on the nature of the EU.

The creation of the European Community is often considered a by-product of the USA's hegemonic policy. Indeed the American government understood that a more cooperative and united Europe would contain Soviet propaganda, supported by communist and left-wing parties. Nevertheless, the process towards a politically united Europe was based on people's abhorrence of the catastrophic consequences of the nation state system. After World War Two, Europeans wished fervently for a peaceful future. Historians usually underline the role of national governments in European integration, but this is a one-sided view: the role of popular movements, especially federalist movements, and the role of convinced Europeans outside of politics, such as Jean Monnet, are ignored. Monnet understood that the only way out of national divisions was to pool coal and steel in a European institution. He proposed his plan to the foreign minister Schuman; the Adenauer governments unhesitatingly accepted. So, on 9 May, 1950, Schuman announced that the Franco-German production of coal and steel was to be placed under a common 'High Authority' as a first step towards a European Federation. The first supranational community was set up.

The drive towards unity did not stop with the European Coal and Steel Community (ECSC). In June 1950 North Korean forces invaded South Korea. The US government decided to move military forces available in Germany to the Asian front. In this situation, Germany, still without its own defence forces, was powerless against a Soviet attack. The issue of German rearmament came to the fore in European politics once again. The French Prime Minister, Pleven, proposed a Plan modelled on the ECSC, a European

Defence Community (EDC) that would represent a common defence force for the six members of the ECSC. However, this time a 'High Authority' would not be suitable for running the EDC, as a European military force would have to be accountable to a political government. In Italy, the leader of the federalist movement, Altiero Spinelli, convinced the Prime Minister De Gasperi to support a federalist solution. In 1953 the Statute for the European Political Community, with a government, an armed force and a budget, was ready. But its ratification was now in doubt, because of a change in the French political majority. In August 1954, in spite of the fact that Germany and the Benelux countries had already ratified the Treaty, the National Assembly, with a majority of Gaullists and Communists, voted against the EDC. The collapse of the EDC and the European Political Community was considered a setback for the federalist project.

This event marked the divide between the political phase and the economic phase of European integration. The federalist project failed due to France's desire to preserve its national military sovereignty. In 1954 the economic reconstruction of Europe got off to a good start thanks to the Marshall Plan and the European Payment Union (EPU); a common defence was no longer required thanks to the creation of NATO. In short, the American government provided Europe with economic, monetary and military security. The American protectorate over Western Europe was exploited by national governments to create a comfortable niche to preserve their national sovereignty, pooling only the minimum powers required for peaceful economic cooperation in the European institutions.

On the basis of this philosophy, in 1957, two new communities were set up: the European Economic Community (EEC) and the Euratom. The EEC was conceived as an extension of the ECSC to cover all sectors of the economy: the supranational feature was maintained with the creation of the Commission, a Parliamentary Assembly, the Council of Ministers and the Court of Justice (ECJ). Here we will confine our analysis to two main achievements: the Single Market (which started as the Common Market) and the Economic and Monetary Union (EMU). These two projects can be considered two European public goods, which require supranational European powers.

The four freedoms of the single market programme – the free movement of people, goods, services and capital – required an impressive effort by the European Commission, the Council and the European Parliament, which had to pass comprehensive legislation establishing a transparent, non-discriminatory regime for procurement and the abolition of restrictive practices, abuses of power and state aid. The achievement would certainly not have been possible without the power of the Commission to regulate competition among private companies and avoid state subsidies that favoured national companies. The ECJ played a crucial role in establishing the doctrine of the supremacy of EU law over national law. One member of the ECJ commented that the ECJ had acquired a power similar to that of the Supreme Court of the USA (Mancini, 2004: 75).

The second European public good to consider is the EMU. The decision to go for fully fledged monetary union was taken at Maastricht in 1991, after the fall of the Berlin Wall and many years of hesitant attempts – and failures – to coordinate national monetary policies. From the political point of view the Maastricht Treaty was a compromise between France, which feared the strength of a united Germany, and Germany, which understood that German reunification was only possible within the European framework. According to Chancellor Kohl the aim of the Treaty was to open the way for a united Germany in a united Europe. However, the Treaty was a limp compromise. At Maastricht the heads of state and government were aware that monetary union could not work without a federal budget and a federal government. In 1984 the European Parliament had already approved the project for the European Union – supported by a majority of MEPs led by Altiero Spinelli – which provided the institutional framework for forging monetary union with a democratic European government; but Mrs Thatcher's veto halted the project. In Maastricht the decision was taken, in spite of UK opposition, but the mechanism of the EMU was in practice similar to the gold standard of the nineteenth century.

The Maastricht Treaty was built on a flawed assumption. After the end of the Cold War it was no longer possible for the European Union to proceed little by little seeking minor degrees of integration. The world political system had changed completely; once the illusion of a unipolar world led by the USA had faded away, the reality of a new multipolar world became more and more evident; and in the new multipolar world the European Union needed a supranational democratic government.

Now let us consider the debate on the nature of the EU. Jacques Delors defined the EU as an unidentified political object. He later proposed considering it as a federation of nation states. In France, some political scientists have attempted to justify this definition by observing that the EU is already past the confederation stage, but is not yet a federal state. However, since the EU is grounded on double legitimacy – the legitimacy of the people, represented in the European Parliament, and the legitimacy of the national governments, represented in the Council – it is correct to define the EU as a new model of federalism, 'intergovernmental federalism' (Quermonne, 2008: 200–202). In the 1990s Federico Mancini criticized Joseph Weiler's conception of the EU as no more than an international organization. Mancini rightly remarked that this judgement was based on an inability to conceive of a state different from the nation state; it is necessary to separate the notion of state from that of nation. If these are separated we can see that the EU is legitimized by a European demos, a pluri-national people. This kind of state already exists, in Canada, South Africa and India, for instance. So why can't the EU, which is based on the principle of the rule of law, human rights and democracy, become a pluri-national democratic federation? (Mancini, 2004: 99–118). Weiler refused to recognize, as Mancini did, that the EU suffered from a democratic deficit and that the creation of a European democratic government could bridge the gap between the European institutions and the citizens. He was against the concentration of powers in the EU and he preferred the status quo of a supranational community to the creation of a new super-state (Weiler, 1999: Chapter IX). Oliver Beaud puts forward a more elaborate theory. He correctly observes that federalism is incompatible with the concept of sovereignty and that a federation should be based on a constitutional pact. Beaud also says that the federation is not a state, but a new form of polity, a federal union of states. The aim of his research is to remove the notion of state from the notion of federation (*désétatiser la notion de fédération*). Beaud says that the EU is a federal union of states, because it is based on a federal pact, which includes the repudiation of war among member states and the acceptance of federal law to regulate their controversies (Beaud, 2010: 77–92). Lastly, Armin von Bogdandy clearly explains why the EU should be viewed as a 'supranational federation'. He says that:

> Unity is constitutive of diversity. Consequently, principles advancing unity were the first to develop in the process of integration. In a constitutionalist reconstruction, the rule of law appears to be the most important principle promoting unity. … [It] is fundamental for the trajectory taken by integration. It constitutes a *differentia specifica* in view of international law.
>
> (von Bogdandy, 2012: 762)

The development under the rule of law explains the primacy of European law and the relative autonomy of the European institutions from national states. Von Bogdandy's general assessment of the nature of the Union is that the EU is neither a state nor an international organization, because the Union is only 'a community of law and not also a community of coercion' (p. 763).

This overview is useful in that it clarifies the differences between the EU as a supranational organization and other international organizations. In our view the EU can be considered a supranational federal state 'in progress', not just a new kind of supranational organization. Nobody denies that the EU is a public authority, for the simple reason that it provides supranational public goods, as we have already shown. But, in order to provide public goods, a public authority needs powers of coercion to prevent the free-rider problem. The EU's powers of coercion are not clearly visible because they are not similar to the traditional powers of coercion of the nation state: the police and army. Yet they do exist: if a member state disregards EU law, soon or later it must abandon the EU, a decision that carries a high political and economic cost for a national government. Therefore, it is possible to assert that the EU is a federal state 'in progress' (for a similar point of view, Telò, 2010), keeping in mind that building a federal state is different from building a traditional nation state, where the centralization of military force is usually the founding act (for an in-depth analysis, Montani, 2014).

We conclude this section with some remarks on the neo-liberal doctrine of European integration. The birth of the European community shows that we cannot agree with the neo-liberal interpretation of various historians who base their narratives on 'the dominant school of political economy, the neo-liberal institutionalist approach of political science' according to which 'by means of "negotiated cooperation", governments and organisations adapt to change in the market' (Gillingham, 2003: xiv). On the contrary, in 1957 the European governments chose the road of economic integration as the first step towards political integration, only after the failure of the EDC and the European Political Community due to the nationalistic drift of French politics. Thus the edifice of the EU remained midway between confederalism and federalism. In 2008, when the world financial crisis struck the European economy, there were calls in the media and from political parties for a federal government to overcome the ineptitude of the existing European governance. During this debate, many Eurosceptics – both right and left wing – called for the dissolution of the EMU. A return to the nation state, which is the best bulwark against market neo-liberalism, appeared to be the most reasonable solution (Streeck, 2013). This stand is based on a thorough lack of confidence in European democracy. For some left-wing critics the real danger for European citizens is not nationalism, but neo-liberalism. For them, the collapse of the EMU does not mean the Balkanization of Europe. These critics do not see that neo-liberalism is only the fig leaf of nationalism and national sovereignty is the fig leaf of vested interests, lobbies and rent-seekers. Europe is at a turning point. If the democratic political parties do not understand what is at stake today in the European debate, if they continue with the old politics of preserving a fading national sovereignty, not only will the achievement of sixty years of integration be lost, but – as Dehio warned – the peoples of the European continent will be condemned to a future similar to that of the Greek *poleis* dominated by the Macedon and Roman empires.

## Supranational political economy: a research programme

The starting point of our analysis was the schism between economics and politics and the relationship between the two up to the supremacy of politics during the age of totalitarian regimes in the twentieth century. After World War Two, thanks to the international institutions created by the USA, a fairer balance between the market and national governments was made possible. In Western societies the Bretton Woods years were considered an age of economic and political stability, despite the menace of a nuclear war between the two superpowers. Today, especially after the global financial crisis, the task is to look for a new balance between state and market, between the public and private lives of citizens. A new centre of gravity must be found, otherwise the market pan of Hamilton's weighing scale will get heavier year by year. In the following pages we discuss three problems: international security and economic integration; economic integration and democracy and, finally, the ecological challenge. Our aim is not to propose clear-cut solutions to these problems, but only to identify some fields for future research into supranational political economy.

*International security and economic integration.* Politicians, diplomats and scholars of international relations rightly pinpoint the risk of war that is embedded in the transition towards a multipolar system of big powers. Past experience shows that if necessary the emerging power will wage a war to assert itself. Emerging powers invest much of their income in armaments and it is clear that their goal is to compete with the old major powers. Chinese foreign policy is a case in point. There is a Chinese school of thought which asserts that China's national interest is to refute globalization, the trap of wealthy imperialist countries, and that it should be ready for a military confrontation (Shambaugh, 2011). Other schools of thought support the view that 'China will serve its interests better if it can provide more common goods to the international community and share more values with other states' (Jisi, 2011: 79).

Faced with an international scenario fraught with risk a wise policy is not to wait for a new world war, but to do everything possible to prevent it, and turn enemies into friends. We do not have to start from scratch. All the states of the world are members of the UN and the UN is – in theory – an international community based on the rule of law. The Secretary-General of the UN, Kofi Annan, said that

> the rule of law is a concept at the very heart of the Organization's mission. It refers to a principle of governance in which all persons, institutions and entities, public and private, including the state itself, are accountable to laws that are publicly promulgated, equally enforced and independently adjudicated.
>
> (Annan, 2004:4)

This declaration should be translated into policies and institutions.

The fundamental task of the nation state is to guarantee the internal and external security to its citizens. Therefore national governments are not inclined to transfer part of their military power to uncertain, weak supranational institutions. The history of European integration clearly shows how bumpy this road has been. Therefore, a reasonable road map for the creation of a world security community is to improve economic integration. As Rajan (2010: 210), notes:

> The WTO has a dispute-resolution process aimed at enforcing participants' adherence to the agreements, and because the rules are relatively clear, adherence can be judged in a quasi-legal setting. Penalties against violators, usually in the form of sanctions on their trade, are easily imposed.

The example of the WTO can be applied to other international organizations, especially in the fields of environmental protection, where the lack of clear rules and commitments, and penalties for violators, is the main cause of the failure of UN policies.

If the main states agreed to create supranational institutions with a view to ensuring a stable, thriving world economy, relations among them could reach a stage that enables a crucial step forward in the field of military security. The nature of international security changed greatly after the end of the Cold War. Today the major threats of war come not from clashes between big powers, but international terrorism, piracy, failed states and civil wars. Here, an old proposal made by Boutros Boutros-Ghali in 1992, just after the fall of the Berlin Wall, could be taken seriously into consideration. In his *Agenda for Peace*, the Secretary-General of the UN, after proposing rules for preventive diplomacy, stated: 'Under the political circumstances that now exist for the first time since the Charter was adopted' it is possible to organize UN armed forces not only on an ad hoc basis but on a permanent basis. 'The ready availability of armed forces on call could serve, in itself, as a means of deterring breaches of the peace, since a potential aggressor would know that the Council had at its disposal a means of response.' These forces would not be enough to hold off a threat from a state equipped with sophisticated weapons, but they would be useful 'in meeting any threat posed by military force of lesser order' (Ghali, 1992: 25). Ghali's proposal was not taken into consideration in 1992; today, twenty years on, it could become a goal for the forthcoming decade.

*Economic integration and democracy*. During the last quarter of the twentieth century people all over the world became aware that a new era was dawning. Globalization was the name given to a more integrated international community. The core of globalization was economic integration, caused by drastically reduced trade tariffs, information technologies, and a vast increase in multinational firms and international finance.

The debate on the benefits and evils of globalization goes beyond economics. Today, following the 2008 financial crisis, there is a widespread sentiment that the traditional balance between public and private life has deteriorated, and that economic problems, especially the recession and unemployment, are wrecking civil society, social solidarity and democracy. The most eloquent warning comes from the philosopher Martha Nussbaum, who reports that a 'crisis of massive proportions and grave global significance' is 'damaging the future of democratic self-government'. This crisis mainly concerns education because 'the humanities and the arts are being cut away, in both primary/ secondary and college/university education, in virtually every nation of the world'. This radical change has been caused by the fact that 'nations prefer to pursue a short-term profit by the cultivation of the useful and highly applied skills suited to profit-making' (Nussbaum, 2010: 2). In such a way national governments hamper the development of the imaginative, creative and critical skills that are needed to keep democracy alive.

Focusing on the relationship between global economic integration and democracy, we need to consider the incisive analysis of Dani Rodrik, and his theorem of the political 'trilemma' facing the world economy. According to Rodrik:

> [W]e have three options. We can *restrict democracy* in the interest of minimizing international transaction costs, disregarding the economic and social whiplash that the global economy occasionally produces. We can *limit globalization*, in the hope of building democratic legitimacy at home. Or we can *globalize democracy* [original emphasis], at the cost of national sovereignty.

This trilemma captures the fundamental choice we are facing for our future: 'we cannot have hyperglobalization, democracy, and national self-determination all at once. We can have at most two out of three' (Rodrik, 2011: 200). Rodrik's analysis can give us more insight into the difference between international political economy (IPE) and supranational political economy. The trilemma is based on two postulates, which are also widely accepted by scholars of IPE: the nation state, as the fundamental subject of international relations, and the 'natural' framework of any democratic political community. Rodrik himself is well aware of these two limits, but he is of the opinion that it is not realistic, at present, to overcome well-established institutions.

Indeed, the nation state, the first postulate, is not the only form of state in existence today: 40 per cent of the world's population lives in federal states, such as Canada, Australia, India, South Africa, Brazil, Germany and, of course, the USA. Within a federal state the trilemma is a problem, because it is not easy to harmonize the three requirements, but it is possible to find an appropriate balance. We can envisage, says Rodrik,

> a form of global governance – the US model expanded on a global scale. Within the United States a national constitution, federal government, federal judiciary, and large number of nationwide regulatory agencies ensure that markets are truly national despite many differences in regulatory and taxation practices among individual states.

But this solution is not possible in the international system because 'real federalism on a global scale is at best a century away' (Rodrik, 2011: 202–203). Rodrik posits the impossibility of overcoming the national framework of democracy, even if he admits that the European Union is following this road. But, the EU is

> at best the exception that tests the rule. The European Union proves that transnational democratic governance is workable, but its experience also lays bare the demanding requirements of such governance. Anyone who

thinks global governance is a plausible path for the world economy at large would do well to consider Europe's experience.

(Rodrik, 2011: 220)

Let us drop these postulates and consider the question of building a new Bretton Woods compromise to guarantee a healthy form of globalization, as Rodrik proposes. In our view the first problem to tackle is the reform of the international monetary system and the financial system. A stable currency and a stable financial system are two global public goods. The 2008 financial crisis showed that the cause of the US crisis was not only poor financial regulation, but the role of the dollar as an international reserve, which allowed the USA to accumulate great external deficits and to keep interest rates very low for a long time, thanks to the flow of dollars coming back from the rest of the world. Moreover the future of the dollar as a key reserve currency is uncertain since, in a multipolar world, new competitive currencies will enter the global market. The euro is already present, but in a few years' time the yuan and the yen could become new competitors. In short, a global market with several monetary areas in competition could become a very dangerous place. For this reason we have posited (Fiorentini and Montani, 2012) the creation of a world monetary union – with a central bank supervising global liquidity – among the main countries willing to lead the new global world order. The world monetary union would be accountable to a Council formed of representatives of the member states. A similar proposal has also been put forward by the Chinese economist Lin (2013: 201), who says that the economic structure of the new monetary system should be based on paper gold, which would be 'an international reserve currency, issued by an international central bank, according to the provisions of an international treaty'. Lin specifies that 'countries could retain their national currencies but would have to fix their exchange rate to paper gold. Parity adjustment would require the permission of the international monetary authority.' A supranational monetary system would stabilize not only the global economy, but also democratic countries.

Here we cannot deal with the wider problem of supranational or cosmopolitan democracy (Archibugi, 2008) and the related problems of regulating global capitalism and cosmopolitan law (Rossi, 2013), although these are undoubtedly topics which can be usefully studied from a supranational perspective.

*The ecological challenge.* National governments have not yet understood the threat overhanging the future of their citizens caused by human destruction of the biosphere. During the last few decades several scientific reports on the impact of human activities on the fragile ecological system of our planet have launched dramatic warnings. In the UN more and more meetings among national governments, NGOs and scientists have discussed the issue and proposed various solutions. The outcome is depressing. One of the most dangerous problems, climate change, gets worse year after year, as the quantity of greenhouse gases in the atmosphere approaches the threshold of irreversibility. Biodiversity is being lost at an unprecedented rate. Some scientists are proposing to call this the *Anthropocene era*, as humans are no longer merely inhabitants of the planet, but now the main cause of its transformation and death.

Here, our aim is not to discuss the ecological challenge in-depth, but only to show the shortcomings of the international approach, which is based on voluntary cooperation among national governments. Ultimately, cooperation among sovereign states can only work to the extent that national governments have an interest in cooperating. When, for whatever reason, national interests change, cooperation ends. This does not mean that cooperation always fails. For instance, when the depletion of the ozone layer became a pressing issue, the Montreal Protocol of 1987 was effective, because it was possible to find a cheap alternative to CFCs. On the other hand the Kyoto Protocol, agreed on in 1997, with governments accepting binding quantitative objectives for the reduction of greenhouse gases, is now moribund.

This failure can be explained. The climate is a global public good. Greenhouse gases do not respect national borders. If a country pollutes, producing an external diseconomy, the atmosphere is endangered for all the inhabitants of the planet. A sustainable environment is a global public good, but without a supranational authority to manage global environmental problems, every nation state can play free rider. To provide a public good to a community of citizens a public authority, enforcing common rules, is needed.

At present this simple solution has been rejected. The problem of climate change is complex. There is no single technique to deal with global warming: renewable energies, the alternative to the massive consumption of coal, oil and gas, are not available in the short run. World population will increase until 2050 and so, unless there is some kind of a turning point, will global pollution. The Kyoto agreement also failed due to the divide between industrialized countries and emerging countries. Moreover, public opinion in some countries is in favour of environmental policy while, in other countries, it is not a priority.

Therefore the international community is not facing a specific problem, such as smallpox or safeguarding the ozone layer, but an existential challenge, where the life and death of humankind is at stake. In order to find a solution it is necessary to avoid the international trap. A group of states must make a pact, similar to the Schuman Declaration, by which they entrust a limited but real power to a supranational Authority, which would be accountable to a Council of member states. Concerning the ecological challenge, the main supranational power, established to combat global warming and the loss of biodiversity, would need a budget of about 1 per cent of GDP (of the member states of the UN or G20) in order to finance mitigation and adaptation policies in developing countries, combat extreme poverty and fund research and development of clean technologies in cooperation with private investors. The budget could be financed by a global carbon tax and, if need be, a financial transaction tax (Fiorentini and Montani, 2012: Chapter 6).

To conclude, the international community, or a leading group of states, must take on the environmental challenge: the key issue of the twenty-first century, as the spectre of nuclear holocaust was for the last century. The internationalist approach must be abandoned because it can only lead to dead ends. The supranational approach is necessary when public goods are at stake, because powers of coercion are required to prevent people or states playing free rider. Nevertheless establishing a supranational authority does not equate to the creation of a world Leviathan. Within the framework of the nation state, citizens have already attained fundamental rights, the rule of law and democracy. Global public goods are now needed to safeguard these national achievements.

## Notes

1 In his book *Hamilton's Paradox*, Jonathan Rodden (2006) examines in-depth the problem of fiscal federalism, i.e. the financial responsibility in a multi-level system of government. In the present chapter we widen the range of the Hamilton's problem, including the relationship between monetary policy and fiscal policy and the impact of the global market on democracy.

## References

Annan, K. (2004). 'The Rule of Law and Transitional Justice in Conflict and Post-conflict Societies'. *United Nations Security Council Report*, S/2004/616.

Archibugi, D. (2008). *The Global Commonwealth of Citizens: Toward Cosmopolitan Democracy*. Princeton: Princeton University Press.

Barnett, M. and Sikkink, K. (2010). 'From International Relations to Global Society.' In Reus-Smit, C. and Snidal, D. (eds.) *The Oxford Handbook of International Relations*. Oxford: Oxford University Press.

Beaud, O. (2010). 'Peut-on penser l'Union européenne comme une Fédération?' In Esposito, F. and Levrat, N. (eds.) *Europe: de l'integration à la Fédération*. Louvain-la-Neuve: Université de Genève, pp. 71–103.

Blyth, M. (2013). *Austerity: The History of a Dangerous Idea*. Oxford: Oxford University Press.

von Bogdandy, A. (2012). 'Neither an International Organization nor National State: The EU as Supranational Federation.' In Jones, E., Menon, A. and Weatherill, S. (eds.) *The Oxford Handbook of the European Union*. Oxford: Oxford University Press, pp. 761–776.

Dehio, L. (1960). *Germany and World Politics in the Twentieth Century*. New York: Alfred Knopf.

Fiorentini, R. and Montani, G. (2012). *The New Global Political Economy: From Crisis to Supranational Integration*. Cheltenham: Edward Elgar.

Freeden, M. (1996). *Ideologies and Political Theory: A Conceptual Approach*. Oxford: Oxford University Press.

Freeden, M. (2003). *Ideology: A Very Short Introduction*. Oxford: Oxford University Press.

Ghali, B. B. (1992). *An Agenda for Peace*. New York: United Nations.

Gillingham, J. (2003). *European Integration, 1950–2003: Superstate or New Market Economy?* Cambridge: Cambridge University Press.

Hale, T., Held, D. and Young, K. (2013). *Gridlock: Why Global Cooperation is Failing when We Need it Most*. Cambridge: Polity.

Hardach, K. (1976). 'Germany 1914–1970.' In Cipolla, C. M. (ed.) *The Fontana Economic History of Europe: Contemporary Economies*. London: Collins/Fontana, pp. 180–265.

Hayek, F. A. (1982). *Law, Legislation and Liberty*, Vol. 1, 2 and 3. London: Routledge & Kegan Paul.

Hoopes, T. and Brinkley, D. (1997). *FDR and the Creation of the UN*. New Haven: Yale University Press.

Ikenberry, G. J. (2004). 'Liberal Hegemony of Empire? American Power in the Age of Unipolarity.' In Held, D. and Koenig-Archibugi, M. (eds.) *American Power in the 21st Century*. Cambridge: Polity.

Jisi, W. (2011). 'China's Search for Grand Strategy.' *Foreign Affairs*, 90 (2), pp. 68–79.

Keohane, R. O. and Nye, J. S. (1989). *Power and Interdependence*. New York: Harper.

Kupchan, C. A. (2002). *The End of the American Era: US Foreign Policy and the Geopolitics of the Twenty-first Century*. New York: A. Knopf.

Lin, J. Y. (2013). *Against the Consensus: Reflections on the Great Recession*. Cambridge: Cambridge University Press.

Mancini, G. F. (2004). *Democrazia e costituzionalismo nell'Unione europea*. Bologna: Il Mulino.

Mayall, J. (1988). 'The Institutional Basis of Post-war Economic Cooperation.' In Taylor, P. and Groom, A. (eds.) *International Institutions at Work*. London: Pinter, pp. 53–74.

Montani, G. (2012). 'Human Nature, Nationalism and Cosmopolitism.' *Il Politico*, 3, pp. 68–90.

Montani, G. (2014). 'The European Federal State: from Utopia to Supranational Democracy.' *Il Politico*, 1, pp. 28–42.

Moravcsik, A. (2010). 'The New Liberalism.' In Reus-Smit, C. and Snidal, D. (eds.) *The Oxford Handbook of International Relations*. Oxford: Oxford University Press, pp. 234–254.

Nussbaum, M. C. (2010). *Not for Profit: Why Democracy Needs the Humanities*. Princeton: Princeton University Press.

Polanyi, K. (1944). *The Great Transformation*. Boston: Beacon Press.

Quermonne, J-L. (2008). *L'Union européenne dans le temps long*. Paris: Presse de Sciences Po.

Rajan, R. G. (2010). *Fault Lines: How Hidden Fractures Still Threaten the World Economy*. Princeton and Oxford: Princeton University Press.

Rodden, J. A. (2006). *Hamilton's Paradox: The Promise and Peril of Fiscal Federalism*. Cambridge: Cambridge University Press.

Rodrik, D. (2011). *The Globalization Paradox: Democracy and the Future of the World Economy*. New York: Norton & Co.

Rossi, G. (2013). 'Capitalismo fra economia e diritto.' *Il Politico*, 1, pp. 17–27.

Sally, R. (1998). *Classical Liberalism and International Economic Order: Studies in Theory and Intellectual History*. London: Routledge.

Schmidt, V. and Thatcher, M. (eds.) (2013). *Resilient Liberalism in Europe's Political Economy*. Cambridge: Cambridge University Press.

Shambaugh, D. (2011). 'Coping with a Conflicted China.' *The Washington Quarterly*, 34 (1), pp. 7–27.

Stein, A. A. (2010). 'Neo-liberal Institutionalism?' In Reus-Smit, C. and Snidal, D. (eds.) *The Oxford Handbook of International Relations*. Oxford: Oxford University Press, pp. 201–221.

Streeck, W. (2013). *Gekaufte Zeit. Die vertagte Krise des demokratischen Kapitalismus*. Berlin: Suhrkamp Verlag.

Supple, B. (1973). 'The State and the Industrial Revolution 1700–1914.' In Cipolla, C. M. (ed.) *The Fontana Economic History of Europe: The Industrial Revolution*. London: Collins/Fontana, pp. 301–357.

Telò, M. (2010). 'Pertinance et limites des theses fédéralistes: verse une constitution mixte?' In Esposito, F. and Levrat,N. (eds.) *Europe: de l'integration à la Fédération*. Louvain-la-Neuve: Université de Genève, pp. 163–175.

Weiler, J. H. H. (1999). *The Constitution of Europe*. Cambridge: Cambridge University Press.

Weingast, B. R. (1995). 'The Economic Role of Political Institutions: Market-Preserving Federalism and Economic Development.' *The Journal of Law, Economics & Organisation*, VII (1), pp. 1–31.

# 12 Dollars, euros and debt in the American and European monetary unions

*Vito Tanzi*

## Introduction

The European Union (EU) was conceived, several decades ago, as a largely *political* project, at a time when the memories of the Second World War were still vivid in the minds of many Europeans and when the effects of the war on the economies were still visible. The dream of a United Europe was not new. In the past, several historical figures, including Napoleon and Metternich, had entertained such a dream. The belief was that a politically united Europe would reduce or eliminate the frictions that in the past had often led to horrible wars and to much destruction and misery.

The decade of the 1950s, when the idea of a European Union was first formulated, was a period when several leading world figures, including Einstein, Churchill, Gandhi, Maritain and others, had come to believe that the world would benefit if some form of world governance came into existence. Given this perception, the idea of creating a European Union, in place of many national, sovereign jurisdictions, was not seen as visionary or strange. It was an idea that made some sense.

The current version of 'globalization' is of course different from the 1950s' concept because it aims at opening the countries' economies and at integrating the economic activities of the nations while leaving them essentially 'sovereign'. The idea of a United Europe (or a European Union), that its creators had, in the decade of the 1950s and in later years, was more radical and reflected the spirit of the time. It was then known that, in the past, several nations, including the United States, Germany, Italy, Canada, Brazil, India and several others had had their *national* origin through the aggregation of previously independent parts, or jurisdictions. The creation of a European Union would simply follow this historical trend.

It was realized that the process toward the creation of a European Union would need to be gradual and that it would require a lot of time and effort, because of the wide historical, cultural, linguistic, religious and economic differences that existed among the countries of Europe and that separated them. Therefore the original founders were aware that the road toward the European unification would be a bumpy one. Many obstacles would need to be removed and many difficulties would be encountered on the way. As one of the original founders of the European Union (Monnet) put it at that time: 'Europe will be forged in crises and will be the sum of the solutions adopted for these crises.' He was aware that the road toward 'nationhood' had not been smooth for other 'federations'. Some of them had come into existence by military conquests or by annexation and some were still undergoing difficulties in becoming fully united political and economic entities, as for example Italy. For an interpretation of that experience, see Tanzi (2012).

The hope that the creators had was that, with time, a 'single market' would be brought into existence that, by facilitating commercial exchanges and movements of workers and capital within the Union, would lead to the creation of a truly European economy and of a functional European identity. Time would create European 'citizens', individuals who would consider themselves 'citizens' of a 'United States of Europe' and not just French, Germans, Italians, Spaniards, or citizens of the many European countries.

The precise road to the final destination, and even the precise characteristics of the final destination, were left to future leaders to determine. It would have been impossible at the beginning to provide a detailed final design and there was no 'constitution' available to guide the process.

## Characteristics of a European Union

A *mature* 'United States of Europe', or a true 'European Union', when it was created could take the characteristics of a *unitary* state, as for example was France, or of a *federation* as was the United States of America. It must have been realized from the beginning that given the existing diversity among the European countries a unitary state could not be a realistic destination. Thus, from the beginning, a realistic assumption was that the final destination would be some 'European federation' made up of member states that would retain *some* political and economic independence and some national characteristics, as 'states' or 'regions' do in other federations. However, as members of the same 'club', they would need to give up various national powers, delegating them to the supra national (i.e. the European) authorities, and would have to observe some common rules for their behaviour.

The member states would necessarily endorse a common trade policy, vis-à-vis the (non-European) rest of the world. They would allow free movements of goods, capital and people within the Union. They would need to adopt a common policy for financing (and for deciding on) European 'public good'. They would need to coordinate, if not to harmonize, the tax systems of the member countries, to reduce, if not eliminate, 'tax competition' and they would need to harmonize many regulations.

They would also need to develop common rules for *measuring* and for *maintaining* given budgetary outcomes and for promoting a European monetary policy. Finally, they would need to create institutions, such as a European executive, a European legislature, a European Court of Justice and some institutions related to monetary and fiscal policies. These institutions would gradually increase their power over the years while the power of the national corresponding institutions would be reduced.

The absence of a Constitution and of a European Supreme Court, with the power to interpret the principles of a Constitution, would make the process more difficult than it could have been. The willingness of the policymakers of different European countries to move at the same speed has not been evident, creating, at various times, different speeds for different parts of Europe. This has been particularly noticeable between the countries that joined the European Monetary Union (EMU) and those that did not.

Over the decades, since the idea of a European Union was first conceived, there has been considerable progress toward the creation of a European Union with characteristics of a federation. However, opposition has continued to be raised to some developments, especially on the part of some countries (such as the United Kingdom and some others) that have been uncomfortable with the goal of moving toward a *political* union and about some of the social and financial policies being proposed. The policymakers of these countries would prefer and would be satisfied with some kind of 'enhanced trade union' that would have limited political power, thus leaving the member countries sovereign but more open within the European context.

For the above reasons progress in some areas has been more rapid than in others. This has led to the prospect of a Europe divided into two parts moving at different speeds toward fuller integration. With the creation of EMU one part has moved much further toward the establishment of a European economic and political entity, having created a uniform monetary policy and a common currency for a growing number of countries and thus reducing the cost of trading among them and reducing the national authorities' power to pursue an independent monetary policy.

A mature, true federal European Union would, of course, require several features: an *executive* that would have access to significant financial resources to promote European objectives. The resources would be obtained from taxation and from borrowing from the financial market. The executive (i.e. the European government) would be able to make some political and economic decisions on behalf of all the member countries; a *legislative* body (a parliament) that could legislate for the whole union; a European *system of justice*; a common *exchange rate policy* vis-à-vis the rest of the world and, thus, a common *currency*; and some other characteristics. So far, progress has been more rapid in some areas than in others. The EMU has acquired more of the characteristics of a mature federation than the EU.

In the rest of this chapter we shall focus mainly on the European Monetary Union and compare it with that other monetary union that is the United States of America. We shall, in particular, discuss the limits that exist to monetary and fiscal policies in these two regions and, consequently, on their bearing for the dollar and the euro.

## The US Monetary Union and the European Monetary Union

The monetary union that is the United States of America is constituted by 50 states and some territories, including Puerto Rico and others. The US Federal government is responsible for a large share of the fiscal action (spending and taxing) of the whole country, and the Federal Reserve System, made up of several regional banks and a Federal Reserve Board, is responsible for the monetary policy of the country. The fiscal action of the Federal government is complemented by that of the sub-national governments (states, counties, municipalities and the territories, Puerto Rico, Guam and the US Virgin Islands).

The Federal Reserve System was created a century ago (in 1913). It has the mandate of promoting the objective of both price stability and full employment with its monetary policy. It prints dollars, provides reserves to commercial banks and supervises the US financial system. The full employment objective was added to that of price stability only in 1948.

The fiscal responsibility of the *Federal* government changed dramatically over the years as a consequence of the Great Depression. Until 1916, or about the time when the Federal Reserve System was created, the fiscal role and the public spending of the Federal government had been limited to the financing of *national* public goods, mainly defence and national infrastructure, and of the public administration. Until 1916, the share of Federal public spending into the USA's GDP had been only about 2 per cent. In 1929 it was still only 3 per cent of GDP. Excluding a few years during World War One and immediately after, the Federal public spending remained below 3 per cent of GDP until the Great Depression. It ought to be realized that this spending included defence spending, which in Europe is still in the hands of the national countries, and also the servicing of the public debt accumulated during World War One. Therefore, until the Great Depression the public spending of the Federal government of the United States was not different from what is today that of the European Union, as a share of GDP.

The increase in public spending by the US Federal government was largely a consequence of *changing views of what the government should do and of timing.* The Great Depression, that was followed by World War Two, came at a time when views of what governments should do to sustain economic activity (the Keynesian Revolution) and to redistribute income and provide some protection against particular economic risks for citizens (the introduction of welfare states) were rapidly changing. These views, which were not universally endorsed, were pushing governments to play a larger role, with their fiscal tools, in stabilization and in income maintenance. In the United States these changes led to the introduction of the Social Security System and to other social programmes by the Federal government.

The role of the local governments and their public spending changed much less. The changes which were introduced by the Administration of President Roosevelt during the Great Recession, in the decade of the 1930s, were amplified by President Johnson, with his 'War on Poverty' programmes, in the middle 1960s. These new policies led to a permanent increase in the role of the *Federal* government in the US economy and in its public spending and reversed the relative positions in public spending that had been held by the sub-national and the national (i.e. Federal) governments. All the new action came at the Federal level.

In Europe the growth of public spending had generally started earlier than in the United States. In the 1930s it was further stimulated by the same forces that influenced the American government. Especially after World War Two, there was a dramatic expansion in public spending accompanied by large increases in the average tax levels. These were connected with the creation of welfare states, that in several European countries tended to be more generous and more expensive than in the USA. This expansion occurred in each country; in some more than in others (Tanzi and Schuknecht, 2000). This development would have important, indirect consequences for the European Union, and especially for the European Monetary Union.

By the time the European Monetary Union was created, in the late 1990s, the countries that became members of EMU had already mature, expensive and highly developed welfare systems. However, and this is important, these systems were *not uniform but diverse*. The countries' welfare systems had specific and highly differentiated national characteristics that required different public spending and tax levels. For example in 2000 the share of taxes in GDP was 31.7 per cent in Ireland and 34 per cent in Portugal and Spain; but it was 47.2 per cent in Finland and 44.4 per cent in France. By comparison, the share of total taxes in GDP was only 29.5 per cent in the United States and much of it was at the federal level.

Given the very wide differences that existed among the European countries, in the shares of total taxes and total public spending in the GDPs, and given the wide differences in the specific characteristics of their welfare and tax systems, it would have been very difficult if not impossible to bring those systems under a uniform, European roof, in a harmonized way, as it had occurred in the United States, under Roosevelt and Johnson where the spending had filled a void. It would be almost impossible to do it now. Just think of the wide differences in public pension systems, in public health systems, in tax systems, and so on that now exist among the member countries that belong to the European Monetary Union.

It would also have been difficult to create a European-wide 'fiscal authority' (one similar to the US Federal government) with the taxing and spending powers that are enjoyed by the US Federal government. The tax revenue that would need to be given to such a European-wide fiscal authority would have to be *additional* to those that are already badly needed by the national governments of the member states. Many of these states already run large fiscal deficits and have high public debts. Unless some important, and now national spending (as for example that for defence) could be transferred from the countries to the European authority, it would be very difficult to transfer to the European fiscal authority the revenue that the national governments now receive. Under current circumstances to give significant revenue to the European fiscal authority would require raising the already very high tax burden in the member countries.

It is also very unlikely that the citizens of countries as diverse as France, Germany, Italy and Spain would agree to accept European-wide common denominators, in their welfare and tax policies, similar, in principles, to those imposed on the Americans by the US social security system and by the US Federal tax system. The 'principle of subsidiarity' and the existing entitlements by pensioners and citizens in general would rule out such possibilities.

The politicians and the economists who, during the recent financial crisis and during the problems encountered by Greece, Ireland, Spain, Portugal and some other European countries, have continued to argue in favour of the creation of a European fiscal authority, one that would conduct a European-wide fiscal policy and that would play the role of a 'transfer union' (transferring major resources from some countries to countries in difficulties), have failed to fully understand the limitations and the obstacles that exist to such a proposal. Only a truly radical revolution – one that destroyed the existing welfare and the entitlements that they have created and the tax systems that now exist at the country level in Europe – that created, from scratch, a new European welfare and tax reality could allow the creation of the desired policy. Such a revolution has very little chance of happening.

## Rules for federations and monetary unions

To work well, federations, like most clubs, need rules. When the needed rules do not exist, or are not followed or enforced, problems are likely to develop. The bad behaviour by some parts of the federation will create negative spillovers for the other parts (Tanzi, 2004). This happened in the United States, in the first part of the nineteenth century; in Brazil, in the 1980s; in Argentina, in the 1980s and 1990s; in Spain, in recent years; and even in some parts of the USA very recently.

In all the cases in which federations (and monetary unions) got into financial difficulties it was because parts of them overspent and overborrowed, and attempted to pass the costs to the whole federation. For this reason there must be rules to prevent this behaviour and, equally importantly, rules that are observed and enforced. The most important and, potentially, the most effective among the rules must be a *credible* 'no-bailout rule'. If such a rule exists but is not credible, it will not prevent behaviour that will lead to difficulties.

The 'no-bailout rule' must be accompanied by restrictions on borrowing, for the parts that make up the federation. It may also be necessary to put limitations to the level of public spending of each part as a share of GDP. The reason is that a high public spending and the high tax burden that must accompany it are likely to reduce the efficiency of the economy and the growth rate of the high spending jurisdiction, compared with the growth rate of the rest of the federation. This differential growth is likely to lead to difficulties.

### Rules in the American Monetary Union

In the United States an implicit and credible no-bailout rule was introduced in the first half of the nineteenth century when 'several states ... defaulted on their debt and [when the Federal government refused to help them] had to undertake painful adjustment measures [without the assistance of the Federal government]' (Bordo *et al.*, 2013: 459). This experience led to the introduction of balanced-budget rules by most of the states. However, while most of the 'states' introduced such rules, counties and municipalities did not and continued to depend on the automatic enforcement mechanism of the market, or on the hope that other levels of government would come to assist them. As a consequence, several of them over the years continued to experience occasional defaults. In recent months, the most important, but not the only one, has been the City of Detroit that declared bankruptcy.

The rules that constrain the behaviour of the states in the USA have, however, received more praise than they may deserve, so that a few comments on them may be appropriate.

The first comment is that, as mentioned earlier, the balanced-budget rule applies only to 'states'. It does not apply to the Federal Government, to the counties, to the municipalities and to the 'territories' (Puerto Rico, Guam, Virgin Islands) that the United States controls. Attempts over the years by Congress to apply that rule to the US Federal governments have not been successful.

The second comment is that, for the 49 states in which the rule applies, it covers only the 'operational' or the 'current' budget, and excludes capital spending on infrastructures. It is thus a kind of 'golden rule'. This means that the states can and do accumulate debt obligations for spending classified as 'capital spending'. It also means that the rule encourages attempts by the state authorities to reclassify some current expenditures or capital spending. Because of this 'capital' spending is often favoured over spending for 'operation and maintenance'. The consequence has been that, as several recent reports have commented and as some recent accidents have indicated, the quality of the existing American infrastructure has been decaying creating enormous potential costs for the future and reducing the productivity of the American economy. The rule may also have encouraged the building of very expensive structures, such as a reported $600 million high school in California. It has also encouraged occasional 'roads to nowhere' when some Federal subsidies were received by the states.

The third comment is that the rule may have led to increasing political pressure in Congress to shift some spending upward, to the Federal government, and some taxes downward, to the sub-national government, reducing the Federal government's ability to cover its essential spending. Excises, sales and property taxes have remained largely at the sub-national level and the United States is now one of the very few countries in the world (and the only one among industrial countries) without a value added tax. The reason is that the states would oppose the introduction of such a tax at the Federal level. Federal taxes have encountered growing difficulties to cover federal spending resulting in large recent fiscal deficits.

The fourth comment is that the recent financial crisis and the Federal policies to deal with its consequences may have contributed to changing political attitudes and to make some rules less rigid in the future. The government bailout of 'too large to fail' banks and other financial institutions, during the financial crisis, might have created a 'moral hazard' problem. Should a 'too large to fail' state (say, California or Illinois) face major financial difficulties, imposing great costs on the citizens of that state, many are likely to ask why the US Federal government was so ready to help 'too large to fail' financial institutions and not 'too large to fail' states.

Additionally, Puerto Rico has accumulated a public debt that exceeds $70 billion, a debt that is larger than that officially reported by all US states except California and New York. Puerto Rico is now facing very high interest rates on its borrowing and major financial difficulties. Puerto Rico is becoming for the United States a problem similar to that of Greece for the EMU.

Finally and perhaps more importantly (and generally less well understood) is the fact that the balanced-budget rule that the American states are required to respect not only excludes investments but is applied on a 'cash' and not on an 'accrued' concept of the fiscal deficit. If a state makes an investment it can finance it with borrowing without breaking the rule because of the 'golden rule'. However, if it accumulates obligation for pensions to be paid in the future (which do not require immediate cash spending) and if it does not accumulate enough assets to be able to fully pay the pensions when they fall due, the balanced-budget rule does not force it to set aside the required amounts. This can create large intergenerational liabilities which in some ways are similar to public debt but do not show up in debt statistics.

Many states as well as other levels of sub-national governments (countries and municipalities) have accumulated enormous future obligation vis-à-vis public employees (school teachers, firemen, policemen, etc.) without setting aside enough assets to be able to meet those obligations when they fall due. This has created a situation that some have defined as a future 'tsunami wave' that at some point will hit the sub-national governments. For example, it has been estimated that California is already short of $80 billion for teachers' pensions and that the shortfall will grow to $500 billion by 2043, unless money is now set aside. It is an open question how these obligations will be covered and what impact they will eventually have on the sustainability of the US fiscal policy and on the value of the US dollar. The Detroit recent bankruptcy is not likely to remain an exception. It ought to be added that some European countries are facing similar situations. Let us now look at the EMU's rules.

### Rules for EMU

The European Monetary Union adopted a no-bailout rule from the beginning. It also tried to impose some limits to the borrowing by the member states, through the Maastricht Treaty and through rules imposed on the European Central Bank, which prevented it from lending directly to government. However, the behaviour of market operators and of some countries indicated that the enforcement of the rules was doubted and that the rules or borrowing were not as strict as they could have been. The rules and the difficulties that developed are reviewed briefly below.

In the EMU, the most important rules were imposed by the Stability and Growth Pact negotiated at Maastricht and endorsed by the governments of the member countries. The rules set a limit of 3 per cent of GDP to the fiscal deficit of the *general* government (a limit measured following guidelines established in 1995 by EUROSTAT) and a goal of 60 per cent of GDP for the measure of the public debt of the *general* government (also following the EUROSTAT guidelines). Because, at the time when the Maastricht Treaty was negotiated, several countries (especially Belgium, Italy and Greece) had public debts that were much larger than 60 per cent of their GDPs, the rule on public debt was set as a goal, to be reached in a realistic, but unspecified, time and not as an immediate limit.

Difficulties soon developed with the way the Maastricht rules were set. The first difficulty was that it was not specified how soon, or at what speed, the ratio of 60 per cent of GDP for the public debt would have to be reached. Therefore, the rule became a *soft* rule and the objective of the 60 per cent of GDP a *distant* one. Governments paid little attention to it. The second difficulty was that the limit of 3 per cent of GDP, imposed on the fiscal deficit and that had been intended to be reached only under exceptional circumstances, soon came to be seen as a target and not as a hard inflexible ceiling. The third was that the penalties for breaking the deficit rule were not automatic. Rather they were imposed only if the finance ministers of the member countries as a group agreed. It also became more difficult to impose the penalties on large countries, such as France and Germany, than on smaller countries making the rule less fair and thus less applicable on anyone.

Finally, and perhaps as importantly, the technical complexity of measuring fiscal deficits and public debts, following the EUROSTAT principles, which were partly based on *cash* transactions and partly on *accrual* commitments, and for *general* governments, allowed countries to easily hide some spending that did not require immediate cash payment and to enhance some revenue, through sales of public assets and through other ad hoc manoeuvres, thus manipulating the accounts to make them look better than they were. The EUROSTAT guidelines of 1995 had tried to prevent this problem from arising. However, given the complexity of the principles, it had been only partly successful. The rule depended on the full, informed and honest collaboration of national experts. For example the *reporting* of debts, to private enterprises that had done public works or had supplied goods and services to the public sector, could be delayed and often so were the *payments* to them. Various other manoeuvres were also possible, reducing the value of the rule (Tanzi, 2013: Chapter 6). Another problem was that, while the rules attempted to set limits to fiscal deficits and public debts, they did not set limits to the level of public spending, that keep growing in several countries.

A different but also significant problem that developed within EMU was that private banks were allowed to lend money to their own governments without the need to keep equity capital against that lending, as it was necessary for other kind of lending, and they could borrow from the European Central Bank. Thus, indirectly the ECB ended up financing some public spending. Given the often incestuous relations that existed between banks and governments in several European countries, governments used banks to promote some of the objectives that they wanted to promote and that could have been promoted more directly with government spending. This created mutual obligations between banks and governments and consequently 'moral hazards'. These became evident during the financial crisis in several countries and not just EMU countries (Spain, Ireland, Portugal but also in the United States and the UK).

The conclusion of this section must be that neither the United States nor the European Monetary Union have had in place rules sufficiently rigorous to prevent problems from developing. In both monetary unions (EMU and USA) the rules should have been more precise and should have been applied with greater rigour.

## Outcomes for the dollar, for the euro and for public debt

In the previous sections we briefly described: (a) the origin of the European Union, which, for a growing number of countries, became the European Monetary Union, (b) some of the objectives and characteristics of that Union; (c) some of the, major differences in the American and European monetary unions; and finally, (d) some of the rules that have guided the two unions and that were supposed to prevent difficulties from developing in them.

Perhaps it ought to be recalled that, while the American monetary union (the USA) was created in a country that was largely empty at the time the union was created and in which the relatively few occupants had a fairly homogeneous cultural and linguistic background, the EMU was created in a territory that was densely populated, that had been populated for a long time, and that had populations that had very different histories, languages and traditions. It was thus normal to expect, as Monnet had predicted, that the European Union would experience difficulties and would 'be forged in crises'.

From the beginning, the creation of EMU attracted many sceptical and negative comments, especially from American economists and financial operators. For some of them it was an article of faith that EMU would fail.

*Table 12.1* Some essential statistics

| Year | Exchange rate | Euros in central banks' holdings | Share of public debt in | |
|------|---------------|----------------------------------|-------------------------|------|
| | | | US | EMU |
| 1995 | 1.34 | n/a | – | – |
| 1996 | 1.27 | n.a | – | – |
| 1997 | 1.09 | n.a | – | – |
| 1998 | 1.17 | n.a | – | – |
| 1999 | 1.01 | 18.1 | – | – |
| 2000 | 0.94 | 18.4 | – | – |
| 2001 | 0.89 | 19.0 | – | – |
| 2002 | 1.05 | 23.3 | – | – |
| 2003 | 1.26 | 23.1 | – | – |
| 2004 | 1.36 | 22.9 | – | – |
| 2005 | 1.18 | 21.2 | – | – |
| 2006 | 1.32 | 22.2 | 63.8 | 68.6 |
| 2007 | 1.46 | 24.2 | 64.4 | 66.5 |
| 2008 | 1.40 | 23.3 | 73.3 | 70.3 |
| 2009 | 1.43 | 25.4 | 86.3 | 80.1 |
| 2010 | 1.34 | 23.9 | 95.1 | 85.7 |
| 2011 | 1.30 | 22.3 | 99.4 | 88.2 |
| 2012 | 1.32 | 24.4 | 102.7 | 93.0 |
| 2013 | 1.37 | 24.5 | 106.0 | 95.7 |

Source: IMF, Fiscal Monitor and Bloomberg Net.

Milton Friedman gave EMU no more than 10 years before it would break up (Friedman, 1997). Martin Feldstein wrote several articles in which he provided various reasons why the union had little chance of surviving (Feldstein, 1997). A brief survey of the arguments advanced by these critics is provided in Tanzi (2013: Chapter 10). In this connection it may be worthwhile to point out that the United States did not always have a good sailing, in spite of its more propitious beginning. It experienced defaults by several states, a civil war that almost broke it up, a Great Depression that was a terrifying experience, and various other difficulties.

An analysis of the rules that now guide the two monetary unions has concluded that there is no obvious or clear superiority of the US over the European rules. There are problems in both of them and these problems have led to different difficulties. In this section we shall provide a few but important statistics that give some indication of recent economic developments in the two unions. They are provided in Table 12.1 and refer to (a) the behaviour of the exchange rate between the euro and the dollar; (b) the use of these two currencies in the foreign exchange holdings by the world's central banks; and (c) the share of the public debts of general governments in the two monetary unions. These statistics are indicative of the performances of the two monetary unions in recent years.

If the expectations of disaster for the EMU had been correct: (a) the euro would have progressively lost value with respect to the dollar: (b) the world's central banks would get rid of their euro holdings; preferring the dollar as the safer world currency; and (c) the EMU would experience a faster growth in public debt, as a share of the area's GDP, compared to the USA.

As to the exchange rate, in the first few years of the creation of EMU, the euro lost value with respect to the dollar, probably reflecting the doubts about the survivability of EMU and the euro that many entertained. The euro had an average value of only 0.89 in respect to the dollar in 2001, but its value rose rapidly afterwards. With some fluctuations it reached an average value of 1.46 in 2007. The financial crisis that brought daily predictions of the near collapse of the euro made its value fall to 1.30 in 2011 but, since that time, its value increased to around 1.37 in 2013 and was 1.39 on 18 March, 2014.

As to the share of the euro-denominated assets in the reserves of the world's central banks, it rose from around 18 per cent in the first years to reach 25.4 per cent in 2009. The financial crisis led to some fall (to 22.3 per cent) in 2011 but since that time it has been rising and in 2013 it was 24.5 per cent of the total, or close to the maximum reached in 2009. In 2014 the rating given by Moody to the ECB bonds was raised to AAA. There was much less talk about the near collapse of the euro.

As to the share of public debts in the GDPs of the two areas, the data available from the IMF indicate that, in 2006, the general government of the EMU had a public debt that was larger than that of the USA, 68.6 per cent of GDP versus 63.8 per cent of GDP. By 2013, the estimated percentages were 106.0 per cent for the USA and 95.7 per cent in the EMU. Public debt had increased much faster in the USA.

The above data, though limited, seem to indicate that the disaster for the EMU, that had been widely predicted, simply did not happen. It can be concluded that, in relative terms the EMU area has done better than it had been expected, in spite of a truly major shock to the system that had come from the financial crisis that, it should be recalled, originated in the USA. As Monnet had predicted, the crises were forging the European Union and, in some ways, were bringing about solutions and needed reforms in several of the countries and especially to those most hit by the financial crisis. Also surprisingly, the number of countries that became part of the EMU and that used the euro as their currency kept rising.

## Concluding comments

This chapter has compared the experiences of two important monetary unions. The first, the USA, has been a federation for more than two centuries and has been a true monetary union for a century, after the creation of the Federal Reserve System in 1913. The second, the EMU, has been in existence for less than two decades and has had a central bank and a formal common currency only since 2002. The EMU is still developing institutions and norms (such as the recent Banking Union) that in time should transform it into a real federation, with a federation-wide budget and fiscal policy.

Both of these monetary unions operate in geographical and political areas and both have established rules for the behaviour of the parts that make up these unions. As is true for any club, the rules are expected to be followed to prevent difficulties, but some difficulties have developed in both of them. A view that has been shared by various economists and financial operators, especially in Anglo-Saxon countries, has been that the arrangements and the rules that exist in the American monetary union are more consistent with those needed by an optimal currency area and a mature federation. The European monetary union has been considered a far from-optimal currency area and the euro has been widely expected to fail. The difficulties that in recent years were encountered by some of the countries belonging to EMU seemed to back this expectation of failure of the euro.

This chapter has argued that while at first look the USA seems to have better institutional arrangements and rules – such as a market that is closer to a single market; a Federal government with strong powers that finds it easier to pursue stabilizing policies; an efficient central bank with fewer constraints than the European Central Bank; and 'good' budgetary and other rules that should lead to better policies – a closer look gives a less sanguine conclusion.

There is little convincing evidence that the economic outcome has been and will continue to be better in the USA compared to Europe. From the time of the creation of the EMU: (a) the euro has increased in value with respect to the dollar; (b) the euro has increased its share in the holdings of foreign reserves by the world's central banks and (c) the public debt for the general government has increased more in the USA than in the EMU area. It also seems that, in spite of the presumably balanced-budget rules that are supposed to discipline the fiscal policies of American states, the US subnational governments have accumulated large current debts (for investment projects) and large and worrisome future obligations with respect to public pensions that do not show up in official debt statistics. This is of course also a European problem.

The conclusion from the above analysis seems to be that, in spite of the recent and continuing difficulties that the European Monetary Union and the euro have encountered they are both likely to survive. The jury is still out as to which monetary union and which currency will perform better over the long run.

## References

Bordo, M. D., Jonung, L. and Markiewiez, A. (2013). 'A Fiscal Union for the Euro: Some Lessons from History.' *CESifo Economic Studies*, 59 (3), pp. 449–488.

Feldstein, M. (1997). 'The Political Economy of the European and Monetary Union: Political Sources of an Economic Liability.' *Journal of Economic Perspectives*, 11 (4), pp. 23–42.

Friedman, M. (1997). 'Why Europe Can't Afford the Euro: The Danger of a Common Currency.' *The Times*, 19 November.

Tanzi, V. (2004). 'The Stability and Growth Pact: Its Role and Future.' *Cato Journal*, 24 (Spring/Summer).

Tanzi, V. (2012). *Italica: Costi e Conseguenze dell' Unificazione d'Italia.* Torino: Grantorino Libri Editore.

Tanzi, V. (2013). *Dollars, Euros, and Debt: How We Got Into the Fiscal Crisis, and How We Get Out of It.* London: Palgrave MacMillan.

Tanzi, V. and Schuknecht, L. (2000). *Public Spending in the 20th Century.* Cambridge: Cambridge University Press.

# 13 Against EUrocentrism

## A new stage in the building of the European Republic[1]

*Fernando Iglesias*

### The two halves of the European twentieth century and the end of nation-building

Building European unity was never a simple or a linear process, nor a completely democratic one. However, a quick glance at the European twentieth century, split into two almost equal halves by the Schuman Declaration (1950), allows an understanding of the basic facts. Comparing the first half of the century, meaning the Europe of nations based on national autarchy and national sovereignty, with the second half, characterized by the progressive development of a common economic market and supranational institutions, is expressive enough. The effects of nation-building and nationalism, in the first case, and of federalism and regional integration, in the second one, reveal the progressive obsolescence of the national paradigm within an increasingly globalized world.

The year 1950 represented the exact split between two antithetical realities: the Europe of hunger, war and genocide that preceded the Schuman Declaration of 9 May; and the Europe of peace, human rights, democracy and prosperity that emerged from the European Community of Coal and Steel and arrived to its current form, the European Union (EU). The opposite outcomes of these two Europes demonstrate that the success of the European process of integration was not the achievement of a particular ethnicity or cultural tradition, but of a political method for articulating the increasing need of political unity with the human-social preference for cultural diversity and plural identities.

Nothing that innovative: the equality of rights of people from different ethnicities, cultures and religions was the paradigm that had structured the creation of national states from the Peace of Westphalia to the end of the nineteenth century, when national states were 'refeudalised' on behalf of a common ethnicity, culture and identity (Iglesias, 2000: 403). That kind of political unity able to conciliate cultural diversity with equality of rights at a scale able to deal with the existing techno-economic reality, meaning then the national scale and state, was abandoned at the beginning of the twentieth century in the name of nationalism. History will show soon the consequences of that.

The history of the EU is the story of a post-national entity that was built upon the tragedies nationalism caused in an increasingly globalized world. Its development was contemporaneous to the failure of the two main post-war nation-building projects. Between 1947 and 1950, India, Palestine and Europe were politically reorganized under opposing models. Whereas the European Community of Coal and Steel was a clear attempt to overcome national structures and national sovereignty, the reorganizations of India and Palestine were melded on the traditional nationalistic principle: the ethnic and cultural unity of the state. Thus, three decades after the adoption of the Wilsonian nationalistic paradigm to the reorganization of European borders at the end of the First World War, the old-fashioned generator of protectionism, nationalism, militarization, totalitarianism and war was put again on its feet outside the European territory, in India and Palestine.

By 1947, a big part of the Asian territory was divided in a Hindu India and a Muslim Pakistan, and by 1948, Palestine was split into a Jewish Israel and a Muslim Palestine. The guiding idea (political unity is only possible under common identity and cultural uniformity) was a prolongation of the pre-Westphalian *cuius regio, eius religio* principle to the modern context, constituting a clear denial of the original nation-building process. The development of these three different experiments of institutional-building, Europe, Palestine and India, and their outcomes were meaningful. The results of these renewed versions of nation-building within the second half of the twentieth century confirmed the obsolescence of the nationalistic paradigm: a long period of peace and progress was opened in Europe based on a *cosmopolitanism of difference* (Marramao, 2012: 232), but endless conflicts arose in Palestine and India, whose effects still threaten world peace (Iglesias, 2011: 400).

Six decades of peace and prosperity in Europe and racism, terrorism and war in India and Palestine say nothing on the idiosyncrasies of Europeans, Indians, Pakistanis, Israelis and Palestinians. They express the results of two different responses to the need of establishing political unities in a globalized world: the cosmopolitan strategy of regional integration and the decimononic nation-building-as-usual. Unfortunately, things got even worst at the beginning of the twenty-first century due to the events of September 11, 2001 and the risk of a nuclear war between India and Pakistan, by 2002.

Therefore, if we want to avoid past mistakes and horrors, the proposals on the current situation of the EU should avoid throwing out the baby of regional integration with the dirty bathwater of the economic crisis. In order to do so, there are at least five strategies those who support the EU as the most advanced form of civilization that humanity has reached insofar should utilize:

1   Diachronic comparison between the situation in Europe before and after the beginning of the process of integration (1950).
2   Synchronic comparison between the current situation in Europe and other simultaneous political reorganizations such as India–Pakistan and Israel–Palestine.

3   Diachronic comparison between the way the Europe of Nations 'solved' its previous biggest financial crisis (1930) and the way the EU is trying to solve its biggest financial crisis (2008); this is to say: by peace, cooperation and increased integration and not by nationalism, genocide and war.
4   Diachronic comparison between the current difficulties of building the EU and the nation-building processes of the nineteenth and twentieth centuries, which included, in almost all the cases, decades of war, discrimination and forced assimilation, when not ethnic cleansing and genocide.
5   Promotion of a public debate centred on globalization and on the global dynamics of technology, finance and production, in order to facilitate the comprehension of the new hypercompetitive inter-national scenario, in which the problem of the EU is not about being too big and united, but too small and disunited.

Beyond the unforced errors that were committed during the process, the results achieved by the European integration are extraordinary: according to the UNDP-HDI,[2] in spite of the crisis, sixteen of the twenty-eight EU countries are among the top thirty nations in human development.[3] Another ten are a little behind this but still on the list of the Very-High-Human-Development Countries ranked by the UNDP. All of these ten countries (except Portugal) were incorporated into the EU by 2004 and by 2013. Finally, Bulgaria and Romania, the only two EU countries which still have not reached the Very-High-Human-Development Countries standard, entered the EU in 2007, after a long period behind the Iron Curtain. Since then, despite the crisis, they have improved their situation from the sixty-first to the fifty-seventh place (Bulgaria) and from the sixty-third to the fifty-sixth place (Romania) on the UNDP-HDI table, at a speed of one place per year.

Now, the old Europe of Nations from which millions ran away to seek refuge in the Third World has become the preferred destination for migrants from all corners of Earth. And the political consequences of the building of the EU were as profound as these socio-economic achievements. EU efforts aimed at creating a continent based on cooperation were awarded by peace and the defeat of the totalitarian systems developed by the times of the Europe of Nations. The fail of the Iron Curtain and the Berlin Wall, the largest territorial barriers that humans had ever built, was the result of a new conception of the relation among economy and politics that overcame the limitations of wild capitalism and communism. Neither of these extraordinary results for the future of liberty and democracy in the world were the result of any European particular tradition or ethnic specificity, as the similar success of the other political experiences on both democracy and federal unification at a continental scale (USA and Canada) confirm. If history is not an opinion, the amalgam between democracy and continental-scale federalism is a universally valid paradigm. Their absence or failure in other regions due to balkanization should be considered the main cause of their delay and poverty with respect to Europe and North America. Stretching this argument to its extreme, it suggests the lack of democracy and large-scale federalism at the global level is the main reason for the social structure of the world continuing to be similar to the national ones prior to the triumph of democracy and federalism.

## The European Union as a fortress

The building of a united Europe has allowed two-centuries-old enemies to become peaceful and cooperative neighbours and the development of human societies in which the respect for democracy and human rights, as well as the average living conditions, are the best in history. Yet, the consideration of this breath-taking success must not result in the sacralization of the European Union.

European history demonstrates the worst experiences used to be the product of the reification of a political model (then, the national state) and the irrational attempt of prolongation of its successes beyond the original historical frame. The binomial between nation and state, which by the nineteenth century had been the archetypical social device for economic development and social prosperity, became the nightmare of the early twentieth century. In a more comprehensive perspective, as soon as the Second Industrial Revolution overcame national boundaries nationalism, the ideology that consecrated the marriage between the state and the nation changed during the transition from the monarchical Agrarian age to the democratic Industrial era, from a progressive and inclusive practice into a reactionary devil.

1913 meant the end of the *belle époque*, the start of increasing commercial protectionism and restrictions to the circulation of people through national frontiers. It was also the beginning of a new political age characterized by the exaltation of national, ethnic and cultural specificities, which led to the militarization of societies and totalitarianism and, finally, to war and genocide (Hobsbawm, 1995). Of course, as Keynes correctly marked (Keynes, 1992: 308), mercantilist economists had no illusions on the nationalistic character of the policies they advocated and its intrinsic tendency to promote war which, predictably, started in 1914. Unfortunately, at the end of the First World War, the post-war period saw the reorganization of Europe under the same nationalistic bases that had caused the tragedy. Removed from the collective memory by a sort of nationalistic curse, four pan-European conferences (Vienna 1926, Berlin 1930, Basel 1932 and Vienna again, 1935) failed during that period in the attempt to build a Europe immune to nationalism. This political impossibility of overcoming the national frame was the cause of the development and consolidation of Nazism, the political force which would lead to the ultimate consequences the logic of Wilsonian nationalism (Hobsbawm, 1995: 143)."

Many decades have passed from the 1920s and 1930s, and the current political situation is very different. A complete revival of Fascism and Nazism is unthinkable right now. However, the EU that was born from the ruins of the Second World War should not decline its cosmopolitan fundamentals on behalf of a continental nationalism based on what Andersen and Björklund called *welfare chauvinism*.[4] This danger is not theoretical but expressed by the project 'Fortress Europe' that populists use to claim for and conciliate with their insults against the 'Brussels bureaucracy' and the coming back of the 'good old times' of the Europe of nations. The apartheid through which millions of Europeans pretend to protect the exclusivity of their rights to residence and employment; the criminalization of illegal emigrants; the pogroms against extra-communitarians; the spread of a new type of 'leftist' anti-Semitism; the reappearance of neo-Nazi groups and the rise of a nationalistic populism and authoritarian leaders, constitute an alarm that should not be ignored. They all represent a betrayal of the principles on which the unity of the European continent was forged: peace, universal human rights, cosmopolitanism, free movement of people and goods, transnational democracy, abolition of borders, frontiers and limits to human interaction.

All over Europe, nationalism is reinvigorating at the national level as well as some kind of continental nationalism claims for the building of a 'Europe for the Europeans'. An innovative mix between a confederal-intergovernmental Europe with some kind of European continental nationalism under the appellation of a 'Fortress Europe' is going on, and rising. Therefore, not only disintegration threatens the future of Europe, but also the tendency to focus on EU internal affairs and the promotion of some kind of 'continental nationalism', which is what I mean by 'EUropeism'. Consequently, the insistence on the unity of Europe is not anymore a sufficient guarantee against the demons of the past. Now, the idea of a European Fortress should let us recall that Fascism and Nazism did not only mean a form of nationalistic overreaction against globalization, but also a project for the unification of Europe.

### What is Europe about?

In this context, in which the European unity is at stake and a nationalistic and confederal Fortress Europe project pushes for being its future design, the controversy over the true character of the European Union acquires particular importance. While some argue that the EU is a State in the making, others support the confederal vision and prestigious academicians say that the EU is a cosmopolitan empire (Beck and Grande, 2004: 85). 'We created Europe, let's create the Europeans' shout some of the defenders of the European *Demos*, paraphrasing the famous phrase claimed by Massimo D'Azeglio during the first session of the Italian Parliament.

However, the EU is not a continental nation, neither a true state nor an empire. The EU is not an in-the-making state in the sense of an artefact destined to rebuild the top-down sovereignty of the monarch at the continental level, but rather a set of institutional devices whose main capability is reinforcing the bottom-up sovereignty of the citizens. The EU is a republic, meaning a progressively integrated political unity founded on human rights, rule of law, common policies, public debate and increasing democracy within an ever-rising institutional structure. The EU is a republic, this is to say not a conglomerate that tends to its unitary assemblage at the state level but a constellation of different institutional devices able to deal with the proliferation of orders (Sassen, 2006: 9) that is prototypical of the twenty-first century political universe. The EU is a republic showing supranational powers can be built without creating any kind of Leviathan. The EU is a Republic, the first of this kind at the continental level, whose history demonstrates that democracy, federalism and citizenship are not tied anymore at the national scale.

The present of Europe speaks for itself. Every time the EU tends to the proliferation of a centralized bureaucracy, to the top-down intervention of Brussels in affairs which should not be subjected to regional control, to the promotion of a uniform cultural identity, to the building of a traditional army or to the militarization of European borders, it goes back towards the mix between territory and State over whose ruins the EU was built. On the contrary, whenever the EU enforces its economic and political unity, emphasizes the rule of law, reinforces the centrality of the European Parliament, empowers its *corpus* of rights linked to a transnational cosmopolitan citizenship and promotes a constitutional federalism based on subsidiarity, it strengthens the sovereignty and autonomy of its citizens and embodies a powerful force able to substantially change the global landscape. This way, the European model continues to propose itself as the only suitable modern answer to the end of the space-age (Bauman, 2004). Let us consider now then the reasons why the EU is not a state in-the-making.

Although every state implies the existence of institutions, the existence of institutions within the frame of a political unity does not necessarily imply the existence of a state. The most expressive example of this assumption is the EU, which, for more than half a century, progressed towards a transnational democratic-republican order without having shaped a European State. Indeed, six decades after the Schuman declaration there is not a bureaucratic centralized administrative system, nor a continental monopoly of violence, nor a sovereign power that rules over citizens, nor any kind of military compulsion, collective identity or uniform culture based on the territory and the past (Rifkin, 2005: 255); which are the marks of any(?) every(?) traditional state. At the bazaar dominated by national-states, the European Community of Coal and Steel, and then the European Economic Community, and then the EU, appear to be something completely different to the old-fashioned national structures; a new form of political unity closer to Levi's 'laboratory of supranational democracy' (Levi, 2002) than to the traditional Leviathan (see Table 13.1).

Among the many elements that constitute a universal Republic similar to the one that was figured out by Immanuel Kant in *The Perpetual Peace* (Kant, 1999), the EU must emphasize its constitutional order, rule of law, politic and economic unity, equality of rights, sovereignty of citizens, democratic principle

*Table 13.1* Differences between State and Republic

| STATE | REPUBLIC |
| --- | --- |
| Top-down sovereignty of the state (monarchic sovereignty) | Bottom-up sovereignty of the citizens (democratic sovereignty) |
| Territorial unity | Economic and political unity based on a constitution |
| Rule of power | Rule of law |
| Concentration of power | Division of powers |
| Military security | Human security |
| Centralized government | Federalism and subsidiarity |
| Centrality of the Executive | Centrality of the Parliament |
| State secrecy | Transparency |
| Raison d'état | Accountability |
| Hierarchy and heteronomy | Respect to minorities and to individual autonomy |
| *Jus solis – jus sanguis* | Free circulation and residence Universal equality of rights |
| Collective close identity | Open identity, individual rights and universal citizenship |
| Independence | Interdependence |
| Impermeable frontiers | Connectivity and integration to the world |
| Cultural uniformity | Cosmopolitanism and multiculturality |
| Military forces | Institutional structures |
| Bureaucracy | Democracy |
| Isolationism and belligerence | Cooperation, integration and multilateralism |
| Inter-governmentalism and multi-polarity | Supranational democracy and federalism |

of majority, respect for minorities, open identity (Beck and Grande, 2004: 158), freedom of movement and residence, federal-subsidiary form of government and centrality of the Parliament. At the same time, following the lessons given by the twentieth century, the EU should reject like the plague other components of the state order, such as the vertical concentration of power in a few hands, the sovereignty of the state over individuals, the abuse of secrecy, the centralization of decision-making in a bureaucracy, the promotion of cultural uniformity and collective identity hidden behind the concept of 'European demos', the attempt of sealing its frontiers and developing a real army and a military-territorial conception of human security. History shows that, with few exceptions, these are the usual characteristic of any state. Undoubtedly, the unitary model of national states developed in Europe by the beginning of the twentieth century was paradigmatic in terms of authoritarianism and militarism. But the history of the world shows that –sooner or later – every state tends to develop all these elements unless it is integrated within a larger federal-democratic-republican entity.

Finally, federalism and democracy are close friends but not lovers, as the seven decades of history of the Union of Soviet Socialist Republics demonstrate. Therefore, the classic statement 'separated states who claim to be sovereign are a sufficient cause for war' (see Reves, 1945) that was the central federalist claim at the end of the Second World War, should be complemented by another principle: 'separated states who claim to be sovereign are a sufficient cause for authoritarianism, bureaucratism, territorialism, exaltation of common identity and cultural uniformity, militarism and, finally, war'. This should be both a warning on the risks of going back to a purely inter-governmental Europe as well as to the interpretation of the EU as a state (including an in-the-making state) in the traditional sense.

Under this perspective, the difficulties emerged in the attempt to unite Europe had dialectically the virtue to avoid any risk of continental statism and nationalism. The discussion on the dangers of 'continental nationalism' for the peace of the world, which was vibrant between European federalists and world federalists during the 1940s,[5] was rationally closed in favour of Europeans, given the need of focusing then on the European scale. Yet, the question is acquiring a renovated topicality. The fact that the EU is not only a model for supranational democracy but also for a post-state republican one deserves the maximal attention today, when new ideas and strategies are urgently required at the international and global level.

## Regional integration and late industrialism

A further reflection on Europe, and on regional integration processes in general as well, should connect them to a particular stage in human development. We are starting to live in a society based on the production of immaterial goods produced by human intelligence for which the cost of transportation is asymptotically close to zero. Within this software-phase (Iglesias, 2011: 253), the reasons for *any kind* of territorial unity hesitate. Looking back, regional integration was the product of a specific period of history: late industrialism. The two worldwide conflicts that destroyed Europe as well as the process that reshaped the continent from the post-war to the present were related to the increased scale of land, natural resources and markets in the age of the Third Industrial Revolution, when European techno-economic forces needed to reach a continental dimension in order to fully develop their potential (as they have successfully done in the Soviet Union and the United States of America).

The point is: regional integration works in a window of history, after the early industrialism led to the building of national states but before the global society of knowledge and information. The economy of scales for standardized late-industrial production pushed for the extension of the European political units from the beginning of the twentieth century, which was pursued *manu militari* by the Nazi-Fascism and *manu federali* by the European Community of Coal and Steel, the European Economic Community and the

EU. Yet, when a big part of the industrial production has been relocated to Asia and Europe is engaged in the shift to an economy based on knowledge, information, cultural diversity, communication, innovation and subjectivity, the links that tied European nations to the EU become fragile. Predictably, they will get more fragile unless new reasons for the union are founded.

The second half of the twentieth century was the moment in which Europe and North America showed the benefits of the marriage of late industrialism and continental-scale political unity, but the fall of the Berlin Wall and the consequent acceleration of globalization altered the scenario. As soon as the market globalized but democracy remained national, the social-democratic consensus (Dahrendorf, 1993) that had reigned in North America and Europe all along the Thirty Golden Years was broken, the Keynesian multiplier drained its positive effects to foreign economies, the Phillips curve became a crazy sinusoid, and the impossibility of any kind of territorially limited Keynesianism within a global economy opened the door for a new paradigm. This new order announced by George Bush where everything became global but democracy (Monbiot, 2003: 83), this universe defined by the increasing unbalance between democracy and politics, on one hand, and capitalism and economy, on the other, was the cradle of the Neo-liberal Consensus that still rules the world (Iglesias, 2011: 210).

There are good practical reasons – both economic and ecological – for avoiding the costs of transportation of objects across distant points of the planetary surface, but none of them subsists for the communication through a planetary network such as the Internet. That is why an economy based on the production of knowledge, information, diversity, communication, innovation and subjectivity tends to overcome regional frames at the same speed and with the same facility than national ones. A mode of production that creates immaterial goods rather than objects tends to be global, not regional. And a global market supposes a global political power able to regulate it in order to prevent the chaos and anarchy that are typical of unregulated markets. This is exactly what is happening nowadays, wich establishes a necessary shift in the way the unity of Europe has to be pursued. All this implies, necessarily, the formulation of new reasons and goals for the regional integration in order to limitate the risks of the EU becoming the mere prolongation of a glorious but dead past.

Defending jobs created inside the EU by any tradable production while the cost of labour in Asia is about eight times lower is becoming more problematic every year. The building of an EU economic common policy is necessary and positive but it is not going to change this fact. In short, the option 'First-world salaries for the first-world workers and third-world salaries for the third-world workers' is over. The new alternative is 'First-world salaries for the third-world workers or third-world salaries for the first-world ones'. If the global dumping on wages, environment and labour has any chance of being abolished, the balance between politics and economy, democracy and capitalism, state and markets, must be recreated at the global scale.

A sort of new global social-democracy (Held, 2005: 155), or – at least–a new global social-democratic consensus, must rule the world, Keynesian expansive and socially progressive policies must be elevated to the global level[6] and some sort of planetary welfare state must be established (Held, 2005: 204). Unless it happens – in the best case, *meanwhile* it happens – the reasons for European nations to stay inside the EU in order to protect national welfare will get weaker every year. Assuming that, there is no better way for reinforcing them than the transformation of the EU into a political actor capable of pushing it's own model to the global scale.

## Looking for a new stage in the building of the European Republic

At the sunset of the nation-state monopoly of politics, two concepts that were joined by history deserve to be separated: the republic and the state. For centuries, the valid rule was: every republic is a state but not all states are republics. The experience of the European Union suggests now, in addition, that a republic could exist without a real and proper state, not even an in-the-making state. If this is correct, the understanding of the current EU crisis under the *internal* viewpoint of a fight between Europeist-federalist forces and anti-Europeist national-populist forces is misleading, and implies an alteration of the federalist methodology, which supposes to consider first and foremost the *external* scenario, meaning here the *global* one. In this broad prospective, the crisis that begun by 2008 has shown the limits, and perhaps the end, of three basic strategies that were successful for more than half a century:

1  The strategy of building Europe without taking care of the involvement of their citizens (let's call it 'elitarianism');
2  The strategy of building Europe by giving priority to the economy (let's call it 'functionalism');
3  The strategy of building Europe focusing on internal matters regardless of the world (let's call it EUrocentrism).

The limitations of the elitarian and the functional strategies had been adequately criticized by many intellectuals, as well as balanced by the action of federalist organizations. Yet, EUrocentrism has not been adequately contrasted by any of them. However, the reasons for incorporating the topic of the global order to the EU agenda differ today from those invoked by world federalists during the 1940s and 1950s. The burning new fact is that each and any of the main European troubles (financial instability and low economic growth, rise of youth unemployment, social inequalities and undemocratic political forces) had reached a global scale in which even a theoretical European Federation would be impotent to cope with. Yet, the global scenario and its unavoidable consequences on the EU situation are not at the centre of the European debate, which is surprising in the case of a supranational entity whose organizations and functionaries should be used for cosmopolitan approaches. This is what I call EUrocentrism. On the contrary, there subsists a vague insistence on the development of a common security and defence policy and on the need that the EU 'speaks with one voice', with no emphasis in which its predicament should be.[7] Consequently, the extension of the European model[8] of integration to other regions of the world and to the global level itself (Rifkin, 2005: 465) seems to be completely out of the question nowadays. This is a predictable consequence of a state-centric approach to the question, which leads to similar misleading conclusions as methodological nationalism (Beck, 2005). EUrocentrism has alienated the EU from the progressive forces around the world that should be its allies, facilitating the emergence of an international scenario hostile to the EU experience.

Far from being the rational extension of the federalist approach, EUrocentrism is contrary to the inheritance of the EU's Founding Fathers. Let's just consider the most well-known statement made by Altiero Spinelli, Eugenio Colorni and Ernesto Rossi at the Ventotene Manifest:

> The dividing line between progressive and reactionary parties no longer follows the formal line of greater or lesser democracy, or of more or less socialism to be instituted; rather the division falls along the line, very new and substantial, that separates the party members into two groups. The first is made up of those who conceive the essential purpose and goal of struggle as the ancient one – that is, the conquest of national political power – and who, although involuntarily, play into the hands of reactionary forces, letting the incandescent lava of popular passions set in the old moulds, and thus allowing old absurdities to arise once again. The second are those who see the creation of a solid international State as the main purpose; they will direct popular forces toward this goal, and, having won national power, will use it first and foremost as an instrument for achieving international unity.
>
> (Spinelli *et al.*, 1941: 8)

In this amazingly advanced statement made at the abysm of June 1941, Spinelli *et al.* affirm the supremacy of the regional scenario over the national ones, stating that those who wanted to see more democracy and social justice *inside* their nations must pursue the unity of Europe *beyond* their nations instead of focusing on internal strategies.

But Spinelli *et al.* did not proclaim the eternal centrality of the regional prospective. They rather affirmed the Copernican principle (Reves, 1945: 25) that enlarged scales determine the situation inside minor ones (Iglesias, 2011: 207), meaning 'regional over national' by then and '*global over regional*' by now. Let us try again: in the middle of the twentieth century the Italian founding fathers of European federalism realized that there was no chance for a democratic Italy amidst a Europe in the hands of totalitarian forces.

*Mutatis mutandis*, current Europeist and federalist forces must recognize that there is not space for a democratic Europe within a global scenario marked by financial crises, global warming, nuclear proliferation, uncontrolled migrations and international terrorism. Therefore, the impotence of international agencies such as the UN Security Council, the IMF, the WTO and the G20 to effectively deal with global crises should not be an external secondary matter for the EU, but its new 'first and foremost' concern.

The dawn of the *Pax Americana* (Steel, 1970) that had determined the second part of the twentieth century adds a worrying note to this panorama. The emerging international arena is reminiscent of the last part of the nineteenth century, marked by the end of the *Pax Britannica*. Today, as then, the decreasing power of the most democratic political unit and the increased power of non-democratic entities constitute a source of instability and conflict, as the recent crisis in Libya and Syria demonstrated. Nowadays, as then, the decreasing hegemony of the democratic nations of the age is not likely to be replaced by a fair *multilateral* order but rather by a belligerent *multipolar* one marked by international tension and determined by the dispute about the succession of the outgoing monarch.

Within this context, the project of a United States of Europe or European Federation able to cope with its own problems in isolation is illusory and misleading as the project of a democratic and socially fair Italy was within the frame of a Europe marked by nationalism and warfare in the early twentieth century. Consequently, at the beginning of the twenty-first century the principle for which 'The question that must be resolved first, failing which progress is no more than mere appearance, is the definitive abolition of the division of Europe into national, sovereign States' has overcome the regional level and gets valid for the entire world, following the federalist fundamental 'first and foremost ... achieving international unity' (Spinelli *et al.*, 1941: 8).

## The European legacy

No matter the road that the European Union will take the post-war European experience remains a turning point in the dialectic between socio-economic processes, political institutions and territory. European unity is the missing link between the previous nation-state order grounded on territorial unity and top-down sovereignty and a future we still ignore, but which components have appeared in our horizon. The expansion to the East, the acceptance of Turkey as a candidate to membership and the current negotiation with the United States about a Transatlantic Trade and Investment Partnership (TTIP) are significant steps in a new direction. They open the door to fascinating questions. For instance: once the TTIP is signed, could the USA and the EU start to walk together the same path that led from the European Community of Carbon and Steel to the EU? Could a USA–EU agreement be – as Bertrand Russell, Altiero Spinelli and many others expected a long time ago ((Spinelli *et al.*, 1941; Russell, 1953) – the seed of a democratic world order or, at least, a political alliance working in favour of global democratic governance?

Hence, what if a democratic not-European country (say: Canada, Japan or Brazil) asks in future to be incorporated into the EU? In the long run, is not the incorporation into the EU a reasonable road map for the North African countries that could have recently started their own path to freedom and democracy? Why Turkey and not Egypt, for instance? What about Israel? Palestine? Could not this perspective provide a stimulating input for a pacific resolution of the Israeli-Palestine conflict? Could not a progressive partnership between Israel, Palestine and the EU with the final perspective of the incorporation of both into the EU open the way towards an end of the conflict under the condition of immediate peace and increasing democracy? So far, all these developments are just mere speculation. But perhaps they are such important speculations as those that Spinelli, Rossi and Colorni had resumed in the 'Manifesto for a free and united Europe' by June 1941 (Spinelli *et al.*, 1941), when they were prisoners of the Fascist regime within a Europe ruled by the Nazis.

The analysis of the causes of the success of regional integration and the failure of traditional forms of *nation-building* have particular importance at the beginning of the twenty-first century, when the problems that beset humanity are similar to those that Europeans faced at the dawn of the twentieth century. All of them were produced by the growing tension between a techno-economic apparatus that tends to the expansion and a political system anchored to the territorial dimension of the state. Predictably, that contradiction got destructive in Europe at the beginning of the twentieth century because Europe was both the most advanced region in technology and economy and the most fragmented one in politics.

Today, when the digital revolution has made the entire planet smaller than Europe at the time of its crashes, the question of lack of any kind of worldwide federal-democratic-republican unity transcends the theoretical field, causing the emergence of big five global crises: economic, ecological, demographic, military[9] and technological.[10] In this worrying context, the EU experience could provide two contributions in terms of global politics, as a part of the EU legacy to the world:

1 The peaceful construction of a supranational democratic political unity.
2 A model for the worldwide widening of the federalist experience.

Most of the anti-Europeist forces have fully understood the unpopularity of insisting on the United States of Europe, the European Federation, a European State and so on. These concepts are often difficult to explain and allow anti-Europeists to agitate the ghosts raised by the twentieth century. Paradoxically, the risk of an enormous and totalitarian state evoked by Huxley and Orwell, which the European unity defeated, is used by its nationalistic enemies to criticize the same EU.

The model of a traditional territorial state and the prospective of a European State must not be considered anymore as a suitable solution of European dilemmas, but as a part of the problem. The political forces that were the first to criticize nationalism should also be the first to question the state model, remarking on its increasing incapacity to achieve deeper levels of regional and worldwide integration.

> The sovereign nations of the past can no longer solve the problems of the present: they cannot ensure their own progress or control their own future. And the European Community itself is only a stage on the way to the organized world of tomorrow.
>
> (Monnet, 1988)

## What is to be done with the world?

Within a global universe, the classical political question 'What is to be done?' means, above all, what is to be done *with the world*. Of course, European troubles can be diminished through an 'internal' damage reduction strategy, but they cannot have a reasonable expectance of being solved unless an 'external' global prospective is adopted.

Let us start by considering the main troublesome aspects of the current period of human history: climate warming, financial crisis and nuclear proliferation. In an ecologically damaged world, the battle for natural resources and permanent stop-and-go in the economy necessarily provoke international disputes and conflicts. In this rapidly changing universe, nobody can make precise predictions, but the risk of a catastrophic scenario during the coming decades is high. A global cataclysm is likely to happen unless a global political action is taken, and not a single country or region would be safe in such scenario within an interconnected world. In other words, any 'every nation or region of the world for herself' strategy has become as irrational as it was the idea of 'every European country for himself' at the beginning of the twentieth century.

Global warming, financial crisis and nuclear proliferation: none of the three more urgent aspects of the global crisis can be managed at the national or regional level; none can expect to have a positive evolution through the same international agreements and intergovernmental institutions that have failed on regulating global capitalism and protecting global common goods; not a single one is going to stop worsening thanks to the interventions of the current model of global governance, the main characteristics of which are duplication, ambiguity, overlap and confusion (Goldin, 2013: 102). But, more important, none of them can be solved separately, as so many global

NGOs seem to expect to happen. As soon as we consider the real dimension of the economic, ecological and military aspects of the global crisis, it gets evident that a global strategy – *both* planetary and inter-systemic (Iglesias, 2011: 329) – is the previous condition for every rational attempt of controlling, diminishing and – hopefully – solving any global issue.

For a better explanation, let us enter the field of the counterfactual to ask a crucial question: how would a government rationally manage the three main global crises in the case in which there were no 'external' entities?[11] Likely, in this situation a government with no exterior menace (which is the case for Earth) would reduce the military budget in order to redirect the savings to the research on clean technologies and the development of a sustainable global energy system (Iglesias, 2011: 324). The pact with the military industry could be as simple as this: the government guarantees, for a certain period of time, the usual amount of money to the military corporations, under the condition they do not build any of those technologically wonderful weapons that we humans do not need at all.

During that period, as part of the bargain, the military corporations must become competitive in the field of clean sustainable energies and be ready to compete in this market without any further support from the government (in, for example, five to ten years). This strategy, adequately complemented by a tax on the use of all petroleum products, would dramatically diminish the gap between renewable sources and fossil fuels, accelerating the necessary shift between the two systems and impacting positively on climate change. This way, an enormous economic market could be promoted, helping to solve *simultaneously* the three most urgent global crises: economic, ecological and military. A safer, more stable and prosperous world should result for this amalgam of politics, technology and economy at the global level.

A similar strategy could be adopted for the management of the global financial crisis, which in the long term is insolvable without regulating the global financial market, without redirecting monetary and human resources from finance to the rest of the economy,[12] without reconnecting finances and the rest of the economy and without transferring (as happened during the Golden Thirty) a big part of the economic resources from the production of private goods (objects for individual consumption) to the production of common social goods (stable weather, clean air, clean water and universal satisfaction of basic human needs).

What should a government do rationally in order to achieve all these goals? Taxing any kind of speculative transaction in order to diminish the profitability of the financial sector with respect to the rest of the economy must be the first thing. This should result in the diminution of the capital with no application to the rest of the economy and a reduction of the financial volatility, which are mutually linked and reinforcing. That would suitably redirect highly qualified human resources from finance to other sectors and increase the amount of available capitals for productive investment. The resources that a tax on speculation could raise must be added to other incomes, such as those originated in abolishing fiscal paradises and taxing transcontinental first-class air tickets, the production of arms, the capital plus valences of multinational corporations and unhealthy habits such as the consumption of alcohol and cigarettes (Attali, 2012: 339).

Any smart government would use these resources to finance infrastructure and education (say: water, housing, hospitals, schools, electricity, public transportation, broadband digital networks and cheap laptops, etc.) for everybody, in order to guarantee the full satisfaction of human basic needs. Predictably, this must provoke a jump in production, starting a virtuous circle of increased productivity and better living conditions. Likely, the fulfilment of unsatisfied basic needs of the poorest two-thirds of the population, together with the building of a new and sustainable energetic matrix, would allow a colossal expansion of the market. They should do it faster and better than the current economy based on the hyper-consumerism of the richest third of the world population and the misery of the last third.

Clearly, the solutions for the economy, the ecology and the military-spending reduction of the world are linked. Clearly, they are directly connected with the building of institutions able to consider the protection of environment and the fulfilment of basic human needs as priority and to operate all over the global market. If this is correct, the resolution of the three big crises that menace our future depends on a political power expanded to the maximum scale of the territory (global) and able to represent the interests of the majority of the population (democratic). Pushing this argument to its ultimate consequence, a progressively globalized world implies that there will not be long-term solutions for any crisis without the progressive building of some kind of global democratic order, which doesn't mean a world state or global government (Habermas, 2005: 130), but global judicial and parliamentary institutions able to democratize globalization (Boutros-Ghali, 2002) and globalize democracy (Iglesias, 2006).[13]

You may say I am a dreamer. But the fact is that the obsolete political structure of the world – not the economic voracity of capitalism, which could be better fed by this programme than by the business-as-usual strategy – is the only obstacle to a plan like this. 'What is to be done with the world?' therefore, is not anymore a rhetoric question or a utopian science-fiction programme usable for Star Trek or Star Wars style films. 'What is to be done with the world?' is the rational question to be posted as soon as the technologies developed by humanity have reached a global scale of causes and effects.

Consequently, a renewed EU must work on:

1   The positive conclusion of the Transatlantic Trade and Investment Partnership (TTIP) *and its politicization*, including a compact on the defence of democracy and human rights inside its limits and its promotion by pacific means beyond them (Attali, 2012: 337),[14] as well as the

commitment of the USA and the EU in the leading of a Global Marshall Plan For the Fourth world (Radermacher, 2004) funded by global taxes.

2    The active support to the proposal of the Governor of China's Central Bank, Zhou Xiaouchuan, about substituting the American dollar as a means of payment in international trade and financial transactions with an international currency[15] (Fiorentini and Montani, 2012: 20). This should be the first step towards the creation of a) a global currency able to secure global stability by combating global imbalances through an automatic mechanism, as proposed by Keynes by 1945 at the Bretton Woods conference, b) a global lender of last resort in order to allow countercyclical global policies and stabilize the global GDP growth, and c) a suitable instrument for the creation of global sovereign debt bonds to finance the production of global public goods such a safe environment and the satisfaction of basic human needs for all the members of the human community.

3    The extension of federalism and democracy to the global level, which implies an active role of the EU in the progressive building of a demo-cratic global order. The democratization of the United Nations (includ-ing the regionalization of the UN Security Council (Held, 2005: 154)), the reform of the Bretton Woods organizations and the creation of a United Nations Parliamentary Assembly (UNPA) (Bummel, 2005; Heinrich, 2010)[16,17] as the first stage towards a world parliament (Iglesias, 2006; Falk and Strauss, 2011) must constitute its basic elements.

4    The support to the generalization and deepening of regional integration process in all continents and regions of the world, starting by concrete EU actions in favour of the ongoing processes in Africa and South America.

As the European Union is the leading experience for regional integration, the last point of this catalogue deserves a particular consideration. Given the close links among Europe and Africa and Latin America, the success of the EU was one of the main factors that favoured the start of African and Latin American processes of integration. Unfortunately, the EU crisis has got also one of the main causes of the blockade in their development. The Community of Andean Nations, the Mercosur, the Unasur, the Community of Latin American Countries and many other promising initiatives initiated by the foundation of the Latin American Parliament (1964) are detained. The only active initiatives within the region – the NAFTA (North American Free Trade Agreement) and the Pacific Alliance – are only commercial treaties with no relation to the EU model of integration that combines the economic, social, political and institutional dimensions.

This, of course, is not a direct EU responsibility. Endogenous causes such as the rise of populist governments led by Venezuela are the main reason for the freeze of the Mercosur, for instance. While abstractly claiming for the Patria Grande,[18] they have concretely split the continent by ideologizing the integration process. This is also the most important cause of the reduction of the Unasur to occasional inter-governmental summits. Having said that, the EU has almost no initiative in favour of the Latin American and South American integration, including commercial, politic and civil society levels.[19] The most important of them – the EU-Mercosur negotiations initiated by 2000 and stopped by 2004, which should have led to the constitution of the largest free-trade zone of the world – were discontinued after having been re-launched by the 2010 Madrid Summit. The reason is not only the hostility of some South-American governments to any form of integration, but also the scarce flexibility of EU countries favoured by the Common Agricultural Policy (CAP), the most regressive part of the European integration process itself.

The EU has also lost its pre-eminence in Africa, and the space that Europe had as the most significant partner for African countries is being occupied by China. The lack of a common EU strategy about the Arab spring, the disagreements of its national governments on the Libyan situation and the irrelevance of the EU in the Syria issue are an expression of the nonexistence of the EU as an actor at the global scale. The divergent visions and interests of the European countries made it impossible to reach agreements on the conflicts in Iraq, Libya and Syria, so close to the European territory. And three years after the creation of the European External Action Service (EEAS) the EU is still lacking any active strategy on matters that all its members should share and support, such as the promotion of the regional integration in all the regions of the world and the extension of the European model to the global political arena.

## Conclusion

The history of the European integration is the history of an internal success and an external failure. More than half a century after the Schuman declaration there is no concrete EU external policy, no real support for the regional integration in Africa and Latin America, nor a single coordinate initiative in favour of the adoption of the European Union model at the global level. The necessary and urgent steps that must be taken for a more federal Europe and in order to increase the citizen participation in the process of building a very European republic must be completed by an active EU policy at the global scenario. The elitarian and functionalist orientation of the European process of integration must also be overcome by leaving behind EUrocentrism.

At the beginning of the past century there was no opportunity for European national democracies within the warfare frame of the Europe of Nations. At the beginning of the twenty-first century there is no opportunity for any regional democracy within the anarchic framework created by the failures of the national/international system. The new fact is that the industrial civilization is becoming outdated not only at its early dimension, whose political expression was the national state, but also at its later stage, the political expression of which was the continental-scale units born pluri-national and multicultural by immigration, such as the USA, or by aggregation, such as the EU. The democratic nations and regions of the world face now the alternative between collaborating in the building of a democratic global order or progressively losing their democratic capabilities as the consequences of global crises invade their territories. The current effects of global financial volatility, climate warming, nuclear proliferation, uncontrolled migrations and fundamentalist terrorism demonstrate that this is not a prophecy for the future but a crucial part of the existing reality.

The emerging global society of information and knowledge implies the Copernican paradigm has worldwide implications. Therefore, the progressive building of a planetary federal republic and a global democracy is the condition for the keeping of democracy and civility inside all the nations and regions of the world. The political challenge of the twenty-first century, thence, is not about pushing the *Pax Americana* to its end, but about overcoming the *international monarchy*, replacing the *ancienne regime* of nations and states by a republican democratic global order.

Among the menaces of these unpredictable volatile times, humanity is facing an extraordinary challenge: putting an end to the hegemonic system that ruled the past century without crossing through a big crisis generated by a monarchical dispute on its succession, as happened at its beginnings. The connection among the internal and external aspects of the European reality is getting as evident and relevant for its future as the link between the European unity and the democratization of European countries was at the end of the *Pax Britannica*. No matter how difficult this complex panorama is to be publically explained and politically pursued, it is not more complicated than spreading the federal concept during the *second war of the thirty years* (1914–1944) (Dahrendorf, 1993: 119). The only difference between the first post-war period (1919) and the second one (1945) depended on the amazing capacity of a group of a few federalists thinkers and activists to convince national leaders to change the old paradigm.

What is to be done with the world means a political programme to face the challenges of the global society of knowledge and information; a prospect for the rest of the twenty-first century for which the EU and its internal developments must not be considered as a separate container but as a crucial part. A new global institutional network system, both republican and democratic, must be built, so that the EU's DNA is required. The shorter denomination of such a political structure is 'global democracy', which does not mean the concentration of power at the global scale but rather a democratic system of decision-making at each and every level in which political decisions must be made and public policies must be deliberated and delivered. This is the necessary, pragmatic and institutionalizing answer to the need of multi-layered multilevel governance for different political challenges at the local, national, regional and global levels (Held, 2005: 147); an expression of the emerging global commonwealth of citizens (Archibugi, 2009); a concrete way of satisfying the need of global policies that the complexity and contingency of the current social universe generates (Innerarity, 2012: 102); and a rational strategy for avoiding the risks of global anarchy and international tyranny.[20]

Within a global world ruled by Copernican paradigms, what is good for the world is good for my country (Fiorentini and Montani, 2012: 43). Betting on 'every country – or every region – by himself' is not just egoistic, but stupid. This was what the European nations and the United States discovered at the end of the Second World War. This is where the Marshall Plan and the European unity were grounded on. And these are the promises that the European Republic brings to the future of the world.

The time has come for the EU works in promoting to the global level the two principles – federalism and democracy – which are part of its most important contribution to humanity. The legacy of European federalist founding fathers could give us an important address on this road. At least, this seems to be what Spinelli, Colorni and Rossi were thinking about when they wrote

> it must be recognized that the European Federation is the only conceivable guarantee ensuring that relationships with American and Asiatic peoples will work on the basis of peaceful co-operation, waiting for a more distant future when the political unity of the entire world will become possible.
>
> (Spinelli *et al.*, 1941: 8)

Of course, whether working for the political unity of the entire world is already possible or not is a debatable issue. However, if not the EU, who? If not now, when?

## Notes

1  This text has been corrected by Ken Kostyo.
2  The Human Development Index of the United Nations Development Program.
3  See UNDP, Human Development Index Report http://www.undp.org/content/undp/en/home/librarypage/hdr/.
4  In 1990, Jörgen Goul Andersen and Tor Björklund were the first to use this expression (Andersen and Björklund, 1990).
5  World federalists claimed, basically, that focusing on the building of regional federations would lead to the repetition of the tragedies of nationalism at a bigger scale. European federalists answered with the urgent need of avoiding a third world war in the European territory and sustaining, rationally, that the danger marked by world federalists was still far from any concrete manifestation.
6  The amazing change in Keynes' conceptions, from the closed economy approach of the General Theory of employment, interest and money (Keynes, 1992: 302) to the proposal of the Bancor, which Keynes and Schumacher elaborated by 1940–1942 and Keynes defended during the foundation of the Bretton Woods institutions, show how far he went in this direction.
7  The UEF Manifesto 2014 that was delivered by the Union of European Federalist at its XXV Congress (Berlin, 16–17 November) is meaningful in this regard. http://www.federalists.eu/fileadmin/files_uef/Congress_2013/Adopted_Resolutions/UEF_MANIFESTO_2014.pdf.

8  By European model I mean: both economical and political integration based on democracy, federalism and subsidiarity and matched with high welfare-state standards.

9  Meaning: loss of control of the monopoly of violence by national States.

10  Meaning: loss of control on technology by the human society.

11  A perspective like this is perfectly matchable with Keynes' definition of the 'art of government', which consists on 'taking in account the entire system as a whole and trying to reach the optimal use of all its resources' (Keynes, 1992: 301), and to the Habermas–Beck proposal of an inner world politics (Beck, 2005: 91; Habermas, 2005: 100).

12  Any demonization of the finances, such as the habit of speaking on a 'real economy' –which suggests that the financial economy is 'unreal' – should be avoided. Many things have happened these years that show that the financial part of the economy is real and will be progressively more real in an economy based on information and knowledge. As Fiorentini and Montani stated, the aftermath of the US crisis shows that the financial system is an integrated sector of the world economy (Fiorentini and Montani, 2012: 15).

13  A viewpoint under this perspective, as well as a concrete programme for its realization, could be found in the Manifesto for a Global Democracy signed by Abdullahi Ahmed An-Na'im, Daniele Archibugi, Jacques Attali, Bertrand Badie, Zygmunt Bauman, Ulrich Beck, Noam Chomsky, Roberto Esposito, Richard Falk, Susan George, David Held, Fernando Iglesias, Daniel Innerarity, Mary Kaldor, Mathias Koenig Archibugi, Lucio Levi, Raffaele Marchetti, Giacomo Marramao, George Monbiot, Toni Negri, Heikki Patomäki, Saskia Sassen, Fernando Savater, Richard Sennett, Vandana Shiva, Andrew Strauss and Teivo Teivainen, among others. See http://globaldemocracymanifesto.wordpress.com/english-2/.

14  This implies necessarily, for instance, that the European Union urges the USA to adopt the Rome statute of the International Criminal Court and that it pushes in favour of a reform of the UN chart, according to article 109.

15  An IMF super-sovereign reserve currency developed from the IMF Special Drawing Rights (SDR).

16  The UNPA campaign webpage is http://www.unpacampaign.org/.

17  The European Parliament's Committee on Foreign Affairs (AFET) urged the EU Council to put the UN Parliamentary Assembly on the UN's agenda on 08/05/2001 and a recommendation to the EU Council to support UN Parliamentary Assembly was adopted at the plenary session of 08/06/2011. http://en.unpacampaign.org/news/563.php.

18  The Big Homeland. Meaning the project of a united South America that was raised by South American Founding Fathers such as Simón Bolívar and José de San Martín at the times of the war for national independence of South American nations from the Spanish Crown.

19  A personal experience is useful in order to describe this situation: as chair of the World Federalist Movement, director of the Altiero Spinelli Chair (CUIA) and vice-president of Democracia Global (Movimiento por la Unión Sudamericana y el Parlamento Mundial) I used to look for any kind of economic support by the EU to the activities we develop in the city. But beside the good will of the EU ambassadors here, the EU allocates no financial resources to civil-society initiatives in favour of regional integration, even if funds for the promotion of democracy, human rights and other general values exist.

20  Similar viewpoints can be found in Iglesias (2000, 2006, 2012), Patomäki and Teivainen (2004), Held (2005), Archibugi *et al.* (2011), Attali (2012), among others.

# References

Andersen, J. G. and Björklund, T. (1990). 'Structural Changes and New Cleavages: The Progress Parties in Denmark and Norway.' *Acta Sociological*, 33 (3), pp. 195–217.

Archibugi, D. (2009) [2008]. *Cittadini del mondo*. Milano: Il saggiatore.

Archibugi, D., Koenig-Archibugi, M. and Marchetti, R. (2011). *Global Democracy – Normative and Empirical Perspectives*. Cambridge: Cambridge University Press.

Attali, J. (2012) [2011]. *Domani, chi governerà il mondo?* Roma: Fazi.

Bauman, Z. (2004) [2002]. *La sociedad sitiada*. Buenos Aires: Fondo de Cultura Económica.

Beck, U. (2005) [2002]. *Poder y contrapoder en la Era Global*. Barcelona: Paidós.

Beck, U. and Grande, E. (2004). *La Europa cosmopolita*. Barcelona: Paidós.

Boutros-Ghali, B. (2002). *Democratiser la mondialisation*. Paris: Rocher.

Bummel, A. (2005). *Developing International Democracy*. Stuttgart: KDUN.

Dahrendorf, R. (1993). *El conflicto social moderno*. Barcelona: Mondadori.

Falk, R. and Strauss, A. (2011). *A Global Parliament*. Berlin: KDUN.

Fiorentini, R. and Montani, G. (2012). *The New Global Political Economy*. Northampton: Edward Elgar.

Goldin, I. (2013). *Divided Nations*. Oxford: Oxford University Press.

Habermas, J. (2005) [2004]. *L'Occidente diviso*. Roma: Laterza.

Heinrich, D. (2010). *The Case for a United Nations Parliamentary Assembly*. Berlin: KDUN.

Held, D., Barnett, A. and Henderson, C. (2005). *Debating Globalization*. Cambridge: Polity Press.

Hobsbawm, E. (1995) [1990]. *Naciones y nacionalismo desde 1780*. Barcelona: Grijalbo-Mondadori.

Iglesias, F. A. (2000). *República de la Tierra*. Buenos Aires: Colihue.

Iglesias, F. A. (2006). *Globalizar la Democracia*. Buenos Aires: Manantial.

Iglesias, F. A. (2011). *La modernidad global*. Buenos Aires: Sudamericana.

Innerarity, D. (2012) [2009]. *The Future and its Enemies*. Stanford: Stanford University Press.

Kant, I. (1999) [1795]. *Toward Perpetual Peace*. Cambridge: Cambridge University Press.

Keynes, J. M. (1992) [1936]. *Teoría general de la ocupación, el interés y el dinero*. Buenos Aires: Fondo de Cultura Económica.

Levi, L. (2002). *Il pensiero Federaliste*. Bari: Laterza.

Marramao, G. (2012) [2003]. *The Passage West*. London: Verso.

Monbiot, G. (2003). *The Age of Consent*. London: Harper-Collins.

Monnet, J. (1988). *Mémoires*. Paris: Fayard.

Patomäki, H. and Teivainen. T. (2004). *A Possible World: Democratic Transformation of Global Institutions*. London: Zed Books.

Radermacher, F. J. (2004). *Global Marshall Plan*. Hamburgo: GMP Foundation.

Reves, E. (1945). *Anatomy of Peace*. New York and London: Harper and Brothers Publishers.

Rifkin, J. (2005) [2004]. *El sueño europeo*. Buenos Aires: Paidós.

Russell, B. (1953). *Nuevas esperanzas para un mundo en transformación*. DF México: Hermes.

Sassen, S. (2006). *Territory, Authority, Rights*. New Jersey: Princeton University Press.

Spinelli, A., Rossi, E. and Colorni, E. (1941). *The Ventotene Manifesto*. Torino: The Altiero Spinelli Institute. http://www.altierospinelli.org/manifesto/en/manifesto1944 en_en.html.

Steel, R. (1970). *Pax Americana*. Barcelona: Lumen.

# Index

For Product Safety Concerns and Information please contact our EU
representative GPSR@taylorandfrancis.com Taylor & Francis Verlag GmbH,
Kaufingerstraße 24, 80331 München, Germany


Printed and bound by CPI Group (UK) Ltd, Croydon, CR0 4YY

01/06/2025

01858459-0003